CORTÉS

CORTÉS

The Life of the Conqueror
by His Secretary

FRANCISCO LÓPEZ DE GÓMARA

Translated and Edited by

LESLEY BYRD SIMPSON

from the ISTORIA DE LA CONQUISTA DE MEXICO

Printed in Zaragoza, 1552

UNIVERSITY OF CALIFORNIA PRESS
BERKELEY, LOS ANGELES, LONDON

University of California Press
Berkeley and Los Angeles, California

Cambridge University Press
London, England

© *1964 by The Regents of the University of California*
First Paper-bound Edition, 1966
Library of Congress Catalog Card Number: 64-13474
Published with the assistance of a grant from the Rockefeller Foundation

Designed by Adrian Wilson
Printed in the United States of America

2 3 4 5 6 7 8 9 0

Contents

Illustrations

following page 236

PLATE 1. The Mexicans attack the house where Moctezuma is held a prisoner. Cortés, a mounted captain, and four Tlaxcalans are defending the house. Doña Marina is on the roof speaking to the assailants. A stone is flying through the air on its way to kill Moctezuma. The date is June 27, 1520. The inscription reads: "Now they begin the attack upon the house where Moctezuma is." (Gómara, Chapters 103–107)

PLATE 2. After the defeat of his wooden towers, Cortés attacks the main temple. The Castilians are thrown down; the air is filled with beams, arrows, and stones; the temple is burning. The inscription reads: "The Marqués burns the temple of the idols." (Gómara, Chapter 108)

PLATE 3. After the disastrous retreat of La Noche Triste (June 30–July 1, 1520), Cortés leads the remnants of his army to Tepotzotlán, on the shore of Lake Zumpango. The Spaniards attack the temple and defeat the Aztec defenders (July 3). (Gómara, Chapter 111)

PLATE 4. Cortés, having survived the critical battle of Otumba, finally reaches Xaltelolco, where he is warmly received by the Tlaxcalan nobles, who are bringing him gifts of food for men and horses. Cortés is seated, Doña Marina at his side, and several Spanish and Tlaxcalan captains stand behind him. He is receiving the Tlaxcalan lord Citlalpopoca. (Gómara, Chapter 112)

PLATE 5. Cortés begins his new campaign against Mexico–Tenochtitlán by destroying the Aztec garrisons in the Valley of Puebla. He is shown here attacking Acatzingo. (Gómara, Chapter 115)

PLATE 6. Cortés continues his strategy of strangulation of the Aztec Empire by taking Huaquechula. (Gómara, Chapter 116)

PLATE 7. Having cut off the eastern and southern provinces, Cortés returns to the Valley of Mexico and attacks Xochimilco, from which he again circles the lakes and re-enters Texcoco, April 15, 1521. The painting represents the four cities taken in this last sweep: Tepatepec, Xochimilco, Coyoacán, and Tacuba. (Gómara, Chapter 133)

PLATE 8. Final assault on the city. Cortés establishes headquarters at the fortress-temple of Xoloc, on the Ixtapalapa causeway, from which he directs operations. The painting represents the battle in the main square, June 16, 1521. The inscription reads: "Now they take the streets between the houses." (Gómara, Chapters 141–142)

Introduction

ONE MIGHT THINK that, after four hundred-odd years, the furious row stirred up by Francisco López de Gómara, the great biographer of Cortés and first historian of the conquest of Mexico, would let up a bit. On the contrary, not long ago it was blown into a white heat when, in 1946, a young Spaniard named Fernando Baeza discovered the bones of Cortés buried in the chapel wall of the Hospital de Jesús in Mexico City, where they had been hidden by Lucas Alamán during the War of Independence, to secure them from desecration at the hands of the insurgents. The occasion was seized upon by the pious to pronounce eulogies of Cortés, whom they hold to be the lay founder of the Mexican Church, and by professional patriots to denounce him for all the atrocities of the conquest, as, indeed, has been the fashion since 1810. It was, perhaps, not a coincidence that not long afterward the bones of Cuauhtémoc, the Aztec hero and opponent of Cortés (whom Cortés had hanged), were reported to have been found reposing beneath the altar of the parish church of Ixcateopan, Guerrero, brought thither by his grief-stricken followers over some thousand kilometers of exceedingly rough country. The inconsistencies and anachronisms with which the story is fairly studded were ignored, and it is now firmly embedded in the folklore of the Revolution, and woe to the unlucky scholar who scoffs at it!

Gómara started the thing back in 1552, with the publication of his *Historia de las Indias,* and its second part, *La Crónica de la Nueva España,* or *Historia de la Conquista de México,* as it is more generally known. The book was promptly suppressed by Prince Philip (later Philip II, then governing overseas affairs for his father), who could have been annoyed by the author's irreverent treatment of the Emperor Charles V. Prince Philip may have been persuaded to take this action by Fray Bartolomé de las Casas, then at the height of his influence, whose hatred of Cortés and Gómara was phenomenal in its intensity. Las Casas was not at all reticent in stating his motives: "Gómara, a secular priest, who wrote the *History* of Cortés, and who, after Cortés was made a marqués, lived with him in Castile, who was never in the Indies, and who wrote nothing but what Cortés himself told him to write, fabricated many stories in Cortés' favor which are manifestly false. . . . Gómara's whole book was composed in this vein; he put down only what Cortés testified about himself; so Cortés and Gómara bedazzled the world, which knew nothing whatsoever about the matter; and all this, with the help of God, lover of truth, will appear below."[1]

Gómara's dislike for the Dominican firebrand was no less apparent. Their antagonism arose from their irreconcilable difference over the best method of converting the Indians: Las Casas condemning all use of force and all those who employed it; Gómara holding that conquest must precede evangelization, as he makes quite clear in his Dedication and in Chapter 13, where, in a passage evidently aimed at Las Casas, he says: "Truth to tell, it is war and warriors that really persuade the Indians to give up their idols, their bestial rites, and their abominable bloody sacrifices and the eating of men (which is directly contrary to the law of God and nature), and it is thus that of their own free will and consent they more quickly receive, listen to, and believe our preachers, and accept the Gospel and baptism, which is what Christianity and faith consist of."

There may have been more behind the suppression of Gómara's book than the annoyance of Prince Philip. Its sponsor, Martín Cortés, second Marqués del Valle, could hardly have enjoyed its Dedication, in which Gómara lectures him like a silly schoolboy, which, in fact, he was. At any rate, Philip repeated the edict of suppression in 1566, and in 1572 ordered the confiscation of all Gómara's papers, among which was found the Latin manuscript of his *Life of Cortés*.[2]

---

[1] Las Casas, *Historia de las Indias,* Vol. III, p. 529.
[2] *De Rebus Gestis Ferdinandi Cortesii.* This fragment, long considered anonymous, was established as Gómara's by Ramón Iglesia in a brilliant essay published in 1942,

Like most prohibitions, these had little effect upon the circulation of the *History,* except, perhaps, in Spain. "Gómara," says Iglesia (p. 97), "was the first historian to devote a separate book to the conquest of Mexico. It was the first to be printed on the subject; it was discussed and censured from the moment of its appearance; it was suppressed and withdrawn from circulation; it was republished many times, translated into various languages, and today in Mexico is condemned to an almost total oblivion." Rather surprisingly, only one contemporary English version appeared, that of Thomas Nicholas, which may have been suffocated by its title, *The Pleasant Historie of the Conquest of Weast India, now called New Spayne, Achieved by the worthy Prince Hernando Cortés, Marques of the Valley of Huaxacac, most Delectable to Reade: Translated out of the Spanishe tongue, by T. N. Anno 1578.* Nicholas mutilated the book unmercifully, omitting 101 of its 252 chapters and limiting the narrative to the capture of Mexico, thus destroying the author's design, which was to portray Cortés fully, in defeat as well as victory. Certainly, Nicholas' excision of the heroic, tragic, and enthralling account of the march to Honduras is difficult to excuse or explain. In any event, and for whatever reason, *The Pleasant Historie* was republished only once, in 1596, and then lay forgotten until 1940, when it was reproduced in facsimile.[3] But Gómara's significance did not escape the great Prescott, who wrote: "The two pillars upon which the story of the conquest mainly rests, are the Chronicles of Gómara and of Bernal Díaz."[4]

Iglesia demonstrates, in his thoroughly documented and unanswered argument, that the eclipse suffered by Gómara's *History of the Indies* had causes quite unrelated to the merits of the book. They were, in brief: (1) its condemnation by Las Casas, already mentioned; (2) the uncritical disparagement of Gómara by the eighteenth-century historians, Antonio de Solís and Juan Bautista Muñoz, and their modern followers, who, while dipping into Gómara's works with both hands, complain that he was the paid chaplain of

---

Cronistas e Historiadores de la Conquista de México, Appendix, pp. 225-287. Since I shall be quoting from Iglesia's essay freely through this Introduction, I shall cite it henceforth merely as "Iglesia."
[3] *Scholars' Facsimiles and Reprints,* ed. Herbert I. Priestley (New York, 1940).
[4] William H. Prescott, *History of the Conquest of Mexico,* Book V, Chapter VII.

Cortés, from whom he got a large part of his story, and that therefore he could not be expected to tell the truth about the Conqueror
(Las Casas' thesis); (3) a process that Iglesia calls the "democrati-
zation of history," a kind of leveling movement, in which it is the
fashion to take as gospel the tirades of Bernal Díaz del Castillo, in
his *True History of the Conquest of Mexico,* and depress the importance of Cortés, to the extreme of making him hardly more than
chairman of the board, faithfully carrying out the plans approved by
his subordinates, including, naturally, Bernal Díaz, who, it is inter-
esting to add, failed to be noticed by any chronicler of the conquest
except himself.

One of the gravest charges brought against Gómara by the level-
ers, beginning with Las Casas and Bernal Díaz, is that he was not
present at the events he describes and that, therefore, he could not
know what he was talking about, an absurdity that would force us
to throw out the work of Solís, Muñoz, and Prescott, among others.
That Gómara is carried away at times by his admiration of the Conqueror and gives scant space to the rank and file, Iglesia readily ad-
mits, as he also recognizes that in Gómara's view great men make
history. What else could Gómara be expected to believe? He was,
after all, writing in the middle of the sixteenth century, when history was thought of as the record of God's will operating through
great and excellent men, as he informs us in his Dedication.
And (who can deny it?), judged by any objective standard, Cortés
did make history. And what if Gómara did draw heavily upon
Cortés? What historian in his right mind would not jump at such
an opportunity? Iglesia submits, finally, that Gómara's conciseness,
clarity, and vigor and command of language make him one of the
great writers of the Spanish Renaissance, for which, indeed, he was
recognized in his own day, as he is in ours.[5]

In view of the immense and deserved popularity of the *True
History* of Bernal Díaz, and the parallel neglect of Gómara, it is a
temptation to collate the two and note their divergencies; but that
would only get us lost in a maze of minute and not very significant

---

[5] *"Obra culta, humanística, de proyección heroica de las empresas de Cortés, escrita
en una prosa clásica, es la* Historia General de las Indias (1552) de Francisco López
de Gomara . . ." Angel del Río, *Historia de la Literatura Española,* 2 vols. (New York,
1948), Vol. I, p. 176.

details, and would require another volume besides. In fact, Bernal Díaz and Gómara correspond so closely in their narratives of the conquest that their fundamental difference turns out to be one of style: Bernal's rugged, garrulous, and extremely effective colloquialism, against Gómara's more disciplined restraint. My own conviction is that taking sides in the controversy is foolishness. Each strengthens and supplements the other, and between the two of them they form a body of literature unparalleled in military history.

Iglesia probes Bernal's motives with his usual acumen: "Bernal has the attitude of a resentful man. He reproaches Cortés always with having appropriated for himself the lion's share of the spoils of conquest. He cannot abide not seeing his name stand out in the narrative of the enterprise. Since his part must have been minor, he is obliged, in order to place himself in the front rank, to raise the general level of the participants, and to lower that of Cortés; for it was not only lust for riches that moved Bernal, but thirst for glory, which was typical of the men of the Renaissance. . . .

"If Cortés deprives his companions of their earned reward, Gómara's account deprives them of their last hope of obtaining it, for he makes no mention of their deeds. Hence Bernal includes both in his reproaches. He frequently repeats that Gómara wrote as he did, exalting Cortés alone and failing to record the deeds of the other captains and soldiers, because 'his palm had been greased'. . . .[6]

"There are other aspects [of Bernal's criticism] that merit a more careful consideration, those having to do with the part played by Cortés. Here, beyond a doubt, Gómara's pen ran away with him. His book would have gained if he had entitled it *The Life of Hernán Cortés,* instead of *The History of the Conquest of Mexico,* for he concentrates his attention exclusively on the Extremaduran hero and credits him with all manner of exploits, thus causing Bernal to erupt in justifiable indignation: 'Cortés never said or did a thing without seeking our advice and agreement, although the chronicler Gómara says "Cortés did this, went there, and came from yonder," and adds a great many other nonsensical things. Even if Cortés had been made of iron, as Gómara would have us believe, he could not have been everywhere. . . .' "

_____

[6] Martín Cortés paid Gómara 500 ducats for the *History* (Iglesia, p. 152).

This is all very well, concludes Iglesia, but Bernal's own text proves that it was Cortés who made the plans and then discussed them with his captains, modifying, adapting, or amplifying them, but in the end imposing his decision. One example: Bernal Díaz tells us that Cortés made up his mind to capture Moctezuma *after* having canvassed the opinions of Bernal and the other captains; but Cortés, in his second letter to Charles V, dated at Segura de la Frontera, October 30, 1520, states that in his first letter (i.e., the lost letter written at Vera Cruz in July, 1519) he had said: "I recollect that in my quest for this lord [Moctezuma] I undertook to do a great deal more than I could possibly do, for I certified to Your Highness that I would have him either a prisoner, or dead, or subject to the royal crown of Your Highness."[7] In short, Cortés had planned the capture of Moctezuma well over a year *before* he mentioned it to his companions. This is the mark of a great captain, and it was as a great captain that Gómara saw and portrayed him.

Given the author's subsequent eminence, we know extraordinarily little about him. He tells us (in his *Annals of Charles V*) that he was born in Gómara, in the province of Soria, Old Castile, February 2, 1511. He may have begun his excellent classical education at the University of Salamanca, and he almost certainly perfected it in his ten years' residence in Italy, 1531-1540, where he became the protégé of Diego Hurtado de Mendoza, one of the most eminent humanists and stylists of the century.[8] He accompanied Charles V in the disastrous expedition against Algiers in 1541, when he met Cortés and entered his service. He acted as Cortés' private secretary and chaplain for the next six years, until his employer's death, in 1547. It is a reasonable guess that during this interval Gómara gathered the materials for his *History of the Indies*. After Cortés' death he removed to Valladolid, where he spent the rest of his life writing, and died there some time before 1566.

Gómara tells us virtually nothing about his sources, except to mention that he had talked with Andrés de Tapia, an old companion of Cortés. We do know that he quotes extensively from Cortés' *Letters* and Motolinía's *Memoriales*. His most important source was

[7] Iglesia, p. 150.
[8] H. R. Wagner, "Francisco López de Gómara and His Works." In *Proceedings of the American Antiquarian Society for October, 1948*.

probably Cortés himself, although it may be doubted that Cortés "dictated" the book to his secretary, as charged by Las Casas. In the first place, his style is utterly different from that of the Conqueror, whose marvelously vigorous *Letters* are masterpieces of reporting, but worlds removed from the harmonious prose of Gómara. The task that Gómara set for himself was to give form to the history of the conquest and to make it one with the life of Cortés. He succeeds supremely well, and the secret of his success is his style.

I ventured to state a while back that the principal difference between Bernal Díaz and Gómara is in style: between the homely colloquialism of Bernal and the disciplined classicism of Gómara. The difference is played up by Bernal Díaz himself, between envy and contempt: envy of Gómara's elegance, contempt for the priest writing in his closet. "Whoever reads his *History*," writes Bernal, "will believe that what he says is true, such is the eloquence of his narrative, although it is very contrary to what happened." Again, "Let the reader pay no attention to his rhetoric and polish which, of course, is more agreeable than this coarse style of mine." Besides, in Bernal's mind nothing good can be expected of a *clérigo*, a secular priest. "The Indians," he writes, "at first welcomed the seculars, but later, when they got to know them and saw the greed of some, nay, all, and the outrages they committed in the villages, they turned away from them and would not have them for parish priests, but only Franciscans or Dominicans; and it does the poor Indians no good to inform the bishop of these things, for [the priests] will not listen to him. Oh, what I could say about this business! But it will have to remain in the inkwell."[9] I suspect that this outburst is directed against Gómara.

The "rhetoric and polish" resented by Bernal Díaz and widely accepted as a defect in Gómara is worth looking into, for Gómara tries with all his might to achieve a nobility of expression worthy of his theme. The most outstanding characteristics of his style are dramatic tension, loftiness, pity, irony, and humor. He is a master of dramatic tension. His narrative is a carefully thought-out series of crises, each of which is exploited for maximum effect, and the purpose of which is to portray the hero in every conceivable situation.

---

[9] Iglesia, p. 145.

Most of the time, to be sure, Cortés emerges triumphant, which has given rise to the widely held notion that Gómara is a kind of lickspittle; and certainly in his book Cortés is portrayed as a superb leader of men and an empire-builder, which he was. On the other hand, Gómara is too fine an artist to make an immaculate godling of his hero. When the occasion demands (as it frequently does), he has Cortés intriguing, lying, cajoling, bullying, and threatening—anything to accomplish his purpose. Cortés' policy toward the Indians is an astonishing blend of ferocity, flattery, double-dealing, and magnanimity, and is, moreover, immensely successful. After the horror of the siege of Mexico, his address is such that the conquered become his worshipful followers (always excepting their unreconciled leaders). In this, incidentally, Gómara is fully sustained by Bernal Díaz. His description of the Indians' reception of Cortés upon his return from Honduras in 1526 is the happiest chapter of the book: "The Indians . . . at once came to him loaded with turkeys, fruits, and cacao for him to eat, and brought him plumes, mantles, and silver and gold. . . . He was welcomed at Cempoala, and wherever he passed, even though most of the country was uninhabited, he found an abundance of food and drink. Indians came to greet him from eighty leagues away, bringing presents. . . . They showed the greatest joy at his return; they swept the road and scattered flowers before him, so beloved was he." And in Mexico: "His entrance . . . was the occasion for the greatest outburst of jubilation that you can imagine. All the Spaniards, with Alonso de Estrada [at their head] sallied forth in military array, while the Indians flocked to see him as if he had been Moctezuma himself. They filled the streets to overflowing; they showed their joy by dancing, by the beating of drums and the blowing of conches, trumpets, and many fifes; and all that day and night they surged through the streets making bonfires and illuminations" (Chapter 187).

The jubilation was all the more poignant because Cortés had been given up for dead and his return from Honduras was considered little less than a miracle. The reader will agree that it was, I think, after reading Gómara's heartbreaking account of the expedition, an account that deserves a place beside Xenophon's March of the Ten Thousand. Indeed, I am convinced that Gómara was consciously writing a prose epic and that virtually everything in the book was designed with this end in view, even the breathing spaces, in which he describes the landscape, the people, their customs, dress, and religion, and draws thumbnail sketches of their leaders.

Of Gómara's loftiness of language the Dedication is a fine example, as is the eloquent defense of Christianity that he puts into the mouth of Cortés (Chapter 86), both too long to quote here. Cuauhtémoc's short speech to Cortés upon his surrender is kingly: "I have done everything in my power to defend myself and my people, and everything that it was my duty to do, to avoid the pass in which I now find myself. You may do with me whatever you wish, so kill me, for that will be best" (Chapter 143).

In one of the few places in which I take issue with Iglesia, he accuses Gómara of a frigid indifference toward the Indians (p. 182), although he saves himself later on (p. 215). On the contrary, if only to enhance the achievement of Cortés, Gómara repeatedly shows his admiration and respect for them, except in various aspects of their "abominable religion." Their arts and handicrafts, their skill in government, their fortitude in adversity, their loyalty are praised in the warmest terms, while his compassion for the wretched people of Mexico toward the end of the siege would be monstrous if feigned: "As [the Spaniards] rode through the city they found dead bodies heaped up in the houses and streets, and floating in the water. They also saw a great deal of gnawed bark and roots, and men who were so emaciated that the Spaniards were filled with pity for them. Cortés proposed a truce but they, although their bodies were starved, were strong of heart and told him that . . . if a single one of them survived, he would die fighting" (Chapter 142).

Irony is one of Gómara's favorite and most successful devices, sometimes used playfully and sometimes as a weapon wielded with devastating effect against Cortés' enemies. His contempt for Diego Velázquez, Governor of Cuba and villain of the piece, is compressed into one scalding sentence. The disgruntled Velázquez men in Cortés' army had plotted a mutiny. "Some of these were servants of Velázquez, others his debtors, and a few were his friends" (Chapter 41). Gómara's playfulness can be macabre. During the siege of Mexico, the Tlaxcalan allies of the Spaniards get tired of inaction and decide to stage a raid on their own. As they retreat they are attacked by the Mexicans, "and a very pretty skirmish ensued, in which both sides fought stoutly with equal arms. . . . Both sides lost many dead and wounded, upon whom all dined well!" (Chapter 141).

Gómara is especially fond of the ironical ending. Francisco de Garay, frustrated in his ambitions and captured by Cortés, comes to Mexico and has dinner with his captor on Christmas Eve, 1523. They go to Mass, returning from which Garay catches a cold and shortly after dies of pneumonia. "So died the Adelantado Francisco de Garay, poor and unhappy, in the house of a stranger and the land of his adversary, when he might, if he had not been restless, have died rich and happy in his own house, surrounded by his wife and children" (Chapter 155). His epitaph for Cristóbal de Olid is of a piece. This misguided lieutenant of Cortés had ventured to set up an independent satrapy for himself in Honduras, but the long arm of Cortés overtook him, and he was captured and beheaded by Francisco de las Casas and Gil González de Avila, who, while prisoners in his house, had had the effrontery to warn him of their intention. "So he lost his life because he despised his opponent and did not take his enemy's advice" (Chapter 171).

The Licenciado Luis Ponce de León, armed with a decree of the Council of the Indies, comes from Santo Domingo in 1526 to take the residencia of Cortés. Outmaneuvered by that master of intrigue, and sick besides, he takes to his bed and dies within a few days, to the evident satisfaction of Gómara, who gaily describes his last moments: "Cortés' enemies spread the rumor that the Licenciado had died of poison; but the Licenciado Pero López and Dr. [Cristóbal] de Ojeda, who attended him, treated him for modorra (lethargy) and swore that it was the cause of his death. They even testified that in the afternoon before he died he had the drums rolled for the dying, and that during the ceremony he kept time with his feet, as was witnessed by many. . . . Few have died dancing as this lawyer did!" (Chapter 189).

Gómara's deplored "elegance" of style might give the impression that he was one of those Latinizing pedants who became the plague of Spanish letters, but the truth is that his command of the vernacular is in no sense inferior to that of Bernal Díaz. He wrote in the great popular tradition of Castile. His stay in Italy coincided with the ascendancy of the Erasmian school and the Valdés brothers, Alfonso and Juan, particularly the latter, whose charming *Diálogo de la Lengua*

(1535) could well have served as Gómara's textbook. Whether or not Gómara knew Valdés (and it is quite frustrating that he tells us nothing about himself) he is plainly in the Valdés camp, for he sprinkles his pages with homely and apposite Castilian proverbs, which Valdés recognized as the linguistic treasure house of Spain. Thus, in the speech that Cortés (*via* Gómara) makes to his wavering troops before their assault on Tlaxcala: "If we abandon this country, this war, this adventure that we have undertaken, and turn back, as some of you desire, are we by chance going to be left to disport ourselves in idleness and sloth? Certainly not, you will say, for it is foreign to our Spanish nation to do so when we are engaged in war and our honor is at stake, for *Where goes the ox that he will not draw the plow?*" (Chapter 52).

With humorous incongruity Gómara even puts a Spanish proverb into the mouths of Moctezuma's captains. Pánfilo de Narváez has just landed at Vera Cruz with a large force, and Moctezuma calls a council of war to consider what is to be done. The council is split between those who favor killing the Spaniards piecemeal and those who would wait and kill them all at once. The latter win the debate, clinching their argument with *"The more Moors the greater the spoils!"* (Chapter 95).

In editing the text I have adopted several devices. Gómara, in common with the Spanish writers of his day, tends to abuse relative pronouns, which become quite confusing when strung out indefinitely, their antecedents lost in the distance. So to spare the reader the bother of guessing at the identity of a pronoun, I have in a number of instances repeated the antecedent. Also, Gómara is fond of rambling chapter headings, which sometimes stray from the contents, so I have substituted shorter and more descriptive headings for most chapters. Finally, to keep the book within the bounds of its proper structure, that is, the life of Cortés, I have omitted some ninety pages (Chapters 200 to 248, inclusive), in which the author repeats almost verbatim Motolinía's account of Aztec society and religion, which not only interrupts the narrative but which is redundant and has long since been rendered obsolete by the researches of modern scholars, such as Spinden, Thompson, and Vaillant, whose works are readily available in popular editions.

The translator's task, as I see it, is to build a bridge between author and reader (in this case a bridge 400 years long), for what may have been a commonplace in the sixteenth century may be unintelligible to a reader in the twentieth. It is not, on the other hand, the translator's business to obtrude his own notions of the matter translated. Hence, I have limited my occasional footnotes to the correction of names and dates, and to the clarification of a small number of obscure passages. For the easier identification of place names I have followed the nomenclature in Jorge L. Tamayo's *Geografía General de México* and other standard authorities. The text I have utilized is that of the primitive edition of 1552, as published by Joaquín Ramírez Cabañas. Spanish terms adopted in the translation are defined in the accompanying Glossary.

The eight plates reproduced in the text were selected from the unique and beautiful *Lienzo de Tlaxcala,* a picture story of the conquest painted probably at the order of Viceroy Luis de Velasco about 1552. It was preserved in the municipal archives of Tlaxcala for three hundred years, but disappeared a century ago. Fortunately, several copies had been made, one of which Alfredo Chavero utilized in his edition of 1892. Of the eighty-seven scenes, forty-six depict the actions leading up to the fall of Mexico-Tenochtitlán. Several others are concerned with the conquest of Guatemala by Pedro de Alvarado, and the rest with Nuño de Guzmán's frightful destruction of Michoacán and New Galicia. The theme of the *Lienzo* is, in effect, the conquest of New Spain by the Tlaxcalans (with the assistance, to be sure, of the Spaniards), for the Tlaxcalans were not at all backward about reminding the Crown of their services, for which they were rewarded with privileges and exemptions that lasted throughout the colonial régime. The Bancroft Library of the University of California, Berkeley, courteously placed the Chavero reproductions at my disposal.

I have been helped over many rough spots by my generous and learned colleagues, Professors Carl O. Sauer and Luis Monguió. My greatest debt, however, is to the late Ramón Iglesia, who first acquainted me with the excellence of Gómara's work, and whose tragic and untimely death in 1948 deprived us of one of finest minds in the historiography of Spanish America.

Berkeley, 1963   Lesley Byrd Simpson

xxvi

CORTÉS

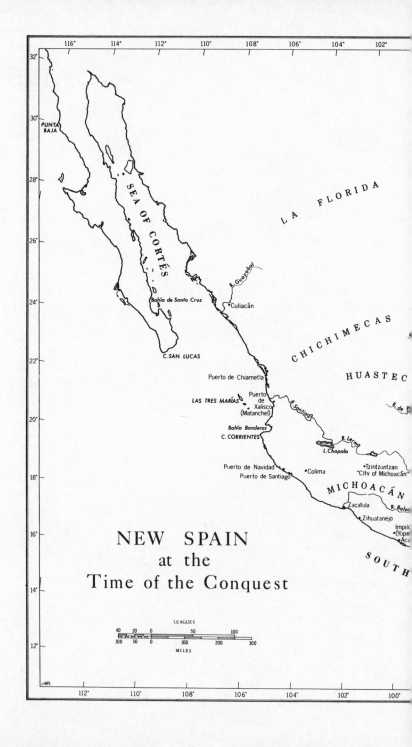

NEW SPAIN
at the
Time of the Conquest

PUNTA
BAJA

SEA OF CORTÉS

Bahía de Santa Cruz
•Culiacán
R. Guayabal

C. SAN LUCAS

LA FLORIDA

CHICHIMECAS

HUASTEC

Puerto de Chiametla

LAS TRES MARÍAS

Puerto
de
Xalisco
(Matanchel)

R. Santiago

R. de P

Bahía Banderas
C. CORRIENTES

R. Lerma
L. Chapala

Puerto de Navidad
Puerto de Santiago

•Colima

•Tzintzuntzan
"City of Michoacán"

MICHOACÁN

Zacatula
Zihuatanejo

R. Balsa

Impilc
•(Yope
•Aca

SOUTH

LEAGUES

40 20 0   50   100
100 50 0   100   200   300

MILES

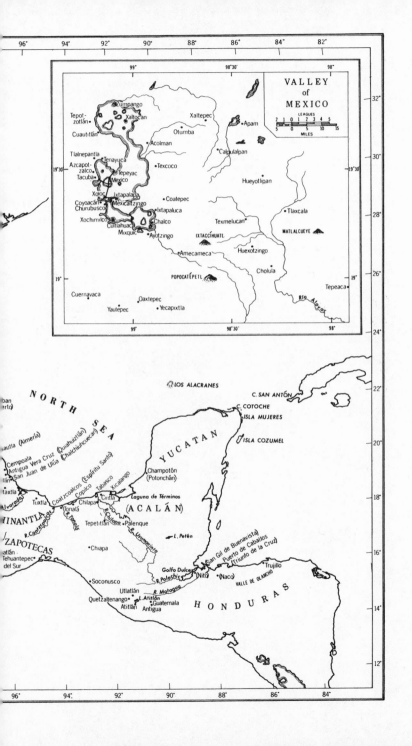

VALLEY of MEXICO

LEAGUES
2 1 0 1 2 3 4 5
5 0 5 10 15
MILES

Tzumpango
Tepotzotlán
Xaltocan
Xaltepec
Apam
Cuauhtitlán
Otumba
Acolman
Tlalnepantla
Tenayuca
Azcapotzalco
Tepeyac
Texcoco
Calpulalpan
Tacuba
Mexico
Hueyotlipan
Xoloc
Ixtapalapa
Coatepec
Coyoacán
Mexicaltzingo
Churubusco
Ixtapaluca
Tlaxcala
Xochimilco
Chalco
Texmelucan
MATLALCUEYE
Cuitlahuac
Mixquic
Ayotzingo
IXTACCÍHUATL
Amecameca
Huexotzingo
Cholula
POPOCATÉPETL
Tepeaca
Cuernavaca
Oaxtepec
Yecapixtla
Yautepec
Río Atoyac

LOS ALACRANES
C. SAN ANTÓN
C. COTOCHE
ISLA MUJERES
NORTH SEA
YUCATAN
ISLA COZUMEL
autla (Almería)
Cempoala
Antigua Vera Cruz (Quiahuiztlán)
San Juan de Ulúa (Chalchiuhcuecan)
taxtla
Champotón (Potonchán)
Tuxtla
Coatzcoalcos (Espíritu Santo)
Copilco
Tabasco
Xicalango
Alvarado
Tonalá
Chilapa
Laguna de Términos
R.Coatzacoalcos
MINANTLA
R. Tonalá
(ACALÁN)
ZAPOTECAS
Tepetitlán
Palenque
R. Chiapas
Usumacinta
L. Petén
Chiapa
atlán
Tehuantepec
del Sur
San Gil de Buenavista
Puerto de Caballos
(Triunfo de la Cruz)
Golfo Dulce
Trujillo
Soconusco
R. Polochic
(Nito)
(Naco)
VALLE DE OLANCHO
Utlatlán
R. Motagua
HONDURAS
Quetzaltenango
L. Atitlán
Guatemala
Atitlán
Antigua

¶La Istoria de las Indias.
Y conquista de México.
1552.

Title page from sixteenth-century edition

Dedication

To the Very Illustrious
Don Martín Cortés, Marqués del Valle

To NO ONE, MY LORD, could I dedicate *The Conquest of Mexico* more fittingly than to your Illustrious Lordship, son of the Conqueror, to the end that along with your patrimony you may inherit its history. In the first instance you have wealth; in the second, fame, for honor and riches here go hand in hand. At the same time your inheritance obligates you to emulate the deeds of your father, Hernán Cortés, and to spend well what he left you. It is no less praiseworthy or virtuous, or perhaps laborious, to retain one's wealth than to increase it. Thus one's honor is sustained; and it was to conserve and perpetuate honor that entails were invented, for it is certain that estates diminish with many divisions thereof, and that with their diminution nobility and glory are lessened and even brought to an end. Late or soon, to be sure, entails and kingdoms must all come to an end, as do all things that had a beginning, either because of failure of the succession, or because of war, in which a change of masters always occurs. But history endures much longer than an estate, because friends are never lacking to keep it fresh, nor do wars interrupt it. The more it ages, therefore, the more it is esteemed.

The kingdoms and lines of Ninus, Darius, and Cyrus, who founded the empires of the Assyrians, Medes, and Persians, ended, but their names and renown live on in the histories. The Gothic kings of our Spain ended with Roderick, but their glorious deeds survive in the chronicles. We should not include among such the kings of the Jews, whose lives and misfortunes are filled with mystery, for they did not long remain in the state of David, who was a man after the heart of God. Kingdoms and seigneuries are of God: He changes them, removes them, and gives them to whom He pleases and as He pleases. Indeed, through His Prophet, he said so Himself. He desires, moreover, that wars, and the deeds and lives of kings and captains, be written down as a memorial and counsel and example for other mortals, and this is what Moses, Esdras, and other saints did.

The Conquest of Mexico and the conversion of the peoples of New Spain can and should be included among the histories of the world, not only because it was well done but because it was very great; and because it was good I am writing its history apart from the others, to serve as a sample of them. It was great, not in time so much as in the fact that many and powerful kingdoms were conquered with little bloodshed or harm to the inhabitants, and many millions were baptized who now live, thanks be to God, as Christians. Men gave up their many wives and took one alone; they gave up sodomy, for they were taught how filthy and how unnatural a sin it is; they cast down their infinity of idols and believed in Our Lord God; and they abandoned the sacrifice of living men and learned to abhor the eating of human flesh, for they had been captives of the devil and would sacrifice and devour a thousand men in a single day in Mexico, and a like number in Tlaxcala and every great provincial capital—a piece of cruelty so unheard-of that it staggers the mind.

Long live, then, the name and memory of him who conquered so vast a land, converted such a multitude of men, cast down so many idols, and put an end to so much sacrifice and the eating of human flesh! Let not oblivion obscure the capture of Moctezuma, a most powerful king, or the taking of Mexico, a strong city, or its rebuilding, which was a very great deed!

Let this suffice for a memorial of the Conquest, and let me not seem to be praising my own work when I write of it, for he who considers the matter will sense its greatness more than I can praise it in a letter. Let me say only that your Lordship, whose life and estate may Our Lord prosper, should feel as proud of the deeds of your father as of his wealth, which he so honorably won in a Christian cause.

To the Reader

EVERY HISTORY, even a badly written one, pleases. Hence it will not be necessary to recommend this one of mine, but only to assure the reader that it is as enjoyable as it is curious, because of its variety, and as notable as it is delightful, because of the many strange happenings it records. The Spanish in which it is written is plain and such as is now current; its order is methodical and simple; its chapters are brief, to avoid wordiness; its sentences, clear and short. To recount when and where a thing happened, and who did it, offers no difficulty; but to explain the why of it is another matter, and so in this particular there is commonly a difference of opinion. He who reads histories, therefore, should content himself with learning what he wishes to learn, briefly and accurately, for he knows indeed that a history which gives elabo.ate details is deceitful and even odious. A general account, if it is public knowledge, does not offend, even though it may annoy a few. Brevity pleases all, except only the curious, who are of small number, and the idle, who are dullards. And so I have written this book of mine in two styles, being brief in my *History* and more lengthy in my *Conquest of Mexico.* I have not described the expeditions and conquests that many others have made at great cost, omitting some because they are of little importance and because most of them are alike, and also because of my ignorance, for otherwise I should not have omitted them. For the rest, no historian ever pleased everybody. If he should deserve a little praise he would be unhappy if he got none and would repay the neglect with churlishness, and if he has written what he would not like to see repeated, he would disown it and thereby truly condemn himself.

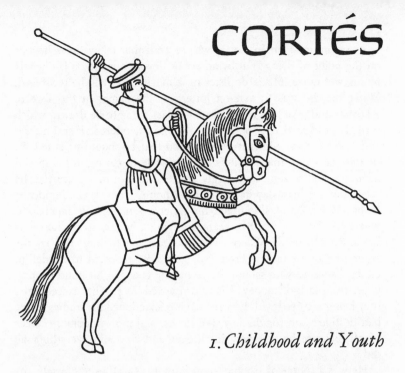

CORTÉS

1. Childhood and Youth

IN THE YEAR 1485, during the reign of the Catholic Monarchs of Castile and Aragon, Don Ferdinand and Doña Isabella, Hernán Cortés was born in Medellín. His father was Martín Cortés de Monroy; his mother Doña Catalina Pizarro Altamirano, both noble, for the four lines of Cortés, Monroy, Pizarro, and Altamirano are very ancient, noble, and honorable. They had little wealth but much honor, a thing that rarely occurs except among those of virtuous life. Their neighbors respected them for their goodness and piety, and they themselves took pride in being honorable in all their words and deeds, by which they earned the love and esteem of everyone. She was a very honest woman, pious, strong-minded, and parsimonious; he was devout and charitable, and during his youth had served in the Army as lieutenant in a company of horse under the command of his kinsman, Alonso de Hermosa, one of the captains of Alonso de Monroy. This last-named attempted to make himself Master of his Order, against the wishes of the Queen, and because of it, Don Alonso de Cárdenas, Master of Santiago, made war upon him.

7

As an infant Hernán Cortés was so frail that many times he was on the point of dying; but by an act of devotion made on his behalf by his wet nurse, María de Esteban, a native of Oliva, he recovered. What she did was to make a lottery of the names of the Twelve Apostles and give him as advocate the last name to be drawn, which turned out to be that of St. Peter, to whom she offered several masses and prayers, with which it pleased God that he should be cured. So he took St. Peter, that glorious Apostle of Jesus Christ, as his special advocate, and became so strongly attached to him that every year he celebrated his feast day in church or at home, wherever he happened to be. When he was fourteen his parents sent him to Salamanca, where he remained for two years, studying grammar in the house of Francisco Núñez de Valera, who was married to Inés de Paz, the sister of Cortés' father. From Salamanca he returned to Medellín, either disgusted with school life or having changed his mind or, perhaps, from lack of money. His return vexed his parents exceedingly, they being annoyed with him for having abandoned his studies. They had destined him for the law, the richest and most honorable career of all, because he was very intelligent and clever in everything he did.

He was a source of trouble to his parents as well as to himself, for he was restless, haughty, mischievous, and given to quarreling, for which reason he decided to seek his fortune. Two ways were open to him at the time, both of which suited his purpose and his inclination: one, to go to Naples with Gonzalo Fernández de Córdoba, known as *El Gran Capitán;* the other, to go to the Indies with Nicolás de Ovando, who was being sent there as Governor. Considering which of the two would be best for him, he finally decided on the Indies, because Ovando knew him and would give him a place, and also because it struck him as the more promising on account of the quantity of gold that was being brought in from there. But, while Ovando was arranging his departure and the fleet was being readied, Cortés went to a house one night to visit a woman and, as he was walking along the badly cemented wall of the garden, it gave way with him. At the noise made by the falling wall and the arms and shield, a young husband, jealous of his wife, ran out and, seeing Cortés lying near the door, tried to kill him, but was prevented from doing so by his old mother-in-law. Cortés was injured by the fall, and besides was stricken with a quartan fever, which kept him in bed for a long time, so he was unable to go with Governor Ovando. Upon his recovery he decided to go to Italy, as he had first thought of doing, and set out for Valencia. He did not get to Italy, however, but wandered idly about for nearly a year, not without hardship and privation. He then returned to Medellín resolved to go to the Indies, and his parents gave him their blessing and money for the voyage.

2. Cortés Goes to the Indies

HERNÁN CORTÉS was nineteen when he went to the Indies in the year of Our Lord 1504, and as young as he was he dared to make this long voyage alone. He took passage on a ship belonging to one Alonso Quintero, of Palos de Moguer, which was accompanied by four other vessels laden with merchandise. Their voyage was prosperous from San Lúcar de Barrameda to Gomera in the Canary Islands, where they took on sufficient supplies for the rest of the passage. But Alonso Quintero, from greed, sailed off by himself in the night without speaking to his companions, thinking to reach Santo Domingo before them and sell his goods. He had no sooner sailed, however, than a storm came up, so severe that it carried away his mast, for which reason he had to put back to Gomera and beg the others, who had not yet sailed, to wait for him while he repaired his mast. This they did, and all sailed together and remained in sight of one another for a great stretch of the sea.

Quintero, however, seeing that the wind was in his favor, again sailed off ahead of his companions, hoping to profit by his speed; but his pilot, a certain Francisco Niño de Huelva, had lost his bearings and they were soon in complete confusion. The sailors were filled with anxiety; the pilot was sad; and the passengers wept, not knowing how much of their voyage they had accomplished, or how much of it lay before them. The captain blamed the pilot, and the pilot the captain, for it seems they were at odds. Meanwhile, provisions were getting scarce and water was giving out, and they had only rain water to drink. All confessed; some cursed their luck; others awaited the death that some had already suffered, or they expected to be cast away in the land of the Caribs, where men are eaten. While they were thus troubled, on Good Friday about sunset a dove flew to the ship and alighted on a yardarm. All took this as a good omen; they considered it a miracle and wept with joy. Some said that the dove had been sent to console them; others, that land was near. So they gave thanks to God and set the ship's course in the direction of the dove's flight. But the dove flew off and all were greatly downcast thereat. Nevertheless they did not despair, and on Easter Sunday they sighted the Island of Española, whereupon the steersman, one Cristóbal Zarza, shouted "Land! Land!"—a word that delights and comforts voyagers. The pilot looked and recognized Punta de Samana, and three or four days later they dropped anchor at Santo Domingo, as they had so longed to do, and there they found the other four ships, which had arrived many days ago.

3. Santo Domingo

WHEN CORTÉS ARRIVED at Santo Domingo Governor Ovando was not in the city, but one of his secretaries, Medina by name, gave Cortés lodgings, informed him of conditions on the island, and gave him a piece of advice: that Cortés should register as a citizen, by which he would acquire a caballería, that is, a building lot and certain lands for cultivation. But Cortés, whose notion was that he had only to arrive in order to be weighed down with gold, scorned the advice, saying he preferred mining. Medina told him to think it over, for getting gold was a matter of luck and hard work.

Upon the Governor's return, Cortés called to pay his respects, explain his presence there, and give an account of affairs in Extremadura. On the advice of Ovando he remained in Santo Domingo, and a little later joined Diego Velázquez in a campaign against Aniguaiagua, Buacaiarina, and other provinces [of Española] which, because of the rebellion of the widow Anacoana, a great lady, had not been pacified.

Ovando gave Cortés some Indians of the province of Daiguaio and appointed him notary of the town council of Azúa, a villa he had founded, where Cortés engaged in trade for five or six years. During this time he planned to go to Veragua with Diego de Nicuesa, but was prevented by an abscess on his right leg behind the knee, a circumstance to which he owed his life, or at least it saved him from the many hardships and perils suffered by those who did go, as we have related in our *History.**

4. Adventures in Cuba

ADMIRAL DON DIEGO COLUMBUS, Governor of the Indies, sent Diego Velázquez on the conquest of Cuba, supplying him with arms, men, and provisions. Hernán Cortés accompanied him as clerk of the treasurer, Miguel de Pasamonte, to keep account of the royal revenues and the King's fifth. He did so at the request of Diego Velázquez himself, for Cortés was able and diligent. In the distribution of Indians that Velázquez made after the conquest, he gave his brother-in-law, Juan Xuárez, and Cortés jointly the Indians of Manicarao.

Cortés settled in Santiago de Baracoa, which was the first town on the island. He raised cattle, sheep, and mares, and was the first to own a herd and a house. He extracted a great deal of gold with the labor of his Indians and soon was rich enough to put 2,000 castellanos into a partnership with Andrés de Duero, a trader. His influence and authority with Diego Velázquez were so great that the latter entrusted him with his affairs and the supervision of the erection of several buildings, including a smelter and a hospital.

Now, a certain Juan Xuárez, a native of Granada, had brought to Cuba his mother and three or four sisters, who had gone to Santo Domingo in the year 1509 with the Vicereine, Doña María de Toledo, thinking to pick up some rich husbands there, for they were poor. One of the sisters, whose name was Catalina, even said quite seriously that she was going to be a great lady, having either dreamed it or heard it from some astrologer, although it was said that her mother knew a good many things. The Xuárez girls were pretty, for which reason and because there were few Spanish women about, they

---

* Gómara, here and elsewhere, refers to his *Historia General de las Indias.*

were much sought after; and Cortés courted Catalina and eventually married her, although there was some trouble about it and he was imprisoned, because he had refused to marry her and she had sued him to force him to keep his promise. Diego Velázquez favored her, because he was in love with one of her sisters who had an unsavory reputation, he being excessively under the influence of women. Cortés was also sued by Baltasar Bermúdez, Juan Xuárez, two men both named Antonio Velázquez, and a certain Villegas, to force him to marry Catalina, and, since they hated him, they accused him before Diego Velázquez of many wicked deeds in the affairs that had been entrusted to him; moreover, [they said] that he had had some strange and secret dealings with several people.

All this, though it was false, bore the color of truth, for many men had gone to the house of Cortés complaining that Diego Velázquez had given them no allotments of Indians, or very small ones. And Diego Velázquez believed their charges because of his annoyance at Cortés' refusal to marry Catalina Xuárez, and he scolded him severely in the presence of many, even arresting him and putting him in the stocks. Cortés feared a trial before false witnesses, as commonly happens in those parts, so he broke the padlock, seized the guard's sword and shield, opened a window, let himself down, and took sanctuary in the church.

Diego Velázquez was angry with the guard, Cristóbal de Lagos, saying that Cortés had bribed him. He then attempted to get Cortés out of sanctuary by trickery and even by force, but Cortés saw through his words and resisted the force. One day, however, he got careless and was picked up, while walking without the church door, by the constable, Juan Escudero, and others, who locked him in a vault in irons. At that time many favored Cortés, because they thought the Governor was acting from passion. When Cortés found himself imprisoned he doubted that he would be set free, and was convinced that they would send him either to Santo Domingo or to Spain. After many attempts to free his foot from its shackle he finally succeeded, although it cost him a good deal of pain. That same night he exchanged clothing with the boy who served him and escaped from the vault, slipping out a side door to a skiff and making off in it. In order to prevent pursuit he also cut loose the boat of another ship near by. The current of the Macaniagua, the river that flows past Baracoa, was so swift that he could not make headway against it, he being tired and rowing alone; nor did he dare attempt to land, fearing he would drown if the skiff should capsize. So he took off his clothes, tied up in a bundle on his head certain documents unfavorable to Velázquez that he had written as notary of the town council and clerk of the treasurer, took to the water and swam ashore. Then he went to his house, spoke with Juan Xuárez, and once again took sanctuary, armed, in the church.

Diego Velázquez sent word to Cortés to let bygones be bygones and to be friends as before, and to join an expedition against certain islands that had rebelled. Cortés married Catalina Xuárez because he had promised to do so, and also because he wished to live in peace, but he refused to speak to Diego Velázquez for many days. Diego Velázquez assembled many men and marched against the rebels.

Cortés told his brother-in-law, Juan Xuárez, to get him a lance and a crossbow and conceal them outside the city. He left the church at nightfall and, picking up his crossbow, he went with his brother-in-law to a farm where Diego Velázquez, attended only by his servants, was staying, for the rest of the men were lodged in a village near by, not all of them having reported yet, since it was the first day of the expedition. Cortés knocked at the door, which was unlocked, and told the servant who answered that he wished to speak with the Lord Governor, after which he entered. Diego Velázquez, seeing him armed and at such a late hour, was alarmed, but he begged Cortés to stop and eat with him, and to rest without fear. Cortés said that he had come only to learn the nature of the charges the other had made against him, and to assure Velázquez that he was his friend and servant. So they shook hands and after a long talk lay down together in the same bed, where they were found the next morning by Diego de Orellana, who had come to tell the Governor that Cortés had escaped.

In this fashion Cortés regained the confidence of Diego Velázquez which he had formerly enjoyed, and went with him to the war. Upon his return he almost got drowned in the Bocas de Bani, where he had put in to see the shepherds and Indians at his mines of Baracoa, for his canoe had capsized at night half a league from land during a storm. He escaped by swimming, guiding himself by the light of a fire, about which some shepherds were eating near the shore. It is by such adventures and roundabout means that excellent men make their way to the goal of the good fortune that awaits them.

5. Discovery of New Spain

FRANCISCO HERNÁNDEZ DE CÓRDOBA (as we have related in the other part of this book) discovered Yucatan in 1517, while on a slaving and trading expedition, in three vessels that he and Cristóbal Morante and Ochoa de Caicedo had fitted out. Although he got nothing out of the expedition but wounds, he did bring back word of a land rich in gold and silver, and people wearing clothes. The next year, Diego Velázquez, Governor of the Island of Cuba, sent his nephew, Juan de Grijalba, with two hundred Spaniards in four vessels, to the land described by Francisco Hernández, thinking to acquire a great deal of gold and silver in exchange for merchandise. So Juan de Grijalba went to Yucatan, where he fought a battle with the men of Champotón, and was wounded. He sailed into the River of Tabasco, which has since been named the Grijalba after him, and there exchanged things of little value for cotton garments and beautiful pieces of featherwork.

Thence he sailed to San Juan de Ulúa, took possession of the land in the name of Diego Velázquez for the King, and traded his goods for gold, cotton cloth, and featherwork. If he had been aware of his good fortune he would have planted a colony in that land, as his companions begged him to do, and would have become what Cortés became. But this great good was not for one who could not recognize it, although he excused himself by saying that he had not gone there to found a colony, but to trade and to discover whether the land of Yucatan was an island or not. He gave it up also because of his fear of the many people and great size of the country, which he saw was not an island, and so he did not penetrate Tierra Firme.

There were [in his company], moreover, many men who wished to return to Cuba, such as Pedro de Alvarado, who was madly in love with an island girl. So Grijalba set out on his return voyage to Diego Velázquez, with an account of what had happened thus far, making his way up the coast as far as Pánuco, and trading with the natives for gold, feathers, and cotton, against the wishes of the others, and he even wept because they did not want to return with him, so weak-spirited was he. Five months had elapsed between his departure from the island and his return to it, and eight since his departure from Santiago, and when he arrived Diego Velázquez refused to see him—a fate that he deserved.

6. Grijalba Trades with the Indians

JUAN DE GRIJALBA acquired from the Indians of Potonchán, San Juan de Ulúa, and other places along the coast so many and such valuable things that the men of his company would have been glad to stay there, and he got them so cheaply that his men would willingly have traded everything they had for them. The workmanship of many of the articles was worth more than the materials. In brief, what he acquired was the following:

  1 small hollow idol, gold
  1 same, with horns and hair, with a chain about its neck, a fly-flap in its hand, and a small jewel in its navel
  1 piece like a gold medallion, with several stones set in it
  1 helmet, gold, with two horns and black hair
22 earrings, gold, each with three gold pendants
22 more of same, smaller
  4 very wide bracelets, gold
  1 large purse of thin gold
  1 string of hollow beads, gold, with a frog of same, well made
  1 string of same, with a small gold lion
  1 pair of large gold pendants
  2 small eagles, gold, well molded
  1 small salt cellar, gold
  2 pendants of gold and turquoise, each with eight pendants
  1 woman's necklace of 12 pieces, with 24 stone pendants
  1 large necklace, gold
  6 small necklaces of thin gold
  7 gold necklaces, with stones
20 gold fishhooks

12 gold nuggets, worth 50 ducats
1 gold braid
Several thin gold plates
1 gold vessel
1 hollow idol of thin gold
Several thin gold brooches
9 thin gold beads, with fastenings
2 strings beads, gilded
1 string wooden beads, gilded, with small gold tubes
1 small gold cup set with 8 purple stones and 23 of other colors
1 two-faced mirror trimmed with gold
4 gold bells
1 small gold salt cellar
1 small gold vessel
Several small gold necklaces of little value, and several earrings of base gold
1 hollow piece resembling an apple, gold
40 axes of gold and copper, worth as much as 2,500 ducats
All the pieces necessary for a man's armor, of thin gold
1 suit wooden armor, gilded, set with small black stones
1 small feather ornament of leather and gold
4 cuisses covered with gold leaf
2 gilded wooden containers
2 shields, covered with feathers of many beautiful colors
Several other shields of gold and feathers
1 large feather piece in colors, with a small bird in the middle, very lifelike
1 fan of gold and feathers
2 feather flyflaps
2 small alabaster vessels filled with various stones, among them one worth 2,000 ducats
Several tin beads
2 strings pottery beads, round, covered with very thin gold leaf
130 hollow gold beads
Many strings of pottery and wooden beads, gilded
Many gilded beads
1 pair gilded wooden scissors
2 gilded masks

1 mask inlaid with gold and mosaic

4 gilded wooden masks, one inlaid with two straight bands of turquoise; another, with ears of the same, although with more gold; another, inlaid in the same way from the nose up; a fourth, from the eyes up

4 wooden plates covered with gold leaf

1 dog's head covered with little stones

1 head of some other animal, of stone and gold, with a crown and crest and two pendants, all of gold, but thinner

5 pairs of shoes, like grass sandals

3 skins, dyed red

7 flint sacrificial knives

2 painted wooden bowls; 1 pitcher

1 jacket with short sleeves, made of feathers of many colors, very fine

1 garment like a dressing gown, of fine cotton

1 large feather mantle, fine

Many thin cotton mantles

Many others of coarse cotton

2 headdresses, or veils, of good cotton

Many delicate perfumes

A great deal of chili and other fruits

Besides all this, he brought back a woman they gave him, and several men that he captured, for one of whom he was offered a ransom of his weight in gold, which Grijalba refused.

He also brought back word of the Amazons who lived on certain islands, and many believed it, for they were astonished at the things they had got at absurd prices, all of them together costing only six shirts of coarse linen. [In exchange the Spaniards gave only:]

5 kerchiefs

3 pairs of drawers

5 [pairs of] women's slippers

5 wide leather belts worked with colored threads, with their leather pouches and bags

Many small skin purses

Many leather straps, with one or two metal fastenings

6 small mirrors

4 glass medallions

2,000 green glass beads, which they consider fine
  100 strings of many-colored beads
   20 combs, highly prized
    6 pair scissors, much esteemed
   15 knives, large and small
1,000 sewing needles; 2,000 pins
    8 sandals
    1 pair tongs; 1 hammer
    7 colored capes
    3 coats, striped and colored
    1 coarse coat, with its cape
    1 green velvet dress, worn, with a black velvet cap

7. Cortés Fits Out His Fleet

SINCE JUAN DE GRIJALBA delayed longer in returning than had Francisco Hernández, and had not sent him word of what he was doing, Diego Velázquez dispatched Cristóbal de Olid in a caravel, to help him and learn of his actions, charging Olid to return immediately with any letters of Grijalba. Cristóbal de Olid, however, sailed very little about Yucatan and did not encounter Grijalba, but returned to Cuba. This was a heavy loss for both Diego Velázquez and Grijalba, for if Olid had gone as far as San Juan de Ulúa or farther, he might perhaps have induced Grijalba to found a colony there; but he said he had to turn back because he had lost his anchors.

After the departure of Olid, Pedro de Alvarado arrived with the news of [Grijalba's] discovery, and with many articles of gold, feathers, and cotton that they had acquired. At the sight of them, and with what Alvarado told him, Diego Velázquez was delighted and astonished, as were all the Spaniards in Cuba. He feared that Grijalba would return, as certain invalids who had come [with Alvarado] told him that Grijalba was unwilling to plant a colony in that country, which was heavily populated and warlike; and Velázquez even distrusted the prudence and courage of his kinsman [Grijalba]. So he decided to send off several ships, well supplied with men and arms and merchandise, thinking to enrich himself by trading and founding a colony in that country by force. He begged Baltasar Bermúdez to undertake it, but because Velázquez demanded of him three thousand ducats for arms and provisions Bermúdez refused to accept, saying that the cost would be greater than the profit. Diego Velázquez, in fact, was somewhat stingy and had little stomach for spending, and wished to dispatch a fleet at the expense of others, as he had done with Grijalba. [In that expedition] Francisco de Montejo had fitted out a ship with a great stock of provisions, as had Alonso Hernández Portocarrero, Alonso de Avila, Diego de Ordaz, and many others who had gone with Grijalba.

Diego Velázquez now proposed to Hernán Cortés that they share the cost of the expedition, because Cortés had two thousand castellanos in gold in the company of Andrés de Duero, a trader; and, since Cortés was a diligent, discreet, and valorous man, Velázquez begged him to command the fleet and spoke enthusiastically of the voyage and the expedition. Hernán Cortés, who had the courage as well as the desire for it, accepted the partnership, the expense, and command of the expedition, in the belief that its cost would not be excessive, and so they promptly reached an agreement. They sent Juan de Saucedo, who had returned with Alvarado, [to Santo Domingo] to get the permission of the Jeronymite Fathers, who were governing at the time, to trade in order to cover their expenses, and seek out Juan de Grijalba, for without such permission no trading could be done, that is, the exchange of merchandise for gold and silver. Fray Luis de Figueroa, Fray Alonso de Santo Domingo, and Fray Bernardino de Manzanedo, the Governors, issued a license to Hernán Cortés as captain and outfitter, in company with Diego Velázquez, commanding him to include a treasurer and inspector to collect and hold the King's fifth, as was the custom. While awaiting the Governors' license, Hernán Cortés set about his preparations for the expedition: He approached his friends and many others to inquire if they would go along, and found three hundred who were willing to do so; he bought a caravel and a brigantine; he already had the caravel in which Pedro de Alvarado had returned, as well as another brigantine belonging to Diego Velázquez, all of which he stocked with arms, artillery, and munitions. He bought wine, oil, beans, chickpeas, and other things; he acquired, on credit, from Diego Sanz, a shopkeeper, a store of merchandise, for six hundred pesos gold; Diego Velázquez gave him a thousand castellanos from the estate of Pánfilo de Narváez, for whom he held a power-of-attorney during the latter's absence, claiming he had not a penny of his own, and he gave money, joint notes, and securities to many soldiers who were to go with the fleet. Both Cortés and Velázquez stipulated, in the presence of Alonso de Escalante, public and royal notary, what each was to do, and signed the agreement on October 23 of the year '18.

In the meantime, while all this was going on, Juan de Grijalba returned to Cuba, and with his arrival Diego Velázquez changed his mind and decided not to spend any more money on the fleet that Cortés was fitting out; nor did he even wish Cortés to complete its preparation. His reasons for doing so were that he wished to send out the ships of Grijalba on his own account; that he was alarmed by the expenses incurred by Cortés and the freedom with which Cortés was spending money; that he thought Cortés had a mind to take over the affair, as he had done with Admiral Don Diego Columbus;* that, following the advice of Bermúdez and the other two Velázquez, he thought he could not trust Cortés, who was, after all, an Extremaduran, crafty, haughty, touchy about his honor, and who would seek vengeance for past wrongs. Bermúdez was very regretful that he had not accepted command of the expedition when he had been begged to do so, for he could now see the great and beautiful spoils that Grijalba had brought back, and how rich the newly discovered land was. The various Velázquez relatives would have liked to be captains and commanders of the fleet, although they were not fitted for it, as was said. Diego Velázquez also thought that if he should turn cool toward the expedition, Cortés would give it up, and he sent Amador de Lárez, a very prominent man, to persuade him to do so, now that Grijalba had returned, and to assure him that he would be reimbursed for all his expenses.

Cortés, who saw through the motives of Diego Velázquez, told Lárez that he would not give up the expedition if only on account of his honor; nor would he withdraw from the pact; that, if Diego Velázquez wished to send another in his place who would fit out the expedition at his own expense, he might do so; but that Cortés had already procured the license of the governing Fathers. So Cortés

---

* Rather, the Jeronymite Fathers, as in the preceding paragraph.

spoke with his friends and certain influential persons who were preparing to go on the expedition, to see whether they would follow and favor him, and as soon as he was assured of their support he began to collect money. He borrowed four thousand pesos in gold from Andrés de Duero, Pedro de Jerez, and Antonio de Santa Clara, merchants, as well as from certain others, and with it he bought two ships, six horses, and a great deal of clothing. He engaged many men, took a house, entertained, and began to go about armed and with a great company, at which many grumbled, saying that he was acting like a great lord, although he had no title.

It was about this time that Juan de Grijalba arrived at Santiago, and Diego Velázquez refused to see him because he had abandoned that rich land. Velázquez was also worried because Cortés was going there with such a great force, but he was unable to stop him, because everyone was going along, not only the men of Santiago, but also Grijalba's men. Indeed, if he had pursued the matter rigorously there would have been an uprising in the city, and even killings. And so, since he had been left out of it, he concealed his feelings, but even so he ordered that no provisions should be given them, as many said.

Cortés decided to leave at once, and proclaimed that he was going on his own authority, now that Grijalba had returned. He told his soldiers not to have anything to do with Diego Velázquez and to embark with whatever provisions they could find. He took from Fernando Alfonso the swine and sheep that Alfonso was going to weigh the next day at the slaughterhouse, giving him in payment a gold chain with a thistle design, which would also cover the penalty of depriving the city of its meat supply. He departed from Baracoa the eighteenth of November [1518], with more than three hundred Spaniards, in six ships.

8. Men and Ships That Cortés Took on the Conquest

CORTÉS LEFT SANTIAGO very short of provisions for his many men and for the voyage, which was still uncertain. As soon as he had sailed he sent Pedro Xuárez Gallinato de Porra, a native of Seville, to Jamaica with a caravel, ordering him to bring his purchases to Cape Corrientes, or to Punta de San Antón, which is the last point of the island toward the west. He himself went with the rest to Macaca, where he bought 300 loads (*cargas*) of bread and a few pigs from Tamayo, the King's treasurer. From there he went to Trinidad and bought a ship from Alonso Guillén, and from private citizens he bought three horses and 500 loads of feed. At Trinidad he learned that Juan Núñez Sedeño was passing with a shipload of provisions, so he sent Diego de Ordaz in a well-armed caravel to intercept it and bring it to Punta de San Antón. Ordaz captured it in the Canal de Jardines and brought it there as he had been instructed. Sedeño and others came to Trinidad with manifests of their cargoes, which included 4,000 arrobas of bread, 1,500 flitches of salt pork, and many fowl, for which Cortés gave them in payment several knots of gold and other pieces, and to Sedeño an agreement by which he became a member of the expedition. At Trinidad, Matanzas, Carenas, and other places Cortés picked up nearly 200 of Grijalba's men, who were living there.

Sending his ships on ahead, Cortés went by land with his men to Havana, which was then situated on the south bank of the mouth of the Onicaxinal; but the people there, out of loyalty to Diego Velázquez, refused to sell him any provisions, notwithstanding which, Cristóbal de Quesada, the Bishop's tithe collector, in company with a vendor of papal bulls, sold him 2,000 flitches of salt pork and a like number of loads of maize, yucca, and chili. With all this, Cortés supplied his fleet reasonably well and then set about assigning crews and provisions to the ships.

About that time, Pedro de Alvarado, Alonso de Avila, Francisco de Montejo, and many others who had gone to see Diego Velázquez, arrived, among them a certain Garnica carrying letters from Velázquez to Cortés, begging Cortés to wait a little, because Velázquez would either come himself, or send him word of things important to them both. Velázquez also sent letters to Diego de Ordaz and others, telling them to arrest Cortés. So Ordaz invited Cortés to dine on board the caravel he commanded, thinking to bring him to Santiago in it; but Cortés, smelling a trap, pretended to have a stomach-ache and did not appear at the dinner, and to avoid further trouble went on board his own ship. There he gave the customary signal to retire, and ordered all to follow him to San Antón, where they soon arrived in good order.

At Guaniguanico Cortés reviewed his troops and counted 550 Spaniards, including 50 sailors. He divided them into eleven companies, to which he appointed as captains, Alonso de Avila, Alonso Hernández de Portocarrero, Diego de Ordaz, Francisco de Montejo, Francisco de Morla, Francisco de Salceda, Juan de Escalante, Juan Velázquez de León, Cristóbal de Olid, and a certain Escobar. Cortés himself, as General, took command of one company. He appointed eleven captains because there were eleven vessels. He named as senior pilot, Antón de Alaminos, who had been with Francisco Hernández de Córdoba and Juan de Grijalba. There were also 200 islanders from Cuba to act as bearers and servants, several Negroes and a few Indian women, and 16 horses and mares. He also counted 5,000 flitches of salt pork and 6,000 loads of maize, yucca, and chili. Each load is two arrobas, the weight that an Indian can carry on the road. There were also many chickens [turkeys] and a great deal of sugar, wine, oil, chickpeas, and other legumes; a quantity of merchandise, that is to say, bells, looking glasses, strings of glass beads, needles, pins, purses, leather thongs, ribbons, clasps, buckles, knives, scissors, tongs, hammers, iron axes, shirts, kerchiefs, headdresses, neckcloths, breeches, and linen handkerchiefs; shirts, capes, hose, and woollen hoods—all of which he distributed among the ships.

The flagship was a nao of 100 tons; three others ranged from 70 to 80 tons; the rest were small open vessels and brigantines. The flag that Cortés hoisted was of white and blue flames with a cross in the middle, and about the margins a Latin motto which, translated, said: "Friends, let us follow the Cross, and with faith in this symbol we shall conquer." Such was the ceremony with which Cortés began his expedition, and with such scant means did he win such a great kingdom. And such, neither larger nor better, was the fleet that he led to strange lands that he did not yet know; and with such a small company did he vanquish innumerable Indians. Never did a captain with such a small army do such deeds, win so many victories, and win so vast an empire. Nor did he even have money with which to pay his men; rather, he was heavily in debt. It is not necessary to pay the Spaniards who go to war and the conquest of the Indies; if they had to be paid they would go to places nearer at hand. In the Indies every man seeks an estate or great riches.

The fleet now being readied and the men distributed, as you have heard, Cortés made a short speech to his men, the substance of which is as follows.

9. Cortés' Speech to His Troops

"CERTAIN IT IS, my friends and companions, that every good man of spirit desires and strives, by his own effort, to make himself the equal of the excellent men of his day and even those of the past. And so it is that I am embarking upon a great and beautiful enterprise, which will be famous in times to come, because I know in my heart that we shall take vast and wealthy lands, peoples such as have never before been seen, and kingdoms greater than those of our monarchs. Certain it is also that the lust for glory extends beyond this mortal life, and that taking a whole world will hardly satisfy it, much less one or two kingdoms.

"I have assembled ships, arms, horses, and the other materials of war, a great stock of provisions, and everything else commonly needed and profitable in conquests. I have spent large sums, for which I have put in pawn my own estate and those of my friends, for it seems to me that the less I retain of it the greater will be my honor. Small things must be given up when great things present themselves. As I hope in God, more profit will come to our King and nation from our expedition than from those of all the others. I hardly need mention how pleasing it will be to God Our Lord, for love of whom I have willingly offered my toil and my estate; nor shall I speak of the danger to life and honor to which I have exposed myself getting this fleet together, because I would have you know that I do not seek gain from it so much as honor, for good men hold honor dearer than riches.

"We are engaging in a just and good war which will bring us fame. Almighty God, in whose name and faith it will be waged, will give us victory, and time will see the accomplishment that always follows upon whatever is done and guided by intelligence and good counsel. We must, therefore, employ a different way, a different reasoning, and a different skill from those of Córdoba and Grijalba. I shall not pursue the matter further because of the pressure of time, which urges us onward. There we shall do as we shall see fit, and here I offer you great rewards, although they will be wrapped about with great hardships. Valor loves not idleness, and so, therefore, if you will take hope for valor, or valor for hope, and if you do not abandon me, as I shall not abandon you, I shall make you in a very short time the richest of all men who have crossed the seas, and of all the armies that have here made war. You are few, I see, but such is your spirit that no effort or force of Indians will prevail against you, for we have seen by experience how God has favored the Spanish nation in these parts, and how we have never lacked courage or strength, and never shall. Go your way now content and happy, and make the outcome equal to the beginning."

10. Cozumel Expedition

THE DISCOURSE OF CORTÉS filled his companions with great hope, as well as with admiration for himself, and now they felt such a keen desire to accompany him to a land that hardly anyone had even seen, that it seemed to them they were not going to war, but to certain victory and spoils. Cortés was very pleased to see his men contented and happy to be with him on his expedition, and he boarded his flagship and ordered them all to embark at once. As soon as the wind was favorable he set sail, having first heard Mass and prayed to God for guidance, on the eighteenth day of February of the year of Our Lord, Redeemer of the world, 1519. When they were under way he gave his captains and pilots, as is customary, the name of their patron saint [for the voyage], that is to say, his advocate, St. Peter, and told them to keep the flagship always in sight, for which purpose he hung up a great lantern as a beacon and guide for them to follow. He set the course due west from Punta de San Antón, the last point of Cuba, to Cape Catoche, the nearest point of Yucatan, for which he commanded them to steer directly, and from there to follow the coast between north and west.

On that first night, after Cortés had begun the passage of the strait that lies between Cuba and Yucatan, a matter of 60 leagues, a violent northwester came up and blew the fleet off its course; the ships were scattered, and each one ran on as best it could. Following the orders given to the pilots, all the ships save one found their way to the island of Cozumel, although they did not keep together, nor did all arrive at the same time. Those most delayed were the flagship and one commanded by Captain Francisco de Morla which, either through the negligence or weakness of the steersman, or because of the violence of the wind and waves, lost her rudder. Morla hoisted a flare as a distress signal. Cortés saw it and brought up his flagship, and, seeing the necessity and danger the other was in, hove to and waited for daylight, to encourage the crew and lend aid. At dawn, by the grace of God, the sea was calmer and not so rough as it had been during the night. As soon as there was light enough they found the rudder floating between the two ships. Captain Morla plunged into the water with a rope tied around him and swam to the rudder, which was hoisted on board and secured in its proper place, whereupon they set sail again.

They sailed all that day and the next without sighting land, but the day following they reached Punta de las Mujeres, where they found a few of their ships. Cortés ordered them to follow him, and set his course in the direction in which the wind and weather had probably driven the missing ships. He anchored at Cozumel, where he found them, all but one, which was not heard of for many days. The people of the island, frightened, had packed up their effects and taken refuge in the woods. Cortés sent a number of his men inland, to a town near the place where the fleet was at anchor. The town was of stone and mortar, with good buildings, but they found no one in it. They did find, however, cotton garments and some gold jewelry in several of the houses. They also entered a high stone tower near the sea, thinking they might find men, women, and treasure, but it contained nothing but clay and stone idols. They returned and told Cortés of the many maize fields and cultivated plots they had seen, large beehives, and groves and orchards, and gave him the trifling bits of gold and cotton they had picked up.

Cortés rejoiced at the tidings they brought, although at the same time he was astonished at the flight of the people, because they had not fled when Juan de Grijalba was there, and he suspected it was because his fleet was larger. He also feared it might be a ruse to trick him into a skirmish, so he ordered the horses landed: this for two reasons: to reconnoiter the country and, if necessary, to fight; otherwise, to let them rest and put them out to pasture. He also landed his men and sent a number of them to explore the island; and some of them discovered, in a very thick part of the forest, four or five women and three children, whom they brought back. Cortés could not understand them, or they him, but by signs and gestures he learned that one of the women was mistress of the rest and the mother of the children. Cortés used her gently, because she was weeping at her captivity and that of her children: he dressed her in the best garments he had, after the Spanish fashion; to her servants he gave looking glasses and scissors, and to each of the children playthings with which to amuse themselves. He treated her indeed with such respect that she expressed a desire to send one of her servants to summon her lord and master and show him how well his wife and children were being treated.

Thereupon, by command of the *calachuni*, several natives approached to see what was going on, and to get tidings of his wife. Cortés gave them a few trifles for themselves and others for their chief, and sent them back to the *calachuni* to beg him, for his own sake and that of his wife, to present himself before the Spaniards, from whom he had fled without cause, promising him that no one of his household would be harmed or molested. The *calachuni*, when he understood this, moved by love of his wife and children, came the next morning with many men of his village, where a number of Spaniards were already lodged. He refused to allow his people to vacate their houses; rather, he ordered them to return and to provide the Spaniards thenceforth with plenty of fish, bread, honey, and fruits. The *calachuni* addressed Cortés with great ceremony and humility, and was well received and lovingly treated. Cortés gave him to understand the good things the Spaniards wished to do for him, not only by signs and words, but also with gifts of merchandise from his stock, for himself and his people, things of little value among us, but much esteemed by them and held more precious than the gold that the Spaniards were seeking.

Besides this, Cortés ordered all the gold and garments taken in the village to be brought before him; and when each islander identified what was his, it was returned to him, an action which filled them with joy and astonishment. The Indians considered themselves happy and rich with the trifles brought from Spain, and went about the island showing them to others, and commanding everyone, by order of the *calachuni,* to return to their houses with their wives and children, which they could do in safety and without fear, because the strangers were good and kind. So each Indian returned to his own house and village, for others had fled [from their own villages] with the people of this village, and little by little they lost their fear of the Spaniards; and in this fashion they became friendly and carefree, and abundantly supplied our army with honey and wax, bread, fish, and fruits the whole time it was on the island.

11. News of Bearded Men

AS SOON AS CORTÉS saw that they no longer feared him, and were very peaceful and willing, he decided to take away their idols and give them instead the Cross of Jesus Christ Our Lord, and the image of His Glorious Mother and Virgin, St. Mary; and for this purpose he spoke to them one day through his interpreter, a certain Melchior, whom Francisco Hernández de Córdoba had brought back with him. This fellow, however, was uncouth, being a fisherman, and it seemed he knew neither how to speak nor to answer. Even so, Cortés told them he desired to give them a better law and a better God than those they had, and they replied, very good. So saying, he called them to the temple, had a Mass said, and broke up their idols, which they replaced with Crosses and images of Our Lady, whom they worshiped devoutly; and while he was there they did not sacrifice as they had used.

The islanders could not get their fill of gazing at our horses and ships, and never ceased their coming and going. They were equally astonished at the beards and color of our men, and even came up to touch them; and they made signs toward Yucatan with their hands, giving our men to understand that many days' journeys away there were four or five other bearded men. Hernán Cortés, considering how important it would be to have a good interpreter, begged the *cala-chuni* to let him have a man to carry a letter to the bearded men they had spoken of. But the *calachuni* was unable to find one willing to carry such a message, for fear that the great and cruel chieftain who held our men captive would kill and eat the messenger. When Cortés saw how things were, he coaxed three islanders who had been serving him in his lodging, giving them a few trifles and begging them to take the letter. They made many excuses, saying they were sure to be killed; but, finally, they were persuaded by entreaties and gifts, and consented to go. So he immediately wrote a letter, which said, in effect:

"Noble lords, I departed from Cuba with a fleet of eleven vessels and 550 Spaniards, and arrived here at Cozumel, where I am writing this letter to you. The people of this island have assured me that in your country there are five or six bearded men, like us in every respect. They cannot give me more details, but judging by what they have told us, I suspect and consider as certain that you are Spaniards. I and these gentlemen who have come with me to explore and colonize these lands, beg you, within six days from the time you receive this letter, to come to us, without delay or excuse. If you will come, we shall recognize and reward the favor that this fleet will receive from you. I am sending a brigantine to pick you up and two ships to act as escort.

Hernán Cortés."

This letter having been written, a new difficulty arose to prevent its delivery, namely, that the Indians did not know how to carry it so secretly that it could not be seen or detected by spies, of whom they were afraid. Then it occurred to Cortés that it could safely be carried in the hair of one of the messengers (which is commonly worn long for war and festivals, braided over the forehead), so he chose the one who looked more intelligent and clever than the others, and hid the letter in his hair. Captain Juan de Escalante commanded the brigantine that carried the Indians, and Diego de Ordaz the ships and the 50 men of the escort, to be used in case of need. The ships sailed, and Escalante landed the messengers where he had been told. Our men waited a week, although they had been told to wait only six days, but the messengers did not appear, so it was feared they had been killed or captured, and our men returned to Cozumel without them. This was a great disappointment for the Spaniards, especially for Cortés, for they now thought that the story of the bearded men was a fiction and that they would have to do without an interpreter. Meanwhile, the damage the ships had suffered in the storm was repaired and they were made ready for sea. As soon as the brigantine and the two ships returned, the fleet set sail.

12. Arrival of Jerónimo de Aguilar

THE PEOPLE OF COZUMEL were much afflicted, especially the *cala-chuni,* by the departure of the Christians, for in truth they had been treated very well as friends. The fleet had fair weather from Cozumel to the coast of Yucatan, where Cortés anchored at Punta [Isla] de las Mujeres, to see what the land and the people were like. He was not pleased. The next day, which was the first day of Carnival, they heard Mass on shore and spoke to the Indians who came to see them. They reëmbarked and made an attempt to round the point and go to Cape Catoche, to see what kind of place it was; but, before they had cleared the cape, Captain Pedro de Alvarado's ship fired a distress signal, and the others came up to see what was wrong. Cortés learned that the ship had sprung a leak, such a bad one that the water could not be kept down with two pumps, and that the ship would be lost unless it could make port. [So they sailed back to Cozumel] and the islanders ran happily down to the shore to find out what was wanted or had been forgotten. Our men told them of their trouble, disembarked, and repaired the ship.

The next Saturday all the men, save only Cortés and 50 others, embarked again; but the weather turned ugly, with strong and contrary winds, so they did not sail that day. The storm lasted all that night, but abated in the morning, and the sea was calm enough to let them sail. Since, however, it was the first Sunday in Lent, they decided to hear Mass and eat before embarking. While Cortés was eating he was told that a canoe had been sighted sailing from Yucatan to the island, and heading straight to where the ships were anchored. He went down to see where it was going, and when he saw it was sailing away somewhat apart from the ships, he told Andrés de Tapia to take some men and hide near the beach and, if any men should land from it, to bring them to him. The canoe touched behind a point or cove and four men landed, entirely naked except for a breechclout, their hair braided and curled over their foreheads like that of women, and with bows and many arrows in their hands. Three of them were frightened when they saw the Spaniards who had run to capture them with swords drawn, and tried to get back to their canoe; but the fourth stepped forward and, speaking a language that the Spaniards did not understand, told the others not to run away or be afraid. And then he said in Spanish: "Gentlemen, are you Christians?" They replied that they were Spaniards, and he was so overcome at their words that he burst into tears. He asked if it was Wednesday, for he was accustomed to devoting several hours to prayer on that day, and he begged them to join him, sank to his knees, and raised his hands and eyes to Heaven. Then, with tears in his eyes, he offered up a prayer to God, giving Him infinite thanks for His mercy in liberating him from those infidels and hellish men, and for restoring him to the Christians and men of his nation.

Andrés de Tapia approached him, helped him to his feet, and embraced him, and the other Spaniards did the same. The stranger told the three Indians to follow him, and went with the others to Cortés, talking and asking questions. Cortés, who was exceedingly glad to have him among them, welcomed him, gave him clothing and whatever else he needed, and asked him about his misfortunes and what his name was. And the other answered joyfully:

"Sir, I am Jerónimo de Aguilar, of Ecija, and I was cast away as I shall relate: I was in Darien, involved in the wars and quarrels and mischances of Diego de Nicuesa and Vasco Núñez de Balboa, in the year 1511, and set sail with Valdivia for Santo Domingo in a small caravel to acquaint the Admiral Governor with what was going on in Darien; also, to make an accounting of the men and supplies, and to bring 20,000 ducats belonging to the King. We had got as far as Jamaica when the caravel struck on the shoals called Las Víboras, and twenty of us barely escaped in the ship's boat, without sails, without water, without bread, and with only one miserable pair of oars. We drifted in this fashion for thirteen or fourteen days, when we were caught in the current that runs very fast and strong to the west, and were cast ashore in a province called Maya. Seven of us had died, or, as I believe, eight. A rascally cacique, into whose power we had fallen, sacrificed Valdivia and four others to his idols, and then ate them, making a fiesta of it and offering a share to his friends. I and six others were placed in cages to be fattened for the next banquet, and to avoid such an abominable death we broke out of our prison and fled to the woods. And it was God's will that we should meet another cacique, a mortal enemy of the first, a humane man, chief of Xaman-zana, called Aquincuz, who sheltered us and spared our lives, although he kept us in servitude. He died not long afterward, and since then I have been with Taxmar, his successor. One by one five of our companions died, and no one remained but myself and a certain Gonzalo Guerrero, a sailor, who is with Nachancán, lord of Chete-mal, and he is married to a rich lady of that land, by whom he has children, and is one of Nachancán's captains, greatly esteemed for his victories over their neighbors. I sent your Worship's letter to him and begged him to come with me, now that we had the means and opportunity; but he refused, from shame I believe, because his nose and ears had been pierced, and his face and hands painted in the manner of that country and people, and also because of his attachment to his wife and love of his children."

Jerónimo de Aguilar's story caused the greatest astonishment among his listeners, and also fear, because of his account of the sac-rificing and eating of men, and the hardships that he and his compan-ions had endured. But they thanked God to see him out of the hands of these barbarous and cruel people; also, because they saw in him a true and trustworthy interpreter. And most certainly they thought it a miracle that Alvarado's ship had sprung a leak and obliged them to return to the island, and that contrary winds had kept them there until Aguilar's arrival, for doubtless through him they would learn about the land that Hernán Cortés was to invade. This is why I have related the occurrence at such length, as a notable event in this history. I shall also relate how Jerónimo de Aguilar's mother went mad when she learned he was in the hands of people who ate men, and how from that time on, whenever she saw meat being roasted or broiled, she would shriek: "Woe is me! That is my son and my darling!"

13. Cortés Casts Down
the Idols of Cozumel

THE NEXT DAY after Aguilar's arrival, Cortés again spoke with the people of Cozumel, in order to inform himself better about the island, now that he could understand them with the help of his faithful interpreter; also for the purpose of encouraging them in the veneration of the Cross and persuading them to put aside their idols, in the belief that this was the best way to get them to abandon the sooner their heathenish customs and become Christians. Truth to tell, it is war and warriors that really persuade the Indians to give up their idols, their bestial rites, and their abominable bloody sacrifices and the eating of men (which is directly contrary to the law of God and nature), and it is thus that of their own free will and consent they more quickly receive, listen to, and believe our preachers, and accept the Gospel and baptism, which is what Christianity and faith consist of.

So Jerónimo de Aguilar preached to them about salvation, and, either because of what he told them, or because of the beginning they had already made, they were pleased to have their idols cast down, and they even assisted at it, breaking into small pieces what they had formerly held sacred. And soon our Spaniards had left not a whole idol standing, and in each chapel they set up a Cross or the image of Our Lady, whom all the islanders worshiped with prayer and great devotion, burning incense to her and offering partridges, maize, and fruits, and the other things they were accustomed to bring to their temples. Such was their devotion to the image of Our Lady that ever afterward, when Spanish ships touched at their island, they would run out to them, shouting "Cortés, Cortés!" and singing "María, María!" —which they did when Alonso de Parada and Pánfilo de Narváez passed that way. Even more, they begged Cortés to leave someone behind to teach them to believe in the God of the Christians; but he did not dare consent, for fear they might kill the preacher, and also because he had few priests and friars with him. And in this he did wrong, in view of their earnest request and supplication.

THE NATIVES call the island Acuzamil, and, corruptly, Cozumel. Juan de Grijalba, the first Spaniard to land there, called it Santa Cruz, because he had sighted it on the third of May. It is ten leagues long and three wide, although some say more and some say less. It lies at 20°N. Lat. or thereabout, and five or six leagues from Punta [Isla] de las Mujeres. Its three towns contain as many as three thousand people. The houses are of stone and mortar, roofed with straw or branches, some of them even with stone. The temple and towers are also of stone and mortar, very well constructed. There is little water, and what they have they get from wells and rain.

Calachuni means cacique or king. The people are dark and go about naked, or, if they wear any clothing, which is of cotton, it is only to cover their private parts. They wear their hair long, neatly braided over their foreheads. They are expert fishermen, and fish is their principal diet, although they also have a great deal of maize for bread, and many and good fruits. They also have much honey, although it is somewhat bitter, and their apiaries contain a thousand and more small hives. They were not acquainted with the use of candles for lighting, and were pleased and astonished when our men taught them. They raise dogs with foxlike faces, which they castrate and fatten for eating. The dogs do not bark. In the hills and flat country, deer, wild pigs, rabbits, and hares abound, although they are small. Our Spaniards killed a large number of them with crossbows and arquebuses, and with dogs and hounds. Some of the meat they ate fresh, but they dried and cured a great deal of it in the sun. The natives slash themselves; they are idolaters; they sacrifice children, although few, and often sacrifice dogs instead. For the rest, the people are poor but kindly, and very devout in that false religion of theirs.

15. Religion of Cozumel

THEIR TEMPLE resembles a square tower, wide at the base, with steps on all sides; it rises vertically from the middle up, and at its top there is a hut with a straw roof and four doors or windows, each with its sill or gallery. In this hut, which seems to be a chapel, they house their gods, or paint them on the walls. Such, at least, was the one on the shore, where they kept a very strange idol, very distinct from the others, which are many and differ widely among themselves. The body of this great idol was hollow, made of baked clay and fastened to the wall with mortar, in back of which was something like a sacristy, where the priests of the temple kept their implements. The priests had a small secret door cut in the side of the idol, into which one of them would enter, and from it speak to and answer those who came to worship and beg for favors. With this trickery simple men were made to believe whatever their god told them. Him they honored above the rest; they burned before him a very fine incense made of perfume or copal, and offered him bread, fruits, and sacrifices of partridges and other birds and dogs, and sometimes even of men. Attracted by this oracle or idol, a great many pilgrims and devout and superstitious people came from distant lands to the island of Cozumel, and this is the reason for such a multitude of temples and chapels there.

At the base of that same tower there was a wall of stone and mortar, very well built, with battlements, and at its center a plaster cross about ten spans high, which they held to be the god of rain and worshiped as such; and when water was scarce and the rains failed, they went to it in very devout processions and sacrificed partridges, to placate its wrath with the blood of that one small bird. They also burned before it a certain resin, like incense, and sprinkled it with water, in the belief that rain would fall at once.

Such was the religion of these people of Cozumel, but it could not be learned how or in what manner they had acquired their devotion to the Cross, for it is certain that, before the coming of the Spaniards, there was not a vestige of the preaching of the Gospel in that island, or, for that matter, in any part of the Indies, as will be explained at greater length in another place. The people of Cozumel, from that time on, were very reverent in the presence of the Cross, as if accustomed to this symbol.

AFTER LEAVING CUBA Cortés spent a month and a half in the activities we have described. Having made the natives of Cozumel firm friends of the Spaniards, he departed from the island, taking with him a large store of wax and honey that they had given him, and sailed to Yucatan, keeping well in while he searched for his missing ship. The wind died just as he had made Punta [Isla] de las Mujeres, and he lay becalmed there for two days while he gathered salt from the many salt pans there and took a tiburon with hook and ropes. It could not be hoisted on board because it caused the ship to list, the ship being very small and the fish very large. Our men killed it in the water from their boat, cut it into small pieces and hoisted it on board with block and tackle. In the belly of the tiburon they found more than five hundred rations of salt pork, including, they said, ten flitches that had been hung in the water to get rid of the salt. Now, since the tiburon is a glutton (for which reason some call it a *ligurón* [Ligurian=glutton]), and had found that great quantity of food, it could stuff itself as much as it pleased. Our men also found in its gullet a tin plate that had fallen from the ship of Pedro de Alvarado, three ruined shoes, and a cheese.

This is what they tell of the tiburon, and certain it is that the tiburon swallows such masses of food that it seems incredible. I have heard honest men swear that they have killed and cut open tiburones and found so many things in their bellies that they would have considered it impossible if they had not seen it; for example, they say that a tiburon will swallow one, two, or more whole sheepskins, complete with head and horns, just as they had been thrown into the sea, to save the bother of dressing them. The tiburon is a long, thick fish, some of them measuring eight spans through the middle and twelve feet long. Many of them have two rows of teeth, one behind the other, which look like a saw or a crenellation. Its mouth is proportionate to its body, monstrously huge. Its skin is like that of the dogfish. The male has two reproductive organs, the female only one, but she will bear as many as twenty, thirty, or forty little tiburones at one time. This fish will attack a cow or horse that may be grazing or drinking on the bank of a river, and will eat a man, as one tried to eat the *calachuni* of Cozumel but did not entirely succeed, because he was rescued, but not before losing two of his toes. The tiburon is so voracious that it will follow a ship for five hundred or even one thousand leagues, swallowing whatever is thrown overboard; and it is so swift that it swims faster than a ship can sail, however favorable the wind—even, they say, three times as fast, because when a ship is sailing before the wind a tiburon will swim two or three times around it, and so close to the surface that it can be followed with the eye. Its flesh is not very good to eat, being tough and tasteless, although when it is cut into strips and dried it will add greatly to a ship's store of provisions. The men of the fleet tell how they ate the salt pork they had taken from the belly of a tiburon, and how it had a better flavor than the other, and how some of them recognized their own rations by the knots and cords.

17. *The Great Tides at Campeche*

WITH THE GOOD WEATHER that now prevailed, the fleet sailed in search of the lost ship, and Cortés had the brigantine and the ships' boats look for it in the rivers and estuaries. But while the ships lay at anchor off Campeche, awaiting the return of the boats and the brigantine, suddenly they were left stranded, although they were almost a league out to sea, such is the flow and ebb of the tide there. Nowhere, except in Labrador and Paria, does the tide rise so high, and no one knows what causes it, although many guesses have been made, none of them satisfactory. If it had not been for the tide, our men said, they would have landed at Campeche to avenge the defeat that Francisco Hernández de Córdoba had suffered there.

Keeping always close inshore, they ran into a large lagoon now called Puerto Escondido, in which there are several small islands, and behind one of them they found the ship they were looking for. Cortés and the rest rejoiced greatly to see it unharmed, and all its men safe and in good health. The latter on their part were equally glad to be found, for they had begun to fear for themselves, being alone and short of provisions, and thinking perhaps that the fleet had been lost or had passed them by. And doubtless they would have perished of hunger if it had not been for a greyhound that brought them food; but, since she did, and since they were on the fleet's course, they waited for their Captain, even though they feared he might have run into some such trouble as Grijalba and Francisco Hernández de Córdoba had experienced.

The whole fleet anchored near the ship, and all hands were in high spirits, as one might have expected. The men of the lost ship were asked about the many pelts (rabbit, hare, and deer) that were hanging in the rigging, and they said that no sooner had they arrived than they saw a dog running along the beach, scratching in the sand, and looking at the ship; and that the captain and several others had landed and saw that it was a large greyhound, which came up to them wagging her tail, running from one to the other, barking, and jumping up on them with her forepaws. Then she ran into a wood near by and came out with a mouthful of rabbits and hares. The next day she did the same, from which they concluded there was plenty of game about, so they gathered up all the crossbows in the ship and followed her, and hunted so diligently that they were able to provide themselves with fresh meat all the time they were there (although it was Lent), and they dried enough deer and rabbit meat to last them for many days. And as a reminder they had hung the pelts in the rigging and stretched the deerskins out to dry in the sun. They did not know whether the greyhound had belonged to Córdoba or to Grijalba.

18. Battle and Capture of Potonchán

THE FLEET did not stop there but set sail immediately, everyone being happy at having found the men they had considered lost, and went on to the Río de Grijalba, which in the native language is called the Tabasco. They did not enter it, because the bar looked too shallow for the larger ships, but anchored off its mouth. A great many Indians gathered on the shore to stare at the ships and men, some of them armed and wearing feathers. Viewed from the sea they appeared to be handsome and magnificent men, but they did not seem at all astonished to see our men and the ships; indeed, they had seen them before when Juan de Grijalba had been there. Cortés liked the looks of these people and the lay of the land, so, leaving a strong guard in the large ships, he embarked the rest of his men in the brigantine and the ships' boats, with several pieces of artillery, and made his way up the river against the swift current.

A little more than half a league upstream they came to a large town of adobe houses thatched with straw, surrounded by a thick wooden wall and battlements, which were pierced with loopholes for shooting arrows, stones, and darts. Just before our men reached the place, a large number of little boats (called *tahacup*) put out, filled with armed men, who looked very fierce and eager for a fight. Cortés approached them making signs of peace, and spoke to them through Jerónimo de Aguilar, begging them to receive the Spaniards well, for our men had not come to molest them, but to get fresh water and provisions, because they had been at sea and were in want, and he urged them to let him have what was needed, for which they would be paid very gladly. The Indians in the boats replied that they would bear his message to the town and return with the answer and some provisions; whereupon they departed and soon came back in five or six boats, bringing bread, fruit, and turkeys, which they offered as a gift. Cortés conveyed to them that in view of the need this was a very scant provision for the many men in the great ships (which the Indians had not yet seen, since they had been shut up in their town), so he asked them to bring more and to allow him to enter the town himself to purchase food. The Indians asked to be given that night in which to decide one way or the other, while Cortés stopped on an islet in the river to await their reply.

Each side thought to deceive the other: The Indians utilized the interval to remove all their goods and to hide their women and children in the woods and thickets, while Cortés had all his arquebuses and crossbows landed on the island, as well as many men from the ships, and sent a scouting party up the river to look for a crossing. He accomplished both objects during the night, while the enemy, occupied in their own affairs, did not hear them. All the men from the ships joined Cortés, and the scouting party made its way along the bank observing the currents, and less than half a league upstream they found a place where they could cross by wading waist-deep. They also found such thick woods and undergrowth on both banks that they were able to approach the town unseen and unheard. When

Cortés got this intelligence he ordered two of his captains, Alonso de Avila and Pedro de Alvarado, with fifty men each, to take a guide that same night and conceal themselves between the river and the town: this for two reasons: one, so that the Indians might think there were no more men on the island than there had been the previous day; two, so that our men, at a prearranged signal, could attack the town from the rear.

At daybreak no fewer than eight boatloads of Indians put out, more heavily armed than the first, and approached our men. They were bringing a trifling amount of food and said they could bring no more because the townspeople had run away for fear of the Spaniards and the huge ships. The Indians begged our men to accept what they had brought and go back to the sea, and not to bother or disturb the people of the country, or upset them further. The interpreter answered them, saying it was a cruel thing to let the Spaniards perish of hunger, and that if the Indians would listen to the reason for their coming, they would see how much good and profit they would get from it. The Indians replied that they did not seek the advice of strangers, and still less did they wish to receive them in their houses, because the Spaniards seemed to them to be terrifying and domineering men; and that if they wanted water they could dip it out of the river, or dig wells, which is what they themselves did when they needed it.

At this, Cortés, seeing that further words were useless, told them that in no circumstances would he desist from entering their town and exploring the country, for the purpose of bringing word of it to the greatest lord on earth, who had sent him there; that, therefore, they should give their consent, for he desired only their good; otherwise, he would place himself in the hands of God, in his own, and in those of his companions. The Indians said nothing more, except to tell the Spaniards again to leave and not to play the bully in someone else's land, and in any case they would not be allowed to invade their country or enter their town; rather, they warned Cortés that if he did not depart at once they would kill him and his men.

Cortés endeavored to treat these barbarians with every civility, as is right and as is laid down in the instructions issued by the monarchs of Castile: that is, to offer them peace one, two, and many times before making war upon them or invading their lands and taking their towns. So he repeated his offer of peace and friendship, promising them freedom and good treatment, and to teach them so many things of profit to their souls and bodies that they would consider themselves fortunate; but, on the other hand, he warned them that if they stubbornly refused to receive and admit him (setting a limit of that afternoon before sundown for their decision), he, with the help of God, would sleep in their town that night, at whatever cost to its inhabitants, who had spurned his peace and friendship.

The Indians laughed heartily at his words and mocked him, and returned to their town to tell of the boasting and madness they had heard. As soon as the Indians had withdrawn, the Spaniards ate, and a little later armed themselves and went on board the boats and the brigantine to await the Indians' reply. Toward sunset, when the Indians failed to appear, Cortés alerted the Spaniards who were in ambush, embraced his shield, and, calling upon God, St. James, and his advocate St. Peter, attacked the town with about two hundred men. They reached that part of the wall which was on the river, beached the brigantine, landed the artillery, jumped into the water up to their thighs, and began their assault on the wall and the battlements. The enemy, who had for some time been shooting their arrows and darts at them, and throwing stones with their slings and by hand, seeing their foes upon them, fought bravely from their ramparts, plying their spears and shooting many arrows through the loopholes and openings in the wall, wounding almost twenty Spaniards. The smoke, fire, and reports of the guns confused them and knocked them to the ground (such was their fright at hearing such a fearful noise, something they had never before experienced), but they did not abandon the wall or the defense, even though they died; rather, they bravely faced the blows of their enemies, whom indeed they would have successfully stood off if they had not been attacked from the rear.

When the three hundred Spaniards in the ambuscade heard the firing, which was their signal to attack, they rushed upon the town and, since all its men were occupied with the enemy in front of them and with trying to drive them into the river, the three hundred met no resistance and ran in shouting and striking down everyone they encountered. The men of the town now realized their carelessness and tried to meet the new threat, but in so doing they weakened the part that Cortés was attacking, and he and his men entered unopposed. In this fashion, with some Spaniards attacking at one side and some at the other, they reached the square at the same time, still fighting with the inhabitants, of whom none remained in the town but the dead and the prisoners. The rest, who were few, abandoned the place and took refuge in the surrounding woods, with their women who were already there.

The Spaniards searched the houses and found little, only some maize, turkeys, and a few cotton things, but no sign of gold. The town had been defended by no more than four hundred warriors, and a great deal of Indian blood had been spilled, because they fought naked. Many were wounded but few captured, and the dead were uncounted. Cortés and his men took up their quarters in the temple of the idols, where there was room for all of them, because it had a courtyard and several large apartments. There they slept well that night, but under a heavy guard, for they were in the enemy's house. The Indians, however, did not molest them.

And that is how Potonchán was taken, the first city Cortés won by force of arms in his expedition and conquest.

19. Cortés Treats with the Men of Potonchán

THE NEXT MORNING Cortés had the wounded and captured Indians brought before him, and through his interpreter commanded them to go to their chief and the other inhabitants of the town, and tell them of the harm that had been done, all through their own misconduct, because the Christians had begged them many times and peacefully to admit them. He said they might return to their houses and their town in safety, if they so wished, and promised them in the name of his God that no harm would come to them, rather, all pleasure and good treatment. Cortés told them also that he desired to make the acquaintance of their chief and learn from him several things he had to know; that, if the chief did not trust him to keep his word and pledge, he would give hostages; but that, if the chief refused to come to him, he might be sure that Cortés would seek him out to purchase provisions from him.

With these words Cortés dismissed the Indians and sent them on their way happy and free, which they did not think he would do; so they departed very joyfully and told the others what they had been commanded to tell; but not a single one returned. On the contrary, the Indians gathered their forces to attack our men by surprise, thinking to find them careless and confined in their quarters, which the Indians intended to burn if they could not avenge themselves otherwise.

But Cortés had sent at the same time several Spaniards, by three paths that seemed to lead, as afterward was seen to be the case, to the farms and maize fields of the town. Many Indians were gathered there, and our men attacked them for the purpose of capturing their leader and bringing him to town to be interrogated. They said that all the men of the surrounding country were being assembled to fight and give battle with all their might to those few strangers, and to kill and eat them for the enemies and robbers that they were. Moreover, they said, they had made a pact among themselves, to the effect that if it was their bad luck to be vanquished, they would serve their conquerors from that time on as slaves.

Cortés sent them back free, as he had done with the others, to urge the council and lords not to embark upon such a course, for it was utmost folly for them to think they could vanquish and kill those few men they saw before them, and to tell them that, if they would lay aside their arms, he promised to hold and treat them as his brothers and good friends; but that, if they persevered in their hostility, he would punish them in such wise that they would never again take up arms against such men as he and those Spaniards of his.

Either because of what the messengers said to the Indians, or because of what they had learned from their spies, the next day some twenty persons of authority or nobility came to the town. Touching the ground with their fingers and then raising them to the sky (which is their customary sign of greeting and respect), they told Captain Cortés that the lord and the other noble citizens were his friends; they begged him not to burn their town, and they promised to bring him provisions. Cortés replied that his men were not such as would pick a quarrel with walls, or with other men, except for very strong and just reasons; nor had they come to do harm, rather, good; and that if their lord would come to him he would soon learn how truly Cortés had spoken, and how soon the lord and the others would learn great mysteries and secrets of things they had never known, and would rejoice to learn them. At this the twenty ambassadors, or spies, took their leave, saying they would return with the answer. And so they did, for the next day they came with some food, excusing themselves for not bringing more, because, they said, their frightened people were scattered and in hiding. They did not demand payment for the provisions, but only a few bells and other trifles. Their lord could not come, they said, because, from fear and shame, he had gone away to a remote place, but would send persons of credit and responsibility with whom Cortés could talk, and Cortés was invited to come and buy provisions.

Cortés was very pleased with this reply, because it gave him the opportunity and justification to penetrate the country and learn what it was like. So he dismissed the Indians, telling them that he would come the next day with his men to get supplies for his army, and that they should tell the natives to have a good stock on hand, for which they would be well paid.

But on both sides there was trickery: Cortés was interested less in getting provisions than in discovering gold, of which up to that time he had seen little; and the Indians were temporizing, while getting their army together. The next day in the morning Cortés mustered three companies of eighty men each, put over them as captains Pedro de Alvarado, Alonso de Avila, and Gonzalo de Sandoval, and gave them also some Cuban Indians for servants and carriers, in case they should find maize and fowl to bring back. He sent his companies off by different routes, with orders to take nothing by force or without payment, and to go no farther than a league and a half, at most two, so that they could return by nightfall. He himself stayed behind to guard the town and the artillery.

One of the captains led his company to a village where an infinite number of Tabascans were under arms, guarding their maize fields. He begged them to exchange their grain for merchandise, but they refused because, they said, they needed it for themselves. At this both parties took up their arms and a fierce encounter ensued; but, since the Indians greatly outnumbered the Spaniards and shot a vast cloud of arrows at them, wounding them badly, the Spaniards retreated to a house, where our men defended themselves very well, although with evident fear and danger of fire. And certain it is that they would have perished there, or most of them, if the two routes taken by the other companies had not led to the same fields. But it pleased God that the two companies should arrive together, while the Indians were attacking the house and making a great noise and hubbub; and with their coming the Indians abandoned the fight and milled off to another village. Then the besieged Spaniards ran out and joined the others, and all set out for the new village, still skirmishing with the enemy, who kept up their discharge of arrows. Cortés was already on his way with a hundred companions and the artillery to rescue them, for two of his Cuban Indians had reported the plight of the eighty. He came upon them a mile from the village and, seeing that the enemy was still attacking their rear, he had two small cannon fired, at which they stopped and came no nearer, and he and his men took shelter in the village. A few Indians died that day, and many Spaniards were wounded.

20. Battle of Cintla

CORTÉS DID NOT SLEEP that night; rather, he had all the wounded carried on board the ships, together with their clothing and other baggage, and sent ashore the men who were guarding the fleet, and 13 horses. All this was accomplished before dawn, but not without the Tabascans' knowledge. By sunrise Cortés had already heard Mass and put nearly 500 men, 13 horses, and six pieces of artillery in the field. (These horses were the first to land in the country now known as New Spain.) He formed his men, readied his guns, and set off for Cintla, where the fight had taken place the day before, thinking to find the Indians there. By the time our men arrived, the Indians had also formed their squadrons in good order, of 8,000 men each. The meeting place of the two armies was cultivated land, cut up by many ditches and deep streams, difficult to cross, among which our men became confused and disorganized, so Hernán Cortés took his cavalry to find a better ground to the left and to seek cover among the trees, from which he might attack the enemy in the rear or from one side, as from an ambush. The foot went to the right, crossing ditches at every step, and shielding themselves from the enemy's missiles. Our men did some mischief among the Indians and killed a few with their crossbows, arquebuses, and artillery (which was being fired as fast as possible), but even so could not force them to retreat, because the enemy took cover behind trees and fences. Now, since the men of Potonchán had selected that evil spot to wait for ours, as is to be believed, they were not barbarians or unskilled in war.

Our men extricated themselves and found a somewhat better position, spacious and flat, with fewer streams, where they were able to make better use of their cannon, which they fired at point-blank, and of their swords, for now they were fighting at close quarters. The Indians, however, were in such great numbers and pressed our men so hard that they crowded them into a corner and forced them to fight back to back. Our men were now in grave danger, lacking room in which to work their guns, and horsemen to drive off the enemy. While they were thus disheartened and about to yield, Francisco de Morla rode up on a dapple-gray and attacked the Indians, forcing them to give way a little, and the Spaniards, thinking it was Cortés, charged the enemy and killed a few. But the horseman disappeared, and the Indians again closed with the Spaniards, and soon had them in the same plight as before. Again the horseman returned and took his place with the Spaniards, driving the Indians back, at which our men attacked the Indians with spirit and killed and wounded a number of them. In the thick of the fight, however, the horseman disappeared again and could not be seen, and since the Indians could not see the centaur either (for such they believed him to be), for fear of whom they had fled, they turned upon the Christians with great bravery and handled them worse than before. Then the horseman returned for the third time and drove off the frightened Indians with loss, and our foot attacked them at the same time, wounding and killing.

At this juncture Cortés rode up with the rest of his mounted companions, tired of wandering about among the endless streams and woods. Our men told him what that single horseman had done and asked him whether it was one of his company. Cortés answered that it was not, and they believed, since no other horseman had appeared, that it was the Apostle St. James, patron saint of Spain. And now Cortés shouted: "Forward, my friends, for God and the glorious St. Peter are with us!" So saying, he and his horsemen charged into the enemy and drove them out of the ditches to a place where he could lance them at will and put them to flight. The Indians then abandoned the open ground and took refuge in the woods and underbrush, no two together, and our foot took up the pursuit and killed well over 300 of them, not counting the many wounded by arquebus and crossbow.

More than seventy Spaniards were wounded by arrows and stones that day, and, either because of the fatigue of battle and the excessive heat of the place, or because of the water our men drank in the creeks and puddles, above a hundred of them were struck by such a sudden pain in the loins that they fell to the ground and had to be carried off the field on men's backs, or in cradles made by joining hands. It was God's will, however, that the sickness should leave them that night and that by the next day they should be quite recovered. Our men gave heartfelt thanks to God Our Lord when they saw themselves once more free of the arrows and the multitudes of Indians they had been fighting, for He had miraculously saved them. And all of them said they had seen the man on the dapple-gray join them three times in their fight, as has been said, and that it was St. James, our patron saint. Hernán Cortés preferred to believe it was St. Peter, his special advocate. But, whoever it was, it was considered a miracle, as it truly turned out to be. And not only did the Spaniards see him, but the Indians felt the weight of his attack upon their squadrons, which he seemed to dazzle and render stupid. This was learned later from the prisoners we took.

21. Treaty Between Tabasco and the Christians

CORTÉS RELEASED some of the prisoners and sent word by them to their chief and the others that he regretted the harm done to both sides by their culpability and stubbornness, and he called God to witness his own innocence in the matter. Nevertheless, he said, he would forgive them if they should come to him within two days to make amends for their wrongdoing and make a treaty of peace and friendship with him; also, to hear certain mysteries he wished to explain to them. He warned them, on the other hand, that, if they did not appear within that time, he would invade their country, and destroy and burn it and cut down all the men he might encounter, great or small, armed or unarmed.

When these men had been sent on their way with this message, Cortés and his Spaniards withdrew to the town, where they rested and treated their wounds.

The messengers did their work well, and the next day more than fifty respectable Indians came to ask pardon for what had happened, and to beg permission to bury their dead and a safe-conduct for their lords and nobles. Cortés granted their request, but warned them not to deceive him or lie to him again, and not to attempt another conspiracy, which could only result in greater misfortunes for them and their country; moreover, he said, he would not treat with them again through third parties.

These fierce and cruel threats and protests, and the Indians' feeling that they lacked the arms to fight or resist those few Spaniards whom they now considered invincible, induced the lords and nobles to come and parley with the captain. And so, at the end of the term set by Cortés, the lords of the town, accompanied by four or five others and a sizable body of Indians, came to see him, bringing bread, turkeys, fruits, and other provisions for his camp, and little jewels worth as much as four hundred pesos gold, as well as some turquoises of small value, and twenty female slaves to work for our army, by which they thought to do our men a great favor, seeing them without women to grind and bake maize bread daily, a necessary occupation that keeps the Indian women busy a good part of their time.

The lords begged forgiveness for everything they had done; they entreated Cortés to receive them as friends; and they put themselves into his hands and those of the Spaniards, offering them their lands, their estates, and their persons. Cortés received them warmly and gave them presents, with which they were delighted, and he distributed the twenty female slaves among his men for companions.

Now the horses and mares that were tied to trees in the temple court-yard began to neigh, and the Indians asked Cortés what they were saying. He replied that they were scolding him for not punishing the Indians, at which the Indians offered the horses roses and turkeys to eat, and begged their pardon.

22. Cortés Interrogates the Tabascans

OUR MEN and the Indians talked together a great deal, but, since they did not understand one another, the effect was very laughable. Now that the Indians had talked with our men unmolested, they brought their wives and children to camp, these latter being very numerous and about as dirty as gypsies.

Among the questions and proposals that Cortés, through his inter-preter, Jerónimo de Aguilar, put to the Tabascans were these five: Was there any gold and silver in their country, and how and where did they get the little they were wearing? Why had they withheld their friendship from him, but had not refused it to that other cap-tain who sailed there the year before? How did it happen that they, with their great numbers, had fled from so few? Then he attempted to explain to them the greatness and power of the Emperor and King of Castile. Finally, he preached them a sermon on the religion of Christ.

They answered that, with respect to the gold mines and treasures of the country, they gave little importance to living as rich men, but only to be contented and happy, for which reason they could not even tell him what a gold mine was; nor did they seek any gold but what they could pick up, which was very little; but that farther inland toward the setting sun a great deal of it was to be found, and that the people there valued it more than they did.

As for that other captain who had passed that way, they said that, since his men and ships were the first of the kind brought to their country, they had spoken to the captain and asked him what he was seeking, and when he told them he only wanted to trade for gold, they had willingly consented. But that now that more and bigger ships had come, they thought it was for the purpose of taking what was left, and they felt insulted that such a trick should be played on them, for we had not so treated lords of less importance than they.

For the rest, with regard to the war, they said they considered themselves a mighty people, and valiant as compared with those of the back country, because nobody dared to take their goods and women by force, or their children for sacrifice. This was their thought when they saw those few strangers, but they had been greatly undeceived when they measured their strength against them, for the Indians had been able to kill none of ours. Besides, they had been dazzled by the flashing swords, the wounds from which were deep and deadly and incurable, and they found the roar and flames of the guns more stunning than thunder and lightning from the skies, because of the death and destruction they wrought wherever they struck. Also, they were astonished and frightened by the horses, whose great mouths seemed about to swallow them, and also by the speed with which the horses overtook them, although the Indians were themselves swift runners. Moreover, since they had never before seen a horse, the first one that attacked them terrified them, even though it was alone; and when it was joined by many more, they could not stand against the shock and strength and fury of their charge. They thought that man and horse were one.

23. The Men of Potonchán Destroy Their Idols

THIS ACCOUNT convinced Cortés that that land was not for the Spaniards, and that it was not a place to make a settlement, there being no gold or silver or other treasure in it, so he decided to advance into the western country where the gold was. But first he told the Indians that the lord whom he and his companions were serving was King of Spain and Emperor of the Christians, the greatest Prince on earth, served by more kingdoms and provinces, and obeyed by more vassals, than any other, and that his just rule and government was of God, holy, peaceful, and gentle, and that the entire universe was his domain, for which reason the Indians should render him their obedience as his vassals and friends; that, if they did so, many things of great value in law and customs would follow.

Concerning religion, Cortés told them of their blindness and great vanity in worshiping many gods and making sacrifices of human blood to them, and in thinking that those images, being mute and soulless, made by the Indians with their own hands, were capable of doing either good or harm. He then told them of a single God, Creator of Heaven and earth and men, whom the Christians worshiped and served, and whom all men should worship and serve. In short, after he had explained the Mysteries to them, and how the Son of God had suffered on the Cross, they accepted it and broke up their idols. Thus it was that with great reverence, before a large concourse of Indians, and with many tears on the part of the Spaniards, a Cross was erected in the temple of Potonchán, and our men first, kneeling, kissed and worshiped it, and after them the Indians.

Cortés dismissed the Indians, and all retired to eat, and he begged them to come again two days thence to witness the feast of Palm Sunday. The citizens of the town, being devout men and able now to attend in safety, came, and so also did the people of the surrounding country, in such vast numbers that it was a cause of astonishment to see so many thousands of men and women gathered there, all offering their obedience and vassalage to the King of Spain by the hands of Cortés, and declaring themselves friends of the Spaniards. These were the first vassals that the Emperor had in New Spain.

On Palm Sunday, at the proper moment, Cortés had branches cut and arranged as if on a table, although it had to be done in the open on account of the multitude of people; and he had the service read and displayed the best ornaments to be had, and all the Indians attended it and were impressed by the ceremony and pomp of the procession, and rejoiced at the Mass and the celebration. After it our men embarked, bearing the branches in their hands.

Cortés deserved no less praise for this than for his victory, because in both things he had conducted himself wisely and courageously, leaving the Indians to their devotion and the people free and unharmed. He took no slaves, nor did he sack the town, nor did he do any trading, although he was there more than twenty days. The people called the place Potonchán, which is to say, "stinking place," but our men named it Victoria. The name of its lord was Tabasco, which is why the Spaniards called the river Río de Tabasco; but Juan de Grijalba named it for himself, and his name and fame will not soon be forgotten. And this is what future discoverers and settlers were to do, that is, perpetuate their names.

Potonchán is a large town, but it has not twenty-five thousand houses, as some say, although, since each house is separated from the others, it looks bigger than it is. The houses are large and well built, of brick or of stone and mortar, but some are of adobes and sticks, with roofs of straw or boards. The living quarters are raised from the ground because of the mist and dampness from the river. The houses are scattered because of the danger of fire. Outside the town the Indians have better houses, for pleasure.

The people are brown, go about almost naked, and eat human flesh from the sacrifices. Their weapons are the bow and arrow, the sling, and the dart and the spear. They carry shields and wear helmets, and what looks like leg armor: this of wood or bark, but some of very thin gold. They also wear a kind of breastplate made of quilted cotton to protect the soft part of the body.

24. The River of Alvarado

AFTER LEAVING POTONCHÁN, Cortés sailed into the river called the Alvarado, after the captain who discovered it, but those who dwell there call it the Papaloapan. It has its source at Aticpan, at the foot of some low ranges near the Sierra de Culhuacán. Above it is a beautiful peak, round and steep and tapered like a distaff, six hundred feet high, covered with trees, and upon it the Indians make many bloody sacrifices. The river is deep and clear, full of good fish, and more than five hundred feet wide. It is fed by the Quiotepec, Usila, Chinantla, Cuaucuezpaltepec, Tuxtlán, Teyuciyocán, and some smaller streams, all of which are gold-bearing. It flows into the sea by three channels, one through sand, one through mud, and one through rock. The land it drains is good land; its banks are beautiful, and in time of its many floods it creates great estuaries, one of which lies between Otlatitlán and Cuaucuezpaltepec, two good-sized towns.

This estuary or lagoon swarms with fish: shad as big as tunny and many reptiles (called iguanas in the Islands, and here called *cuauhquetzpallin*). This creature looks like a lizard of many colors; its head is round and small; its body thick; it has along its spine a row of spikes; its tail is long and thin, and it twists and curls it like a greyhound. Its four feet have four toes, and claws like those of a bird; its teeth are sharp, but it does not bite, although it makes a noise with them. It is brown in color; it can resist hunger for long periods; it lays eggs like those of a hen, with yolks and whites, small, round, and good to eat. Its flesh tastes like rabbit, only better. It is eaten during Lent instead of fish, for it is said to belong to both elements, and hence to both seasons. It is harmful to syphilitics. These animals leave the water and climb trees and walk on the ground. Their appearance is frightening, even to those who are familiar with them, so dreadful is their ferocity of expression. They are fattened by rubbing their bellies in the sand, a very strange thing.

The lagoon also harbors manatee, turtles, and other fish unknown to us, and tiburones, and sea lions that come out and sleep on the shore and bark very noisily. The females bear two young at a time and nurse them on milk from two teats on their breast between their flippers. There is fierce and perpetual war between the tiburones and the sea lions, the tiburones trying to eat the sea lions, and the sea lions trying to avoid being eaten; but the tiburones greatly outnumber the sea lions. The lagoon shelters many birds, large and small, of a shape and color unknown to us; black ducks with white wings, much prized for their feathers; each of them fetches the price of a slave in those parts where they are not found. There are white herons also, sought for their feathers, and other birds called *teuquechul* [*teoquechol*], which is to say, bird-gods, as big as cocks, of whose feathers and gold the Indians make rich ornaments. If this featherwork were durable nothing would be more precious. Another bird is one resembling a wild pigeon, white and brown, with a beak like that of a duck, one of whose feet is webbed, the other armed with claws like a hawk's, so that it can fish while swimming and hunt while flying. There are cormorants also, marvelously skillful in fishing, and a bird that looks like a swan, only its neck is much longer and more strange; and pelicans of many colors that live by fishing, as big as geese, with a beak about two spans long, only the lower member of which is movable, with a sack that hangs down to their breast; in it they can store more than ten pounds of fish and a pitcher of water. They readily vomit up what they have eaten. I have heard it said that one of these birds swallowed a black baby a few months old, but could not fly away with it, and so was captured.

Round about the lagoon are infinite numbers of hares, rabbits, and monkeys and cats of many sizes; pigs, deer, lions and tigers, and an animal called *ayotochtli,* which is no larger than a cat, but has the face of a duck, the feet of a porcupine, and a long tail. It is covered with plates, which fit together like a cuisse, and into which it retreats like a tortoise. This armor is much like that of a warhorse. Its tail is covered with small scales, and its head with a hood of the same, which leaves the eyes showing. In short, it resembles nothing so much as a horse encased in armor, which is why the Spaniards call it "the armored one" [armadillo], and the Indians, *ayotochtli,* which is to say, "pumpkin-rabbit."

25. Cortés Is Well Received at San Juan de Ulúa

As SOON AS OUR MEN had embarked they set sail to the west, keeping as close inshore as they could, close enough to see the people walking along the beach; but not until Holy Thursday did they find a port where they could anchor their big ships in safety, and that was at San Juan de Ulúa (which looked like a port to them). It is called by the natives of those parts, Chalchiuhcuecan. There the fleet anchored, and it had hardly done so when two *acalles,* which are like canoes, put out seeking the captain of the fleet. When the Indians saw the banners and standard of the flagship, they approached it and asked for the captain, who was pointed out to them. They bowed to him and said that Teudilli, governor of that province, had sent them to find out who those men were and whence they came, and whether they intended to stop or continue on beyond. Cortés, although Aguilar did not understand them very well, had them brought on board his ship, thanked them for their trouble and their visit, gave them refreshments of wine and conserves, and told them that the Spaniards would land the next day to see and talk with their governor, who, he hoped, would not be alarmed at their landing, for Cortés would do him no harm, rather, would bring him much profit and pleasure.

The Indians accepted several trifling gifts, and ate and drank watchfully, suspecting evil but liking the taste of the wine, some of which, as well as some conserves, they begged for the governor, after which they took their leave. The following day, which was Good Friday, Cortés went ashore with the boats full of Spaniards, and then had the artillery and horses landed, and then little by little all the rest of the soldiers and Cuban servants, these last numbering about 200. Cortés selected the best place among the dunes that line the shore, and there pitched his camp and fortified himself. From the many trees in the vicinity the Cubans quickly put together enough branch huts to shelter them all. Then a crowd of Indians from a village near by, and from others, came to the Spanish camp to gaze at what they had never seen before, bringing gold in exchange for trifles such as the first Indians, those of the *acalles,* had brought back, and bringing also a great deal of bread and dishes cooked in their fashion with chili, to give or sell to our men. The Spaniards gave them in exchange little glass beads, looking glasses, scissors, pins, and the like, and the Indians, quite pleased, took them and returned to their houses and showed them to their neighbors. And such was the joy and pleasure that these simple people got from the trifles that they returned the next day with many more Indians, loaded with gold jewels, turkeys, bread, fruits, and cooked dishes in such quantity that they supplied the whole of our army; and in exchange for everything they took only a few strings of beads and needles and ribbons, considering themselves so well paid and rich that they could not contain their joy and contentment; and they even believed they had got the better of the strangers, because they thought the glass beads were precious stones.

Cortés, seeing the great amount of gold they brought and exchanged so foolishly for childish baubles, ordered by crier that, under heavy penalty, no one in the camp might accept any gold; on the contrary, in order to avoid the appearance of avarice on their part, and to dispel the notion that their single motive for coming was to acquire gold, all should pretend ignorance of it. This dissembling was for the purpose of discovering whether the Indians were making that great display of gold merely to see if that was the object of the Spaniards' visit.

The morning of Easter Sunday, Teudilli (or Quintaluor, as some call him) came to the camp from Cotastla, eight leagues away, where he resided, bringing with him more than four thousand men, unarmed, but most of them handsomely dressed: some wearing cotton garments, rich after their fashion; others, almost naked, loaded with provisions in amazing abundance. He greeted Cortés with ceremony, as is their custom, offering him burning incense and straws dipped in his own blood. He presented the provisions to Cortés and gave him several gold jewels, valuable and finely wrought, and other things made of feathers, no less strange and beautiful. Cortés embraced him and received him joyfully, and, saluting the others, gave him a silk coat, a medallion and necklace of glass, many strings of beads, looking glasses, scissors, straps, sashes, shirts, handkerchiefs, and other things of leather, wool, and iron, of little value among us, but highly esteemed by them.

26. Doña Marina

ALL THIS WAS DONE without an interpreter, because Jerónimo de Aguilar did not understand these Indians, who spoke a very different language from the one he knew. This vexed Cortés exceedingly, because he lacked means of communicating with the governor and learning about the country; but he soon recovered from his vexation when he heard one of the twenty women given to them in Potonchán speaking to the governor's men and understanding them very well, as if they were of her own language. So Cortés took her aside with Aguilar and promised her more than her liberty if she would establish friendship between him and the men of her country, and he told her that he would like to have her for his interpreter and secretary; besides which, he asked her who she was and where she came from.

Marina (as she had been named at her baptism) answered that she was from near Jalisco [Coatzacoalcos], from a village called Viluta [Olutla], and that she was the daughter of wealthy parents, who were related to the lord of that country; that, when she was a child, she had been stolen by certain merchants during a war and sold in the market place of Xicalanco, a large town above Coatzacoalcos, not very far from Tabasco, and that afterward she had fallen into the hands of the lord of Potonchán. This Marina and her companions were the first Christians to be baptized in all New Spain, and she and Aguilar were the only trustworthy interpreters between our men and those of the country.

As soon as Cortés was convinced that he had faithful interpreters in the slave girl and Aguilar, he heard Mass at the camp, placed Teudilli next to himself, and they ate together. Which done, they both remained in his tent, with the interpreters and many Spaniards and Indians. Cortés told them that he was a vassal of Don Carlos of Austria, Emperor of the Christians, King of Spain, and Lord of a great part of the world, whom many and great kings served and obeyed, and that all other princes rejoiced to be his friends because of his goodness and power. Don Carlos, he said, having heard of that land and its lord, had sent Cortés as his ambassador to visit Teudilli and inform him in private of certain things (which he had brought along in writing), which Teudilli's lord would be happy to learn. Therefore, Cortés asked, where would Teudilli's lord receive him?

Teudilli replied that he was very glad to hear of the greatness and goodness of the Lord Emperor, but that Cortés should know that the Lord Moctezuma was no less a king and no less good; rather, Teudilli was astonished to learn that there could be another such great prince in the world; but, since such was the case, he would send word to Moctezuma to learn his pleasure toward the ambassador and the embassy, for Teudilli trusted that his lord, in his clemency, would not only be pleased with the message, but would reward the messenger.

After this exchange, Cortés had the Spaniards, armed and in military formation, parade to the music of fife and drum; then he had his men practice mock combat, the horsemen charge, and the guns fired—all this to the end that the governor should tell his lord of it. The Indians stared at the dress, fierce countenances, and beards of the Spaniards; they were astonished to see the horses eat and run; they were frightened by the flashing of the swords; and they fell to the ground at the roar of the cannon, for it seemed to them the sky was falling upon them with its thunder and lightning. They said of the ships that the god Quetzalcoatl had come, bearing his temples on his shoulders, for he was the god of the air who had gone away and whose return they were expecting.

Teudilli sent a message to Moctezuma in Mexico describing everything he had seen and heard, and asking for gold to give the captain of the strangers, who had asked him whether Moctezuma had any gold, and Teudilli had answered yes. So Cortés said: "Send me some of it, because I and my companions suffer from a disease of the heart which can be cured only with gold."

This message was carried from the camp of Cortés to Mexico, that is, seventy leagues, in a day and a half. The messengers also carried a painting, very lifelike, representing a horse with a man on it, the Spaniards' arms and cannon, as well as the number of bearded men. Teudilli had already sent a painting of the ships as soon as he had seen them, showing how many and how large they were, everything represented very naturally on cotton cloth, for Moctezuma to see. The message was delivered in this short time because men had been stationed at intervals along the way, like relays of horses, and they passed the painting and message from hand to hand, so the news flew. Indeed, it is carried in this way faster than it would be by post horses, and the custom is even more ancient. The governor also sent to Moctezuma the garments and other things that Cortés had given him, and they were found later in Moctezuma's apartment.

27. Moctezuma's Answer

WHEN THE MESSENGERS had been dispatched, Teudilli, having promised an answer within a few days, took his leave. At a distance of two or three crossbow shots he had had more than a thousand huts built of branches, under the direction of two nobles, with as many as two thousand persons, men and women, to serve the Spaniards. Which done, he retired to Cotastla, where he resided. The two nobles were charged to look after the Spaniards; the women ground and prepared the *centli* bread (which is of maize), and cooked beans, meat, fish, and other dishes; the men brought the food to the camp, all the wood and water needed, and all the grass that the horses could eat, for the fields of that region are covered with it at all seasons of the year. These same Indians went to the neighboring towns inland and brought back such a quantity of food that it was an amazing thing to see.

Seven or eight days were spent in the many visits of the Indians and in waiting for the governor and the answer of the great lord they were all talking about. The governor soon appeared with rich and beautiful presents: many mantles and garments of white and colored cotton, embroidered in their fashion; many plumes and gorgeous feathers; many objects made of gold and feathers, richly and handsomely worked; a quantity of jewels and pieces of gold and silver; two thin disks, one of silver weighing 52 marks, representing the moon, the other of gold weighing 100 marks, representing the sun, with many decorations and animals carved upon it in relief, a very beautiful thing. In that country they hold the sun and the moon to be gods, and give to each the color of the metal it resembles. The disks measured as much as ten palms in diameter and thirty in circumference, and were probably worth 20,000 ducats, or even a little more. According to what the Indians said, they had been prepared as a gift for Grijalba, if he had not left.

The governor delivered his lord's reply to Cortés: that Moctezuma rejoiced to learn about and be a friend of such a powerful Prince as the King of Spain was said to be; that the latter might, whenever he wished, send more of those unusual, good, strange, and never-before-seen men, whom Moctezuma would receive with all pleasure and honor; that Cortés should determine what he needed for himself and the cure of his sickness, as well as for his men and ships, during the time he expected to be there, and that Moctezuma would command that everything be faithfully provided; moreover, that if there was anything in the country which Cortés might wish to send to that great Emperor of the Christians, Moctezuma would very willingly give it to him. But, as for their meeting and talking together, he considered it impossible, because he was himself ill and could not descend to the sea, and because it would be extremely difficult and laborious for Cortés to come to him, not only on account of the many high mountains that lay between, but also because of the great and sterile deserts Cortés would have to traverse, where he would necessarily suffer from hunger, thirst, and similar hardships. Besides, much of the country through which Cortés would have to pass was in the hands of Moctezuma's enemies, who were cruel and evil people, and who would kill him as soon as they learned that he was traveling as Moctezuma's friend.

Now, all these objections, or excuses, that Moctezuma and his governor made were for the purpose of discouraging Cortés from advancing with his men; or, perhaps, they hoped that bad weather would force the fleet to sail away. But the more obstacles they put in his way, the greater was the desire of Cortés to see Moctezuma, who was such a powerful king in that country, and to explore fully the riches he imagined it contained. And so, upon receiving Moctezuma's gifts and message, he presented Teudilli with a complete suit of clothing for his person, and he begged him to send to Lord Moctezuma, of whose magnificence and liberality he had heard such praises, many of the best pieces of merchandise he had brought along for trading. He also told Teudilli that, if only for the sake of knowing such a great and powerful king, it was proper that Cortés should see him, to say nothing of the embassy entrusted to him by the Emperor of the Christians, who was the greatest King on earth. Cortés told Teudilli, furthermore, that if he failed in his mission and his obligation under the law of right and chivalry, he would incur the disfavor of his King and Lord. Cortés begged Moctezuma, therefore, to reconsider his decision, in the knowledge that Cortés would not change his own because of the difficulties the other had brought up; no, not even because of greater ones that might transpire, for a man who had come two thousand leagues by water could well cover seventy by land.

Cortés importuned Teudilli to send this reply at once, so that the messengers could return quickly, for Teudilli could see that Cortés had many men to feed and little to give them; that the ships were in danger; and that the two were wasting their time in words. Teudilli said that he was sending daily dispatches to Moctezuma, and that Cortés meanwhile should rest easy in his mind, for the reply and decision would soon arrive from Mexico; that, moreover, Cortés need not worry about provisions, which would be most abundantly supplied him where he was. Teudilli then begged Cortés, who was encamped in a very bad spot among the dunes, to go with him to certain villages six or seven leagues distant. Cortés, however, refused to do so, and Teudilli took his leave, while Cortés remained in his camp for ten days awaiting the pleasure of Moctezuma.

28. Cortés Learns of Divisions in the Country

DURING THIS INTERVAL several men were observed on a low hill or sand dune, of which there are many in the vicinity, and, since they did not join or speak to the Indians who were serving the Spaniards, Cortés inquired who they were and asked why they had not approached his camp. Teudilli's two captains answered that they were only farmers who had stopped to gaze. Cortés was not satisfied with this reply and suspected that they were lying, because it seemed to him that the men wanted to approach, but dared not do so for fear of the governor's captains. And so it turned out to be, for the whole coast and even the country as far as Mexico was buzzing with the news of the strange and wonderful things our men had done at Potonchán, so everyone wished to see and speak with them, but dared not for fear of the Culhúans, that is to say, the men of Moctezuma.

Cortés therefore sent five Spaniards to invite them by peaceful gestures to come to him, or, failing that, to bring some of them by force to his camp. The men, who numbered about twenty, rejoiced to see the five Spaniards approach, and, eager to see those strange and unusual people and the ships, they came very willingly to the army and the captain's tent.

These Indians were very different from any that the Spaniards had thus far seen: they were taller than the others, and the cartilage of their noses was so widely pierced that it hung down almost to the mouth, with rings of jet or amber, or some such precious substance, inserted in it. Their lower lips were also pierced, and they wore in them little gold rings set with coarse turquoises, so heavy that the lip was pulled down over the chin, exposing the teeth. All this, which they practice to make themselves handsome, struck our Spaniards as ugliness such as they had never seen, even though the men of Moctezuma also had their lips and ears pierced, and wore little round plugs in them. But these new men had such great holes in their noses and ears that they could put their fingers through them, and in them they wore little gold rings and stones. Their ugliness and strange appearance astonished our men.

Cortés spoke to them through Marina, and they said they were from Cempoala, a city about a day's journey away (for that is how they reckon distances); that the frontier of their country was about half way, on a great river that divided their land from that of Lord Moctezuma; that their cacique had sent them to find out what kind of men or gods had come in those *teocallis,* which is to say, temples; that they had not dared come sooner or alone, not knowing what kind of men they would encounter. Cortés was pleasant to them and treated them with deference. He told them he was glad to see them and to learn of the good will of their cacique. He gave them a few trifling gifts and displayed the arms and horses, something they had never seen or heard of, and they wandered about the camp staring foolishly at one thing or another; and all this time they did not associate with, or speak to, the other Indians.

Our Indian woman interpreter was asked the reason for this, and she told Cortés that they not only spoke a different language but were subject to a different lord, who by force of arms kept himself independent of Moctezuma. Cortés was overjoyed with this bit of intelligence, for he had already guessed, from his talks with Teudilli, that Moctezuma had enemies and war in those parts; so he brought to his tent three or four of the Indians who seemed to him the more understanding and noble, and through Marina asked them about the lord of their country. They replied that all the country belonged to Lord Moctezuma, but that each province or city had its own lord, and that all of them paid tribute to Moctezuma and served as his vassals, or even slaves; but that many of them, for a short while past, recognized him only because they were forced, and now rendered him obedience and tribute, which formerly they had not done. Among them were the lord of Cempoala and his neighbors, who were at war with Moctezuma to free themselves from his tyranny, but at the moment they were stopped, because his forces were too great and his men too strong.

Cortés was well pleased to find the lords of that country at war with each other, which would allow him the better to carry out his plans and intentions. So he thanked them for their information about the state of the country and their description of the land, offered them his friendship and help, and begged them to come back often to his camp. He then dismissed them with many compliments, and gave them presents for their lord, whom he said he would soon go to see and serve.

29. Cortés and Four Hundred Companions Reconnoiter

TEUDILLI RETURNED at the end of ten days, bringing a deal of cotton garments and several pieces of featherwork, well made, in exchange for what Cortés had sent to Mexico, and he told Cortés to take his fleet and leave, because it was useless to try to see Moctezuma at that time. He told him furthermore to see what he needed from the country and it would be given him; that, whenever Cortés should pass that way again, they would do the same. Cortés answered that he would do nothing of the kind and would not depart without speaking to Moctezuma. The governor told him not to insist further in the matter, and with this he took his leave. That same night he took away all the Indians, men and women, who had been serving the Spaniards, and when day broke, all the huts were empty.

This aroused the suspicions of Cortés and he prepared for battle; but nothing happened, so he busied himself with finding a port for his ships and a good spot for a settlement. His intention was to remain there and conquer the country, for he saw excellent signs of gold and silver and other riches; but he was unable to find sites within a long league roundabout, because the country was all sand dunes, which shift with changes of the wind, and the rest was wet swampland, and hence very bad for quarters. For this reason he sent

Francisco de Montejo, in two brigantines, with Antón de Alaminos as pilot, to explore the coast until he should find a reasonably good port and place for a settlement. Montejo sailed as far as Pánuco without sighting a port, except in the shelter of a rock that jutted out into the water. He returned after having spent three weeks in that short trip, flying from the rough sea. The currents were so fearful that, even with sails and oars, the brigantines were driven backward. But he did say that the people of the coast had come out to meet him and offer him straws dipped in their blood, a gesture of friendship or reverence.

Cortés was much disappointed at Montejo's account, but nevertheless decided to seek the shelter that the other had mentioned, because it was near two good rivers, where he could get water and engage in trade. There were also large forests to supply firewood and timber, and building stone, and pasture, and flat land for tillage. Even so, the port was unsatisfactory for trading and accommodating the ships, because it was exposed to the north wind, which blows very hard there and causes much damage.

Now that Teudilli and Moctezuma's men were gone and he was without resources, Cortés was anxious lest his provisions fail or his ships be sunk, so he had all the clothing put on board, and he, with about 400 men and all the horses, set off in the direction taken by the Indians who had been supplying them. After marching some three leagues they came to a very beautiful river, which was not very deep and could be crossed by wading. Immediately beyond the river they came upon a deserted village, whose inhabitants had fled at the approach of our men. Cortés entered a large house, which must have belonged to the lord, made of adobes and timber, with floors that had been raised more than a fathom from the ground, and a roof covered with straw, of a strange and handsome appearance viewed from below. The house had many large rooms, some filled with jars of honey, *centli*, and other grains which they eat and keep in storage all the year, and other rooms filled with cotton garments and feather-work decorated with gold and silver. A great deal of the same was found in the other houses, which were built in the same style. Cortés had the crier announce that, on pain of death, no one was to touch anything but food—this in order to enhance his fame and good will among the natives.

The village had a temple, resembling a house in its living quarters, with a low but massive tower at its summit, and on top of the tower a kind of chapel, access to which was by twenty steps, and in it several large idols were housed. A great many bits of paper, of the kind they make, soaked in blood, were strewn about, and there was much blood from sacrificed men, according to Marina, and a block on which the victims were stretched for sacrifice, and flint knives with which they were cut open, while their hearts were torn out, still palpitating, and cast into the air as if for an offering. This sight aroused the greatest pity and astonishment among our Spaniards.

From this village they proceeded to three or four others, none of which had more than two hundred houses, all abandoned but full of provisions and blood like the first. Cortés then turned back, because he saw no profit in it, and because it was time to unload the ships and send them for more men; also because he wished to make a settlement there. In this activity he spent about ten days.

30. Cortés Resigns His Command

WHEN CORTÉS GOT BACK to the ships where the rest of the Spaniards were, he called them together and spoke to them, saying that God had evidently favored them by guiding and bringing them safely to such a good and rich land (as it truly seemed to be, to judge by what they had seen in the short time since their arrival), abundant in provisions and filled with people, who were better dressed, more civilized, reasonable, and intelligent, with better houses and farms, than all the others thus far seen or discovered in the Indies; that it was likely there was much more to it than they had seen; that for that reason they should thank God and make a settlement there, and penetrate the country and enjoy the grace and favor that Our Lord had shown them. Also, it seemed best to him to settle there for the present, or in the best locality or port they could find, and to make themselves strong with a wall and fortifications, in case they had to defend themselves from the people of the country, who were not happy at their coming and staying there.

Moreover, he said, from that place they could the more easily make friends with the Indians and towns of the neighborhood, and trade with them, towns such as Cempoala and others that were enemies of Moctezuma; that, when they had built their settlement, they could unload the ships and send them back to Cuba at once, or to Santo Domingo, Jamaica, Boriquén, and other islands, or to Spain, for more men, arms, and horses, and clothing and supplies. Besides, it was necessary to send a report to Spain, to the Emperor and King, giving him an account of what was happening, together with samples of the gold, silver, and rich featherwork they had acquired. And so that this might be done with greater authority and better advice, he wished, as their Captain, to appoint a town council, complete with alcaldes, regidores, and all the other officers necessary for the organization and good government of the villa they were about to found, who would rule, prohibit, and command, until such time as the Emperor should provide whatever was most necessary to his service.

So saying, Cortés took possession of the country, and of all the land as yet unexplored, in the name of the Emperor Don Carlos, King of Spain, and he performed the other acts required in such cases, and begged Francisco Fernández, the royal notary, who was present, to bear witness to it. All approved of his plan and told him to proceed, for they had come with him to follow and obey him. Cortés forthwith appointed, in the name of the Emperor, his natural Lord, the alcaldes and regidores, an attorney, a constable, a notary, and all the other officers of a complete town council, and then delivered into their hands their wands of office and gave the corporation the name of Villa Rica de la Vera Cruz, because they had landed in that country on Friday of the Cross.

After executing these legal formalities, Cortés performed yet another in the presence of the same notary and the new alcaldes, Alonso Hernández de Portocarrero and Francisco de Montejo, in which he relinquished, desisted from, and delivered into their hands and power, as justices royal and ordinary, the command and title of Captain and Discoverer that the Jeronymite Fathers (governing in His Majesty's name in the Island of Santo Domingo) had granted him. He further stated that he no longer wished to exercise the authority he had received from Diego Velázquez (Governor of Cuba in the name of the Admiral of the Indies), to trade and explore and to look for Juan de Grijalba, since none of these officers held power or jurisdiction in the new land that he and his companions had just discovered and were now in the act of colonizing in the name of the King of Castile, as his loyal vassals. He asked them to witness his act, and they did so.

31. Cortés Is Elected Captain and Justicia Mayor

THE NEW ALCALDES and officers accepted their wands of authority and took possession of their offices, and at once met in council, as is customary in the villages and towns of Castile. They discussed and spoke of many things concerning the public good and the government of the new villa, and agreed among themselves to make Cortés himself their Captain and Justicia Mayor, and to give him power and authority in all matters having to do with war and conquest, until such time as the Emperor should otherwise dispose. Having reached this agreement and decision, the whole council went to Cortés the next day and told him that (pending the Emperor's disposition), since they had to have a commander to lead them in war, he should continue as such in the conquest and invasion of that country; that he should be their Captain, Chief, and Justicia Mayor, to whom they would have recourse in arduous and difficult situations, and in the differences that might arise among them; that, all this being necessary and obligatory for the good of town and army, they begged and charged him to be their Chief and to rule and govern them, for, with his experience in organizing and preparing the expedition and fleet, and before and since, he had more abilities and qualifications for the post than any of them. This, they said, was their charge to him and, if necessary, their command, because they held it as certain that God and the King would be well served if he accepted this authority; and they would profit by it themselves, contented and satisfied with the knowledge that he would govern them with justice, treat them with humility, and lead them with diligence and boldness. It was for this purpose, they said, that they were electing, naming, and taking him for their Captain-General and Justicia Mayor, giving him all the necessary and possible powers, and submitting themselves to his authority, jurisdiction, and protection.

Cortés, without much persuasion, accepted their election, because at the moment he desired nothing better. He told the council they were quite aware that, until they had founded a settlement in the country and knew more about it, they had no means of sustaining themselves except with the provisions he had brought in the ships. He would, therefore, take what he thought he needed for himself and his servants, and the rest would be appraised at its just value and distributed among his men, who would undertake to pay him for it, or they might take the price of it from the common store [of booty], after deducting the King's fifth. The men then begged him to have the ships and the artillery also appraised, so that they might reimburse him in common; and in common they would bring from the Islands bread, wine, clothing, arms, horses, and the other things needed for the army and the villa. This, they said, would be less expensive for them than if they had to depend on traders, who always demand exorbitant and excessive prices for their goods. In this, they said, Cortés would be doing them a great favor.

Cortés answered that when he had outfitted the fleet in Cuba and supplied it with provisions, he had not done so with the thought of reimbursing himself, as others are in the habit of doing, but had intended to give it all to them as a free gift, even though he had spent his estate and gone into debt; that they should therefore take it without protest, and he would command, as he did thereby command, the masters and notaries of the ships to bring all the provisions to the council, which would distribute them equally among the men, without favoring any, even himself, because at a time of such scarcity of food, hardly enough to sustain life, the need of the small was as sharp as that of the great, of the old as that of the young. And so, even though he owed more than seven thousand ducats, he was giving it all to them freely, and, as far as the ships were concerned, he would dispose of them in whatever way was best for all and would do nothing affecting his men without first informing them.

Cortés did all this especially to win their good will and verbal support, because there were many who disliked him, despite his true generosity with his companions in the matter of war expenses.

32. Reception of Cortés at Cempoala

SINCE THEIR PRESENT ENCAMPMENT was unsatisfactory as a site for the new villa, they decided to remove to Quiahuixtlán, the place in the shelter of a rock that Montejo had reported. So Cortés ordered guards posted on the ships, and the artillery and all the stores reëmbarked, and he sent the ships on to Quiahuixtlán, while he took the horses and four hundred companions, two demi-falconets, and some Cuban Indians by land over the eight or ten leagues that lay between the two points.

The ships sailed, and he set out for Cempoala, which lay due west, although he had to take a roundabout route to get to the rock. After marching three leagues he came to the river that marks the boundary of Moctezuma's territory, but he could not find a ford and had to descend to the sea, where he could cross the river more easily by the bar at its mouth; but even there he had difficulties and had to cross the bar at a run. Once on the opposite side, his men followed the bank upstream, because they could not travel along the swampy beach. They passed some fishermen's cabins and poor huts, and a few cultivated plots, but after a league and a half came out upon some rich and beautiful meadows where they saw many deer.

They continued their march up the river, thinking they might encounter a good town upon its banks, when they espied as many as twenty persons on a hilltop. Cortés sent out four horsemen, with orders to approach the Indians making signs of peace, but, that if the Indians fled, to pursue them and take some prisoners, whom he needed as guides and interpreters, for the Spaniards were marching blindly and feeling their way, not knowing what road to take to the town. The horsemen rode up to the hill shouting and making signs of peace, but the Indians ran away in terror at the sight of such monstrous tall animals, for they believed horse and rider to be one. But the ground was flat and our men soon overtook them; and they surrendered, having no arms, and were all brought back to Cortés.

Their ears, noses, and faces were pierced with great ugly holes, in which they wore rings, like the men of Cempoala, which, indeed, they said they were from, and that the city was not far away. Asked why they had come, they answered, to look; asked why they had fled, they answered, for fear of the strange men. Cortés reassured them, saying that he and his few companions were going to the Indians' town as friends, to see and speak with their lord, whom he was very desirous of knowing, since their lord had refused to come to Cortés, or even to leave the town—which was why Cortés wished to be guided there. The Indians answered that it was too late to reach Cempoala that day, but that they would guide him to the village which he could see on the far bank of the river at no great distance; that it was small, but could feed and lodge the whole company that night.

Upon their arrival at the village several of the twenty Indians, with the permission of Cortés, went to inform their lord where they were, and they told Cortés they would be back the next day with their lord's reply. The rest remained to serve and provide for their strange guests, whom they lodged and fed well. Cortés fortified his position that night as well and strongly as he could, and on the following morning some hundred men came bearing fowl and turkeys, and told him their chief was greatly pleased at his coming, but was so fat and heavy he could not travel, and would await Cortés in the city. Cortés and his Spaniards breakfasted on the fowl and then followed their guides, marching in military order, with the two guns ready for action, in case of need.

They crossed back over the river and followed a fine road to the next ford, waded it, and soon arrived at Cempola, a mile or so away, which was all gardens and greenery and well-watered orchards. Many men and women came out to greet and welcome these strange beings, more than men, and gave them flowers and fruits very different from any that our men knew, and even mingled freely with our squadrons. In this fashion, gaily and joyously, all entered the city, which was like a bower, so covered by great tall trees that the houses could hardly be seen. A group of distinguished-looking men, something like a town council, was waiting at the gate to greet our men and offer them gifts. Six horsemen, who had gone on ahead as scouts, turned back in amazement and reported to Cortés that they had seen the courtyard of a house all plated with silver. He ordered them to re-enter the town and show no surprise at that, or at anything else they might see.

The street by which our men approached was filled with people, gazing open-mouthed at the horses, cannon, and strange men. Crossing a wide square, they saw on their right a high wall of stone and mortar, with battlements, plastered with well-polished gypsum, which shone in the sun like silver, and this is what our Spaniards thought was silver-plated walls. In my opinion, their imagination and desire made them think that everything that shone was gold and silver. It was, of course, an illusion, an illusion, moreover, that lacked the substance of their desire. Inside the courtyard or enclosure was a row of apartments, and at the far side seven towers separated from each other, but one much taller than the rest.

Our men passed by in silence, concealing their surprise, but deceived [as to its cause], and followed their guides to the lord's palace. He came out surrounded by the elders, who were better dressed than the common run, and was escorted by two gentlemen (at least, they seemed to be such, to judge by their dress and manner), who supported him on either side. The lord and Cortés bowed courteously to each other, as is the custom in that country, and, through the interpreters, exchanged a few words of greeting, after which the lord retired to his palace and appointed several of his nobles to look after the captain and his men and arrange lodgings for them. The nobles led Cortés to the walled courtyard on the square, where all the Spaniards were lodged, for the apartments were spacious and good. Once inside, our men realized their mistake about the walls, and were even ashamed to have believed them plated with silver.

Cortés distributed his men among the rooms, had the horses looked after and the guns placed at the entrance—in short, he fortified himself as if he were in the enemy's camp and presence, and ordered that no one, on pain of death, should venture outside. The lord's servants, and the officials and nobles of the council, provided an abundant supper for our men and gave them beds after their fashion.

33. Cortés and the Lord
of Cempoala

THE NEXT DAY in the morning, the lord, accompanied by his nobles, paid a visit to Cortés, bringing him many cotton mantles (which they wear knotted at the shoulder, like gypsy women), and a few gold jewels, worth perhaps two thousand ducats. He told Cortés to rest with his men and enjoy himself. This, he said, was his reason for not wishing to bother him or talk business at that time. The lord then took his leave, as he had done the day before, after telling Cortés to ask for whatever he needed or desired. As soon as the lord had gone, a crowd of Indians, outnumbering the Spaniards, entered bearing a bountiful cooked dinner, with a great abundance of fruits and flowers. In this fashion the Spaniards spent two weeks there, most plentifully provided for.

The day following, Cortés sent the lord some Spanish garments and many little trade articles, and begged to be allowed to come and see him at his house, for it would be discourteous to receive a visit from his worship and not return it. The lord answered that he would be pleased and delighted, with which Cortés took some 50 armed men as an escort and went to the palace, leaving the rest on guard in the courtyard under a captain. The lord came out to greet Cortés and together they entered a low room. (In that country, which is hot, they do not build lofty rooms, but, for reasons of health, raise a dirt platform solidly about a fathom above the ground and climb up into the house by steps. Upon this platform they erect the walls of their houses, made of either stone or adobe and finished with glistening lime or gypsum plaster. The roof is of straw or leaves, so well and cleverly woven that it lends beauty to the house, while it protects it from the rain as well as if it were of tile.) Cortés and the lord sat down upon two low benches resembling chopping blocks, made all of one piece, complete with legs and everything. The lord ordered his men to stand aside or leave the room, and then he and Cortés, through their interpreters, began to talk of their affairs, spending a great while in questions and answers, for Cortés was very desirous of finding out what he could about the country and its great King

Moctezuma; while the lord, though fat, was anything but a fool in his own inquiries.

In brief, the purpose of Cortés' talk was to give the lord an account of his visit and its motive: who was sending him, and to what purpose, just as he had done with Tabasco, Teudilli, and the others. The lord, after listening attentively, made a long and detailed reply, to the effect that his ancestors had lived in peace, quietness, and liberty, but that for several years past his city and country had been tyrannized over and ruined, because the lord of Mexico–Tenochtitlán and the men of Culhúa had taken over everything and no one had been able to prevent or disturb them, especially since they had first come with religious pretexts, and with the same pretexts had later seized all the arms in the country. In this fashion they had made themselves its masters before anyone realized what they were about, and now that his people recognized their mistake they could not prevail against the usurpers or shake off their yoke of servitude and tyranny, although they had attempted to do so by force of arms; but the more they struggled, the greater were the evils they experienced, for [it was the policy of Moctezuma] to receive and protect as friends and allies those who recognized him as their lord, while he took hostages and laid a tribute and head tax upon them. If, on the other hand, after having submitted and delivering themselves into his power, they resisted and took up arms against him, their punishment was terrible, for he killed many and had them eaten after sacrificing them to Texcatlipoca and Huitzilopochtli, the gods of war, and then enslaved as many of the rest as he wished, forcing fathers, mothers, and children to work from sunup to sundown. The men of Moctezuma took all their possessions and, in addition to all these insults and outrages, sent constables and tax collectors to their houses to take whatever they might have overlooked—all this without pity or compassion, leaving them to die of hunger. Such being the way they were treated by Moctezuma, who would not willingly become the vassal, not to say the friend, of such a good and just Prince as the Emperor was said to be, if only to escape these daily vexations, robberies, insults, and outrages, not to mention the favors and benefits which such a great Lord would and could grant them?

Here the lord paused, overcome by emotion, but he soon took hold of himself and went on to expatiate on the strength of Mexico, which was built upon the water, and on the wealth, splendor, greatness, army, and power of Moctezuma. He said, however, that Tlaxcala, Huejotzingo, and other provinces of the country, together with the Totonacs of the mountains, were enemies of Moctezuma and, moreover, had heard something of what had happened in Tabasco; that, if Cortés so desired, he would make a league with all of them that would be so strong that Moctezuma would not be able to stand against it.

Cortés rejoiced to hear all this, which fitted in with his intentions, and he told the lord that he was sorry about the miserable treatment suffered by the land and people, but that the lord might be sure Cortés would put a stop to it and even avenge it, for he had come only to right wrongs and succor the oppressed, favor the weak, and destroy tyrannies; that, furthermore, he and his men had been so well received in the lord's house, in word and deed, that Cortés was under the obligation of doing him every favor and supporting him against his enemies, and would do the same for the lord's friends, who should be told the purpose of Cortés' coming; that, since they were of the lord's party, Cortés would help them in any way they wished. So saying, Cortés took his leave, remarking that he had stayed too long and had to go back to look after his men and ships at Quiahuixtlán, where he intended to establish himself for some time, and where he and the lord could speak further.

The lord of Cempoala replied that if Cortés wished to stay with him, he was welcome to do so; if not, the ships were near by and they could discuss their agreement on board without difficulty or delay. So saying, he had eight girls called, all very richly dressed after their fashion, like Moors, one of whom wore better cotton garments than the others, and was more richly decked out with gold and jewels. The lord told Cortés that these ladies were all noble, and that the one with the gold ornaments was his own niece, who had vassals of her own. Her he gave to Cortés for a wife, and the others to the gentlemen of the company, as a pledge of his love and true and perpetual friendship. Cortés received this gift with a great show of satisfaction, not wishing to offend the giver, and so took his leave, the women being carried on litters, with many other girls to serve them; and many men came along to escort Cortés and guide him to the sea and supply him with provisions.

34. Events at Quiahuixtlán

CORTÉS AND HIS MEN reached Quiahuixtlán on the same day they left Cempoala, and discovered that the ships had not yet arrived. Cortés was much astonished at their taking such a long time to sail such a short distance. Since he had nothing to do and was only a crossbow shot, or a little more, from the rock and cove called Quiahuixtlán, he formed his men and set out for it, accompanied by those of Cempoala, who told him that Quiahuixtlán belonged to one of the lords oppressed by Moctezuma. Cortés went as far as the foot of the rock and met only two men, whom Marina could not understand. The Spaniards started up the slope, which was so steep and rough that they would have preferred to dismount; but Cortés forbade it, lest the Indians get the notion that a horse could not negotiate any slope, however high and difficult. So they climbed slowly up and came to the houses, where they saw no one and suspected some treachery. Still, in order not to show weakness, they rode on into the town, where they met a dozen respectable citizens and an interpreter, who knew the language of Culhúa as well as their own Totonac, which is the one in common use in all the mountain country. They said they had never before seen men like the Spaniards, nor had they even heard of their appearance in those parts—which is why they had hidden—but that as soon as the lord of Cempoala had informed them who the Spaniards were, and had vouched for their peaceful intentions, the Indians had lost the fear they had felt upon seeing them approach, and had come out to welcome them in the name of their lord and show them to their quarters.

Cortés followed them to the square, where the lord of the town was awaiting him with a large company. The lord showed great pleasure at the sight of the strangers with the great beards. Then he picked up a clay brazier filled with coals and threw upon it a kind of resin, which resembles white animé and smells like incense, and perfumed Cortés with the smoke—a ceremony they observe with their lords and gods. While the men were being lodged, Cortés and the lord sat down together beneath the portals of the square, and Cortés gave the other an account of his coming to that country, as he had done all along his route. The lord repeated virtually the same story that the lord of Cempoala had told, and he told it in manifest fear that Moctezuma would be angry with him for receiving Cortés and entertaining him without Moctezuma's express command and permission.

While they were thus conversing, some twenty men looking like constables appeared on the opposite side of the square, each carrying a short, thick wand and a feather flyflap. The lord and his men began to tremble at the sight of them. Cortés inquired the reason, and they told him that those were Moctezuma's tribute collectors, who, they feared, would report the presence of the Spaniards, and this would bring down upon them Moctezuma's wrath and punishment. Cortés reassured them, saying he was a friend of Moctezuma and would persuade him not to punish them; rather, Moctezuma would rejoice at their having received the Spaniards. And, he added, even in the contrary case, he would defend them against Moctezuma, because every one of those men of his was equal to a thousand Mexicans in battle, as Moctezuma himself knew quite well from the Potonchán war. But the lord and his men were not at all comforted by the words of Cortés; on the contrary, the lord wished to rise to his feet and give lodging to [the men of Moctezuma], such was his fear of them. Cortés, however, stopped him and said: "Just to give you an idea of what I and my men can do, order your men to seize these tribute collectors of Moctezuma, for I shall be with you, and not even Moctezuma himself will be able to molest you, even if he wished, so great is his respect for me."

Encouraged by these words, the lord had the Mexicans seized and, when they resisted, had them beaten and trussed up (that is, he had their feet lashed to one end of a long pole, their neck to the other, and their hands tied in the middle), so that they could only lie stretched out on the ground. When Moctezuma's men had been secured, the lord asked whether he should kill them, and Cortés begged him not to, but to keep them as they were and prevent their escape. So Moctezuma's men were thrown into a room where ours were quartered, and in the middle of it a great fire was built and Moctezuma's men were laid around it, under a heavy guard. Cortés also posted guards at the door and then retired to his room to eat, for the lord had provided an abundance of food for him and his men.

35. Cortés' Message to Moctezuma

WHEN IT SEEMED to Cortés that the Indians must be asleep, the night being far advanced, he ordered the Spanish guards to release two of the prisoners and bring them to him, but to do so without awakening the Indian guards. This the Spanards did so quietly that, unheard, they cut the cords (which were made of a kind of rush), freed two of the prisoners and brought them to Cortés. He pretended not to know who they were and asked them through Aguilar and Marina to tell him what their business was there, and why they had been imprisoned. They answered that they were vassals of Moctezuma, charged with the duty of collecting certain tributes that the people of that town and province owed their master; that they were ignorant of the reason for their arrest and abuse; rather, they were astonished at such strange folly, because at other times they had been met on the way and treated with no little respect. It was their belief that the mountain people had rebelled because of the presence of Cortés and his companions, who were said to be immortal. They were even afraid that the other prisoners would be put to death before Moctezuma could be warned, such was the barbarism of these people. The mountain people, they said, would gladly rise against Moctezuma, given the opportunity, if only for the sake of annoying him and putting him to the expense of suppressing them, as had happened before. They begged Cortés, therefore, to see that their companions did not die, or remain in the hands of their enemies, because Lord Moctezuma would be grieved if his old and honest servants should suffer for having served him well.

Cortés answered that he would indeed be sorry if Lord Moctezuma should be grieved, or his servants mistreated, in the presence of Cortés, who would look after them as if they were his own; but, he added, they should thank God and Cortés for their freedom, for Cortés had set them free because of his liking and friendship for Moctezuma, and also because he wished to send them forthwith to Mexico with a certain message. Therefore, he said, they should eat and fortify themselves against the journey, and put their trust in their legs, for if they were caught this time they would fare worse than the first.

The prisoners ate hurriedly, so anxious were they to be off. Cortés sent them at once from the town, they themselves acting as guides, gave them provisions for the journey, and charged them, by the liberty and favor they had received from him, to tell Lord Moctezuma that Cortés considered him as a friend and desired to serve him in every way, now that Cortés was aware of his fame, goodness, and power. Cortés charged them, furthermore, to tell Moctezuma that he was glad he was present at a time when he could demonstrate his good will by liberating them, and by striving to guard and preserve the honor and authority of such a great prince, and by favoring and helping his men. And [continued Cortés], let his Highness beware of spurning his friendship and that of the Spaniards, as Teudilli had done (this fellow having left without ceremony, while he removed his men from the coast), but, even so, Cortés would not fail in his service to Moctezuma whenever the occasion required it, nor would he fail to seek his grace, favor, and friendship by all possible and manifest means. Also, he was firmly convinced, having every reason to believe that nothing but good will and love existed between them, that His Highness would not avoid or deny his friendship. Moreover, he did not believe that Moctezuma had sent his men to see and talk with Cortés, or had provided necessary supplies out of his own pocket; rather, that Moctezuma's vassals had done so on their own responsibility, thinking to serve him. But their desire to hit the mark was so keen that they missed it altogether, for they did not know that God was coming to them in the persons of those servants of the Emperor, from whom Moctezuma and all the rest might expect to receive very great benefits and learn mysterious and holy things. If, however, this should come to naught because of Moctezuma, the blame would be his; but Cortés trusted so much in Moctezuma's wisdom that he was sure Moctezuma would be happy to see and speak with Cortés, and become a friend and brother of the King of Spain, in whose glorious name Cortés and his companions had come. As for the servants of Moctezuma who remained there as prisoners, Cortés would undertake that they should not be endangered, promising to have them set at liberty for the service they had done him; and this he would do at once, as he had done with the two he was sending with this message; only [he would have to delay it a little] in order not to anger the people who had entertained and treated him with such great courtesy, for otherwise it might seem to them that he was requiting them badly by interfering in their affairs. The Mexicans departed very happily, promising to execute punctually everything Cortés had commanded them to do.

36. Cortés Contrives a Rebellion

THE NEXT MORNING, when the two prisoners were found to be missing, the lord scolded the guards and would have put to death the remaining prisoners; but Cortés, who was waiting to see what the people of the town would do or say, came out at the noise of the shouting and begged the lord not to kill them, because, after all, they were public servants and, according to natural law, neither deserved punishment for their acts nor were culpable for what they did in the service of their king. But, he said, to prevent their escaping, as the others had done, they should be given into his charge, and he would be responsible for them. So they were given to him, and he sent them on board the ships, with warnings, and ordered them put in irons.

After this, the terrified people of the town held a council with their lord to discuss what should be done in the circumstances, for they were certain that the runaways would divulge in Mexico the insult and abuse they had suffered. Some said it would be proper and fitting to send ambassadors, with tributes and other offerings, to Moctezuma, to placate his wrath and annoyance, and to excuse themselves by laying the blame on the Spaniards, who had ordered them to take the prisoners, and to ask his pardon for the error and fault they had commited like mad and insolent men, in disrespect of the Mexican majesty. Others said it would be much better to shake off the yoke of servitude and no longer recognize the authority of the wicked and tyrannical Mexicans, now that they had with them these demigods and invincible Spanish knights; also, because they would have many of their neighbors to help them. They finally decided to rebel and not waste this opportunity, and they begged Hernán Cortés to approve their decision and act as their captain and leader, since it was on his account that they found themselves in this predicament;

that, whether or not Moctezuma sent an army against them, they were now determined to break with him and fight.

God knows how delighted Cortés was at this turn of events, for he thought by this means to reach Mexico. He answered that they should carefully consider what they were doing, for Moctezuma, he had learned, was a most powerful king; but that if they so desired, he would command and defend them, for he valued their friendship more than that of Moctezuma. At the same time he would like to know how many men they could muster. They answered, one hundred thousand, counting all those of the league they would make. Cortés then told them to send word to all those of their way of thinking, enemies of Moctezuma, to advise and inform them of their decision, and assure them of the help that the Spaniards would give them; not, he added, that he had any need of them, for he and his men alone were a match for all the men of Culhúa, even though the Culhúans were twice as numerous as they were. Nevertheless, they should be on their guard, lest by chance Moctezuma should send an army against the lands of their allies and do them mischief, taking them by surprise through some carelessness. They should be on the alert also, in case they should need help, to send for it in time.

With the hope and encouragement that Cortés gave them, and also because they were by nature proud and thoughtless, they dispatched messengers at once to all the towns they could think of, informing them of their decision, while they praised the Spaniards to the skies. These appeals and measures led many towns and lords, as well as the whole mountain country, to rebel; not a single Mexican tax collector was left in any part, and open war was declared against Moctezuma. Cortés' thought was to stir these people up in order to win them and their lands over to his support, seeing that without them he could accomplish little. He had the constables arrested; released them; made new overtures to Moctezuma; aroused the town and the country roundabout; and left them in rebellion so that they should have need of him.

DURING THIS WHILE the ships were lying in the shelter of the rock, where Cortés went to inspect them, taking along many Indians from the rebellious town and from another near by, together with the Cempoalans he had brought with him. He got them to cut many branches and logs which, with some stones, were brought in to build houses at the site he had marked out, to which he gave the name of Villa Rica de la Vera Cruz, as had been agreed upon at the election of the council of San Juan de Ulúa. Lots were assigned to the citizens and members of the council; sites were indicated for the church, square, town house, jail, arsenal, wharf, slaughterhouse, and other public buildings necessary for the good government and order of the villa. At an appropriate spot above the port, a fortress was traced out, and the fabrication of bricks for it and the other buildings was begun at once, since the soil lent itself to the purpose.

While this activity was going on, two youths, nephews of Moctezuma, arrived from Mexico, accompanied by four respectable old men as advisers, with many servants to look after their personal needs. They presented themselves to Cortés as ambassadors, and offered him a great many cotton garments, some pieces of featherwork, and a helmet full of loose gold in grains, just as it is gathered from the earth, which weighed 2,090 castellanos. They told him that Moctezuma, their lord, was sending it to him to cure him of his sickness, and as a reward for releasing the two servants of Moctezuma's household and preventing the death of the others. They assured him that Moctezuma would do as much for him; that Moctezuma begged him to procure the release of the prisoners who were still being held; that he forgave him his lack of respect and his insolence, for he loved him well; and that he would overlook the reception of Cortés by the Cempoalans; but he warned Cortés that the character of the Cempoalans was such that they would commit other excesses and crimes, which they would expiate all together, by being beaten like dogs. For the rest [the ambassadors said], Moctezuma was well, but busy with wars and other important matters, and could not say at the moment where or when they might meet, but that in time a way would be found.

Cortés received them cordially and lodged them as best he could in huts and field tents by the river, and sent at once for the lord of the rebellious town of Quiahuixtlán. He came, and Cortés told him to mark how truly he had spoken, and how Moctezuma would not dare to send an army or do any mischief where Cortés was; that, therefore, the lord [of Quiahuixtlán] and his confederates might thenceforth be free and exempt from servitude to the Mexicans, and not be obliged to pay them tributes as they were accustomed to do; but Cortés begged him not to take it ill if he should free all the prisoners and give them to the ambassadors. The lord answered that he would obey Cortés, since they were dependent upon him, and would not exceed his instructions in any respect. Cortés could well afford such negotiations with people who did not understand where the thread of his plot was leading them.

The lord returned to his town, and the ambassadors to Mexico, all very happy. He at once spread the word of these actions and of Moctezuma's fear of the Spaniards throughout all the mountain country of the Totonacs, whom he induced to take up arms, abandon their allegiance to Mexico, and cease payment of tributes. The ambassadors accepted the prisoners and the many gifts that Cortés made them, such as linen, wool, leather, glass, and iron articles, and were filled with wonder at the Spaniards and all their works.

38. Cortés Takes Tizapantzinco

NOT LONG AFTER THIS, the Cempoalans sent word to Cortés, asking for Spanish help against the Mexican garrison that Moctezuma maintained at Tizapantzinco, from which they received a great deal of harm, for their lands and crops were burned and destroyed, and the farmers killed. Tizapantzinco is on the border between the lands of the Totonacs and those of the Cempoalans, in a strong position near a river, with a fortress on a high rock. Because of its strength and its situation among those who were constantly rebelling against him, Moctezuma kept a large force there. When his men saw the rebels under arms, and the tribute collectors and the treasurer in flight taking refuge in the fortress, they sallied forth to put down the uprising, and as a punishment burned and destroyed everything they found, and even captured many people. So Cortés set out for Cempoala and Tizapantzinco, which is two days' journey, or eight or more leagues beyond it, with a large force of his Indian friends.

The Culhúans came to meet them, thinking they had only to do with the Cempoalans, but when they sighted the bearded men on horseback, they fled in a panic. They took refuge in a shelter and tried to get from it to their fortress, but the cavalry cut them off before they were able to do so. The horses, however, could not climb the rock, so Cortés and four or five others dismounted and entered the fortress unopposed, with the Indians of the town. Once inside, they held the gate until the rest of the Spaniards and many more friends came up, to whom Cortés delivered the fortress and town, begging them at the same time not to harm the inhabitants, and to let the soldiers of the garrison go free, but without their arms and standards—which was a novel thing for the Indians—but they obeyed him and he returned to the coast by the same way he had come.

With this exploit and victory, the first that Cortés had won over the men of Moctezuma, the mountain people were relieved of the fear and vexations perpetrated by the Mexicans, and our men gained very great fame and renown among friends and enemies alike. So true was this that afterward, whenever any situation arose, the Indians would send to Cortés requesting one of the Spaniards of his company, saying that one such would suffice for their leadership and security.

This was not a bad beginning for what Cortés had in mind. When he reached Vera Cruz (his men being very proud of their victory), he learned that Francisco de Salceda had arrived with the caravel purchased from Alonso de Caballero, a citizen of Santiago de Cuba, and was careening it. The caravel had brought sixty Spaniards and nine horses and mares, which gave Cortés no little encouragement and pleasure.

CORTÉS PUSHED THE BUILDING of the fortress and the houses of Vera Cruz, so that the soldiers and citizens might live in some comfort, and have shelter against rain and enemies, because he intended shortly to set out for Mexico and meet Moctezuma, and because he wished to leave everything in order and as it should be, so that he might depart in an easier state of mind. He prepared for war as well as for peace. He had all the arms and munitions landed, the merchandise for trading, and the victuals and provisions, all of which he delivered over to the town council, as he had promised.

Then he assembled his men and told them it was now the proper time to send the King an account of what had been accomplished there up to that time, and, along with this account, samples of gold, silver, and other wealth; that, for this purpose they would have to distribute by heads what they had acquired, as was customary in those parts in war, and first to set aside the royal fifth. That this might be done best, he appointed Alonso de Avila King's treasurer, and Gonzalo Mejía that of the army. The alcaldes, members of the council and all the others approved of his action, not only rejoicing at the appointment of the treasurers, but confirming it and begging them to accept. Cortés thereupon had the cotton garments they had accumulated brought out into the square for everyone to see, and the gorgeous featherwork, and all the gold and silver, valued at 27,000 ducats, and he gave it all into the hands of the treasurers by weight and count, and told the council to distribute it.

They all replied, however, that they would not do so, because after the King's fifth should be deducted, the rest was necessary to repay Cortés for the provisions he had supplied, and the guns and ships, which they had used in common. Therefore, they said, he should take it all and send the fifth part of the best to the King. Cortés answered that there would be time later on for him to be reimbursed for his expenditures and debts, but that for the present he wanted only the part due him as their Captain-General; that all the rest should go to those gentlemen so they might pay off the small debts they had incurred when they joined the expedition. He said also that he intended to send the King more than the royal fifth, and he begged them not to take offense, because this was the first present he had sent and included things that could not be divided or melted down, and he was not taking the trouble to compute the fifth by weight or by shares. Finding them all to be in agreement with him, he selected from the heap the following articles:

The two disks of gold and silver that Teudilli had given in the name of Moctezuma.

A gold necklace of eight pieces, in which 83 small emeralds were inlaid, and 232 small stones, like rubies, of no particular value; hanging from it were 27 small gold bells and several ornaments of pearl or small stones.

Another necklace of four twisted strands, with 102 small rubies and 172 small emeralds; ten pearls not badly mounted, and a fringe of gold bells. Both necklaces were notable and had other ornaments besides those mentioned.

Many gold nuggets, none larger than a chickpea, just as they are found in the earth.

A helmet full of unfounded gold, somewhat coarse, plain and not worked.

A wooden helmet plated with gold, encrusted with stones, and a beaver hung with 25 gold bells; on its top a green bird with eyes, beak, and feet of gold.

A casque encircled with gold plates and bells, with stones on top.

A bracelet of very thin gold.

A wand, like a royal scepter, with two gold rings at its ends, adorned with pearls.

Four three-pronged hooks covered with feathers of many colors, their stone points fastened with gold thread.

Many deerskin sandals, sewn with gold thread, the soles fashioned of a kind of white and blue stone, very thin and transparent.

Six pairs of leather shoes of various colors, ornamented with gold, silver, or pearls.

A shield of wood and leather, with little brass bells about the rim; its boss a plate of gold, with the figure of Huitzilopochtli, the god of war, engraved upon it; on its handle, four heads, a lion, a tiger, and eagle, and a vulture, all very lifelike, wearing their original feathers or hair.

Many skins of birds and beasts, also wearing their own feathers and hair.

24 shields of gold, feathers, and mother-of-pearl, very handsome and well made.

5 shields of silver and feathers.

4 fish of gold, 2 ducks, and other birds, hollow, cast in gold.

Two large gold snails, like nothing we have, and a frightful-looking crocodile, wound about with many threads of gold.

One brass [bronze] bar; also several axes and what seemed to be adzes, of the same.

One large mirror with gold trimmings, and several smaller ones; many mitres and crosses worked with feathers and gold, of a thousand different colors, and adorned with pearls and gems.

Many very handsome feather pieces of all colors, not dyed but natural.

Many fans and flyflaps of gold and feathers; also some of a single feather, small and large, of all kinds, but all very beautiful.

One mantle, like a cape, of woven cotton, of many colors and feathers, with a black circle in the middle, with rays; silk on the inside.

Many surplices and priestly garments, palliums, frontals, and ornaments for temples and altars.

Many more cotton mantles, either pure white, or of white and black checks, or red, green, yellow, blue, and so on, but without nap or color on the reverse side; on the obverse, downy, like felt.

Many short shirts, jackets, and cotton gowns for men, and other things.

Many cotton mantles, bed covers, and rugs.

These things were pretty, rather than valuable, although the disks were truly precious, and the workmanship was worth more than the things themselves, because the colors of the cotton cloth were very fine, and those of the feathers, natural. The cast pieces were beyond the skill of our silversmiths (of which we shall speak at greater length later on in the proper place). Included among these articles were several books of painted figures, which the Mexicans use for writing, folded like kerchiefs. Some of them were made of cotton and glue, and others of the leaves of the agave, quite an admirable thing. Since, however, their meaning was not understood, their value was not appreciated.

At this time the Cempoalans were holding many men for sacrifice, to prevent which Cortés begged them to let him send the men as a present to the Emperor; but the Cempoalans refused, saying that their gods would be angry with them and would take away their maize, their children, and their wives if they did so. Cortés, nevertheless, took four, all comely youths, and two women, who were going about the city dressed in feathers, dancing, and begging alms for their sacrifice and death. And it was an amazing thing to see how much they were given and how they were admired. In their ears they wore gold rings set with turquoises, and in their lower lips huge gold rings which exposed their teeth—an ugly thing in Spanish eyes, but beautiful there.

40. The Emperor Is Requested to Make Cortés Governor

As soon as the King's present and fifth were ready, Cortés asked the council to name two delegates to convey them, to whom he would give his power of attorney and his flagship. The council, to the great satisfaction of Cortés, chose the alcaldes Alonso Hernández de Portocarrero and Francisco de Montejo, and Cortés named Antón de Alaminos their pilot. Since the delegates were going in the name of all, they took from the common store the gold they thought would pay their expenses for the journey to and from Spain, as well as their negotiations and provisions for the sea. Cortés gave them a very full and detailed power of attorney, with instructions about what they were to demand in his name, and their actions at court and in his own province: that is, they were to give his father, Martín Cortés, and his mother a certain sum in gold and an account of his prosperous fortunes.

By the hands of the delegates he sent the Emperor a report and notarized statements of events, and he also wrote him a private letter summarizing everything that had transpired since he had left Santiago de Cuba: the quarrels and differences between him and Diego Velázquez, the bickerings in his camp, the hardships they had all suffered, the good they had accomplished in the royal service, the greatness and wealth of the country, and his hope to subject it to the royal crown of Castile. He undertook to win Mexico for the Emperor, and to take the great king Moctezuma dead or alive. Finally, he begged the Emperor's assistance in the performance of his duties, and money for the purchase of the supplies that would have to be sent to that new land, which he had discovered at his own cost, to compensate him for his hardships and expenses.

The council of Vera Cruz also wrote two letters to the Emperor (although at the time they did not know he was Emperor), in one of which, signed only by the alcaldes and regidores, they recounted what that handful of gentlemen had thus far accomplished in the royal service; the second of which was approved and signed by members of the council and by all the more eminent men of the army, which in substance affirmed that they would hold and defend the villa and the land won in his royal name, or die in the attempt, unless His Majesty should otherwise decree. They prayed him humbly to give its government, and that of whatever other lands they should conquer, into the hands of Hernán Cortés, their leader, Captain-General, and Justicia Mayor, whom they themselves had elected, for he was worthy of it, having done and spent more than all of them together in equipping the fleet and the expedition; and, for their improvement and security, they prayed him to confirm Cortés in the office to which, in the name of His Majesty, they had voluntarily elected him. Furthermore, they pleaded, if His Majesty had already appointed another to that office and government, let him revoke it in the interest of the royal service and the well-being and increase of themselves and those parts, also to prevent the quarrels, scandals, risks, and deaths which would follow if another should be given the government and authority, and be appointed captain over them. They begged his prompt reply and attention to the matters which their delegates would present concerning the council of their villa.

Alonso Hernández de Portocarrero, Francisco de Montejo, and Antón de Alaminos set sail from Quiahuixtlán and Vera Cruz, in a fairly good ship, on July 26, 1519, bearing the letters, documents, testimonials, and reports that I have mentioned. On their way they touched at Marién in Cuba and, leaving word there that they would stop at Havana, they did no such thing, but continued on through the Bahama Channel and sailed with very favorable winds until they reached Spain. The members of the council and the army men had written this letter because they feared Diego Velázquez, who enjoyed great favor at court and in the Council of the Indies; also, because the news brought back by Francisco de Salceda was already circulating in their camp, to wit, that the Emperor, after Benito Martín arrived in Spain, had granted Diego Velázquez the government of that land [of Yucatan], which, although they did not know it for certain, was a very hard fact, as has been related elsewhere.

41. Cortés Puts Down a Mutiny

MANY IN THE CAMP, belonging to the party of Diego Velázquez, grumbled at the election of Cortés, because it excluded Velázquez from the country. Some of these were servants of Velázquez, others his debtors, and a few were his friends. They said that Cortés had been elected by trickery, flattery, and bribes, and that his conniving to get himself begged to accept the office was of a piece, because a captain and governor could not be elected except on the authority of the Jeronymite Fathers, Governors of the Indies, and on that of Diego Velázquez, who had already been appointed, as rumor had it, to the governorship of Yucatan. Cortés heard of this talk, informed himself of who had started it, arrested the principals, and put them on board ship. He soon released them in the interest of peace, which was the cause of a much worse situation, for the same men later on attempted to seize a brigantine, kill its skipper, and sail it to Cuba, there to inform Diego Velázquez of what Cortés was doing and of the great gift he was sending the Emperor, so that Velázquez might seize it from the delegates as they passed Havana, together with their letters and reports, to prevent the Emperor's seeing them and getting the notion that he was being well served by Cortés and the others.

Cortés was truly furious. He seized many of the conspirators and took their statements, in which they confessed it was all true. So, after a proper trial, he hanged Juan Escudero and the pilot Diego Cermeño, and had Gonzalo de Umbría, also a pilot, whipped, as well as Alonso Peñate. The rest he released. With this action Cortés made himself more feared and respected than before; and, in truth, if he had been soft, he would never have mastered them, and, if he had been negligent, he would have been ruined, because they would have warned Diego Velázquez in time to seize the ship, the gift, and the letters and reports. Indeed, Velázquez did try to take her later, sending in pursuit an armed caravel, because Montejo and Portocarrero did not pass Cuba so unperceived that Velázquez did not learn what they were up to.

42. Cortés Destroys His Ships

THE PURPOSE of Cortés was to go to Mexico, but he concealed it from his men, lest they refuse to accompany him on account of the difficulties that Teudilli and others had mentioned, especially that the city was surrounded by water and that they imagined it to be very strong, as, in fact, it was. And so, to make them all follow him whether they liked it or not, he resolved to destroy his ships, a bold and dangerous thing to do, and one that gave him a great deal to think about, not that he would regret the loss of the ships, but that his companions might prevent it, as they doubtless would have done if they had realized what he had in mind. Having, however, decided to destroy them, he arranged with several of the sailing masters to have them holed, beyond the possibility of pumping or plugging them. He begged certain other pilots to spread the story that the ships were decayed and worm-eaten and were no longer seaworthy. There was considerable discussion of the matter, after which Cortés ordered them to bring ashore whatever they could, and then let the ships sink or founder, while they were to feign great sorrow at their loss.

So they removed the guns, arms, provisions, sails, ropes, anchors, and all the other gear that might be of use, and then beached five of the best ships. They sank four others a little later, this time, however, with some trouble, because the men now realized what Cortés' plan was and how he had tricked them, and they said that he wanted to send them to the slaughterhouse. But he placated them, saying that those who were unwilling to wage war in that rich country and who did not like his company, could return to Cuba in a ship he had saved for the purpose—this he did in order to discover how many were cowards and enemies, not to be trusted. Many insolently demanded permission to go to Cuba, half of them sailors, who preferred sailing to fighting. A number of others felt the same way, in view of the vast size of the country and the multitude of its people, but they were ashamed to display their lack of spirit in public. Possessed now of this intelligence, Cortés ordered the ship scuttled, thus removing all means of escape, a deed clearly necessary in the circumstances, carried out with the wisdom of a courageous captain, very secretly, to be sure, as conformed with his purpose, even though he lost heavily in the value of the ships and deprived himself of the services of a naval force.

History offers few examples of such exploits, which are the acts of great men, like Omich Barbarossa, the one-armed, who a few years before had sunk seven galliots and foists in preparation for the taking of Bujía, as I wrote at length in my history of the naval engagements of our time.

43. The Cempoalans Cast Down Their Idols

CORTÉS was exceedingly impatient to see Moctezuma. He announced his departure and selected 150 men from the body of the army to leave behind as a sufficient citizenry and guard for the villa and fortress, now almost completed. He appointed Pedro de Ircio captain and left him there with two horses and two arquebuses, plenty of Indians for their service, and 50 towns of friends and allies near at hand, from which 50,000 more fighting men could be drawn in case of need. With the rest of the Spaniards Cortés went to Cempoala, four leagues distant; he had hardly arrived when he got word that Francisco de Garay was sailing along the coast with four ships. At this news he returned at once to Vera Cruz with 100 men, suspecting they were up to some mischief. There he learned that Pedro de Ircio had gone to find out who they were and what they wanted, and to invite them to his town if they were in any need. The ships were anchored three leagues away. Cortés took Pedro de Ircio and a squadron of his company and went there to see whether anyone had been landed to pick up an interpreter, and to discover what they were after, for he suspected some evil intent on their part, because they had anchored so far away and had not entered the port and town, to which they had been invited. He had gone about a league when he encountered three Spaniards from the ships, one of whom said he was a notary, and the other two witnesses. They said they had come to present Cortés with certain documents (which they did not produce), and demand that he share the country with Captain Garay and erect boundary markers in the proper places, because Garay claimed it for himself, with the title of first discoverer, and intended to plant a colony on the coast, twenty leagues to the west [north], near Nautla, now called Almería.

Cortés told them to get back to their ships and tell their captain to bring his fleet to Vera Cruz, where they could talk and he could learn what Garay's intentions were, and whether he was in any need, which would be taken care of as well as possible. And, Cortés added, if Garay was coming in the King's service, as he alleged, Cortés desired nothing more than to favor and guide a man who was acting in the name of His Highness; besides which, they were all Spaniards together. They replied that in no circumstances would Garay or any of his men land there or come near Cortés, who, now seeing what was in the wind, arrested them and hid them behind a high dune opposite the ships. There, it now being almost night, he ate and slept, and remained until a rather late hour the next day, expecting Garay or one of the pilots, or some other person, to come ashore, whereupon he would seize them and learn where they had been and what damage they had done. In the latter case he would send them back to Spain as prisoners; in the former he would discover whether or not they had talked with Moctezuma's men.

Seeing that they were very fearful, he surmised it was because of some mischief they had done, so he had three of his men exchange clothing with the messengers and sent them to the inlet, where they shouted and waved their capes at the men in the ships, several of whom, either recognizing the clothing or in answer to the shouts, came in a skiff, as many as a dozen of them, armed with crossbows and arquebuses. Cortés' men, disguised in the others' clothing, went into the the bushes, as if seeking shade, for it was midday and very hot, but in reality to keep from being detected, and those in the skiff sent ashore two arquebusiers and an Indian, who walked toward the bushes, thinking their companions were there. Thereupon Cortés charged them with many men and took them before they could make it back to the boat, although they did attempt to defend themselves. One of them, a pilot, aimed his arquebus at Captain Ircio, and if it had had a good match and powder it would have killed him. When the men in the ships saw that they had been tricked, they waited no longer, but set sail before the skiff reached them.

From the seven he had taken, Cortés learned that Garay had navigated a great stretch of the coast in search of Florida, and had landed at the mouth of a river, in a country whose king was called Pánuco, where they had seen some gold, although little, and that without leaving the ship they had acquired some 3,000 pesos' worth, as well as a quantity of provisions, in exchange for some trifling bits of merchandise. Garay was not pleased with any of the country he had seen, because he had found little gold, and that of poor quality.

Without further investigation or precaution, Cortés returned to Cempoala with the same hundred men he had brought. Before he left, he persuaded the people of the city to cast down their idols and the sepulchers of their caciques (whom they worshiped as gods), and to worship the God of heaven and the Cross that Cortés had given them. He made a pact of friendship with them and the neighboring towns, against Moctezuma. They gave him hostages as an earnest of their good faith, and promised to provide for the Spanish garrison he was leaving in Vera Cruz. Moreover, they offered to give him as many men as he might need for war and service. Cortés accepted the hostages, who were many, but the most noble were Mamexi, Teuch, and Tamalli. For supplying of wood and water he demanded one thousand *tamemes*. *Tamemes* are porters or carriers who bear on their shoulders burdens of fifty pounds, wherever they are sent. These were the men who hauled the guns and carried the packs and provisions.

44. The Power of Moctezuma

CORTÉS LEFT CEMPOALA (which he renamed Sevilla) for Mexico on August 16 of that same year, with 400 Spaniards, 15 horses, three small guns, and 300 Indians, including warrior nobles and *tamemes,* among whom I count those of Cuba. Cortés no longer had a vassal of Moctezuma to guide him straight to Mexico, for all had fled, either from fear, when they saw that a league had been formed, or because they had been so ordered by their towns and lords, and the Cempoalans did not know the way very well. During the first three days' march, which the army made through friendly territory, they were well received and lodged, especially at Jalapa. The fourth day they arrived at Xicochimalco, a strong place on the side of a very steep mountain, to enter which two paths like two staircases had been cut; and if the inhabitants had defended the entrance, our foot would have had great difficulty in reaching it, to say nothing of the horse. It was learned later that Moctezuma had commanded them to lodge, honor, and feed the Spaniards. They even said that the Spaniards must surely be friends of his, since they were on their way to visit him.

On the plain below this town were many fine dependent villages and farms, from which Moctezuma could draw at need as many as 5,000 fighting men. Cortés warmly thanked the lord of the place for his hospitality and courteous treatment, and for the good will of Moctezuma. He then took his leave and crossed a high range by a pass three miles in extent, to which he gave the name of Nombre de Dios, which was so trackless and rough that Spain has none to equal it. Along it are many grapevines and bee trees. Descending from the pass, Cortés entered Ixhuacán. a fortress and town friendly to Moctezuma, where our men were received as at the previous place. Beyond it, Cortés marched for three days through desert country, uninhabited and saline, where his men suffered somewhat from hunger and a great deal from thirst, because all the water was salt, and many drank it for want of sweet water and fell sick. They also encountered a sandstorm and cold weather, which brought them much trouble and hardship, for the Spaniards who were already sick spent a chilly

94

night, and the Indians almost perished. Indeed, some of the ill-clothed Cubans did perish, not being used to such cold.

After four days in the bad country, they climbed another mountain, not very steep, and at its summit found a great many wagon-loads (or so they seemed) of firewood, cut and stacked, near a low tower containing many idols. They named this place Pass of the Wood. Two leagues farther on, the land again became poor and sterile, but the army soon came to a town they called Castilblanco [Ixtacamaxtitlán] because of the lord's houses, which were of white new-cut stone, the best they had thus far seen in that country, very well constructed, at which they marveled not a little. In its language the town is called Zacotlán [Zautla]; its valley, Zacatami; its lord, Olintetl. He received Cortés very warmly, and lodged and fed all the men very properly, having been ordered to do so by Moctezuma, as the lord himself said later on. In obedience to Moctezuma's word and command (or, possibly, to curry favor with Cortés), in a gay festival he sacrificed fifty men, whose blood flowed fresh and clean, and many of the townspeople carried the Spaniards on their shoulders and in hammocks, which are, as we should say, litters.

Cortés addressed them through his interpreters, Marina and Aguilar, explaining the reason for his journey to those parts, and all the other things he usually told the Indians, and then asked the lord whether he knew or recognized Moctezuma. The lord, as if astonished at such a question, answered: "Why, is there anyone who is not a slave or vassal of Moctezuma?" Cortés then told him of the Emperor, King of Spain, and begged him to become a friend and servant of that very great monarch; also, if he had any gold, to give Cortés a little of it to send as a gift to his King.

The lord answered that he would not abandon his allegiance to his lord Moctezuma; nor would he give him any gold, of which he had a quantity, without Moctezuma's permission. Cortés said nothing to this and concealed his thoughts, for the lord struck him as a man of courage, and his men as good warriors; but he did beg the lord to tell him about the greatness of that king of his, Moctezuma. The lord replied that Moctezuma was lord of the world, that he had thirty vassals, each of whom commanded 100,000 warriors; that he sacrificed 20,000 men a year; that he resided in the most beautiful and strongest city in all the inhabited part of the country; that his palace or court was very large, noble, and generous; his wealth, incalculable; his expenditures, prodigious. And certainly he spoke truly in everything he said, save that in the number of sacrifices he exaggerated somewhat. Even so, the numbers of men killed in sacrifice at every temple constituted a fearful butchery, and there are Spaniards who say that in certain years as many as 50,000 were sacrificed. While Cortés and the lord were engaged in this conversation, two other lords from the same valley came to see the Spaniards, one of them bringing Cortés a present of four slave girls, each of whom wore a gold necklace of no particular value.

Olintetl, although a tributary of Moctezuma, was himself a great lord of 20,000 vassals. He maintained thirty wives in his own house, and had a hundred other women to wait on him. For his service and bodyguard he had 2,000 retainers. The town was large; it had thirteen temples with many different stone idols, before which men, doves, quail, and other creatures were sacrificed, with the burning of incense and great reverence. Here, and throughout this territory, Moctezuma kept 5,000 garrison and frontier troops, and relays of men on the road between it and Mexico.

Up to this point Cortés had not entirely realized the wealth and power of Moctezuma, although he anticipated many obstacles, difficulties, dangers, and other things on his way thither—even so, when he heard all this, which would have dismayed many brave men, he showed no sign of faltering; rather, the more marvels he heard of that great lord, the greater was his desire to see him.

Now, since he had to pass through Tlaxcala on the way, which all assured him was a large city, strong, and filled with warlike men, he sent forward four Cempoalans to speak with the lords and captains of Tlaxcala, representing him, Cempoala, and their allies, offering them peace and friendship, informing them that these few Spaniards were coming to make their acquaintance and serve them, and begging them not to take offense. Cortés thought that the Tlaxcalans would behave toward them as had the Cempoalans, who were true and loyal, and who had, up to this time at least, always told him the truth. So he thought that the Tlaxcalans, being friends of the Cempoalans, would therefore be friends of himself and his companions, for they were deadly enemies of Moctezuma. He even thought they would be glad to join him in his expedition to Mexico, in case of war, because of their desire to free themselves and take revenge for the insults and depredations which the Culhúans over the years had inflicted upon them.

Cortés rested for five days at Zautla, which is watered by a cool stream and filled with friendly people. He set up many crosses in the temples and cast down the idols, as he had done at each place along his route. He left the friendly Olintetl and went on to another town two leagues upstream called Ixtacamaxtitlán, which belonged to the lord who had given him the slave girls and the necklaces. This town has, along the river and in the surrounding plain, so many villages that they are virtually continuous—so, at least, they were where our army passed. The town itself must have more than 5,000 inhabitants. It is situated on a high hill, on one side of which the lord has his house and the best fortress in those parts, as strong as those of Spain, enclosed by a good stone wall, with barbicans and a deep moat. Here Cortés rested for three days to recuperate from the fatigue of the march, and to await the messengers he had sent on ahead from Zautla, to see what kind of answer they would bring.

45. First Encounter with the Tlaxcalans

THE MESSENGERS were so long in returning that Cortés left Zautla without further intelligence of Tlaxcala. Our army had not proceeded far, however, when at the mouth of a valley it came upon a great wall of uncemented stone, about a fathom and a half high and twenty feet wide, surmounted by battlements along its full length. It stretched across the valley from one ridge to the other and had only one opening, ten paces wide, behind which one section of the wall extended past the other for a distance of forty paces, like a ravelin, making it strong and difficult to pass if defended. Cortés inquired about the reason for the wall and asked who had built it, and Ixtacamaxtitlán,* who was with him, said that his ancestors had built

* Ixtacmixlitán in the text. Gómara confuses the name of the place with the name of its lord, which we do not know.

it for the protection of their territory during a war with the Tlaxcalans, who were coming to rob and kill them for being friends of
Moctezuma. The wall seemed to our men to be as costly and showy
as it was superfluous and useless, because it could easily be flanked.
Even so, they gathered that the Tlaxcalans must be brave and valiant
warriors, to justify such a defense against them.

The army halted to admire this stupendous work, and Ixtacamaxtitlán thought they did so out of hesitation and fear of pushing on.
He begged Cortés not to pass through Tlaxcala, because the Tlaxcalans, knowing that Cortés was his friend and was on his way to see
Moctezuma, would do him some mischief. For this reason he offered
to guide Cortés through the territory of Moctezuma only, where he
would be well received and provided for until he reached Mexico.
Mamexi and the other Cempoalans, on the contrary, urged Cortés
to follow their advice and by no means to take the road by which
Ixtacamaxtitlán wished to lead him, which they said, he was doing
in order to alienate Cortés from the friendship of their province,
the people of which were loyal, good, and brave; and they warned
Cortés not to join Ixtacamaxtitlán against Moctezuma and not to
believe him, for he and his people were false and wicked traitors,
who would lead him into a spot from which he could not extricate
himself, and there would kill and eat him.

Cortés was silent for a while in the face of these conflicting stories,
but finally accepted the advice of Mamexi, because he trusted the
Cempoalans and their allies more than he did the others, and also
because he did not wish to show fear. So he continued the march to
Tlaxcala that he had begun.

He took leave of Ixtacamaxtitlán and accepted three hundred of
his warriors, and passed through the gap in the wall. Then in good
order and with every precaution he pursued his march, keeping the
guns readied for action. He himself went with an advance party,
reconnoitering the country for a league and a half against surprises,
so that in case of need he might return in time to put his men in
battle order and select a good spot for fighting or camping.

Having advanced more than three leagues beyond the wall, he
sent back word to the foot to make haste, for it was getting late, and
went on with his party about another league, where, upon mounting
a slope, the two men in the lead came upon a group of fifteen men

armed with swords and shields, and wearing the feathers they usually don for battle. These men were scouts and, when they saw the horsemen, they ran off headlong, either because they were frightened or to give warning. Cortés then rode up with three other companions, but, regardless of his shouts and signs, the Indians would not stop, and so, to prevent their escape without his taking an interpreter, he pursued them with his six horse and overtook them as they crowded together determined to sell their lives dearly. Cortés motioned to them to stand quiet, thinking to take them alive, but all they did was to brandish their weapons, so the Spaniards had to fight them. The Indians defended themselves so stoutly for a while against the six that they wounded two of ours and killed two horses with two blows of their swords. According to those who witnessed it, they sliced cleanly through the horses' necks, reins and all. At this juncture four other horsemen rode up, and then the rest, one of whom Cortés sent back to tell the infantry to come running, because some five thousand Indians were advancing to aid and reinforce their men, whom they had seen fighting. But they were too late, for, raging at the loss of the two horses, our men had killed them [the fifteen] with lance thrusts, for all of them had refused to surrender. They [the newcomers] fought our horse with great courage and daring, until they saw the infantry advancing, with the guns and the whole body of troops, at which they retired and left the field in our hands. Our horse pursued them and charged among them regardless of their number, killing as many as seventy in complete safety.

As soon as the Tlaxcalans had retreated, the two messengers who, along with several of their men, had been held in Tlaxcala for three days, brought word that the Tlaxcalans said they had not known what those others were doing, they being from different communities and acting without orders; but that the Tlaxcalans regretted it and would gladly receive the Spaniards as friends, because the Spaniards struck them as men of valor. This whole message was a trick, but Cortés believed it and thanked them for their courtesy and good will, saying he would do as they desired and be their friend, and that they need not pay him for the horses, because he would soon have many more of them. But God knows how he felt their loss, and regretted even more that the Indians had discovered horses were mortal and could be killed.

Cortés continued for a league on beyond where the horses had died, although it was almost sunset and his men were tired from having marched such a great distance that day, because he wanted to make camp in a strong and well-watered place. This he did on the banks of a stream, where he spent that night in some trepidation, after having posted sentries both mounted and unmounted; but the enemy did not disturb him, and his men were able to rest more easily than they had expected.

46. Tlaxcalans Against Cortés

CORTÉS SET OUT at daybreak the next morning, his army in good order, the baggage and guns in its midst. As they were approaching a small village, they met the other two Cempoalan messengers who had been sent [to Tlaxcala] from Zautla. These were in tears. They said that the captains of the Tlaxcalan army had tied them up and held them captive, but that they had freed themselves and escaped that same night, for otherwise they would have been sacrificed at dawn to the god of victory and eaten, to make a good beginning of the war, and also as a token of what the Tlaxcalans were going to do to the bearded men and all those who were with them.

The messengers had hardly finished their story when, at less than a crossbow shot, there appeared from behind a low hill as many as a thousand Indian warriors, very well armed, who advanced with a whoop that reached the skies, shooting darts, stones, and arrows at our men. Cortés made them signs of peace and spoke to them through his interpreters, begging them to desist and warning them formally before a notary and witnesses (as if they could profit by it or understand what it was all about); but the more he spoke the greater was their eagerness to close with our men, thinking to defeat them, or to trick them into an ambush of more than eighty thousand men which they had prepared in some ravines that cut the road and made a difficult place to pass. Our men stopped talking and seized their weapons, and a fine skirmish ensued, because their thousand were as many as we had on our side, and were skillful and valiant besides, and had, moreover, a better position from which to attack.

The battle lasted many hours, at the end of which the enemy, either from exhaustion or because they were trying to get our men into a trap and take them without further ado, began to yield and retire toward their own forces, not defeated, but gored. Our men, their blood now up from the fighting and killing, pursued them with all their troops and baggage, and, when they least expected it, found themselves among the ditches and ravines, surrounded by an infinite number of armed Indians who had been waiting for them. In order not to break their formation, our men did not halt, but advanced with great risk and difficulty, in spite of the hustling and opposition of the enemy. Many of the Indians attacked the horsemen and seized their lances, so daring were they, and many Spaniards would have lost their lives if their Indian friends had not come to the rescue. They were also helped by the spirit and encouragement of Cortés, who, although he was ahead with the horse fighting to clear a space, turned back from time to time to re-form and cheer his men. They finally emerged upon a level and open field, where the horses could run and the guns be brought into play, two things that did great damage to the enemy, who were dismayed by the novelty and so fled.

In both encounters that day many Indians died or were wounded, and some of the Spaniards were wounded, but none killed, and all gave thanks to God for saving them from such a multitude of enemies. Rejoicing at their victory, they went on to Teocacingo, where they pitched camp. Teocacingo is a village of a few houses and a small tower and temple, in which the Spaniards fortified themselves and put up many shelters, the straw and branches for which were brought in by the *tamemes*. These Indians of Cempoala and Ixtacamaxtitlán, whether they acted from fear of being eaten or from shame and friendship, did so well that Cortés thanked them heartily.

That night, which was the first of September, our men slept uneasily, fearing an attack; but the enemy did not appear, not being used to night fighting. At daybreak Cortés sent a message of peace and friendship to the Tlaxcalan captains, begging and admonishing them to allow him passage through their country on his way to Mexico, for he would do them no hurt whatever. He left 200 of his men, the guns, and the *tamemes* in camp, and took the other 200, the 300 from Ixtacamaxtitlán, and some 400 Cempoalans, and set out to reconnoiter the country before the Tlaxcalan groups could assemble.

He burned five or six villages, took as many as 400 prisoners, and returned unharmed, although the enemy pursued him all the way back to his tower and camp. There he received the reply of the Tlaxcalan captains, to the effect that they would deliver their answer the next day, as he would see.

Cortés spent the night on the alert, for he thought that the message was threatening and that the enemy were determined to do what they had said, especially since the prisoners assured him that 150,000 men were assembling to descend upon him and eat the hated Spaniards alive, in the conviction that they were friends of Moctezuma, whose death and ruin they desired above all things. This was true: the Tlaxcalans gathered up all their available men to seize the Spaniards and offer them to their gods in the most solemn sacrifice that had ever been made, after which they would all feast upon "that heavenly flesh," as they called it.

Tlaxcala is divided into four quarters or districts, called Tepetícpac, Ocotelulco, Tizatlán, and Quiahuixtlán; that is to say, "Place of the Hills," "Place of the Pines," "Place of the White Plain," and "Place of the Water." Each of these districts has it own head or lord, whom it supports and obeys, and these four make up the government of the republic and city. They command and govern, in peace and in war, so that in this war there were four captains, but the general of the whole army was one of the same captains called Xicoténcatl, from the district of Quiahuixtlán. He it was who bore the standard of the city, a golden crane with outstretched wings, decorated with many figures done in enamel and featherwork. He carried it at the rear of the troops, as is their custom in wartime; at other times it is borne in front. The second in command was Maxixca. The army numbered about 150,000 men. Such was the great horde faced by 400 Spaniards, but in the end they were defeated and eventually became our loyal friends.

Before dawn the next day, then, the four captains assembled their whole army, which covered the plain, and took up a position near the Spaniards, separated from them only by a deep ravine. The men were splendidly armed in their fashion, and their faces were painted with red bixa, which gave them the look of devils. They carried great plumes and maneuvered marvellously well. Their weapons were slings, pikes, lances, and swords (of the kind here called halberds); bows and arrows (these not poisoned); helmets; arm and leg armor of wood, gilded or covered with feathers or leather. Their breast-plates were of cotton; their shields and bucklers, very handsome and not at all weak, were of tough wood and leather, with brass and feather ornaments; their swords, of wood with flints set into them, which cut well and made a nasty wound. Their troops were arranged in squadrons, each with many trumpets, conches, and drums, all of which was a sight to see. Never since the discovery of the Indies had the Spaniards faced a better or larger army.

47. The Tlaxcalans Boast and Threaten

THESE MEN were fierce and full of words. They said: "What foolish and contemptible men are these, who threaten us without knowing us, who dare to enter our country without our permission and against our will? Let us not attack them too soon. Let them rest, for we shall have time later on to take and tie them. Let us send them food, for they are famished, lest they say we were able to take them only because they were hungry and tired." So it was that the Tlaxcalans sent them 300 turkeys and 200 baskets of maize cakes, which are their ordinary bread, weighing more than 300 arrobas, which was a great relief for the hungry Spaniards. A little later the Tlaxcalans said: "Now that they are filled, let us attack, and we shall eat them; and then they shall pay us for our turkeys and cakes, and we shall learn who ordered them to come here. If it was Moctezuma, let him set them free; if they came because of their own foolhardiness, let them pay for it!"

These and similar idle boasts they bandied about, seeing the small number of the Spaniards who faced them, and being as yet unacquainted with their strength and courage. The four captains forthwith sent some two thousand of their best and most experienced soldiers against the Spanish position, thinking to take our men unharmed, or, if they should defend themselves, to bind them and bring them back by force, or kill them. The Indians were reluctant to attack, saying they would gain little honor if so many engaged so few. Nevertheless, the two thousand crossed the ravine and boldly approached the tower. The Spanish horse sallied forth, and after them the foot, and at the first encounter they taught the Indians something of the cutting power of steel; at the second, showed them the strength of those few Spaniards whom they had been insulting a short while before; and at the third, put to flight very handsomely those who had come to seize them. Not a man of the Indians escaped, save some few who succeeded in recrossing the ravine.

The rest of the enemy then came charging toward our position, yelling at the top of their voices, and many of them forced their way in irresistibly and fought hand to hand with the Spaniards. It took some time for our men to drive them out and kill them, which they did by vaulting over the wall and clearing it of its assailants. The fight lasted more than four hours, at the end of which the enemy, having lost many killed and wounded, and not having been able to kill a single one of their opponents, weakened rapidly. Even so, they did not cease their attacks until very late in the day, when they retired, to the great relief of Cortés and his men, who were exhausted from killing Indians. The Spaniards rested and slept that night more tranquilly than at any time before, although they kept careful watch and posted lookouts and sentries on all sides. The Indians, though suffering from the loss of so many men, did not on that account consider themselves beaten, as they proved later on. It could not be learned what their losses were, for our men did not have the leisure to count them, nor did the Indians.

Before daylight the next morning Cortés again set out to lay waste the country, leaving half his force to guard the camp. He burned more than ten towns and sacked one, a place of three thousand houses, in which he found few fighting men, since they were all in the combined army. Those who were there, however, defended themselves, and he killed many of them. Firing the town, he returned to his camp by noon, unharmed but hastily, because the enemy was advancing rapidly to cut him off and attack our position. They came as they had come the day before, bringing provisions and boasting. But, although they attacked for five hours, they did not kill a single Spaniard and lost a large number of their own, for they were so closely packed that the guns played havoc among them. They had their fighting for their pains, and we the victory. They thought our men led a charmed life, for their arrows did no damage.

The day following, the lords and captains sent Cortés three kinds of presents, the bearers of which said to him: "Sir, here are five slaves for you. If you are fierce enough to eat flesh and blood, eat them and we shall bring you more. If you are a benevolent god, here are incense and feathers for you. If you are men, take these fowl and bread and cherries."

Cortés replied that he and his companions were mortal men, precisely like themselves; that he had always told them the truth, while they, on the contrary, had fed him nothing but lies and flattery; that he wished to be their friend, and that they should not be stubborn fools, for they would suffer greatly by fighting. Did they not see how many of them had died without having been able to kill a single Spaniard? With these words he dismissed them. And still the Indians attacked, more than thirty thousand of them, this to test their breastplates against our men in our own camp, as they had done the day before; but all they got out of it was broken heads, as always, and retreated.

It is worthy of note that, although on the first day their whole army had attacked our position in a body, on the succeeding days each group attacked separately, in order to spread the work and suffering among them all, and to keep out of each other's way, for by attacking in such great numbers in a narrow space only a few could fight at a time. So now the fighting was fiercer, for each group strove to outdo the others in valor, and to win more honor if it should kill or capture a Spaniard. It seemed to them, indeed, that all their suffering and shame would be erased by the death or capture of a single one.

Their invitations to eat, as well as their attacks, were also noteworthy, for every day up to this point, and ordinarily every two weeks or so, all during the time the Spaniards were there, they brought them bread, turkeys, and cherries. This they did, not so much for the purpose of feeding the Spaniards, but to discover what harm they had suffered, what was the spirit of our men, and whether they were afraid. And they [the bearers] said that the Tlaxcalans, to whom they belonged, were not the ones who were doing the fighting, but only certain rascally Otomí who were wandering about the country in disorderly bands, recognizing no superior, belonging as they did to several rebellious groups in the mountains, to which the bearers pointed.

48. Cortés Strikes Off the Hands of Fifty Spies

THE NEXT DAY, which was the sixth of September, after sending gifts fit for gods, some fifty respectable Tlaxcalans came to our camp, gazing about as was their habit, and gave Cortés a great deal of bread, cherries, and turkeys, their ordinary fare. They asked him how the Spaniards were doing, what their plans were, and whether they were in need of anything. Then they wandered about our camp, observing the attire and weapons of Castile, the horses and guns, and acting like wonder-struck fools. Indeed, they were astonished, but their real purpose was to spy. Teuch, a Cempoalan, expert and reared on war since childhood, then approached Cortés and told him he did not like the look of those Tlaxcalans who were so closely examining the entrances and exits of our camp, and its weak and strong points, and that Cortés should learn whether or not they were spies.

Cortés thanked him for the timely warning and wondered why neither he nor any other Spaniard had guessed the truth during all the days the Indians had been coming and going with provisions, while the Cempoalan had divined their purpose; not that the Indian was wiser or sharper than the Spaniards, but because he had seen and heard the Tlaxcalans as they mixed with those of Ixtacamaxtitlán and sounded them out.

Thus it was that Cortés came to recognize that the Tlaxcalans were not there to help him, but to spy, so he at once ordered one of them to be seized and separated from his companions. He then interrogated him through Marina and Aguilar, and within an hour the Indian confessed that he was a spy and had come to see and note the places from which they could most easily attack, destroy, and burn our huts. He also said that, since they had tried their luck at every hour of the day without accomplishing anything to further their purpose or add to their ancient renown and glory as warriors, they had decided to attack by night, when perhaps they would have better success; and also, in the night and darkness their men would not be so afraid of the horses, swords, and guns; and that Xicoténcatl, their captain-general, had for this purpose already placed many thousands of troops in a valley behind the hills, opposite and near our position.

When Cortés saw the spy's confession, he had four or five others brought to him separately, and they also confessed that they were all spies, repeating what the first had said, almost in the same words. So, acting on their statements, Cortés had all fifty seized and their hands cut off, and sent them back to their army, threatening to do the same with all the spies he should take, and telling them to inform whoever had sent them that, by day or by night, whenever they should come, they would see who the Spaniards were.

The Tlaxcalan [bearers] were exceedingly frightened when they saw the spies with their hands cut off (a novel thing for them), and they thought our men must have some familiar spirit who revealed what was in their minds. So they all left in haste, lest their own hands be cut off also, bearing the provisions they had brought, to keep their enemies from having the use of them.

49. Moctezuma's Embassy

No sooner had the spies left than a very large party was seen approaching over a hill. These were the men of Xicoténcatl. As it was still daylight, Cortés decided to intercept them, to prevent their firing our huts at their first charge as they had planned, for, if they should succeed, it might be that not a Spaniard would escape burning, or capture by the enemy. He also thought that wounds would be more fearful seen than only felt. So he immediately formed almost all his troops, ordered bells put on the horses, and his men to advance upon the enemy. But the Indians, having seen their men with their hands cut off, and hearing now the strange clamor of the bells, did not dare to wait for them. Our men pursued the Indians through the maize fields for two hours that night, and returned victorious to their quarters.

While this was going on, six Mexican lords, very noble in appearance, arrived at our camp with some two hundred servants, bringing Cortés a present of a thousand cotton garments, several pieces of featherwork, and gold to the value of a thousand castellanos, and with it a message from Moctezuma, saying that he wished to be a friend of the Emperor and Cortés and the Spaniards, and that Cortés should ascertain what tribute the Emperor would like to receive yearly, in gold, silver, pearls, precious stones, slaves, and garments and such other things as his kingdom produced, and that he would pay it punctually without fail, provided that Cortés' men stayed out of Mexico. All this, he said, was not so much for the purpose of excluding them, but because the intervening country was sterile and rugged, and Moctezuma would regret to see such valiant and honorable men suffer hardship in his domain without his being able to prevent it.

Cortés thanked them for their visit and the presents they had brought for the Emperor and King of Castile, and begged them not to depart until the end of the current war, so they might convey tidings of his victory to Mexico, and of the slaughter that he and his companions were about to inflict upon those mortal enemies of their lord Moctezuma.

At this time Cortés was laid low with a fever, because of which he was unable to ravage and burn the fields, and do other damage to the enemy. The only thing he could do was to see that the camp was protected from the hordes of Indians who came to yell and skirmish, which they did every time they brought provisions. The Tlaxcalans always excused themselves by saying it was not they who were annoying the Spaniards, but the scoundrelly Otomí, acting without their permission. Neither the skirmishing, however, nor the fury of the Indians was as bad as it had been at the beginning. Cortés took a quantity of pills he had brought from Cuba, to purge himself; these he divided into five portions, taking one every hour (they are usually taken at night). But it happened that the next day, before the medicine had acted, three very large companies attacked the camp, which they did either because they knew he was ill, or thinking he was afraid to come out. When Cortés was told of this, he, not heeding the fact that he had taken a purgative, mounted and sallied forth with his men to meet them, and fought the enemy all that day until nightfall, forcing them to retreat a great distance, after which he returned to camp; and the next day the purgative took effect, as if only then he had taken it.

I do not relate this as a miracle, but only to tell what happened, and to show how enduring Cortés was in hardship and sickness, being always the first in encounters with the enemy. He was not only a good man with his hands (which is rare enough), but he used great judgment in what he did. Having been purged and rested, he stood night watch when his turn came, like any soldier, as was his habit always. And he was not the worse for it, nor was he the less loved by his companions.

50. Cortés Takes Tzompantzinco

ONE NIGHT Cortés mounted to the top of his tower and, looking about in all directions, espied, some four leagues away, among some mountains in a forest, a large number of smoke columns, which made him think that many people must be dwelling there. He did not mention it to anyone, but ordered two hundred Spaniards and a few Indian friends to follow him, and the rest to guard the camp. He set out three or four hours after nightfall, feeling his way, for it was very dark; but he had not marched a league when the horses were attacked by a kind of cramp and fell to the ground, unable to move.

When the first one fell and Cortés was informed of it, he said: "Well, have its master take it back to camp." Then another fell, and he said the same. But when three or four more fell, his companions began to hesitate, and warned him it was a bad sign; that it would be better to turn back, or wait till daylight to see where or through what they were going. Cortés told them to pay no attention to signs, and that God, whose cause they were supporting, was superior to nature. He said, moreover, that he would not abandon an expedition which, he thought, would bring them great profit that night, and that it was the devil who was putting obstacles in their way to frustrate it. But, while he was talking, his own horse fell, whereupon they halted and considered what was best to do. They decided to send the fallen horses back to camp, lead the rest, and continue on their way. The horses soon recovered, and it was never learned what had happened to them.

Our men marched until they lost sight of the mountains, and got into some rocky ground and ravines, from which they had difficulty in extricating themselves. Finally, after a very bad struggle, the horses bristling with fear, they saw a faint light, toward which they felt their way. The light was issuing from a house where they found two women who, with two men they soon met, guided them to the peaks where they had seen the smoke, and before dawn they came to several small villages. They killed a number of men, but did not burn the houses, so as not to betray themselves by the fire, and also to avoid delay, for they had been told there were two large towns near by. They soon entered Tzompantzinco, a town of twenty thousand houses, as Cortés learned later in an inspection he made. Since the inhabitants were not expecting anything, it was taken by assault before they had got out of bed, and they ran out into the streets naked to see what the lamentations were about. Many of them died at the beginning, but, since they did not resist, Cortés ordered his men to spare them and not to touch the women and clothing. The inhabitants were so frightened that they ran away as fast as they could, fathers abandoning their children, and husbands their wives, houses, and goods. The Spaniards made them signs of peace, motioned to them not to run, and told them to fear nothing, and so the trouble ended.

The town now being pacified, Cortés climbed a hill at sunrise to survey the country, and saw a very large town, which he was told was Tlaxcala and its villages. Thereupon he assembled his men and said: "Look, what good would it do us to kill these people, when so many enemies are at hand?" Doing no further damage to the town, they then went to a very handsome fountain, to which the nobles and governors of the place also repaired, and more than four thousand others, unarmed, who brought a large quantity of provisions. They begged Cortés to do them no further hurt and thanked him for hurting them so little; they said they wished to serve and obey him, and be his friends, and that from then on they would not only cherish his friendship, but would urge the lords of Tlaxcala to do the same.

Cortés replied that it was true they had frequently fought him, although they had brought him food; but that he pardoned them and received them into his friendship and the service of the Emperor. At this he left them and returned to his quarters, joyful at his success after the bad beginning with the horses, and said: "Call not a day evil until it has passed." Then he received the pledge of the people of Tzompantzinco, to the effect that they would urge the Tlaxcalans to lay down their arms and become his friends. So Cortés ordered that in the future no one should vex or harm any Indian [of Tzompantzinco] whatever, and he even told his men he believed that, with the help of God, they had that day ended their war with the province.

51. Certain Spaniards Wish to Abandon the War

WHEN CORTÉS, very joyful, as I have said, reached his quarters, he found some of his companions frightened by the condition of the horses he had sent back, and wondering whether he had not met with some disaster; but when they saw him in good health and victorious, they could not contain their pleasure. At the same time it is true that many of his company were there against their will, discontented, and desirous of returning to the coast, as they had begged him many times to do. Their greatest desire, however, was to leave the country, frightened at its great size and multitudes of people, all armed and determined not to allow them to enter, while they saw themselves few in number and far from the sea, without hope of relief—things certainly bad enough to frighten anyone—which is why some of the men were talking among themselves of the need to speak to Cortés, and even to demand that he proceed no farther but return to Vera Cruz, where little by little they would reach an understanding with the Indians and do whatever circumstances made necessary; meanwhile, to get more men and horses, because without these war was impossible.

Cortés gave little weight to this talk, although he had been informed of it secretly so that he might take measures. Then, one night as he was leaving his quarters to inspect the guard, he heard loud talking in one of the huts, and stopped to listen to what his companions were saying: "If our captain wants to make a fool of himself and get himself killed, let him do it alone; we shall not follow him." Then Cortés called two of his friends as witnesses and told them to listen, for those who dared so to speak would dare to act. He also overheard others talking in the corrals and in groups, and saying that this adventure would be another affair like that of Pedro Carbonerote,* who merely for the sake of attacking the Moors in their own country, had led his men to their death; that they should refuse to follow Cortés, but turn back while there was yet time. Cortés was deeply hurt by this talk, and would have liked to reprimand or punish its authors, but, seeing that the time was not propitious, he elected to overlook the matter and address them.

52. Cortés Addresses His Men

"GENTLEMEN AND FRIENDS: I chose you as my companions and you chose me as your captain, for the service of God and the increase of His Holy Faith, and also for the service of our King and even for our own profit. I, as you have observed, have not failed or offended you; nor, indeed, have you done so to me up to this point. Now, however, I sense a weakening among some of you, and little taste to finish the war we have on our hands, a war which, with the help of God, we have now concluded, or, at least, we now know how little harm it can do us. We have partly seen the good we shall gain from it, although what you shall see henceforth and gain will be greater beyond comparison, so much so that it passes my thought and words. Fear not, my companions, to come with me, for never yet have Spaniards been afraid in these new lands which by their courage, strength, and cunning they have conquered and discovered; nor do I

---

* Pedro Carbonero was a more or less legendary hero of the wars against Granada in the fifteenth century. His romantic exploit, in which he was said to have faced an army of Moors with twelve knights and defended his honor to the death, was celebrated in popular ballads and was made the theme of a play by Lope de Vega, *El Cordobés valeroso Pedro Carbonero*, ed. José F. Montesinos (Madrid, 1929).

entertain such a concept of you. God forbid that I should think, or that anyone should believe, that my Spaniards would be afraid, or disobedient to their captain! One must never turn one's back upon the enemy, lest it appear to be a retreat. There is no retreat, or, to put it more mildly, retirement, which does not bring an infinity of woes to those who make it, to wit: shame, hunger, loss of friends, goods and arms, and death, which is the worst of them, but not the last, for infamy endures forever.

"If we abandon this country, this war, this adventure that we have undertaken, and turn back, as some of you desire, are we perhaps going to be left to disport ourselves in idleness and sloth? Certainly not, you will say, for it is foreign to our Spanish nation to do so when we engaged in war and our honor is at stake, for *Where goes the ox that he will not draw the plow?* Did you think, perhaps, that in some other place you would find fewer enemies, worse armed, and closer to the sea? I warrant you that *You are seeking a cat with five feet,* and that *Wherever we go we shall find three leagues of bad road,* as the saying has it, much worse than the one we are now on. Never since we came to this land, thank God, have we lacked for food and friends, money and honor. You can see how these people hold you to be more than men, immortal, almost gods, if I may say so, for, even though they are so many that they cannot count their own numbers, and are so well armed, as you say, still they have not succeeded in slaying a single one of you. And as for arms, what better luck could there be for us than that they do not poison their arrows, like the Indians of Veragua, Cartagena, the Caribs, and others, which have caused so many Spaniards to die in agony?

"Well, for this one consideration alone you should not seek out others to make war upon. The sea is distant, I admit, and no Spaniard before us has departed so far from it; but at the same time no one has done so much or deserved so much as you. From here to Mexico, where Moctezuma resides, of whose great riches and possessions you have heard tell, it is no more than twenty leagues, and most of our journey thither is behind us, as you know. If we arrive there, as I trust in Our Lord God we shall, not only shall we win for our Emperor and King a country naturally rich, but a vast domain and infinite vassals, and for ourselves great wealth in gold, silver, precious stones, pearls, and other goods. All that aside, we shall win the greatest honor and glory that were ever won up to this time, not only by our own nation, but by any other. The greater the king we seek, the wider the land, and the more numerous the enemy, so much the greater will be our glory, for have you not heard it said, *The more Moors, the greater the spoils?* Besides, we are obligated to exalt and increase our Holy Catholic Faith, which we undertook to do like good Christians, uprooting idolatry, that great blasphemy to our God, abolishing sacrifices and the eating of human flesh, which is so contrary to nature and so common here, and suppressing other abominations which I pass over because of their filthiness.

"So, then, have no fear, and do not doubt our victory, for most of the way is behind us. You vanquished the men of Tabasco and, just the other day, some 150,000 Tlaxcalans, who are reputed to be fire-eaters. With the help of God and your own strength, you will also vanquish the remaining Tlaxcalans, who cannot be many, as well as the Culhúans, who are no better than they, if you will be strong and follow me."

All were pleased with this speech of Cortés. Those who had weakened regained their strength; the courageous redoubled their courage; and those who had wished him ill now began to honor him. In a word, from that moment onward he was the most beloved Spaniard in all the company. His long speech was necessary in the circumstances, for otherwise, so great was the desire of some to retreat that they would have mutinied and forced him to return to the sea, and that would have meant the end of all they had thus far accomplished.

53. Xicoténcatl, Ambassador of Tlaxcala

HARDLY HAD THEY FINISHED discussing this speech, when Xicoténcatl, captain-general of the war, entered our camp, accompanied by fifty noble and honorable men. He approached Cortés, and each saluted the other after the fashion of his own country. After Xicoténcatl had been seated, he said that he represented himself and Maxixca, the other most noble lord of the province, as well as many

whom he named—in short, he was there on behalf of the whole republic of Tlaxcala, to beg Cortés to accept them as friends, to offer
themselves as vassals to the King, and to ask his pardon for having
taken up arms against him and his companions, for they had not
known who the Spaniards were or what they were seeking, and that
if they had resisted him, it was as if they were resisting strangers and
men of a different race, so different, indeed, that they had never before seen their like. The Tlaxcalans had feared that the Spaniards
were in league with Moctezuma, their ancient and perpetual enemy,
for Moctezuma's servants were with Cortés. Or they had feared that
the Spaniards intended to molest them and take away their liberty,
which since time immemorial they had cherished and guarded. In
their struggle to remain free, as all their ancestors had done, they
had spilled a great deal of blood, lost many men and quantities of
goods, and had suffered many evils and misfortunes, especially
nakedness, for their country was too cold to produce cotton. Thus it
was that they had to go about naked as they were born, or to wear
leaves of the agave. Also, they had no salt, without which food is
tasteless, because they did not produce it either. And they had to do
without these two necessities of life because Moctezuma and other
enemies, by whom they were surrounded, had interdicted them.
Moreover, having no gold or precious stones or other valuables to
exchange for salt and cotton, they frequently had to sell themselves
into slavery in order to obtain them. They would not have had to
suffer these wants if they had consented to be subjects and vassals
of Moctezuma, but they would all prefer to die rather than descend
to such an evil and dishonorable act; they were, indeed, as good at
defending themselves from him as their fathers and grandfathers
had been at defending themselves from Moctezuma's father and
grandfather, who were as great lords as he, and who had subjected
and tyrannized the whole country. Also, they said, they would have
defended themselves equally well against the Spaniards, only they
found they could not, although they had employed all their strength
and all their men, by night and by day, and had always found them
strong and invincible, and had no luck against them.

Therefore, they concluded, since their fate was such, they chose
to be subjected to them rather than to any others, because, as the
Cempoalans had informed them, the Spaniards were strong and

good, and had not come to do evil; and, as they themselves had experienced, in war and battle the Spaniards were most courageous and successful. For these two reasons they trusted that the Spaniards would respect their liberty and treat their persons and their women with consideration, and not destroy their houses and fields, and that, if they were attacked, the Spaniards would defend them. At the end of his speech, Xicoténcatl, with tears in his eyes, begged Cortés to remember that Tlaxcala had never acknowledged a king; nor had it had a lord; nor had any man born ever entered it as conqueror, except only those whom they had invited or begged to come.

The delight of Cortés with the ambassador and his embassy passes description, because, apart from the honor of having such a great captain come to his tent and humble himself, it was an exceedingly big step forward in his desire to make that city and province his subject and friend, and because he had ended the war to the great contentment of his men and made a great name and reputation for himself among the Indians. So it was that he gave Xicoténcatl a happy and gracious answer, blaming him at the same time for the harm his country had suffered, for Xicoténcatl had refused to listen to overtures of peace, as Cortés had begged and admonished him to do when he sent the messengers from Zautla. But Cortés forgave him the killing of the two horses, the attacks the Tlaxcalans had made upon him, and the lies they had told when they put the blame on others, as he forgave them for having summoned him to their town in order to kill him from ambush on the way, even though they had given him a safe-conduct and had failed to send him a challenge beforehand, as valiant men would have done. Cortés accepted Xicoténcatl's offer of service and vassalage to the Emperor, and then dismissed him, saying they would soon see each other in Tlaxcala, but that he could not go at once, out of regard for the servants of Moctezuma.

54. Our Men Are Received at Tlaxcala

THE MEXICAN AMBASSADORS were greatly vexed by the presence of Xicoténcatl in the Spanish camp, and by his offer to submit the persons, city, and estates of Tlaxcala to the King. They warned Cortés to believe none of it and not to put trust in promises, for it was all lies, pretense, and treachery, in order to get him safely locked up in their city. Cortés answered that, even if what they said was true, his mind was made up to go to Tlaxcala, because he feared the Tlaxcalans less in town than in the open. At this, the ambassadors begged permission to send one of their number to Mexico to inform Moctezuma of what had occurred and bring Cortés the answer to his principal request, which he would receive within six days without fail. Meanwhile, they would not leave the camp. Cortés granted their petition and waited to see what new offer the messenger would bring, because in truth he did not trust the Tlaxcalans without further guarantees.

Meanwhile, there was much going and coming in the camp, many Tlaxcalans bringing turkeys, others bread; some bringing chili, others cherries; and all gave what they brought freely and with joyful countenances, while they invited the Spaniards to their houses. On the sixth day, as had been promised, the Mexican returned, bringing Cortés a dozen gold jewels very well wrought, and fifteen hundred cotton garments beautifully made, and much better than the first thousand. He begged Cortés most earnestly on behalf of Moctezuma not to expose himself to the danger of trusting the Tlaxcalans, who were poor and who would rob him of the presents Moctezuma had sent, and who would kill him for the single reason that he was in communication with Moctezuma.

At the same time all the chiefs and lords of Tlaxcala came to beg Cortés to afford them the pleasure of going with them to their city, where he would be served, fed, and lodged, because it was a shameful thing for them that such persons should be housed in such miserable huts. And, they added, if he did not trust them, he should indicate what other security and hostages he required, and they would supply them. They promised him on oath that he would be secure in their city, because they did not break their word, nor would they prove false to their loyalty to their republic, or to the promises of so many lords and captains, for anything in the world.

When Cortés saw the good will of these gentlemen and new friends, and saw that the Cempoalans, whom he trusted, were urging and importuning him to go, he had the baggage loaded on the *tamemes* and the guns dispatched, and he left for Tlaxcala, six leagues distant, with as much order and precaution as if for a battle. Meanwhile, he erected crosses and stone markers at the tower and encampment, and on the site of his victory.

So many people came out to meet him on the road and in the streets that they were unable to move. Cortés entered Tlaxcala on the eighteenth of September [1519], and took lodgings in the main temple, which had many and good apartments to accommodate all the Spaniards, and in another he lodged his Indian friends. He also set limits beyond which his men were forbidden to go, on heavy penalties, and he commanded that they were to take nothing but what was given them. They were so obedient that they even asked his permission to go to a creek which was within a stone's throw of the temple. The lords of Tlaxcala performed a thousand kindnesses for the Spaniards and showed Cortés every courtesy. They provided them with everything for their meals, and many offered their daughters as a token of true friendship, so they might bear children by such valorous men and bring into the world a new warrior caste; or perhaps they gave their daughters because it was the custom, or merely to please the Spaniards.

Our men liked the city and the company of these people, and rested there twenty days, during which they studied the peculiarities of the republic and the secrets of the country. They also gathered the best intelligence available about the actions of Moctezuma.

55. Tlaxcala

TLAXCALA means "baked bread," because more maize is harvested there than in the surrounding country. The province is named after the city, or vice versa. Some say it was first called Texcallan, meaning "house in a ravine." It is a very large town, situated on the banks of a river [the Atoyac] which has its source in Atlanátepec. It drains a great part of the province and flows into the South Sea at Zacatula. The province is divided into four districts, named respectively, Tepetícpac, Ocotelulco, Tizatlán, and Quiahuixtlán. The first is situated on a high hill half a league from the river, because of which it is called Tepetícpac, that is, "Top of the Mountain." It was the first town to be built there, and was placed on a hilltop because of wars. The second is on the slope of the same hill among the pines, because of which it was named Ocotelulco, which is to say, "Pine Wood." It was the best and most thickly populated part of the city [province], and in it was the principal square, where the market (called a *tianguis*) was held. There also Maxixca resided. Up the river on a plain was another district, called Tizatlán ["White Land"] because of the quantity of gypsum found there. Xicoténcatl, captain-general of the republic, made his residence there. The fourth district is also on the plain, and because it is marshy is called Quiahuixtlán ["Land of Water"]. It has been almost entirely rebuilt since the Spaniards occupied it; it has better streets and stone houses on the flat near the river.

Tlaxcala, like Venice, is a republic governed by nobles and rich men, and not by one man, which they would regard as tyranny. In time of war, as I have said, there are four captains or colonels, one for each district, and one of them is chosen as general. During battle their standard is carried in the rear, but when the battle is over it is placed where everyone may see it. Those who do not rally to the standard are punished. Two arrows, relics of the first founders, are borne into battle by two brave and noble captains and are used to foretell victory or defeat. One of the arrows is shot at the enemy at the first encounter; if it kills or wounds, it is a sign of victory; otherwise, of defeat. So they say, at least, and they never fail to retrieve the arrow.

The province has 28 villages and 150,000 citizens [heads of families], who are fine-appearing men and warlike beyond all others. They are poor, for they have no wealth or crop other than maize, which is their bread, but they trade enough of it to obtain clothing, tributes, and other necessities. They hold many markets, but the largest, which is held several times a week, is in the square of Ocotelulco, attended by 30,000 or more in a single day, who come to buy and sell, or rather to barter, for they have no knowledge of coined money of any kind of metal. In their markets, as in Spain, they buy what they need for clothing, footgear, food, drink, and crafts. The markets are excellently organized, having silversmiths, feather workers, barbers, and baths; they also have potters, who fashion very good vessels of earthenware, the clay being as good as ours.

The soil is rich for grain, fruit, and pasture, and among the pines there is such a quantity of good grass that our people graze their cattle and sheep together on it, a thing which cannot be done here. Two leagues from the city is a round mountain, to reach the top of which requires a further two hours' climb. It is fifteen leagues in circumference, and snow ordinarily freezes on it. Today it is called San Bartolomé, but formerly Matlalcueye, after the goddess of water [the Aztec Chalchicuitlicue]. They also had a god of wine called Ometochtli, who presided over their drunken orgies. But their greatest idol and principal god was Camaxtli, otherwise known as Mixcoatl, whose temple was in the district of Ocotelulco, where they sacrificed to him in some years as many as eight hundred men or more. In Tlaxcala three languages are spoken: Nahuatl, the language of the court, which is the most widely used in all the lands of Mexico; Otomí, spoken more frequently without than within the city; and in one district, Pinome, a very rude tongue.

Tlaxcala had a public jail, where evildoers were kept in fetters. Sin, or what was considered as such, was punished. It happened that a citizen robbed a Spaniard of a bit of gold. Cortés informed Maxixca of it, and he made an investigation and search, and did so with such diligence that the thief was tracked as far as Cholula (which is a city five leagues distant) and was brought back a prisoner and delivered to Cortés, together with the gold, so that Cortés might punish him according to Spanish custom. This he refused to do, although he thanked them for their diligence, so they paraded the thief through the streets accompanied by the town crier announcing his crime, after which the thief was displayed in the market place, in a kind of theater, and then had his head smashed with a club, at which the Spaniards were no little astonished.

56. The Tlaxcalans Defend Their Idols

CORTÉS, seeing the Tlaxcalans' respect for justice and their piety (although they worshiped devils), preached them a sermon through his interpreters at every opportunity, begging them to abandon their idols and the cruel vanity of killing and eating the victims of their sacrifices, for none of them, he said, would wish to be so killed and eaten, however religious and holy he might be. He told them to accept and believe in the true God of the Christians, worshiped by the Spaniards, the Creator of heaven and earth, who made the rain to fall and all the products of the soil to grow, for the sole use and profit of mankind. Some replied that they would gladly do so, if only to please him, but they feared that the people would stone them. Others said that it would be a terrible thing to reject what they and their ancestors had believed for so many centuries, and that it would ruin them all, and their ancestors as well. Still others said that in the course of time they would do so, after observing the religion of the Spaniards, studying their arguments, and becoming more thoroughly acquainted with the Spaniards' way of life, their laws, customs, and conditions, because in war they had already discovered that the Spaniards were invincible and that their God supported them well.

Cortés answered them, promising that he would send them someone to teach and indoctrinate them, when they would see the improvement and the very great profit and pleasure they would have by following his friendly advice; but that at the moment he could not do so because of his haste to get to Mexico. He did request them, however, to allow him to convert the temple where he was lodged into a church where he and his men might pray and celebrate their services and sacrifices, which the Tlaxcalans themselves might attend. The permission was granted, and many even attended the Mass that was said every day he was there, and came to see the crosses and other images he placed in that temple, as well as in other temples and towers. Some also came to live with the Spaniards, and all the Tlaxcalans were friendly to them; but the one who most truly showed himself their friend was Maxixca, who would not leave Cortés' side, nor could he see or hear enough of the Spaniards.

57. Hatred Between Mexicans and Tlaxcalans

SEEING NOW how willingly the Tlaxcalans talked and associated with them, the Spaniards inquired about Moctezuma and his wealth and grandeur. The Tlaxcalans praised him highly, as men who had tested him. They said they had been at war with him and his father Axayacatl, with various of his uncles and his grandfather, for 90 or 100 years. They all agreed that the gold and silver and other riches and treasures of Moctezuma were beyond description. His domain included all the land they knew. His people were innumerable, and he could muster for battle two or three hundred thousand men, or twice as many if he so desired. Of this the Tlaxcalans were good witnesses, for they had fought him many times. They, and especially Maxixca, had so exalted an opinion of the attributes of Moctezuma that they wanted the Spaniards to avoid the risk of meeting the Culhúans, who were numberless and whom many Spaniards feared.

Cortés answered that, notwithstanding what they had told him, he was determined to go to Mexico and see Moctezuma; that, therefore, they should give thought to what they would like to have him negotiate there for them, because he was in their debt, and because he was convinced that Moctezuma would do what he asked. They begged him to get permission to bring out cotton and salt, which during all these years they had not properly tasted, save only that a few had acquired it secretly at its weight in gold from friendly neighbors, for Moctezuma put to death those who shipped it out of his kingdom to sell to them.

Cortés then inquired about the cause of the wars and churlish behavior of Moctezuma toward them, and they said it was because of an ancient feud, their love of liberty, and their unwillingness to pay tribute. According to the Mexican ambassadors, on the contrary, and according to what Moctezuma and many others said in Mexico later, that was not the way of it at all, but that it had other and very different motives (and it may be that each party was pleading its own cause and justifying its own action), which were to give the Mexican youths exercise in war near at hand, without their having to be sent off to Pánuco and Tehuantepec, which were on distant frontiers. So it was that they sent an army to Tlaxcala to take as many prisoners as were needed for that year to celebrate their festivals and sacrifices, for it was plain that, if Moctezuma had ever wished to do so, he could have killed them all in one day, in a real war. But, since he only wanted to capture men for his gods and for eating, he sent few against the Tlaxcalans, who on that account were victorious.

Cortés was elated to hear of the discords, wars, and hatred between his new friends and Moctezuma, which suited his purpose, for he thought he would be able for that reason to subjugate them all the more easily; so he secretly treated with both sides in order to get the affair well started. Many of the men of Huejotzingo who had fought against us were present at these conversations. They traveled back and forth between their city (which is also a republic) and Tlaxcala, with which they were so friendly and so closely tied that they stood together against Moctezuma, who had oppressed them also and used them in his butcheries in the temple of Mexico. So they offered themselves to Cortés for the service and vassalage of the Emperor.

58. Cholula Receives the Spaniards

MOCTEZUMA'S AMBASSADORS told Cortés that, since he was determined to go to Mexico, he should go by way of Cholula, five leagues from Tlaxcala, for the Cholulans were their friends, and it would be better to wait in Cholula for the decision of their lord, that is, whether or not Cortés might come to Mexico. This they said in order to get him out of Tlaxcala, for it most truly vexed Moctezuma to see peace and amity between Tlaxcalans and Spaniards, from which he feared painful consequences for himself. The ambassadors, to persuade Cortés to leave Tlaxcala and entice him to go more quickly to Cholula, plied him with gifts. The Tlaxcalans were beside themselves when they saw his determination to go to Cholula, and they told him that Moctezuma was a false and treacherous tyrant, that Cholula was a friend of Moctezuma, although a disloyal one, and it might happen that the Cholulans would attack Cortés when they had him in their city. They warned him, therefore, to be on his guard, and they offered him an escort of fifty thousand men in case he should decide to go.

Now, it happened that the women who had been given to the Spaniards upon their entrance into Tlaxcala heard of a plot to kill them in Cholula, with the connivance of one of the four [Tlaxcalan] captains; but his sister, who was in the service of Pedro de Alvarado, divulged it to her master. Cortés at once spoke to the captain and persuaded him to leave his house, whereupon he had him silently strangled, without any disturbance or commotion at all, and so the plot was frustrated. It was wonderful that the Tlaxcalans did not rebel at the death of one of the noblest gentlemen of the republic. The affair was investigated later, and it was learned that Moctezuma had sent to Cholula for the purpose more than thirty thousand men, who were encamped two leagues away, and that they had blocked the streets, piled up many stones on the housetops, closed the main road, and opened another, in which they had dug pits with sharp stakes planted in them to cripple the horses, and then had covered the pits with sand to prevent their detection.

Cortés believed this the more readily because the Cholulans had not come to visit him and had not sent ambassadors, as Huejotzingo and neighboring towns had done. Following the advice of the Tlaxcalans, he sent several messengers to Cholula to invite its lords and captains to come and see him; but they did not appear, sending three or four men to excuse them because of illness. The Tlaxcalans informed him that these men [the messengers] were of no consequence (as, in fact, seemed to be the case), and told him he should not depart before the captains' arrival. So Cortés sent the same messengers back with a written order, to the effect that if the captains did not appear within three days, he would consider them as rebels and enemies, and as such would punish them severely. The next day many lords and captains of Cholula came to present their excuses, saying that the Tlaxcalans were their enemies and that they would not be safe among them; also, they knew how much evil the Tlaxcalans had told him of them, which he should not believe, for the Tlaxcalans were treacherous and cruel; and that if he would accompany them to their town he would see for himself what lies the Tlaxcalans had told him, and how good and loyal the Cholulans were.

After all this, they offered to serve and pay tribute to him as subjects, an offer which Cortés had witnessed by notaries and interpreters.

Cortés took leave of the Tlaxcalans, and Maxixca wept to see him go. He was escorted by one hundred thousand warriors, and many merchants went with him to purchase salt and blankets. Cortés ordered the hundred thousand always to march apart from his men. He did not reach Cholula that day, but encamped on a creek, where many people from the city [of Cholula] came to beg him earnestly not to allow the Tlaxcalans to harm their lands or persons. For this reason Cortés sent all the Tlaxcalans home, save only some five or six thousand. They went unwillingly, warning him to be on his guard with those wicked people, who were not warriors, but merchants and two-faced men. They also told him, now that they had offered him their friendship, that they did not want him to expose himself to danger.

Our men arrived at Cholula the next morning, when more than 10,000 came out to meet him, in groups, many of them bearing bread, fowl, and roses. Each group, as soon as it had welcomed Cortés, withdrew to make way for the next. When he entered the city, all the Spaniards marching in single file, the rest of the people came out to greet them and gape at the men and horses. Next came all the monks, priests, and ministers of their idols, who were many and strange, dressed in what looked like white surplices, some of which were trimmed with spun cotton and fastened in such wise that the arms were left free. Some had trumpets, others bone flutes, still others drums. Some carried lighted braziers, others, covered idols, and all were chanting in their fashion. As they approached Cortés and the other Spaniards, they cast resin and copal on the coals (copal smells like our incense), and perfumed them. After all this pomp and solemnity, which was certainly impressive, they led the Spaniards into the city and lodged them in a house where there was plenty of room for all, and that night gave each of our men a turkey for his dinner. They also lodged and fed the men of Tlaxcala, Cempoala, and Ixtacamaxtitlán.

CORTÉS was very much on his guard that night, because on his way there and in the city he had seen evidence supporting what the Tlaxcalans had told him. Moreover, although on that first night the Cholulans had given them each a turkey, on the three days following they gave them nothing to eat, and the three captains rarely came to see the Spaniards, all of which filled Cortés with misgivings. During this time the Mexican ambassadors urged him, I know not how often, not to go to Mexico, alleging at times that their great lord would die of fear at his sight; at others, that the road was impassable; at still others, that Cortés would find no provisions on the way. Seeing, however, that Cortés answered them only with fair words and arguments, they enlisted the help of the people of the town, who told him that Moctezuma's house was filled with alligators, tigers, lions, and other very fierce animals which, if their master turned them loose, would suffice to tear the Spaniards to pieces and eat them, the Spaniards being so few in number.

All this being of no avail, they plotted with the captains and nobles to kill the Christians, inducing them to do so by promises of great rewards from Moctezuma; they gave the head captain a gold drum and offered him the use of the thirty thousand men who were encamped two leagues away. The Cholulans intended to tie and deliver the Spaniards, but they refused to allow the Mexican troops to enter their town, in the fear that with this pretext the troops would seize it, a common Mexican trick. It was said they wanted to kill two birds with one stone, thinking to catch the Spaniards asleep and keep their town at the same time. They thought that if they should be unable to bind the Spaniards in the city, they could lead them out by a road, not to Mexico, but by one to the left, in which there were many bad spots where ravines twenty, thirty or more fathoms deep cut the road. There they would cut them off and bring them bound to Moctezuma. Now that their plot was well worked out, they began to pack up their belongings and remove their children and wives to the mountains.

Our men by this time were ready to leave the place, not liking the miserable treatment and the black looks they were getting, when it happened that a nobleman's wife who, either moved by pity, or because she liked the looks of the bearded men, told Marina to stay with her, for she would be much afflicted if Marina should be killed along with her masters. Marina dissembled her feelings at this bad news, and got out of her who the plotters were and what they aimed to do. Then she ran to find Jerónimo de Aguilar, and the two of them informed Cortés of the matter. He did not sleep, but had a couple of citizens seized at once and examined, and they confessed that all the lady had said was true. So Cortés put off his departure for two days, to let the matter cool and to dissuade the Cholulans from executing their wicked plot, or to punish them. He called in the governors and told them that he was dissatisfied with their conduct. He begged them not to lie or attempt any tricks with him, and told them he was sorrier about the affair than if they had challenged him in battle, for it became men better to fight than to lie.

They answered that they were his friends and servants, and would always be, and that they had never lied to him and never would; but that he should tell them when he intended to leave, and they would supply him with servants and an armed escort. He said he was leaving the next day and wanted only a few slaves to carry his baggage, because his *tamemes* were tired, and also that he would like some provisions. At this last request they smiled and said to themselves: "Why do these men want to eat, when they themselves will soon be eaten, served up with chili? Indeed, if Moctezuma, who wants them for his own table, would not have been angry with us, we should have eaten them ourselves by this time!"

60. The Cholulans Are Punished

So IT WAS that on the following morning, the Cholulans, very joyful, believing they had their play well staged, brought many men to carry the baggage of the Spaniards, with hammocks for their persons, as if in litters, thinking to seize them thus. For this latter purpose a number of their bravest men stood by to kill any man who resisted, and the priests sacrificed ten three-year-old children to their god Quetzalcoatl, five of them girls, a custom they observe at the beginning of a war. The captains, with a number of armed men, quietly took positions at the four entrances to the courtyard where the Spaniards were quartered.

Very early that same morning, Cortés secretly sent word to the Tlaxcalans, Cempoalans, and other friends, of what was going on. He ordered his horsemen to mount, and the rest of the Spaniards to strike when they heard a shot, for their lives depended on it. When he saw that the men of the town continued to assemble, he had the captains and lords brought to his quarters, on the pretext that he wished to take leave of them. Many came, but he allowed only thirty, whom he judged to be the most important, to come in. He said to them that he had always told them the truth, but that they, on the contrary, had told him lies when they invited and urged him [to come to Cholula], and that when they had begged him, although with evil intent, not to allow the Tlaxcalans to enter their town, he had willingly acquiesced and had even ordered his men to do no harm whatever; that, although they had not supplied him with provisions, as was their obligation, he had not allowed his men to take from them even a chicken; that, to repay him for his good works, they had plotted to kill him and all his men, which, if they could not accomplish it indoors, with the help of the thirty thousand men of Moctezuma's garrison, who were encamped two leagues away, they would do in the bad spots on the road to which they would lead him. For this piece of wickedness they would all die, and as a reminder of their treachery the city would be destroyed and no trace of it would remain. Finally, he said, since they knew this to be the truth, there was no point in their denying it.

The Cholulans were terror-stricken. They stared at one another very red in the face and said: "This man is like one of our gods, for he knows everything; it is useless to deny it." So they at once confessed it was all true—this in the presence of the Mexican ambassadors. Cortés took four or five of them to one side, to keep the Mexicans from hearing them, and they told him the whole story of the plot from beginning to end. He then told the Mexicans how the Cholulans, at the Mexicans' behest and on behalf of Moctezuma, had plotted to kill him, but that he had not believed it, for Moctezuma was his friend and a great lord, and great lords are not in the habit of lying or plotting treachery, and that he intended to punish these vile traitors; but that they, however, had nothing to fear, because they were public officers sent by their king, whom he wished to serve and not to vex, for their king was so good and great that he could not have ordered such a base and infamous thing. All this he said to avoid a break with Moctezuma before he should get to Mexico.

Cortés had several of the captains put to death and the rest bound. He then fired the signal gun, at which all the Spaniards and their friends attacked the Cholulans with great violence and ferocity. They did their best in such close quarters, and within two hours had killed some six thousand or more. Cortés ordered them to spare the women and children. The battle lasted five hours, for the townspeople were armed and the streets blocked, so that they were able to defend themselves. The Spaniards burned all the houses and towers where they met resistance and drove out the inhabitants. They were dripping with blood and walked over nothing but dead bodies. Some twenty gentlemen had climbed to the top of the main temple, the one with the 120 steps, and in company with its many priests did us a good deal of damage with stones and arrows. They were urged to surrender but refused, and so they were burned along with the temple, while they complained to their gods how badly the gods had treated them in failing to come to their aid and the defense of their city and sanctuary.

The city was put to the sack. Our men took the gold, silver, and featherwork, and the Indian friends a quantity of clothing and salt, which is what they most desired, and then destroyed everything they could, until Cortés ordered them to stop.

The captains who had been taken prisoner, seeing the destruction of their city and the slaughter, begged Cortés with tears in their eyes to loose some of them to see what the gods had done with the common people, and to spare those who were still alive and let them return to their houses, for they were less to blame for the damage than Moctezuma, who had corrupted them. Cortés freed two, and the next day the city semed to be as populous as before. Then, at the request of the Tlaxcalans, whom the Cholulans used as their intercessors, Cortés pardoned them all and set the prisoners free; but he told them he would visit a like punishment upon them if they should even again show him ill will, or lie to him and plot treachery. This filled them with no little dread. He persuaded the Cholulans and Tlaxcalans to be friends again, as they had been in the past, before Moctezuma and his ancestors, with promises and gifts, and even by threats, had made them enemies. And the Cholulans, now that their lord was dead, elected another, with the permission of Cortés.

61. Cholula, Holy City of the Indians

CHOLULA, like Tlaxcala, is a republic, and its captain-general, or governor, is elected. It has twenty thousand houses within its walls and as many more in the outskirts. Viewed from without, it is one of the most beautiful cities imaginable, many-towered, with its temples which, it is said, are as many as there are days in the year, each of which has its tower, some of them several, so all told there are some four hundred of these. The men and women are elegant in appearance, handsome in features, and very clever. The women are fine silversmiths, woodcarvers, and the like; the men, very bold and warlike, and also fine workmen in everything they do. They were better dressed than any Indians our men had thus far seen; they wear over their other garments cloaks like those of the Moors, but with armholes. Within the boundaries of the city the land is rich and covered with farms, which are irrigated, and it is so thickly populated that not a palm's breadth is unoccupied, for which reason there were beggars at the doors—something that had not been observed up to this point.

Cholula is the most devout town in all those parts, the holy city of the Indians, where all come on pilgrimages to perform acts of piety, which is why there are so many temples. The principal one is the best and tallest of all New Spain, access to which is by a staircase of one hundred and twenty steps. The most important of their idols is called Quetzalcoatl, god of air and founder of the city, a virgin, they say, of the utmost austerity, who established fasting and the letting of blood from the tongue and ears, and to whom they sacrifice only partridges, doves, and game. He is never dressed otherwise than in a white cotton robe, narrow and long, over it a cloak strewn with red crosses. They keep certain green stones of his as if they were relics. One is in the form of a monkey's head, carved to the life.

This is all that could be learned about Cholula during the scant twenty days that our men were there. So many came to trade and barter that it was a cause of astonishment. One of the most note-worthy things in their market was the pottery, of a thousand different designs and colors.

62. The Mountain Called Popocatépetl

EIGHT LEAGUES from Cholula is a mountain called Popocatépetl, which is to say, "Smoking Mountain," because it often belches forth smoke and flames. Cortés sent ten men to explore it, with many citizens to guide them and carry their provisions. The ascent was rough and difficult. They reached a point from which they could hear the noise, but did not dare go on to the summit, because the earth was quaking and thick ashes blocked the way. Some wanted to turn back, but others, who must have been more courageous or curious, determined to see the mysterious place from which that fearful and wonderful fire issued, and also because they wanted to justify themselves with those who had sent them, lest they be thought timid and poor-spirited. And so, although most members of the party were unwilling and the guides frightened them by saying that no human feet had trod, or human eyes seen, it, they climbed up through the ashes and finally reached the summit in a cloud of heavy smoke. They stayed there a short time looking about, and it seemed to them that the mouth was half a league in circumference. The noise reverberated in it, making the earth tremble, but it was quite shallow and looked very much like a glass oven when it is boiling its hardest. The heat and smoke were so bad that they soon returned, retracing their own footsteps so as not to lose their way.

They had hardly begun the descent when it began to rain ashes and flames, then hot cinders, and finally very large pieces of burning stone, and if they had not found shelter under a rock they would have been burned to death. But, since they brought back good evidence [that they had climbed to the top], and returned alive and well, many Indians came up to kiss their garments and stare at them, as if they were miraculous beings, or gods, and gave them little presents, such was their astonishment at the feat, for those simple people believe it is the mouth of hell, where bad governors and tyrants are sent when they die, to purge their sins before they may rest.

This mountain, which is called Vulcan because of its resemblance to that of Sicily, is tall and round, and is always snow-capped. At night, seen from a distance, it seems to be on fire. Near it are many cities, the closest of which is Huejotzingo. For ten years or more it was quiet, but in 1540 it became as active as before. Upon its eruption it made such a roar that it terrified the people for four leagues roundabout. The smoke was so thick and dense that its like was not remembered, and it vomited up such a fierce fire that the ashes fell as far off as Huejotzingo, Quetlaxcoapan, Tepeaca, Huaquechula, and Tlaxcala, this last being ten leagues distant. It is said that the ashes fell as far as fifteen leagues away; they covered the land, burned crops and trees, and even clothing.

63. Moctezuma Holds a Council

CORTÉS did not wish to quarrel with Moctezuma before entering Mexico; neither did he wish to listen to all the palaver, excuses, and childish nonsense that [the ambassadors] told him. He complained sharply to them that such a great prince, who had sent him assurances of friendship by the hands of so many and such eminent gentlemen, should seek ways to kill him and his men, or have them attacked by others (this only to give him an excuse in case of failure), and that, since Moctezuma did not always keep his word or tell him the truth, Cortés, who had heretofore wished to go to Mexico as a friend and in peace, was now determined to go as an enemy and in war, come what might. The ambassadors made their excuses and begged him to put aside his anger and vexation, and give them leave to send one of their number to Mexico and bring him a prompt answer, for the journey was short. And Cortés sent him on his way and wished him good luck.

The ambassador returned after six days, bringing with him a companion who had gone to Mexico a short while before. They brought Cortés ten gold plates, fifteen hundred pieces of cotton cloth, a large number of turkeys, a quantity of bread and cacao, and a kind of wine they make of cacao and maize. They denied that they had had any part in the conspiracy of Cholula, or that they had ordered or advised it. On the contrary, the local garrison was from Acatzingo and Azacán, two neighboring towns of the province of Cholula, with which it had an alliance and agreement, and they, persuaded by those scoundrels of Cholula, must have plotted this wickedness. The ambassadors said that Moctezuma would continue to be his friend, as Cortés would see, and that Cortés should come to Mexico, where he was expected—a message that greatly pleased Cortés.

Moctezuma was frightened when he heard of the slaughter at Cholula, and said: "These are the men who our god told me would come to take this country." So he went to the temples and shut himself up in one of them, where he prayed and fasted for a week, and sacrificed many men to appease his gods, who must have been angry. There the devil spoke to him and told him to have no fear of the Spaniards, who were few and who, when they arrived, could be dealt with as Moctezuma pleased; that he should not cease his sacrifices, lest some disaster overtake him; that he should keep Huitzilopochtli and Texcatlipoca friendly for his protection, because Quetzalcoatl, the god of Cholula, was angry with the Cholulans for having sacrificed too little and badly, for which reason he had not come to their aid against the Spaniards.

By the time Cortés reached Cholula he was great and powerful, and there he became still more so, because his new reputation had been noised about the whole land and domain of King Moctezuma, so that those who had merely wondered at him up to this point now began to fear him, and more from fear than from love they opened their doors to him wherever he went. In the beginning Moctezuma had tried to induce Cortés not to go to Mexico, thinking to frighten him with tales of the perils of the journey, the strength of Mexico, the multitude of its people, and his own authority, which was the worst obstacle of all, for the lords of the land feared and obeyed him. With this purpose in mind, Moctezuma had a great deal of correspondence with Cortés, but, seeing that it did not avail him, he tried to win Cortés over with gifts, for Cortés demanded and accepted gold. Since Cortés, notwithstanding, continued to insist upon seeing Moctezuma and coming to Mexico, Moctezuma consulted with his captains and priests, and then asked the devil what he should do about it, for it seemed unfitting and dishonorable for him to make war upon Cortés and fight a mere handful of strangers who said they were ambassadors. Another reason was that he did not wish to stir up trouble for himself (and this was the truest reason), for it was clear that he would immediately have to face an uprising among the Otomí, the Tlaxcalans, and many others, who would be all for destroying the Mexicans. So he decided to let Cortés enter Mexico without opposition, thinking to do as he pleased with those scanty forces afterward, and even have them served up for breakfast if they should annoy him.

64. Cholula to Mexico

WHEN CORTÉS received the welcome note brought by the Mexican ambassadors, he gave permission to his Indian friends to go home, and left Cholula with a few of its citizens who wanted to follow him. He did not take the road that Moctezuma's men indicated, because it was bad and dangerous, as the Spaniards who had gone to the volcano had observed, and also because, according to the Cholulans, the Mexicans were planning to attack him upon it, so he chose a different one, smoother and shorter. He scolded the Mexicans, but they answered that they had chosen it, even though it was bad, to avoid passing through the enemy territory of Huejotzingo.

He marched only four leagues that day, so as to spend the night at Huejotzingo, where he was well received and provided for. They even gave him some slaves, clothing, and gold, although not much of this last, for they were poor and had little; besides, Moctezuma had cut off their trade for being friends of Tlaxcala. The next day, after eating, Cortés started up over a pass between two snow-covered mountains, a climb of two leagues. If the thirty thousand soldiers who had come to take the Spaniards at Cholula had waited for them at this pass, they could have taken them with their bare hands, such was the cold and snow that the Spaniards encountered.

From the pass they could see the land of Mexico, the lake, and the towns along its shores, the finest spectacle in the world. But, however great was Cortés' pleasure at seeing it, so much the greater was the fear of certain of his companions, some of whom even doubted they would arrive, and there was some indication of mutiny. Cortés, however, with prudence, dissimulation, and cheerful words, quieted them; and when they saw that he was the first to accept hardships and dangers, their uneasiness diminished. He descended to the plain and came upon a pleasure house in the country, very large and handsome, so large indeed that it easily accommodated all the Spaniards and the six thousand Indians they had brought along from Cempoala, Tlaxcala, Huejotzingo, and Cholula; and Moctezuma's men even put up straw huts for the *tamemes*. They built great fires and provided an abundant supper for everyone, and even women for them.

Many noble lords came from Mexico to talk with Cortés, among them a kinsman of Moctezuma. They brought him gold to the value of three thousand pesos and begged him to turn back because of the poverty of the country and the hunger he would suffer on the miserable road, which he would have to negotiate with boats, so that, in addition to the danger of drowning, he would have nothing to eat, but [if he would turn back] Moctezuma would give him a great deal for himself, besides whatever tributes he might demand for the Emperor who had sent him, delivered yearly to the coast or wherever Cortés should indicate. Cortés received them courteously and gave them presents of Spanish trinkets, especially the kinsman of the great lord. He told them he would gladly serve such a powerful prince, if he could do so without offense to his own King; that nothing but good and honor would result from his visit, since he would only speak to Moctezuma and depart; that what they had brought for themselves would suffice to feed all his men; and that the lake was nothing compared with the two thousand leagues of ocean he had already crossed for the sake of seeing Moctezuma and taking up with him certain matters of great importance.

If the Mexicans had found Cortés off his guard during these conversations they would have attacked him, for they had brought many men along for the purpose, as some say. But Cortés gave the captains and ambassadors to understand that the Spaniards did not sleep at night, or remove their clothing and armor, and that if anyone should be seen standing or moving among them they would kill him instantly, and he would not be able to defend himself; that, therefore, they should tell this to their men for their own good, because Cortés would regret it if any of them should die. On this note he retired for the night.

Cortés was on the road by dawn and marched two leagues to Amecameca, in the province of Chalco, a town which, with its villages, has a population of twenty thousand [householders]. Its lord gave him forty slave girls, three thousand pesos in gold, and abundant food for two days, and secretly complained of Moctezuma. From Amecameca Cortés marched four leagues the next day to a small village, which was half in the water and half on land, at the foot of a rough and stony mountain. A large number of Moctezuma's men went with him and supplied him with provisions. These, together with the men of the village, thinking to attack him, sent spies to learn what the Spaniards did during the night; but Cortés' own spies killed some twenty of them, with which the matter ended, as did the plot to kill the Spaniards. It was a laughable thing to see how at every step they had the notion of killing our men, but were not up to it.

Early in the morning, as the army was setting out, twelve Mexican lords arrived, the most important of whom was Cacama, nephew of Moctezuma and lord of Texcoco, a youth of twenty-five, much respected by everyone. He was carried in a litter borne on men's shoulders, and when he alighted from it, the stones he trod on were cleaned and the ground swept free of straws. They were coming to escort Cortés, and apologized for Moctezuma, saying he was ill and unable to welcome him in person. They insisted again that the Spaniards turn back and not proceed to Mexico, giving them to understand that they would be resisted and the way blocked, which could very easily have been done; but the Mexicans were either blind [to their opportunity] or dared not cut the causeway.

Cortés answered them with due respect and even presented them with certain articles of merchandise. He left the village in a large company of important people and was followed by an infinite number of others, so many that there was not room for them on the road. Many came also to gape at the strange men, now so famous, and at their attire, arms, and horses, and they said: "These men are gods!" Cortés warned them repeatedly not to mingle with the Spaniards and horses unless they wished to die. He did this for two reasons: one, to keep them from getting insolent, and, two, to clear the road for marching, because the Spaniards were surrounded.

Thence he went to a town of two thousand houses, all built over the water, which he approached by a fine causeway more than twenty feet wide. The town had excellent houses and many towers. Its lord received the Spaniards very well and provided for them honestly, and begged them to stay the night. He too complained to Cortés of the many indignities and unjust tributes that Moctezuma had inflicted upon him. He assured Cortés that there was a road, and a very good one, from there to Mexico, over a causeway like the one by which he had come. Cortés halted there, thinking to stop and build boats or brigantines. At the same time he feared they would cut the causeway, and for that reason was very much on his guard. Cacama and the other lords importuned him not to tarry, but to go on to Ixtapalapa, two leagues farther, which belonged to another nephew of the great lord. Cortés was obliged to accede, and besides, it was only two leagues [from Ixtapalapa] to Mexico, which would give him plenty of time and leisure to enter the city. So he spent the night at Ixtapalapa. Messengers from Moctezuma kept coming and going every two hours. Cuitlahuac, lord of Ixtapalapa, and his kinsman, the lord of Culhuacán, came out to meet him. They also gave him slave girls, clothing, featherwork, and even gold to the value of a thousand pesos.

Cuitlahuac lodged the Spaniards in his house, or rather in several very large palaces, all of stone and woodwork, very well carved, with rooms on two floors and excellent service. The rooms were hung with many cotton drapes, rich after their fashion. The palaces were in the midst of cool gardens of flowers and fragrant trees, many paths lined with canes and covered with roses and herbs, and many ponds of sweet water. There was also a beautiful grove of fruit trees and greenery, in it a large shelter built of stone and mortar, measuring some 400 paces to the side and 1,600 roundabout, with a number of staircases leading down to the water and even to the land. The ponds were filled with all kinds of fishes, and many herons, ducks, gulls, and other birds swarmed there, at times covering the surface. Ixtapalapa is a town of ten thousand houses situated on the shore of the salt lake, half over the water, half on land.

65. Moctezuma Receives Cortés

IXTAPALAPA IS CONNECTED with Mexico by two leagues of a very wide causeway, wide enough to accommodate eight horses abreast, and as straight as if drawn with a ruler. The gates of Mexico could be discerned by one with good eyesight. Along its length are Mexicalcingo, of about 4,000 houses, all built over the water; Coyoacán, of 6,000; and Churubusco, of 5,000. These cities are adorned with many temples, each with its tower. They have a rich trade in salt, which they make and sell there, or ship out to fairs and markets. They draw the salt water from the lake through ditches and collect it in pits, in which the salt crystallizes, and with it they make balls or loaves. They also distill it, which is a better method, but more laborious. Moctezuma derived a large income from it. At intervals along the causeway are drawbridges over the channels through which the water flows from one lake to the other.

Cortés, with his 400 companions and 6,000 Indian friends from the pacified towns, advanced along this causeway, marching with great difficulty because of the pressure of the crowds that came out to see them. As he drew near to the city he came to the junction of another causeway which was protected by a large stone bastion [Xoloc], two fathoms high, with towers at the two ends, between them a crenelated gallery and two gates, very strong. Here some 4,000 gentlemen of the court were waiting to receive him, richly dressed after their fashion, all in the same style. Upon his approach each of them touched the earth with his right hand, kissed it, bowed, and passed on in the same order in which he had come. This took an hour and was something to see. The causeway continued beyond the battlement. Before it reached the street it was interrupted by a wooden drawbridge ten paces across, under which the water flowed from one lake to the other.

Moctezuma came as far as this bridge to greet Cortés. He walked under a pallium of gold and green feathers, strung about with silver hangings, and carried by four gentlemen. He was supported on the arms of his nephews, the great princes Cuitlahuac and Cacama. All three were dressed alike, save that Moctezuma wore golden shoes set with precious stones, which were really only sandals held on by straps like those of the ancients. Servants walked ahead of them two by two, laying down and removing mantles, lest Moctezuma should tread on the ground. Two hundred lords came next, as if in a procession, all barefoot, but wearing a richer livery than the 3,000 of the first escort. Moctezuma kept to the middle of the street and the rest followed him, hugging the walls, their eyes downcast, for it would have been an act of great irreverence to gaze upon his face.

Cortés dismounted and approached Moctezuma to embrace him in the Spanish fashion, but was prevented by those who were supporting him, for it was a sin to touch him. Even so, the two men saluted each other, and Cortés threw about Moctezuma's neck a necklace of pearls, diamonds, and other gems made of glass. Moctezuma stepped forward with one of the nephews, and ordered the other to lead Cortés by the hand behind him. As they set off, the men in livery came up one by one to speak to Cortés and felicitate him upon his arrival; and then, touching the earth with their hands, they passed on and took their places as before. If all the citizens had saluted him as they wished, it would have taken the whole day; but, since the king had gone on ahead, they all turned their faces to the wall and did not dare approach Cortés.

Moctezuma was pleased with his glass necklace and, being a great prince and unwilling to accept a present without giving a better one in exchange, he at once commanded two necklaces to be brought. From each of them hung eight gold shrimps (which they greatly esteem) as large as snails and an inch long, of perfect workmanship, and he cast it about Cortés neck with his own hands, which the astonished Mexicans considered a mark of great favor.

By this time they were approaching the end of the street, which is a third of a league long, wide, straight, and very beautiful, lined with houses on both sides; and so many people were crowded at the doors and windows and on the roofs that I know not who was the more amazed, our men at seeing such a multitude of men and women in the city, or they, at the guns, horses, beards, and dress of our men, such as they had never before seen.

The Spaniards then came to a large courtyard in what had been the house of Axayacatl, where idols were kept. At the door Moctezuma took Cortés by the hand and led him to a large room, saying: "You are now in your own house. Eat, rest, and enjoy yourself, and I shall return later."

Such, just as you have heard it, was the reception given Hernán Cortés by Moctezuma, a most powerful king, in his great city of Mexico, on the eighth day of November of the year of Our Lord 1519.

66. Moctezuma Addresses the Spaniards

THIS HOUSE in which the Spaniards were lodged was very large and handsome, having several rather long halls and many small rooms, accommodating them and almost all their Indian friends who had served and escorted them, armed. It was all very clean and shining, covered with mats and hung with cotton and feather drapes. Wherever one looked there was something worth seeing. As soon as Moctezuma left, Cortés assigned quarters to his men and posted guns at the doors, after which they sat down to a good dinner, worthy of such a great king and worthy of being offered to such a great captain.

When Moctezuma had eaten, and learned that the Spaniards had eaten and rested, he came to Cortés, greeted him, and sat down next to him on another bench. He brought many different jewels of gold, silver, and featherwork, and six thousand cotton garments, richly worked and woven with marvelous colors—a gift that proved his greatness and confirmed everything that the Spaniards had imagined of him, judging by his previous gifts. He did all this with the utmost gravity, and with the same gravity, speaking through Marina and Aguilar, said:

"My lord and gentlemen: I am greatly pleased to entertain you in my house and kingdom, and do you the good and pay you the courtesy worthy of you and my estate. If I begged you heretofore not to come here, it was because my people were afraid of you, for you frightened them with your wild beards, and brought animals that swallow men, and because, since you came from heaven, you could call down the lightning and thunder, making the earth to tremble, striking down him who displeased you, or whomever you pleased. But now that I know you to be mortal men and honorable, and do no harm whatever, and now that I have seen your horses, which are like our deer, and your cannon, which are like our blowguns, I know that what I have been told about you is jests and lies, and hold you to be my kinsmen, because, as my father told me, and his father told him, our ancestors and kings, from whom I am descended, were not natives of this country, but newcomers, led by a great lord who, a little while later, returned to his own land. And after many years he came to get them, but they refused to go, because they had settled here and had wives and children and a great ascendancy in the land. So he departed in great annoyance, telling them that he would send his sons to govern them and keep them in peace and justice, and within the ancient laws and religion of their fathers.

"For this reason we have always expected and believed that some day men would come from those parts to subject and rule us, and I think you are the ones, for, judging by the direction you came from, and what you tell of the great King and Emperor who sent you, you knew of us. And so, my lord captain, you may be sure that we shall obey you, if you are not deceiving or tricking us, and that we shall share what we have with you. And even if what I am saying were not true, such are your valor, fame, and knightly deeds that I would willing do so [in any case], for I know well what you did in Tabasco, Teocacingo, Cholula, and elsewhere, vanquishing so many with so few. And if you come believing that I am a god, and that the walls and roof of my house, as well as my service, are all of fine gold, as I understand you were told by those of Cempoala, Tlaxcala, Huejotzingo, and other places, I wish to disabuse you, even though I do not think you are the kind of men who would believe such nonsense. You know that with your advent there have been rebellions against me, and that some of my vassals have become my mortal enemies. But I shall clip their wings! Touch my body, then, which is of flesh and bone. I am a man like any other, and not a god, no, although as king I hold myself high in order to maintain my dignity and position. The houses that you see are of sticks and mud, or at most of stone. Do you not see how you have been lied to? For the rest, it is true that in the treasure of my father and grandfather I have silver, gold, featherwork, arms, jewels, and riches, guarded for long years, as is the custom of kings. All of it you and your companions shall have whenever you like. Meanwhile, take your rest, for you are tired."

Cortés made him a low bow, and with a cheerful countenance (the other had tears in his eyes) answered him to this effect: It was his trust in the goodness and benevolence of Moctezuma that had induced him to insist upon seeing and speaking with him. He knew that what Moctezuma's enemies had told him was all lies and wickedness, just as Moctezuma had discovered for himself what rubbish and old wives' tales had been told him about the Spaniards. Nevertheless, Moctezuma should most truly believe that the Emperor and King of Spain was that natural lord whom he was expecting, ruler of the world and heir to the titles and lands of his ancestors. Finally, with regard to the treasure, Cortés would accept it as a precious gift.

Moctezuma then asked Cortés if the bearded men were all his vassals or slaves, so that each might be treated according to his station. Cortés answered that they were his brothers, friends, and companions, save only some few who were servants. At this, Moctezuma went to his palace of Tecpan and inquired through his interpreters who were gentlemen and who were not, and accordingly sent to each his gift: to the hidalgo and good soldier, a good present by the hand of a majordomo; to others and to sailors, lesser gifts by the hand of a lackey.

67. Moctezuma

MOCTEZUMA was a man of middling size, thin, and, like all Indians, of a very dark complexion. He wore his hair long and had no more than six bristles on his chin, black and about an inch long. He was of an amiable though severe disposition, affable, well-spoken, and gracious, which made him respected and feared. Moctezuma means a furious and solemn man. The Mexicans add the suffix *tzin* to the given names of kings, lords, and women as a mark of courtesy or dignity, as we do with *don,* the Turks with *sultan,* and the Moors with *mulei;* so they call Moctezuma *Moctezumatzin.* His people endowed him with such majesty that they would not sit in his presence, or wear shoes, or look him in the face, with the exception of only a few great lords. But he would not permit the Spaniards to remain standing, either because he enjoyed their society, or because of his high regard for them. When he took a notion to dress in the Spanish fashion, he would exchange garments with them. He changed his own four times a day and never wore the same garment twice. His used garments were saved and given as rewards and presents to servants and messengers, or, as a token of favor and privilege, to soldiers who had fought and captured an enemy. The many and beautiful mantles that he sent to Cortés were of such.

Moctezuma was naturally clean and neat; he bathed twice a day. He seldom left his chambers except to eat, and always ate alone, but gravely and abundantly. His table was a cushion or a couple of dyed skins; his chair a bench of four legs, made from one piece, the seat hollowed out, very well carved and painted. His dishes were brought in by four hundred pages, gentlemen's sons, who served them all at once in his dining hall. Moctezuma would enter and look them over, pointing to those he liked, whereupon they would be set on braziers of live coals, to keep them warm and preserve their flavor. He would seldom touch other dishes, unless it was a well-prepared one recommended by his majordomo.

Before he sat down to eat, as many as twenty of his wives would enter, the most beautiful or shapely, or those serving their weekly turn, who very humbly brought him his food, after which he sat down. Then the steward would enter and draw a wooden screen to keep the people from crowding in, and only the steward could serve him, for the pages were not permitted to approach the table or utter a word; nor could any of those present speak while their master was eating, save only his jester, or someone who had a question to ask; and all waited on him barefoot. His drinking was not done with such pomp and ceremony.

Some six old men, with whom Moctezuma would share portions of the dishes he liked, were always at the king's side, although somewhat withdrawn. They accepted the food reverently and ate it even more respectfully, not looking him in the face—which was the greatest mark of humility they could show him. During his meals he would listen to the music of pipes, flutes, conches, bone fifes, drums, and other instruments of the kind, for they have no better ones; nor can they sing, I say, because they do not know how, and their voices are bad besides.

Always present at his meals were dwarfs, hunchbacks, cripples, and so on, all for his entertainment and amusement, and these, along with the jesters and mountebanks, were given the leavings to eat at one end of the hall. Whatever else was left over was eaten by the three thousand men of the regular guard, who stayed in the courtyards and square—which is why it is said that three thousand dishes were always served, and three thousand pitchers of the beverage they drink, and that the cellar and pantry were never closed. It was a wonderful thing to see what they contained. Everything obtainable in the market was cooked and served daily without fail. There was, as we shall relate elsewhere, an infinite variety, in addition to what was brought in by hunters, tenants, and tributaries.

The plates, bowls, cups, pitchers, and the rest of the service were of very good pottery, as good as that of Spain, and were never used for more than one of the king's meals. He also had a large number of gold and silver vessels, which he seldom used, because to use them more than once would seem a low thing to do. Some have said that Moctezuma cooked and ate babies, but the only human flesh he ate was that of sacrificed men, and this not commonly. When the table linen was removed, the men and women, who were still standing, would approach to offer him water for his hands, which they did with equal respect, and then retired to their own chambers to eat with the others, as they all did, save only the gentlemen and pages who were on duty.

68. The Foot-Jugglers

WHILE MOCTEZUMA was still seated and the table had been taken away and the people departed, the merchants entered, barefoot, for all removed their shoes upon entering the palace, save only great lords such as those of Texcoco and Tacuba, and a few of his kinsmen and friends. All came very poorly dressed: if they were lords or great men, and it was cold, they wore old blankets, coarse and tattered, over their fine new mantles. They bowed three times, but did not look him in the face, and spoke humbly, always facing him. He answered them with great dignity, in a low voice and few words. He did not always speak or answer them, whereupon they would leave, walking backward.

Then Moctezuma would amuse himself by listening to music and ballads, or to his jesters, as he was very fond of doing, or by watching certain jugglers who use their feet as ours do their hands. They hold between their feet a log as big as a girder, round, even, and smooth, which they toss into the air and catch, spinning it a couple of thousand times, so cleverly and quickly that the eye can hardly follow it. Besides this, they perform other tricks and comical acts with astonishing skill and art. (Cortés brought several of these foot-jugglers to Spain and showed them at court.) They also perform grotesque dances, in which three men mount one above the other, resting upon the shoulders of the bottom man, while the top man does extraordinary things.

Sometimes Moctezuma would watch the game of *patolli,* which closely resembles our game of *tabas.* It is played with broad or split beans, used like dice, which they shake between their hands and cast upon a mat, or upon the ground, where a grid has been traced. They put pebbles down to mark the place where the dice come to rest, removing and adding them [according to the cast]. Gamblers will wager all their goods in this game, and at times will even put up their bodies to be sold into slavery.

69. The Ball Game

AT OTHER TIMES Moctezuma went to the *tlachtli,* or ball court. The ball itself is called *ullamalixtli,* which is made of the gum of the *ulli* [*hule*], a tree of the hot country. This tree, when slashed, oozes thick white drops that soon harden, and are gathered, mixed, and treated. The gum turns as black as pitch, but does not stain. It is rolled into balls which, although heavy and hard to the hand, bounce and jump very well, better than our inflated ones. The game is not played for points, but only for the final victory, which goes to the side that knocks the ball against the opponents' wall, or over it. The players may hit the ball with any part of the body they please, although certain strokes [e.g., with the hands] are penalized by loss of the ball. Hitting it with the hips or thighs is the most approved play, for which reason they protect those parts with leather shields. The game lasts as long as the ball is kept bouncing, and it bounces for a long time. They play for stakes, wagering, say, a load of cotton mantles, more or less, according to the means of the players. They also wager articles of gold and featherwork, and at times even put up their own bodies, as in the game of *patolli*.

The ball court is a low enclosure, long and narrow, higher at the sides than at the ends, built so purposely for the game. It is kept always whitewashed and smooth. Stones resembling millstones are set into the side walls, with holes cut through them, hardly big enough to allow passage for the ball. The player who shoots the ball through them (which rarely happens, because it would be a difficult thing to do even if one threw the ball by hand) wins the game and, by ancient law and custom of the players, also wins the capes of all the spectators. He is then, however, obliged to sacrifice to the gods of the game and the stone. The spectators say that this fellow must be an adulterer or a thief, and will soon die.

Each ball court is also a temple, and images of the god of the game are set upon the two lower walls. This is done at midnight on a day of favorable omen, with certain ceremonies and magic rites, while the same rites are celebrated in the middle of the court, and ballads are sung to commemorate the occasion. Then a priest from the main temple, accompanied by other religious, comes to bless it. After speaking a few words, he throws the ball four times around the court, which is thus consecrated and can be used for playing, but by no means before. Even the owner of the court, who is always a lord, cannot play without first performing I know not what rites and making offerings to the idol, so superstitious are they. Moctezuma took the Spaniards to see this game and showed the greatest pleasure at its performance, as he also showed at the Spaniards' games of cards and dice.

ANOTHER PASTIME of Moctezuma's much enjoyed by the court and even by the whole city (because it was very good, long drawn out, and open to the public), was a dance performed after he had dined, either at his command or [voluntarily] by the townspeople for his service and pleasure. It was called *netotelixtli*, a dance of rejoicing and merriment, and was performed in the following manner: Long before it began, a large mat was spread in the courtyard and upon it two drums were placed, a large one called a *teponaxtli*, made of a single piece of wood, very well carved, hollow, but without a skin or parchment head, although it is played with drumsticks like our own. The other is very large, tall, round, and thick, like our drums, hollow, carved, and painted. Over one end a tanned deerskin is very tightly stretched: the more tightly, the higher the tone; the more loosely, the lower. It is played with the hands, without sticks, and has a deep bass tone. These two drums, accompanied by voices (although these are not very good), are loud and not at all ill-sounding. The songs are joyful and merry, or they are ballads in praise of past kings, reciting their wars, victories, deeds, and the like. It is all done in rhyme and has a very pleasing effect.

When the time comes to start, eight or more men whistle very loudly and beat the drums softly. Then the dancers come on, dressed in rich mantles woven of many colors, white, red, green, and yellow; in their hands, bunches of roses or plumes, or fans of feathers and gold. Many carry wreaths of flowers, very fragrant; others wear feather caps or masks made to represent the heads of eagles, tigers, alligators, and other wild beasts.

At times there are as many as a thousand dancers, or at least four hundred, all of them noble and important persons, and even lords; the greater and higher they are, the more closely do they gather around the drums. They dance in rings, their hands joined, one ring within the other. They are led by two agile and skillful dancers, and all obey these two leaders: if the leaders sing, the whole chorus responds, sometimes more, sometimes less, just as is done here and elsewhere. Everyone follows the time set by the leaders, save only the outer ranks, which, because they are so far away and so many, must dance twice as fast as the others and work twice as hard. Nevertheless, all of them raise and lower their arms, their bodies, or their heads alone, at the same moment. It is done with no little grace, and with such a feeling for unity that no one gets out of step. So wildly do they dance, indeed, that it is quite amazing. At the beginning the dancers sing ballads and move slowly, playing, singing, and dancing quietly and with much gravity; but as they get warmer they sing popular ditties and gay songs; the dance is livelier, and they move quickly and vigorously. Since the dance lasts a long while, [they get thirsty] and drink from mugs and pitchers served them by cup-bearers. At times also the buffoons come out, mimicking other peoples in dress and speech, playing the drunk, the fool, or the old woman, to the vast entertainment of the spectators.

Everyone who has seen this dance says it is a fine thing to watch, better than the *zambra* of the Moors, which is the best dance we know here. It is much better when performed by women than by men, but in Mexico women do not dance it in public.

71. Moctezuma's Women

MOCTEZUMA had many houses in and out of Mexico, some for display and recreation, some for dwellings. I shall not describe them all, for it would take too long. The one where he had his permanent residence was called Tecpan, that is to say, palace. It had twenty doors opening on the square and public streets, and three large court-yards, in one of which was a beautiful fountain. It had many halls and a hundred rooms 25 to 30 feet square, and a hundred baths. It was constructed without nails, but very solidly. The walls were of stone, marble, jasper, porphyry, black stone shot with veins of ruby red, white stone, and a translucent stone [alabaster]; the ceilings, of wood, well finished and carved to represent cedars, palms, cypresses, pines, and other trees. The chambers were painted; the floors, covered with mats; the drapes, of cotton, rabbit fur, and feathers; the beds, poor and uncomfortable, being merely blankets laid over mats or straw, or mats alone.

Few men slept in these houses, but there were a thousand

women—some say three thousand, counting the ladies and their servants and slaves. Of the ladies and their daughters, who were very numerous, Moctezuma took for himself those whose looks he liked; the others he gave to his servants for wives, or to other gentlemen and lords. Thus it happened, they say, that he had one hundred and fifty women with child at one time, who, persuaded by the devil, took exercises and medicines to get rid of the babies; or perhaps [they did so] because their children could not inherit. These women were guarded by many old ones, who would not permit a man even to look at them, for the king would have nothing but chastity in his palace.

The coat of arms above the palace doors (where the banners of Moctezuma and his ancestors were hung) was an eagle in combat with a tiger, its claws extended as if to capture its prey. Some say it is a griffin and not an eagle, for there are griffins in the mountains of Tehuacán that depopulated the valley of Ahucatlán by consuming the people. They base their argument on the fact that these mountains are named Cuitlachtépetl, from *cuitlachtli,* which is to say, a griffin resembling a lion. I do not now believe that there are such, for no Spaniard has seen them. The Indians represent these griffins (which they call *quetzalcuitlachtli*) in their traditional form, covered with fur, not feathers. The Indians say that griffins can break the bones of men and deer with their claws and teeth. They closely resemble lions, and look somewhat like eagles; they are represented as having four feet and fur, more like wool than feathers, and beaks and claws, and wings to enable them to fly. In all these respects the Indian paintings agree with our own writings and pictures; that is to say, this animal is neither bird nor beast. Pliny considers this business of griffins to be a fable, although there are many stories about them. Other lords also put the griffin on their coats of arms, showing it flying with a deer in its talons.

72. The House of Feathers

MOCTEZUMA had another house with many fine apartments and several galleries resting upon pillars of jasper (these cut from a single piece), opening upon a spacious garden, in which there were ten or more ponds, some of salt water for sea fowl, others of sweet water for birds of the rivers and lakes. The ponds were frequently emptied and filled, to keep the feathers clean. So many birds lived there that they overflowed the place, and they were of such different plumages and kinds that the Spaniards were astonished, for most of them they had never known or seen before.

Each species of bird was fed the things it had eaten in its wild state: if herbs, it was given herbs; if grain, maize; if beans, these and other seeds; if fish, fish, of which the ordinary ration was ten arrobas a day, caught in the lakes of Mexico. They were even fed flies and other vermin, if such was their diet. Three hundred persons were assigned to take care of the birds: some cleaned the ponds; others caught fish for them; others fed them; others deloused them; others guarded the eggs; others threw out the brooders; and still others had the most important duty of plucking them. Of the feathers, rich mantles, tapestries, shields, plumes, flyflaps, and many other things were made, adorned with gold and silver, of exquisite workmanship.

73. House of the Hunting Birds

MOCTEZUMA had another house with very large rooms and apartments which was also called the bird house, not because there were more birds than in the first, but because they were larger or, perhaps, being birds of prey, they were held to be better and nobler. In the many upper rooms dwelt men, women, and children who were white in body and hair from birth, and who were considered unusual to the point of being almost miraculous, so seldom did they occur. Dwarfs, hunchbacks, cripples, and monsters were also kept there in large numbers for the king's amusement. It is said even that they were broken and made crooked in babyhood as if for the glory of the king. Each of these monsters had an apartment to himself.

In the lower rooms were many cages of stout timbers: in some, lions were kept; in others, tigers; in others, lynxes; in still others, wolves. In short, there was no kind of four-footed beast that was not represented, and all for the purpose of Moctezuma's being able to boast that, however fierce they might be, he [dared] to keep them in his house. They were fed turkeys, deer, dogs, and game. In other rooms, in great eathenware jars, pots, and vessels of the kind, filled with water or earth, reptiles were kept, such as boa constrictors (*muslos*), vipers, crocodiles (which they call *caimanes,* that is to say, water lizards), lizards of other kinds, and such-like vermin, as well as land and water snakes, fierce and poisonous, and ugly enough to frighten the beholder.

In another apartment and in the courtyard, in cages with round perches, were kept all manner of birds of prey, such as lanners, hawks, kites, vultures, goshawks, nine or ten varieties of falcons, and many kinds of eagles, among which were some fifty a great deal larger than our red-tails. At one feeding each of them would eat a turkey of the country, which is larger than our peacock. There were many birds of each kind, and each kind had its own cage. They consumed some 500 turkeys every day. They had three hundred servants to wait on them, not counting the hunters, who were numberless. Many of these birds were unknown to the Spaniards, but it was said they were all good hunting birds, as was manifest by their aspect, size, talons, and the prey they caught. The snakes and their mates were given the blood of men killed in sacrifice, to suck and lick, and some even say they were fed on the flesh, which the lizards devoured with great gusto. The Spaniards did not witness this, but they did see the ground all encrusted with blood, as in a slaughterhouse, which stank horribly and quaked if a stick was thrust into it.

An amazing number of men were in and out of this house, caring for the birds, beasts, and serpents. The diversity of the birds, the ferocity of the beasts, and the serpents swelling with poisonous fury delighted our Spaniards, who, however, did not enjoy their frightful hissing, the hideous roaring of the lions, the howling of the wolves, the screams of the tigers and lynxes, and the yelps of the other animals, owing to hunger or perhaps to the thought that they were caged and could not give vent to their fury. And truly, at night the place was a picture of hell and abode of the devil; and so it was, in fact, for in one of the rooms, 150 feet long by 50 wide, was a chapel thickly plated with gold and silver, all set with pearls and precious stones: agates, cornelians, emeralds, rubies, topazes, and the like.

Here Moctezuma often came in the night to pray, and the devil appeared and gave him advice on petitions and requests.

Moctezuma had another building, for the storage of grain and feathers and mantles brought in as rents and tributes. It was also something to see. Above its doors was the coat of arms, or device, of the rabbit. It housed the majordomos, treasurers, accountants, secretaries, and all those employed in the management of the royal estate. All these buildings without exception had their chapels and oratories of the devil, who was prayed to for the protection of their contents. For these reasons the buildings were very large and accommodated many people.

74. The Armories

MOCTEZUMA had several armories, the sign for which was a bow and two quivers above each door. The arms were of many kinds, to wit: bows, arrows, slings, lances, pikes, darts, clubs, and swords; shields and bucklers, these handsome rather than strong; helmets, greaves, and armlets, but not in such great numbers, made of wood, gilded or covered with hide. The wood of which the arms were made was very tough, hardened in the fire. The points were tipped with flints, or with the bones of the *pez libiza*,* which are poisonous, or with certain other bones which, if left in the wounds, inflame them and render them almost incurable.

The swords were of wood, with sharp flints set into them and glued. The glue is made of a certain root called *zacotl,* and *texualli,* a coarse sand like that from a vein of diamonds, which is mixed and kneaded with the blood of bats and I know not what other birds. It sticks, holds, and hardens extremely well, so much so that it cannot be broken even with heavy blows. Points are made of the same materials, [so hard that] they will cut any wood or stone, even diamonds. The swords could cut cleanly through a lance or the neck of a horse, and even penetrate or nick iron, which seems impossible. In the city no one bore arms, which were worn only for war, the hunt, or guard duty.

---

* Possibly the *liza* or skate (sting ray?), the dorsal spines of which can inflict a dangerous and painful wound.

75. Moctezuma's Gardens

BESIDES THOSE JUST MENTIONED, Moctezuma had many pleasure houses with lovely gardens, some of medicinal and aromatic herbs, others of flowers, roses, and sweet-smelling trees in infinite numbers. It was something to make one praise the Creator to see such variety, coolness, and perfume, and the skill and delicacy with which a thousand different figures had been fashioned out of leaves and flowers. Moctezuma did not permit any vegetables or fruits to be raised in these gardens, saying it was not fitting for kings to operate farms for profit in his pleasure spots, and that it was the duty of slaves or merchants to raise such fruits. Nevertheless, and despite what he said, he did own orchards, but at a distance, which he seldom visited. Outside of Mexico he also possessed great houses in the woods, surrounded by water, with springs, rivers, fishponds, rabbit warrens, breeding grounds, and crags and rocks where stags and deer, hares, foxes, wolves, and other such animals roamed free, in the hunting of which the Mexican gentlemen exercised themselves much and often. So many and so great were the houses of Moctezuma that they were equaled by those of few kings.

76. Moctezuma's Court and Bodyguard

MOCTEZUMA had daily a company of 600 gentlemen and lords to act as his bodyguard, each with three or four armed servants to wait on him, some even with as many as 20 or more, according to their rank and wealth; so altogether they numbered 3,000 (some say many more) in the palace guard. All of them were fed with the leftovers from the king's table and his rations. The servants did not retire to their quarters until he had finished eating, and then not until night. The guard was so numerous that it quite filled the courtyards, squares, and streets [of the palace]. It could be that, to impress the Spaniards, they put on this guard and show of power, and that ordinarily it was smaller. The truth is, however, that all the lords under Mexican rule, who, as has been said, numbered thirty, each with 100,000 vassals, resided a part of each year in Mexico at the court of the great lord Moctezuma, out of obligation and gratitude, and when they returned to their own lands and dominions, they did so with the permission and at the choice of the king. Even so, they had to leave behind a son or brother as insurance against their rebellion, and for this reason they all maintained houses in Mexico–Tenochtitlán. Such, then, were the estate and household of Moctezuma, and such was his generous and noble court.

77. Tributes of the King of Mexico

THERE WAS NO ONE in all his dominions that did not pay some tribute to the lord of Mexico: the lords contributing their personal service; the peasants (called *macehuales*), their persons and goods. This they did in two ways: either as renters or as owners; the owners gave a third of their yearly produce, to wit: dogs, fowl, birds of plumage, rabbits, gold, silver, precious stones, salt, wax and honey, mantles, featherwork, cotton, cacao, maize, chili, sweet potatoes, broad beans, kidney beans, and all kinds of fruits, greenstuff, and cereals, by which they live. The renters paid by the month or the year whatever they must, and because it was a great deal they were all called slaves. These, even though they had nothing to eat but eggs, yet thought the king was doing them a favor. I have heard that tributes were even assessed against their foodstuffs, and that everything else was taken from them, because of which they dressed very poorly. In fine, they possessed a single pot for cooking herbs, a stone or two for grinding maize, and a mat to sleep on. The renters and owners not only paid this tribute, but served with their persons whenever the great lord wished, although he did not call them up except for war and hunting.

Such was the ascendancy that the kings of Mexico had over them that they were silent even when their sons and daughters were taken from them for any purpose. This is why some say that, of the three children of every farmer or non-farmer, one was given for sacrifice. This is manifestly false, for in that case there would not have been a man left in the whole country, nor would it have been as populous as it was. Besides, the lords ate only the sacrificial victims, who were rarely free men, but slaves and prisoners of war. Still, they were cruel butchers, and killed during the year many men and women, and some children, not, however, as many as some have said. We shall estimate their numbers later on by days and heads.

All these tributes were brought to Mexico on the backs of men or in canoes, at least enough to maintain the household of Moctezuma. The other tributes were used to feed the soldiers, or were exchanged for gold, silver, precious stones, jewels, and other valuables, which the kings esteemed and kept in their apartments and treasuries. In Mexico, as I have said, there were storehouses and buildings in which the grain was kept, with a majordomo and assistants to receive it, distribute it in an orderly manner, and keep the records in picture books. Each town had its tribute collector, something like a constable, who carried a staff of authority and a fan. He listed the goods and numbers of people in the towns and provinces of his district, and brought the accounting to Mexico. If any collector made an error or cheated, he died for it, and even the members of his family would be penalized as kinsmen of a traitor to the king. Farmers failing to pay their tribute were arrested. If they were poor because of sickness, they were allowed to defer payment; if it was because of laziness, they were forced to pay. In short, if they did not fulfill their obligation and pay on the appointed days, they might be taken as slaves and sold for their debts and tributes, or even sacrificed.

Moctezuma had many provinces that paid him some tribute and recognized his authority in certain things of importance, although this was more for his honor than for his profit. So it was that he had enough and to spare, for the support of his household and army, and the maintenance of his great wealth and pomp, his great court and service. Moreover, of all this he spent nothing in the building of all the houses he wanted, because for many years back, the neighboring towns that paid no tribute built his houses, kept them up at their own expense, gave their labor, paid the workmen, and carried on their backs, or dragged, the stone, lime, lumber, water, and everything necessary for their construction. They also provided abundantly all the firewood that was burned in the kitchens, bedrooms, and braziers of the palace, which were many, necessitating, as some have said, 500 *tameme* loads, that is, 1,000 arrobas daily, and during many days of the winter (which is not severe), many more. For the braziers and fireplaces of the king they supplied the bark of oaks and other trees, which made a better fire, either to make it different (for they are great fawners), or to give themselves more work.

Moctezuma had a hundred large cities, with their provinces, from which he received the rents, tributes, homage, and vassalage I have spoken of. In some of them he maintained fortresses, garrisons, and treasurers to receive the services and taxes they paid him. His domain extended from the North Sea to the South, and two hundred leagues inland. It is true, to be sure, that in the midst of it were several provinces and large towns, such as Tlaxcala, Michoacán, Pánuco, and Tehuantepec, which were his enemies and paid him no tributes or services, but the trade he carried on with them when he pleased was worth a great deal to him. There were likewise many lords and kings, such as those of Texcoco and Tacuba, who owed him nothing but obedience and homage; they were of his own lineage and were the ones to whom the kings of Mexico gave their daughters in marriage.

78. Mexico-Tenochtitlán

AT THE TIME of Cortés' coming, Mexico was a city of sixty thousand houses. Those of the king and lords and courtiers were large and fine; those of the others small and miserable, without doors, without windows, but, however small they might be, seldom containing fewer than two, three, or ten inhabitants, so that the city had an infinitely large population. The main part of the city was surrounded by water. Its thoroughfares were of three kinds, all wide and splendid: one of water alone, with a great many bridges; others of earth alone; the third kind was of earth and water; I mean, they were half on land, where men could walk, and half in the water, where canoes could circulate. The waterways were naturally clean, and the streets frequently swept.

Almost all the houses had two doors, one opening on the causeway, the other on the water, where they kept their canoes for transport. The city was built upon the water, but the water was not used for drinking. Drinking water was brought in from a spring in the hill of Chapultepec, a league distant, at the foot of which were two large statues carved in the rock, of Moctezuma and (it is said) his father Axayacatl, armed with lance and shield. The water was conveyed in two pipes, each supplying an ox [a large volume] of water. When one of the pipes became foul, they used the other until it too got foul. The city was served by this spring, which also supplied water for the ponds and fountains of many houses. The water was also sold from canoes, for which certain taxes were levied.

The city was divided into two districts: one called Tlatelolco, which means island; the other, Mexico, where Moctezuma resided, which means source. It was the nobler district, for it was larger and the residence of the king. The city was known by this name, although its proper and ancient one is Tenochtitlán, which means stony fruit, composed of *tetl* (stone) and *nochtli* (the fruit known in Cuba and Haiti as *tuna*). The tree (cactus, rather) that bears this fruit is called *nopal* among the Mexicans of Culhúa. It is nothing but leaves, somewhat round, a span wide and a foot long, a finger or two thick, more or less, depending upon where it grows. It is covered with many dangerous and poisonous spines. The color of the leaf is green, that of the spines, brown. The leaf is planted, and from it others grow, one springing from the other, and it gets so thick at the base that it comes to resemble a tree. It not only produces leaves growing out of those at the top, but laterally. Since, however, it is now known here, there is no need to say more about it.

In some parts of the country, as, for example, in the land of the Teuchichimecas [in the north], the earth is barren and without water, so the sap of the nopal leaves is drunk. The fruit *nochtli* is something like a fig, full of seeds, with a thin skin, but longer, and crowned like a medlar. It comes in many colors: some are green on the outside and red within, of a good flavor; others are yellow; others, white; still others are called *picadillas* because they are streaked with a mixture of colors. These last are excellent, better than the yellow ones; but the most perfect and delicious are the white ones, which are abundant in season. Some taste like pears and others like grapes, and are very refreshing, for which reason the Spaniards eat them in hot weather while traveling and pay more for them than the Indians do. The fruit is better when cultivated, so only the very poor eat the wild ones, called *montesinas* or *magrillas*. Another kind of *nochtli* is red, but is not much prized, though tasty. It is eaten by some because it ripens earlier and is the first of all the *tunas* to appear. They are not avoided because they are bad or tasteless, but because they stain the fingers, lips, and clothing, making spots very hard to remove, and they turn the urine as red as pure blood. Many Spaniards, new to the country, have been dismayed upon eating these red *tunas*, thinking they were losing all their blood in their urine—which caused great hilarity among their companions. Many physicians, recently arrived, have also been taken in, deceived by the color of a person's urine who had eaten this red fruit and, ignorant of the cause of it, have prescribed for healthy men remedies for stanching the flow of blood, to the vast amusement of the bystanders who were a party to the joke.

The name Tenochtitlán is composed of *nochtli*, the fruit, and of *tetl*, a stone, for when the place was founded it was near a rock upon which a huge nopal was growing—which is why the Mexicans have a nopal growing upon a rock for their coat of arms and device, which closely corresponds to its name.

Some, on the other hand, say that the city got its name from that of its founder, Tenuch, the second son of Ixtacmixcoatl, whose sons and grandsons, as I shall explain later on, settled this land of Anahuac, now called New Spain. Others even think that it was named after the cochineal (called *nochtixtli*), which grows on the nopal and its fruit *nochtli*, from which the cochineal gets its name. The Spaniards call it *carmesí*, from its very bright color, and prize it highly. However it was, it is certain that the town and its site are called Tenochtitlán and its citizens and natives, Tenochcas. Mexico, as I have said, is not the whole city, but only half of it and one district, although the Indians ordinarily call the whole place Mexico–Tenochtitlán, as I believe it is referred to in the royal writs. Mexico means source or fountain, depending upon what language is used, and so it is also said that the place was named by its first founders after the many little springs and pools of water roundabout. Still others affirm that Mexico took its name from that of the first founders, the Mexiti, for even now the people of the district are known as the Mexica, who in turn took theirs from that of their principal god and idol, Mexitli, who is the same as Huitzilopochtli. Tlatelolco had already been founded, which, because it was on a high and dry piece of land in the lake, was given its name which means islet, deriving from *tlatelli,* island.

Mexico–Tenochtitlán is completely surrounded by water, standing as it does in the lake. It can be approached by only three causeways: one, about half a league long, entering from the west; another from the north, about a league long. There is no causeway from the east, and one must approach by boat. To the south is the third causeway, the one by which Cortés and his companions entered, as I have said. The lake upon which Mexico is situated, although it seems to be one, is really two, very different from each other, for one is saline, bitter, and stinking, and has no fish in it, while the other is of sweet water and does have fish, although they are small. The salt lake rises and falls, and has currents caused by the winds. The fresh-water lake is higher, so that the good water flows into the bad, and not the other way around, as some have thought; it flows through some six or seven large channels cut in the causeway that separates them. These channels are crossed by some very fine wooden bridges. The salt lake is five leagues wide and eight or ten long, and is more than fifteen leagues in circumference. The fresh-water lake is about the same size, so that the whole measures more than thirty leagues roundabout. On its shores are more than fifty towns, many of them of five thousand houses, some of ten thousand, and one, Texcoco, as large as Mexico. The water that collects in this depression comes from a ring of mountains that can be seen from the city. It picks up its salt from the saline earth through which it flows. Its salinity is caused by the soil and the place, and not by something else, as many think. A great deal of salt is gathered from the lake, and is the source of a large trade.

Upon these lakes float some two hundred thousand small boats, called by the natives *acalli,* which is to say, water-houses, from *atl,* water, and *calli,* house, the word being composed from these two terms. The Spaniards called them *canoas,* a word to which they had become used in the language of Cuba and Santo Domingo. They are shaped somewhat like a trough, cut out of one piece, large or small, depending upon the size of the log. I am understating rather than exaggerating the number of these *acalli,* for some affirm that in

Mexico alone there are commonly some fifty thousand of them, used for bringing in provisions and transporting people. So the canals are covered with them to a great distance beyond the city, especially on market days.

79. The Markets of Mexico

THE MARKET PLACE is called a *tianquiztli*. Each district and parish has its square for the exchange of merchandise, Mexico and Tlatelolco, the largest districts, having vast ones, especially the latter, where markets are held on most weekdays. [In the rest,] one every five days is customary, and, I believe, in the whole kingdom and territory of Moctezuma. The market place of Mexico is wide and long, and surrounded on all sides by an arcade; so large is it, indeed, that it will hold seventy thousand or even one hundred thousand people, who go about buying and selling, for it is, so to speak, the capital of the whole country, to which people come, not only from the vicinity, but from farther off. Besides, all the towns about the lake [have their own markets], because of which there is always the vast number of canoes and people that I have mentioned, and even more.

Each trade and each kind of merchandise has its own place reserved for it, which no one else can take or occupy—which shows no little regard for public order—and because such a multitude of people and quantity of goods cannot be accommodated in the great square, the goods are spread out over the nearest streets, especially the more bulky materials, such as stone, lumber, lime, bricks, adobes, and all building materials, both rough and finished. [In the market proper] many kinds of mats are to be found, both fine and coarse; pottery of different clays and glazes, all very pretty, and every kind of vessel, from great jars to saltcellars; charcoal, firewood, and faggots; deerskins, raw or tanned, with hair or without, stained in many colors, for shoes, bucklers, shields, jackets, and coverings for wooden armor. Besides all this, there are skins of other animals: birds with their feathers still in place, dried and stuffed with straw, large and small, an astonishing thing to see because of their colors and strangeness.

The most valuable goods are salt and cotton mantles, these being white, black, and of every color, some large, some small; some designed for bed coverings, others for capes, still others for drapes, drawers, shirts, headdresses, tablecloths, handkerchiefs, and many other things. There are also mantles of maguey fiber, palm fiber, and rabbit fur, which are good, esteemed, and worn, although those made of feathers are better. The most picturesque thing in the market is the birds: some used for food, others for their feathers, and still others for hunting. They are so many that they cannot be counted, and of such different species that I cannot name them: tame birds, birds of prey, birds of the air, land, and water. The most beautiful things in the market are the gold and featherwork, in which they make replicas of everything in every color. The Indians are such masters of the craft that they will make a butterfly, an animal, a tree, a rose, flowers, herbs, and rocks, all done with feathers, and with such fidelity that they seem alive or natural. So absorbed are they in placing, removing, and adjusting the feathers, scrutinizing them from one side or the other, in the sun, in the shade, or in the half-light, that sometimes they will not eat all day long. In a word, they will not let the work out of their hands until it is absolutely perfect. Few nations have such patience, especially the short-tempered ones, like ourselves.

The craft of the highest rank and greatest skill is that of the silversmiths, who bring to the market cast pieces of fine workmanship, set with precious stones: an octagonal plate, half of gold, half of silver, not soldered together, but joined in the casting; a small kettle, cast with its handle, as is done here in the casting of bells, but separately; a fish with silver scales and another with gold, regardless of how many scales it may have. They can cast a parrot that moves its tongue, head, and wings; a monkey that moves its feet and head, and holds a distaff in its hands, so naturally that it seems to be spinning, or an apple that it appears to be eating. All this was much admired by our men, for our silversmiths have not such skill. They also make lacquer ware; they set and carve emeralds, turquoises, and other stones, and bore pearls, but not so well as we do.

To resume: In the market there is a great deal of precious featherwork, gold, silver, copper, lead, brass [bronze], and tin, although the last named three metals are not prized; many pearls and other precious stones; a thousand kinds of conches, periwinkles, bones, pebbles, sponges, and other trifles. And true it is that the toys, baubles, and knickknacks of these Indians of Mexico are many, different, and amusing. There is also a wonderful variety of herbs and roots, leaves and seeds, which are sold for food as well as for medicines, the men, women, and children being very wise in the use of herbs, because they are so poor that they must find them for eating and for curing their ills. They have little to spend on doctors, although there are plenty of doctors and apothecaries who bring to the market their ointments, syrups, waters, and other little things for the sick. They treat almost all diseases with herbs, and even have a special and well-known herb for killing lice.

The kinds of foodstuffs sold are numberless. They will eat virtually anything that lives: snakes without head or tail; little barkless dogs, castrated and fattened; moles, dormice, mice, worms, lice; and they even eat earth which they gather with fine nets, at certain times of the year, from the surface of the lake. It is a kind of scum, neither plant nor soil, but something resembling ooze, which solidifies. It is very plentiful and a great deal of it is gathered; it is spread out on floors, like salt, and there it dries and hardens. It is made into cakes resembling bricks, which are not only sold in the market [of Mexico] but are shipped to others far outside the city. It is eaten as we eat cheese; it has a somewhat salty taste and, taken with *chilmole*, is delicious. It is said that so many birds, attracted by the food, come to the lake in winter that they quite often cover it over in some places.

Deer are sold there, either whole or quartered; wild sheep, hares, rabbits, muskrats (which are smaller than rabbits), dogs, and certain creatures that bark like them, called *cuzatli* [weasels]. To be brief, there are many animals like these that are either bred or hunted. There are so many eating places, and hovels where bad food is served, that it is wonderful to consider where so much food, cooked and uncooked, disappears to: meats and fish, baked or fried in batter, pies, and omelets made of the eggs of various kinds of birds; and the quantity of baked bread, or grain in the ear, that is sold, together with broad beans, [kidney] beans, and other legumes, is beyond reckoning. Neither is it possible to estimate the many and different fruits, fresh or dried, that are sold there every market day; but the most important of all, which is used for money, is one that resembles the almond, which they call *cacahuatl*, and we *cacao*, as we knew it in the islands of Cuba and Haiti.

We must not omit to mention the large number of dyes known to us here, and the many others that we lack, which they manufacture from roses, flowers, fruits, roots, bark, stones, wood, and from so many other things that one cannot remember them all. They make syrups from maize (*centli*), which is their wheat, from the agave, and from other trees and plants, better than our boiled honey. They press oil from the seeds of the *chian,* which some compare to our mustard, and others to the fleawort, and with it cover their paintings to protect them from moisture. They extract oil from other things as well and use it for cooking and greasing, although they prefer lard, animal fat, and tallow. They also make and sell many kinds of wines, which will be described elsewhere.

I should never finish if I were to list all the things they offer for sale, or the various craftsmen in the market, such as stovemakers, barbers, cutlers, and others, whom many think these strange people did not have among them. All the things I have mentioned, many that I am ignorant of, and others that I pass over in silence are sold every day in every market in Mexico. The vendors paid the king something for their place, either for the right to sell or for protection against thieves, for which purpose certain men like policemen were always walking about the market place. In one house, where all might see them, were a dozen old men sitting as judges, hearing suits. Buying and selling consisted merely of exchanging one thing for another: this man offers a turkey for a sheaf of maize; that one, mantles for salt or money (rather, for cacao beans, which circulate as money throughout the country), and in this fashion their trading is done. They kept accounts: so many cacao beans for a mantle or a turkey, and they used a string for measuring things like maize and feathers; pots for other things, such as honey and wine. If anyone gave short weight, he was fined and his measures were broken.

80. The Temple of Mexico

THE TEMPLE was called a *teocalli,* which is to say, the house of god, the word being composed of *teotl,* god, and *calli,* a house, a very proper word if theirs had been the true God. The Spaniards who did not know the language called the temple *cúe,* and *Huichilobos* the god Huitzilopochtli. In its parishes and districts Mexico had many temples, with towers, surmounted by chapels and altars, where the idols and images of their gods were kept. These chapels were also used as sepulchers by the lords who owned them, the rest of the people being buried in the earth roundabout and in the courtyards. Since all the temples were of the same form, or almost, it will suffice to describe the principal one, which, although its form was general throughout the country, had, I believe, never been seen or heard of before.

The temple site was a square, measuring a crossbow shot to the side. Its stone enclosure had four gates, three of them opening on the main streets, which were a continuation of the causeways I have described. The fourth one did not open on a causeway, but on a very good street. Within this enclosure was a structure of earth and heavy stones, square, like the enclosure itself, measuring fifty fathoms to the side. As it rose from the ground, it was interrupted by great terraces, one above the other. The higher it went, the narrower became the terraces, until it resembled a pyramid of Egypt, save that it did not end in a point, but in a square platform eight or ten fathoms wide. The west side had no terraces, but a stairway leading to the top, each step of which was a good span in height. Altogether there were 113 or 114 of the steps, which, being many and high and made of handsome stone, gave the structure an imposing appearance. To see the priests climbing and descending them during some ceremony, or carrying a man up to be sacrificed, was a spectacle to behold.

At the summit were two very large altars, separated from each other, and set so close to the edge of the platform that there was hardly enough room to allow a man to pass easily behind them. One of these altars was at the right, the other at the left. They were not more than five spans in height, and their stone walls were painted with ugly and horrible figures. Each altar had a very pretty chapel built of carved wood, and each had three lofts, one placed above the other, quite high, of carved paneling. The chapels stood well above the pyramid and, viewed from a distance, gave it the appearance of a tall and handsome tower. From it one had a fine view of the city and the lake with all its towns, the most beautiful sight in the world. This was the spectacle that Moctezuma showed Cortés and the Spaniards when he took them to the top of the temple. Between the head of the stairs and the altars was a small square, but more than wide enough for the priests to celebrate their rites without crowding.

All the people prayed with their faces toward the rising sun, which is why the great temples are so placed. In each of the altars was a very large idol. Apart from the towers formed by the chapels on this pyramid, there were forty or more others, large and small, raised upon the lesser *teocallis* which surrounded the great one. These, although of the same design, did not face the east, but other parts of the sky, to differentiate them from the great temple. Some were larger than the others, and each was dedicated to a different god, one to the god of air, called Quetzalcoatl, whose temple was round, for the air encompasses the sky. Its entrance was through a door carved in the form of a serpent's mouth, diabolically painted, with fangs and teeth exposed, which frightened those who entered, especially the Christians, to whom it looked like the mouth of hell. There were other *teocallis*, or *cúes*, in the city, with staircases on three sides, and some with small stairs at each corner. All these temples had adjoining houses for the service of their priests and particular gods.

At each entrance of the great temple there was a large hall containing sizable chambers on its two floors. They were filled with arms, for the temples of every town were community houses and served as defenses and fortresses, which is why munitions and stores were kept in them. There were also three other halls of equal height, with flat roofs, tall and large, their walls of painted stones, the ceiling joists fancifully carved; and within, many chapels or chambers with very small doors, very dark inside, where an infinite number of idols were kept, great and small, made of many kinds of metals and materials. All of them were black with blood, for they were smeared over and sprayed with it whenever a man was sacrificed. They stank horribly, in spite of which the priests entered the chapels daily and, when they were preparing to kill and sacrifice a man, would allow no one else to enter, unless it was some great personage. These ministers of the devil had a large pond, fed by a pipe leading from the principal drinking fountain, where they washed off the blood of the sacrifices, from themselves and their robes. This pond was also used for the kitchens and the poultry. The rest of the great square was empty and open, and was used for the raising of birds, for herb gardens, sweet-smelling trees, rose bushes, and flowers for the altars.

Such, just as I have described it, was the great temple of Mexico, so vast and so strange, which these deluded men raised to their false gods. It housed continually five thousand people; all slept within it and ate at its expense, for it was very rich, having many towns whose obligation it was to build and maintain it in service. By common accord all the people of these towns collected and stored bread and fruits, meat and fish, for the needs of the temple were very much greater than those of the palace. In spite of this heavy duty, they lived more carefree [than the people of the palace], in short, as vassals of the gods, they said.

Moctezuma took Cortés and the Spaniards to this temple to show it to them and explain his religion and piety, of which we shall speak at greater length in another place, for it was the strangest and most cruel religion you ever heard of.

81. The Idols of Mexico

THE GODS OF MEXICO, it was said, numbered two thousand. The most important of them were Huitzilopochtli and Tezcatlipoca, whose images stood upon the altars at the summit of the *teocalli.* They were of stone, of gigantic size, thickness, and height, covered with mother-of-pearl, in which many pearls, precious stones, and gold were set, held in place by a cement made of *zacotl,* decorated with mosaics representing birds, snakes, animals, fishes, and flowers, done in turquoises, emeralds, chalcedonies, amethysts, and other small stones, which made a very handsome design against the mother-of-pearl. Each of the idols wore about its waist thick snakes of gold, and each wore a necklace of golden hummingbirds, a golden mask with mirror-like eyes, and, at the back, a dead man's face—all having their meaning and symbolism. The two gods were brothers: Texcatlipoca, god of plenty, and Huitzilopochtli, god of war, who was worshiped and esteemed above all the others.

Another very large idol stood in the chapel of the said gods which, according to some, was the greatest and best of them. It was made of all the edible and useful seeds found in the country, which were ground and kneaded with the blood of innocent babes and virgins, who had been sacrificed and their hearts offered to the idol as first fruits. The priests and ministers of the temple consecrated the idol with the utmost pomp and ceremony. The people of the whole city and country attended the consecration with incredible rejoicing and devotion, and many of the pious approached the idol after it had been blessed, to touch it with their hands and press into the dough precious stones, small pieces of gold, and other jewels and ornaments taken from their persons. After the ceremony, no layman might touch the idol or enter its chapel, not even the monks, but only the *tlamacazque,* that is, the priest. They replaced the idol from time to time and broke up the old one, and blessed were they who could obtain a piece of it for a relic and precious memento, especially the soldiers. At the time of the consecration of the idol, a flask of water was also blessed; it was piously guarded at the foot of the altar to sanctify the king when he was crowned, and to bless the captain-general when he was elected during a war, he being given some of it to drink.

82. The Ossuary

OUTSIDE THE TEMPLE, more than a stone's throw from the principal gate, was an ossuary built of the skulls of men taken in battle and sacrificed. It was in the form of a theater, longer than it was wide, of stone and mortar, with its benches, between the stones of which skulls were set, teeth outward. At the ends of the theater were two towers, built entirely of mortar and skulls, the walls of which, containing, so far as could be seen, no stone or other material, were strangely handsome. In the upper part of the theater stood seventy or more tall poles, four or five spans apart, into which pegs had been driven from top to bottom. These pegs stood out like studs, and each of them had five skulls impaled on it through the temples. Andrés de Tapia, who described it to me, and Gonzalo de Umbría counted them one day and found them to number 136,000 skulls, including those on the poles and steps. Those in the towers could not be counted. This was a cruel custom, although it had some color of humanity, because it was a reminder of death. Certain persons had the duty of replacing the skulls that fell out, so the number did not diminish.

83. Moctezuma Is Arrested

HERNÁN CORTÉS and the Spaniards spent six days viewing the city and learning its secrets, as well as the notable things we have described, and others that we shall describe later on. They were frequently visited by Moctezuma and the gentlemen of his court, as well as others, and were very well provided for, as on the first day. The Indian friends were also looked after, and the horses were fed green *alcacer,* a fresh grass that grows all the year round, flour, grain, roses, and everything else their masters requested, and were even bedded down in flowers.

Notwithstanding the fact that the Spaniards were so pampered and were so proud at being in such a rich country where they could fill their hands, not all of them were happy or contented, some being afraid and beset with misgivings. This was especially true of Cortés, who, as their head and chief, had the obligation of watching over and guarding his companions. He was particularly uneasy when he contemplated the situation of Mexico, its size and numbers of people, and when he saw the anxiety of many Spaniards who came to him and told him of the fortress and web in which they were caught, for it seemed to them that not a man could escape whenever Moctezuma should take the notion, or the city should rise. It would only be necessary indeed, for each citizen to throw a stone, or break the bridges of the causeways, or cut off supplies—all of which things the Indians could easily do.

So it was that Cortés, with his anxiety to guard his men, avoid such dangers, and surmount any obstacles in the path of his desires, decided to arrest Moctezuma; further, to build four brigantines to dominate the lake and the canoes: this in case anything had been plotted before his arrival (as he thought and I believe), considering that men in the water were as helpless as fish on land, and that unless he arrested the king he could not take the country. He would have preferred to build the brigantines at once, which would have been easy, but in order not to put off the arrest, which was the key to the whole affair, he left them until later and decided, without informing anyone, to arrest Moctezuma forthwith. The opportunity, or incident, which furthered his purpose was the death of nine Spaniards killed by Cualpopoca. Besides, he had boldly written the Emperor that he would seize Moctezuma and his empire. So he showed Moctezuma the letters of Pedro de Ircio which told of the culpability of Cualpopoca in the death of the nine Spaniards. After reading them [to Moctezuma], he put them in his wallet and paced back and forth a long while, alone and very apprehensive over the great enterprise he was embarking upon, which even to him seemed foolhardy, although necessary to his purpose.

While he was thus pacing, he noticed that one wall of the room was whiter than the others. He approached and saw that it had recently been whitewashed, and that a short while before there had been a doorway in it, now sealed with stone and mortar. He called two servants (the rest of them being asleep, for the hour was very late) and had them open it. He entered and found many rooms, in several of which was a large quantity of idols, featherwork, jewels, precious stones, silver, and an astonishing amount of gold, as well as so many lovely things that he was amazed. He closed the door as well as he could and left, without touching anything, so as not to alarm Moctezuma and interfere with his arrest; besides, [the treasure] was safe where it was.

The next morning certain Spaniards, accompanied by many Indians of Tlaxcala, came to tell Cortés that the people of the city were plotting to kill him and, to ensure their success, to break the bridges over the causeways. At these tidings, true or false, Cortés left half the Spaniards to guard his quarters, posted many others at the street crossings, and told the rest to go to the palace very innocently, in twos and threes, or as they thought best, and tell Moctezuma that he must see him about matters of life and death.

They did so, and Cortés went straight to Moctezuma, concealing his weapons, as did the others. Moctezuma came out to meet him and led him to his reception room. As many as thirty Spaniards entered with him, while the rest remained at the door of the courtyard. Cortés greeted Moctezuma as usual, and then began to jest and banter with him, as he had done before at various times. Moctezuma, who was very easy, giving no thought to what fortune had in store for him, was cheerful and pleased with this discourse. He gave Cortés many gold jewels and one of his daughters, and gave him the daughters of other nobles for the Spaniards. Cortés accepted them to please him, because Moctezuma would have been insulted otherwise; but he told him he was a married man and could not take the girl as his wife, because under Christian law no one was permitted to have more than one, on pain of being dishonored and branded on the forehead. After all this, he showed Moctezuma the letters of Pedro de Ircio and had them translated for him. In them Ircio accused Cualpopoca of having killed so many Spaniards, and accused Moctezuma himself of having ordered it done and of having ordered his men to make public that he wished to kill the Spaniards and cut the bridges.

Moctezuma denied both charges, saying it was a lie on the part of his vassals and a very great falsehood that the wicked Cualpopoca had perpetrated against him. To prove to Cortés that this was the truth, in his great rage he called certain of his servants there and then, and ordered them to bring Cualpopoca before him, giving them a jewel from his arm as a seal, carved with the figure of Huitzilopochtli. The messengers left at once, and Cortés said to him: "My lord, it will be necessary for your Highness to come to my apartment and remain there until the messengers return bringing Caulpopoca, to clear up the matter of the killing of my Spaniards. You will be well treated and served, and will rule, just as you do from here. Be not afflicted, for I shall defend your honor and person as I would my own, or that of my King; and forgive me for this, because I cannot do otherwise. If I should tolerate your conduct, my men here would be vexed with me for not defending and aiding them. And so, order your people not to be angry or make a disturbance, and bear in mind that if any ill befalls us, you will pay for it with your life, for it lies with you whether you will keep silent and not stir up your people."

Moctezuma was profoundly shaken and said with all gravity: "My person is not such as can be taken prisoner and, even if I should consent to it, my people would not suffer it." The two spent more than four hours discussing the matter, at the end of which Moctezuma said he would go [with Cortés], because he had to rule and govern. He ordered a room to be well furnished and prepared for him in the house and court of the Spaniards, and went there with Cortés. Many lords, barefoot and weeping, undressed him, put his clothes under their arms, and bore him off in a rich litter. When it was noised about the city that the king was a prisoner in the hands of the Spaniards, it erupted in a great tumult. But Moctezuma comforted those who were weeping, and told the rest to desist, saying that he was not a prisoner, nor was he there against his will, but much to his liking.

Cortés put a captain and a guard over him and changed the guard daily, so that there were always Spaniards to cheer and entertain him. For his part, Moctezuma greatly enjoyed their company, and always gave them something. He was served there by his own people, as in his palace, and by the Spaniards also, who put themselves out to please him, and Cortés himself brought him every kind of gift, begging him at the same time not to feel badly about it, and leaving him free to hear suits, dispatch his affairs, attend to the government of his realms as before, and to speak publicly and privately with all those of his people who wished to see him—which was the bait that caused Moctezuma and his Indians to take the hook.

Never did Greek or Roman, or man of any nation, since kings have existed, do what Cortés did in seizing Moctezuma, a most powerful king, in his own house, a very strong place, surrounded by an infinity of people, while Cortés had only four hundred and fifty companions.

84. Moctezuma's Hunting

WHILE MOCTEZUMA was a prisoner among the Spaniards, not only did he enjoy the liberty I have mentioned, but Cortés also allowed him to hunt or go to the temple whenever he liked, for he was a very devout man and a hunter. When he went hunting he was carried in a litter on men's shoulders; he had a bodyguard of eight or ten Spaniards, and three thousand Mexicans, including lords, gentlemen, servants, and hunters, of whom he had a very large number: some for beaters, others for starting the game, others for falconry. The hunters looked out for hares, rabbits, and iguanas; they shot at deer, wolves, foxes, and other animals, such as coyotes, with bow and arrow, at which they are very skillful and accurate, especially if they are Teuchichimecas, who rarely miss a target at eighty paces and less. When Moctezuma ordered a drive, it was wonderful to see the multitude of people who gathered for it, and the game they captured and slaughtered, with hands, sticks, nets, and bow and arrow, among the animals, either tame or fierce and frightful, such as lions, tigers, and creatures resembling ounces, which look like cats. It is quite a feat to capture a lion, not only because it is a dangerous beast, but because the hunters have few weapons and little defense against it. Cunning, however, can do more than force; but it takes even more skill to capture birds on the wing, as Moctezuma's hunters do, for they are so cunning and dexterous that they will take any bird in the air, however swift and fierce it may be, if their lord commands it. This happened one day while Moctezuma was with his Spanish guards in a gallery, and they spied a hawk, and one of them said: "Oh, what a fine hawk! How I should like to have it!" Whereupon he called certain of his servants, said to be masters of the hunt, and ordered them to chase the hawk and bring it to him. They left, and put such diligence and cunning into the task that they brought him the hawk, which he gave to the Spaniards—a thing that strains one's credulity, but it is vouched for by many, in words and writing. Indeed, it would be an act of madness in such a king as Moctezuma to issue such a command, as it would be folly on the part of his men to obey it, if the feat was beyond their knowledge and skill; but we have already said that he did these things to display his power and magnificence, [or, possibly, in this case he] had his hunters bring another fierce hawk and swear it was the same he had ordered them to catch. If this is true, as is affirmed, I should praise rather the man who captured it than him who gave the order.

Moctezuma's greatest pleasure in these excursions was hawking, which was done with herons, kites, crows, magpies, and other birds, strong or weak, great or small, and with birds of prey, both theirs and ours, that fly among the clouds, such as eagles and vultures, and some that kill hares and wolves, and even deer. Hunting was also done with nets, snares, lures, and other devices, while Moctezuma himself was good at shooting game with bow and arrow, or killing birds with a blowgun, with which he was a fine marksman.

The places where he went [to hunt] were pleasure houses in the woods at least two leagues from the city, and, although he sometimes entertained the Spaniards in them with festivals and banquets, he never failed to return to Cortés' quarters to sleep; nor did he fail to give something to the Spaniards who escorted him on such days. When Cortés saw how liberally and joyfully Moctezuma distributed his presents, he warned him that the Spaniards were rascals, and that they had taken some gold and other things they had found in certain chambers; and that Moctezuma should consider what he wished to do about it. But Moctezuma generously replied: "All of it belongs to the gods of the city. Do not touch the feathers and things not made of gold and silver, but take everything else for yourself and them, and if you want more you shall have it."

85. Destruction of the Idols

WHEN MOCTEZUMA went to the temple, most of the time it was on foot, accompanied by one companion, or between two who supported his arms, preceded by a lord carrying in his hands three wands of authority, to indicate that the person of the king was there, or as a symbol of justice and correction. If he was borne on a litter, he took one of the wands in his hand when he descended; if he was on foot he carried it, I believe, like a scepter. He was very ceremonious in all his actions and service, most of which, from the time Cortés entered Mexico to this point, have been described.

During the first days after the arrival of the Spaniards, whenever Moctezuma went to the temple, men were killed in sacrifice. To prevent this cruelty in the presence of the Spaniards who now had to escort him, Cortés admonished Moctezuma to order the priests not to sacrifice a human body, unless he wanted Cortés to lay waste the temple and the city. Cortés even told Moctezuma that he desired to cast down the idols in his presence and before all the people. Moctezuma told him to do no such thing, for the people would mutiny and take up arms for the defense and protection of their ancient religion and benevolent gods, who gave them their bread, health, intelligence, and all necessities.

The first time that Moctezuma went to the temple after his arrest, Cortés and the Spaniards went with him and, as soon as they entered, Cortés on one side and they on the other, began to cast down the idols from their pedestals and altars in the chapels and chambers. Moctezuma was violently disturbed at this, and his men were profoundly shocked, and had a mind to seize their arms and kill the

Spaniards then and there. But Moctezuma ordered them to keep calm and begged Cortés to put a stop to such a sacrilege. Cortés complied because, as he explained to them through the interpreters, this did not seem to be the fitting moment for it, nor did he have the force necessary to carry out his intent.

86. Cortés on Idolatry

"ALL THE MEN in the world, most sovereign King, noble gentlemen, and priests, you in Mexico, we in Spain, and those of whatever part who dwell in it, have in life the same beginning and the same end, and derive our being and our lineage from God, almost like God himself. We were all given the same kinds of bodies, souls, and senses, wherefore we are all equal, not only in body and soul, but are kindred in blood. It happens, however, that by an act of that same God some are born beautiful and others ugly, some wise and discreet, others foolish and without understanding, judgment, or virtue. It is just, holy, and in conformity with the will of God, therefore, that the wise and virtuous should teach and indoctrinate the ignorant, guide the blind and the erring, and place them upon the way to salvation, by the path of the true religion. This is the great boon and blessing that I and my companions desire and strive to attain for you, and the more we strive, the closer becomes our bond of friendship. We do this also because we are your guests, and being such, we are obligated, forced and constrained by these considerations, as anyone is anywhere.

"Man and his life consist of three things, as you are already aware, to wit: body, soul, and goods. Of your goods, which is the least of them, we wish nothing; nor have we taken anything except what you have given us. We have not touched your persons and have no wish to do so. It is only your souls that we seek for their salvation, and this we shall now explain to you, and give you as well a full account of the true God.

"No one possessed of natural judgment will deny the existence of God, although some through ignorance may say there are many gods, or may fail to hit upon the true one. But I say and certify unto you that there is no God other than our Christian God, who is one and eternal, without beginning or end, the Creator and Ruler of all things. He alone created the heavens, the sun, the moon, and the stars that you worship. He alone created the sea with all its fishes, and the land with its animals, birds, plants, stones, metals, and the other things which you hold to be gods. He alone, with His own hands, after creating all things, fashioned man and woman, and, when they had come into being, breathed a soul into them, delivered the world into their hands, and gave them a glimpse of Paradise, glory, and Himself. From that man and that woman, then, we are all desended, as I said at the beginning, and so we are all kin and the work of God, are even His children; and if we desire the help of our Father, we must be good, humane, pious, and innocent, and capable of correction—which you cannot be so long as you worship stone images and kill men.

"Tell me, is there a man among you who wishes to be killed? Certainly not! Well, then, why do you put others to death so cruelly? If you cannot create a soul, why do you destroy it? No one among you can create souls or make bodies of flesh and bone, for, if you could, none would be without children, of whom you would have as many as you wished and the kind you wished: big, beautiful, good, and virtuous. Since, however, children are given to us by our God in Heaven, of whom I spoke, He gives them as He pleases and to whom He pleases, for He is God; and that is why you must accept Him, and hold and worship Him as such, for He it is who brings the rain, the dew, and the sunshine, by which the earth yields bread, fruits, herbs, birds, and other creatures for your sustenance.

"But these ugly and frightful images of yours which you vainly worship, fashioned by the filthy hands of your servants and slaves, do not give you such things; nor do they give you the enduring stones, the dry timbers, the cold metals, or the tiny seeds. Oh, what splendid gods are these, and what pretty priests! You worship things made by hands so filthy that you will not eat what they touch or cook! Do you really believe that things which decay, which are eaten by worms, which grow old, and which have no feeling whatever, are gods? Things which cannot kill or heal? There is no reason, therefore, for you to keep these idols any longer, or to kill men before them, or pray to them, for they are deaf, dumb, and blind.

"Do you wish to know who God is and where He dwells? Lift up your eyes, then, and you will understand that there is a Deity above who causes the heavens to move, keeps the sun in its course, commands the earth, fills the sea, and provides men and creatures with water and bread. This is the God whom you can now see in your hearts, and whom you must serve and worship, not with the killing of men, or with blood and abominable sacrifices, but only with devotion and prayer, as we Christians do. Know, finally, that we are here to teach you this."

Such was the discourse by which Cortés softened the wrath of priests and citizens.

Having already cast down the idols, he quickly finished their destruction, while he stipulated to Moctezuma that they should not be set up again, that the chapels should be cleansed of their stinking blood, that no more men should be sacrificed, and that Cortés should be allowed to erect a Crucifix and an image of St. Mary on the altars of the great chapel, that is, the one which is reached by the 114 steps that I have mentioned.

Moctezuma and his people promised to kill no more men in sacrifice, and to keep the Cross and the image of Our Lady, if they might be allowed to retain the gods that were still standing. Cortés agreed, and they kept their word, never afterward sacrificing a man, at least in public or to the knowledge of the Spaniards, and they set up Crosses and images of Our Lady and of the other saints among their idols. The Mexicans, however, were left with a mortal hatred and anger, which they could not hide for long.

This Christian deed won more honor and glory for Cortés than if he had vanquished them in battle.

87. The Burning of Cualpopoca

TWENTY DAYS after the arrest of Moctezuma, his servants, who had been sent with his order and seal, returned, bringing Cualpopoca, Cualpopoca's son, and fifteen other noblemen who, as had been ascertained by inquiry, were guilty participants in the plot to kill the Spaniards. Cualpopoca came to Mexico with a large company, as befitted a great noble (which he was), borne on a rich litter carried on the shoulders of his servants and vassals. As soon as he had spoken to Moctezuma, he, his son, and the fifteen gentlemen were delivered in fetters into the hands of Cortés. He took them to one side and questioned them, and they confessed that they had killed the Spaniards in battle. Cualpopoca was asked whether he was a vassal of Moctezuma, and he answered: "Why, is there some other lord whose vassal I could be?" By which he meant virtually that there was not. Cortés said to him: "Much greater is the King of the Spaniards whom you slew while they were under a safe-conduct, and now you shall pay for it!"

They were more severely questioned [tortured], and they unanimously confessed they had killed the Spaniards, partly in obedience to the instructions of the great lord Moctezuma, partly on their own account, as they had in war killed others who had invaded their country, in which case they could do so legitimately. Cortés, acting on their confessions, sentenced and condemned them to be burned; and they were burned publicly in the great square, in view of all the people, who looked on in complete silence, without rioting, terrified by this novel form of justice imposed in the kingdom of Moctezuma, by strangers and guests of their great lord.

88. Antecedents of the Burning

CORTÉS HAD ORDERED Pedro de Ircio to attempt a settlement where Almería now stands, in order to prevent a new landing by Francisco de Garay, Garay having already been driven away once from that coast. Ircio admonished the Indians [of Nautla] to accept his friendship and yield obedience to the Emperor. Cualpopoca, lord of Nautla, or rather, of the five towns now included in Almería, sent word to Pedro de Ircio that he could not come to offer his obedience, because of the enemies that lay between them, but he would do so if Ircio would send some Spaniards to make the way safe for him, for in those circumstances no one would dare attack him. Ircio sent four, believing it was true, since he was desirous of founding a settlement. When, however, the Spaniards entered the territory of Nautla, a large number of armed men came to meet them and killed two with great rejoicing. The other two, wounded, escaped and brought the tidings to Vera Cruz.

Pedro de Ircio, believing it was the work of Cualpopoca, marched against him with fifty Spaniards and ten thousand Cempoalans, two horses, and two small guns. Cualpopoca heard of his coming and advanced with a large force to drive the Spaniards from the country, and fought so well that he killed seven more Spaniards and many Cempoalans. In the end, however, he was defeated, his country laid waste, his town put to the sack, and many of his men were killed or captured. The prisoners said that Cualpopoca had been acting on the order of the great lord Moctezuma (which could have been true, for they all made this confession at the moment of death), but others said they had put the blame on the Mexicans to excuse themselves.

This is what Pedro de Ircio had written Cortés at Cholula, and his letters were Cortés' justification for the arrest of Moctezuma, as has been said already.

89. Moctezuma in Irons

BEFORE CUALPOPOCA and the others were led to the stake, Cortés told Moctezuma what they had said under oath, that is, that they had killed the Spaniards at his advice and command. He told him also that this was an evil thing to do, the Spaniards being such friends of his and guests besides; moreover, since he had no respect for the love that Cortés bore him, things would now go quite differently. Whereupon he put Moctezuma in irons, saying: "According to God's law, he who kills deserves to die." This he did in order to keep Moctezuma's thoughts on his own troubles, and not on those of others.

Moctezuma turned pale as death and was profoundly shocked by the manacles, a strange thing to happen to a king, and said that he was blameless and knew nothing about the business. And so, that very day, now that the fire had been lighted, Cortés removed the irons and left Moctezuma free to go to his palace. Moctezuma was very joyful at their removal and thanked Cortés for his courtesy;

but he refused to go, either because he thought it was all words and flattery (as it may well have been) or because he dared not, from fear that the people would kill him as soon as they saw him away from the Spaniards, for allowing himself to be arrested and held in that fashion. He also said that, if he went, his people would force him to rebel and kill Cortés and the Spaniards.

Moctezuma must have been a weak man of little courage, to let himself be seized and then, while a prisoner, never to attempt flight, even when Cortés offered him his freedom and his own men begged him to take it. But as weak as he was, he was so obeyed that no one in Mexico dared to annoy the Spaniards, and Cualpopoca had come from seventy leagues away, merely at the word that his lord had summoned him, and at the sight of his seal; and for many leagues roundabout all his wishes and commands were caried out.

90. Explorations for Gold

CORTÉS HAD A KEEN DESIRE to learn the extent of Moctezuma's dominions and rule, and what the neighboring kings and lords thought of him; also, to collect a good sum of gold to send to Spain for the Emperor's fifth, along with a complete account of the land and people, and his accomplishments. For this reason he begged Moctezuma to tell him where the mines were from which Moctezuma and his people got their gold and silver. Moctezuma replied that he would be glad to do so, and straightway appointed eight Indians, four of whom were silversmiths and acquainted with the mines, and four others who knew the country; and he ordered them to go in pairs to Zuzolla [Zacatula?], Malinaltepec, Tenich [Chinantla?], and Tututepec, in the company of the eight Spaniards sent by Cortés to explore the rivers and gold mines and bring back samples.

The eight Spaniards and eight Indians set out, bearing the insignia of Moctezuma. Those who went to Zuzolla, which is eighty leagues from Mexico, were shown three gold-bearing streams and given samples, though few, because little gold is extracted there, either for lack of equipment and diligence, or lack of greed. On their trip there and back, these men passed through three provinces, well peopled, of good buildings and fertile lands. The people of one of the provinces called Tlamacolopan [Tamazulapa?] were very intelligent and better dressed than the Mexicans. Those who went to Malinaltepec, seventy leagues away, brought back samples of gold which the natives gather from a great river that traverses the province. Those who went to Tenich, which is upstream from Malinaltepec and of a different language, were not permitted by its lord to enter or make inquiries about gold, because the lord, who was called Coatlicamatl, did not recognize Moctezuma and was not his friend, and thought, moreover, that the men were spies. But when they convinced him they were Spaniards, he told the Mexicans to get out of his country, and the Spaniards to carry out the orders of their captain and take him a message. The Mexicans warned the Spaniards against that lord, saying he was wicked and cruel, and would kill them. Our men hesitated a little to talk with Coatlicamatl because of what their companions said of him and because the people of the country were armed, some with lances of 25 and 30 spans long. But in the end, having his permission, they entered, for it would have been cowardice not to do so and would have brought suspicion upon themselves and resulted in their death. Coatlicamatl received them very cordially and had them shown seven or eight streams, from which they gathered gold in his presence and were given samples to take back. He also sent ambassadors to Cortés, offering his land and person, and some mantles and gold jewels.

Cortés was better pleased with the embassy than with the presents, seeing that Moctezuma's enemies desired his friendship; but Moctezuma and his people were not pleased, because Coatlicamatl, although not a great lord, still had a warlike people and a rugged country. Those who went to Tututepec, which is near the sea and twelve leagues beyond Malinaltepec, brought samples of gold taken from the two streams they explored, and a report that the land was good for both settlement and mining. For this reason Cortés begged Moctezuma to grant him a site there in the name of the Emperor. Moctezuma at once sent out mechanics and workmen, who within two months had built a large house, and three smaller ones near by for service, a fishpond with 500 ducks for feathers (which are harvested many times a year for the manufacture of mantles), and 1,500 turkeys; and they furnished and equipped the houses so well that their value came to 20,000 castellanos. They also sowed some sixty fanegas with maize, ten with beans, and planted 2,000 *cacahuatl* or cacao trees, which grow there very well. This estate was begun, but not finished, because of the coming of Pánfilo de Narváez and the revolt of Mexico, which happened soon afterward.

Cortés also begged Moctezuma to tell him whether there was a good port where the Spanish ships would be safe. Moctezuma replied that he did not know, but would make inquiries. So he had the whole of that [north] coast painted on a cotton canvas, with all the rivers, bays, roadsteads, and capes in the parts that belonged to him; but in the whole painting and map there was no port or bay, or any safe place, except only a large bay in the province of Coatzacoalcos between the two ranges now called San Martín and San Antón, which some Spanish pilots thought might even be a strait leading to the Moluccas and the Spice Islands. They were, however, much deceived, believing what they wished to believe. Cortés selected ten Spaniards, all pilots and sailors, to go with Moctezuma's men, for it was well worth the cost of the journey. The ten Spaniards went with Moctezuma's men to Chalchiuhcuecan, where they had first landed, now called San Juan de Ulúa. From it they explored seventy leagues of the coast without finding a navigable bay or river where ships might anchor, although they found many others. They arrived at Coatzacoalcos, and the lord of that river and province, named Tuchintlec, although an enemy of Moctezuma, received the Spaniards because he had known of them from the time they had been in Potonchán. He gave them boats for exploring and sounding the river, which the Spaniards found was eight fathoms deep at the deepest point. They ascended the river for twelve leagues and found large towns on its banks, and land which looked fertile. Tuchintlec, moreover, sent Cortés several gold articles, precious stones, cotton, feather, and tiger skin garments, and informed him that he wished to be his friend and pay an annual tribute to the Emperor, provided that the Mexicans were kept out of his territory.

Cortés was well pleased with this message and the discovery of the river, because the sailors had told him that between the Grijalba and Pánuco rivers there was no navigable stream; but I think they were mistaken also. He sent more Spaniards with gifts for Tuchintlec, to get a clearer notion of what Tuchintlec had in mind, and to learn more fully the advantages of the land and port. They went, and returned very happy and certain of everything, so Cortés at once dispatched Juan Velázquez de León and a hundred and fifty Spaniards to make a settlement and build a fortress there.

91. Arrest of Cacama, King of Texcoco

THE COWARDICE of Moctezuma, or the love he bore Cortés and the Spaniards, brought it about that his people not only grumbled but plotted uprisings and rebellion, especially Cacama, his nephew and lord of Texcoco, a fierce, courageous, and honorable youth, who had been greatly afflicted by the arrest of his uncle, and who, when he saw his uncle at liberty, had begged him to free himself and be a master, not a slave. Seeing that Moctezuma would not consent, he mutinied and threatened to kill the Spaniards. Some say he did so in order to make himself lord of Mexico; others, because he wanted to kill Spaniards. For one reason or the other, or for both, he took up arms, gathered many of his own men and those of friends to serve against the Spaniards, and proclaimed that he intended to release Moctezuma from captivity and to drive the Spaniards out of the country, or kill and eat them.

This was a terrifying piece of news for our men, but Cortés did not quail, even in the face of such ferocity; rather, he wished to fight Cacama at once and lock him up in his own house and town. But Moctezuma prevented it, saying that Texcoco was a very strong place surrounded by water, and that Cacama was proud and turbulent, and had with him all the people of Culhúa, for he was lord of Culhuacán and Otumba, which were strong forts, and Moctezuma thought it would be best to use a different approach. Cortés followed the advice of Moctezuma in the whole affair, and sent a message to Cacama begging him earnestly to remember the friendship between them since the time Cacama had received him and escorted him into Mexico. He told him that peace was always better than war for a man who had vassals, and that he should lay down his arms (which are always alluring to one who has never wielded them), because by so doing he would be rendering a great service to the King of Spain. Cacama replied that he felt no friendship for one who had taken away his honor and kingdom; that the war he was about to embark on was for the profit of his vassals and the defense of his country and religion; that, before he would lay down his arms, he would avenge his uncle and his gods; that he did not know who the King of Spain was, had no desire to hear about him, and less to know him.

Cortés admonished and warned Cacama many more times, but the other refused to listen to him, so Cortés had Moctezuma order him to do so. Moctezuma sent word to Cacama to come to Mexico and settle the differences and quarrels between him and the Spaniards, and to make friends with Cortés. Cacama replied bitterly that if Moctezuma had blood in his veins he would not now be a prisoner or captive of a handful of strangers, who with honeyed words had bewitched him and usurped his kingdom; nor would the religion of Mexico and the gods of Culhúa be cast down and trampled under the feet of bandits and imposters, or the glory of his ancestors defamed and destroyed by his cowardice and lack of spirit; but that Cacama would willingly take the field to restore religion, re-establish the gods, protect the kingdom, and liberate both Moctezuma and Mexico, not with his hands crossed over his breast, but wielding the sword and killing the Spaniards who had brought such shame and dishonor to the nation of Culhúa.

Our men were in the greatest danger, not only of losing Mexico, but their own lives, if this war and mutiny could not be stopped, because Cacama was brave, rough, and stubborn, and had with him many excellent fighting men; besides, there were many others in Mexico eager to rebel, release Moctezuma, and kill the Spaniards or drive them from the city. Moctezuma met the situation very well, for he knew that war and violence would avail him nothing, and that in the end everything would rest with him; so he arranged for certain captains and lords who were with Cacama in Texcoco, to seize him and bring him to the city. And they, either because Moctezuma was still king and still alive, or because they had always served him in war, or because they had been suborned with gifts and promises, seized Cacama one day during a council of war and put him in a canoe they had armed and ready, and brought him to Mexico—this without killings or tumults, even though it happened in his own house and palace on the lake. Before delivering him to Moctezuma, they placed him upon a rich litter, as is the custom among the kings of Texcoco, who are the greatest and noblest lords of all that country except Mexico.

Moctezuma refused to receive him and handed him over to Cortés, who put him in irons under guard. Then, at the advice and with the consent of Moctezuma, Cortés appointed as lord of Texcoco and Culhuacán, Cuicuitzcatzin, younger brother of Cacama, then with his uncle in Mexico, having fled from Cacama. Moctezuma gave him the title and performed all the ceremonies customary upon the election of a new lord, which we shall describe later on, and in Texcoco he was obeyed by command of Moctezuma, and also because he was better liked than Cacama, who was violent and headstrong. So the danger was avoided, but if there had been many Cacamas I know not how it would have come out. Cortés was now making kings and exercising as much authority as if he had already won the Mexican empire; indeed, he had had this in mind from the moment he entered the country, for he had a fixed idea that he would win Mexico and subject the state of Moctezuma.

92. Moctezuma's Speech to His Nobles

AFTER THE SEIZURE of Cacama, Moctezuma summoned a council, which was attended by all the lords of Mexico and the country round, and either of his own volition, or urged by Cortés, he spoke to them in the presence of the Spaniards, as follows:

"Kinsmen, friends, and servants: Well you know that I have been your king for these eighteen years, as my ancestors were before me, and that I have always been a good lord, and you my good and obedient vassals, as I trust you are now and will be all the days of my life. You surely remember what your fathers told you, that is, that we are not natives of this country and that our kingdom is not an enduring one, because our forebears came from distant lands, and that their king or chieftain returned to his own country, saying he would send one to rule and reign over them if he did not come himself. You may be certain that the king whom we have been expecting for so many years is the one who has sent these Spaniards you see before you, who say they are our kinsmen and have known about us for a long time. Let us give thanks to the gods that those whom we have so desired to see have come in our day. You will please me by giving yourselves to this captain as vassals of the Emperor and King of Spain, our sovereign lord, to whom I have already submitted as his servant and friend. And I implore you to obey him henceforth, as you have obeyed me, and give and render him the tributes, taxes, and services that you have rendered me, for you cannot give me greater pleasure."

Moctezuma could say no more, because of his tears and sobs, and all the people wept so bitterly that for a good while they could not answer him. They sighed and groaned so heavily that they even moved the hearts of our men; but in the end they said they would do as he commanded.

Then Moctezuma, first, and after him all his people gave themselves as vassals to the King of Castile and promised to be loyal to him (all of which was duly recorded with notary and witnesses), and each man retired to his own house, with God knows what feelings, as you can imagine. It was a notable thing to see Moctezuma and so many lords and gentlemen in tears, and to see how each one suffered. But they could not do otherwise, not only because Moctezuma desired and commanded it, but because they had received signs and portents, announced by their priests, of the coming of strange men, white and bearded, from the east, to subject the country; also because it was rumored that with Moctezuma not only would the line of the Culhúans end, but their rule also. And this is why some said that he should not have been king, nor should he have been named Moctezuma, which means "the fretted one," because of the ill fortune it brought him.

They also said that Moctezuma had heard the oracle of his gods say many times that in him the Mexican emperors would end, and that no son of his would succeed to the kingdom, and that he would lose his throne after eight years; that for this reason he had never wished to make war on the Spaniards, in the belief that they would succeed him; although on the other hand he thought it might be false, for he had been king for more than seventeen years. Whether this was the reason, or whether it was the will of God, who gives and takes away kingdoms, this is what Moctezuma did, for he greatly loved Cortés and the Spaniards and could not bear to trouble them.

Cortés thanked Moctezuma most courteously, on behalf of the Emperor and himself, and comforted him, for Moctezuma was sad after his speech, and promised him that he would always be king and lord, and would rule as he had hitherto, and even better, not only in his own domain, but also in that which Cortés would win and bring into the service of the Emperor.

93. Moctezuma's Gifts to Cortés

A FEW DAYS after Moctezuma and his people had tendered their obedience, Cortés spoke to him about the heavy expenses incurred by the Emperor in the wars and enterprises he was engaged in, and that it would be well if everyone should contribute to them and begin to serve in some way; hence it was fitting that Moctezuma should send throughout his dominions to collect tributes in gold and see what the new vassals would give; also, that Moctezuma should himself give something if he had it.

Moctezuma replied that he would gladly do so and that several Spaniards should go with his servants to the House of Birds. Many went and saw a large quantity of gold in plates and bars, jewels and carved pieces, in the hall and two chambers that were opened for them. Daunted by the sight of such a treasure, they did not dare to touch it until Cortés should see it; so they called him, and he went there, took it all, and brought it to his quarters. In addition, Moctezuma gave him many rich garments of cotton and featherwork, marvelously woven, unequaled in color and design, beyond anything the Spaniards had ever seen. Moctezuma also gave him a dozen blowguns, inlaid with wood and silver, which he used for hunting, some of them decorated with various kinds of birds, animals, roses, flowers, and trees, all done so perfectly and in such minute detail and with such workmanship that they delighted the eye. Others were cast and were more neatly and finely chased than the painted ones. The nets for carrying [blowgun] pellets and turquoises were of gold, and some of silver.

Moctezuma also sent his servants, by twos and fives, to the provinces, accompanied by Spaniards, and to the lands of his vassals, 80 and 100 leagues from Mexico, to collect the gold of the regular tribute and their new contribution for the Emperor. Each lord and province gave the measure and amount designated by Moctezuma, in sheets and ingots of gold and silver, jewels, precious stones, and pearls. The messengers returned after many days, bringing to Cortés and the [Spanish] treasurers the tribute they had collected, and they melted it down and recovered in fine gold 160,000 pesos or more, and in silver more than 500 marks. It was divided among the Spaniards by heads, but not all of it, each receiving what his rank entitled him to. The horsemen received twice as much as the foot soldiers, and officers and persons of importance were given preference. Cortés was paid in a lump what had been agreed upon in Vera Cruz, and the King's fifth came to more than 32,000 pesos in gold and 100 marks in silver plates, cups, pitchers, saucers, and other pieces, made in the Indian fashion for the Emperor.

Besides all this, Cortés set aside from the heap, before it was melted down, to send as a present to the King, along with his fifth, pearls, precious stones, garments, feathers, gold and feather work, silver and feather work, and many jewels, such as the blowguns, which were strangely beautiful over and above their value, for they were carved with fishes, birds, serpents, animals, trees, and such things, copied from nature in gold or silver, stones or feathers, quite unequaled. Most of it, however, was not sent, or was lost, along with the effects of everybody else, at the time of the retreat from Mexico, which we shall describe in detail later on.

94. Moctezuma Begs Cortés to Leave Mexico

NOW THAT CORTÉS saw himself rich and powerful, he formed three plans: One was to send to Santo Domingo and the other islands news of the country and his good fortune, this in order to get more men, arms, and horses, because his forces were too small for such a great kingdom. The second was to seize Moctezuma's domain, for he already held him prisoner; besides, Cortés now had the support of the Tlaxcalans, Coatelicamatl, and Tuchintlec, and knew that the people of Pánuco, Tehuantepec, and Michoacán were deadly enemies of the Mexicans and would help him in case of need. The third was the coversion of all the Indians to Christianity, which he began at once as his most important task. Although, for the reasons given, he had not destroyed the idols, he prohibited the killing and sacrificing of men, placed Crucifixes and images of Our Lady and other saints in the temples, and had his priests and friars celebrate Mass daily. Few Indians, to be sure, had been baptized, either because they were stubbornly devoted to their old religion or because our men were too busy in other matters and had to await a more opportune moment. Cortés himself heard Mass daily in his quarters, and ordered all the Spaniards to do likewise.

His plans, however, came to naught at the time, because Moctezuma changed his attitude (at least, he tried to do so), and because Pánfilo de Narváez came against him, and, finally, because the Indians drove him out of Mexico. These things, all of which were important, we shall take up in their order. Moctezuma's change of attitude, according to some, was manifested by his telling Cortés to leave the country, unless he wished to get himself killed along with all the rest of the Spaniards. He was moved to do so [he said] by three considerations, two of which were public knowledge. One was the heavy and unremitting pressure of his people to get him to leave his prison and drive out the Spaniards, or kill them, for they said it was a great affront and insult to him and to all of them for him to be held thus a prisoner and humiliated, and that he should order them to drive out that handful of strangers who had dishonored them, stolen their goods, and fraudulently made away with all the gold and wealth of their towns and lords (all this for themselves and their king, who must be a beggar); that if Moctezuma granted their petition, very well; if not, they would do so whether he liked it or not, for if he no longer wished to be their lord, neither did they wish to be his vassals; and that he should not expect better treatment [from the Spaniards] than Cualpopoca and Cacama had received, even though he was treated with more flattering words and adulation.

The second consideration was that the devil, whenever he appeared to Moctezuma, urged him repeatedly to kill the Spaniards or drive them out, warning him that if he did not do so, he [the devil] would not speak to him again, because he was tormented and enraged by the Masses and the Gospel, the Cross and the baptizing of Christians. Moctezuma replied that it would not be good to kill them, for they were his friends and honest men, but that he would try to persuade them to leave, failing which, he would kill them. To this the devil answered that this would give him great pleasure, because either he or the Spaniards would have to go, for they were sowing the seed of the Christian Faith, a religion very contrary to his, and the two could not exist together.

The third consideration, which was not made public, was, as many suspected, that men are fickle and never remain the same or keep to the same purpose, and that Moctezuma had repented of what he had done, particularly the arrest of Cacama, whom he had once greatly loved, and who, since Moctezuma had no sons, was to succeed him. He also recognized that what his people were saying was the truth—this besides what the devil had told him, that is, that he could not do the devil a greater service, or make a sacrifice more acceptable to the gods, than to kill and drive out the Spaniards, because, once they were gone, the line of the kings of Culhúa would not perish with him and his descendants would reign after him; that Moctezuma should pay no heed to the auguries, for the eighth year [of the prophecy] had passed and he was now in the eighteenth year of his reign.

For these reasons, then, or for others that we do not know, Moctezuma secretly made ready a hundred thousand men, so secretly that Cortés did not get wind of it, this for the purpose of seizing and killing the Spaniards if they refused to depart after being warned. Moctezuma decided to have a talk with Cortés and slyly went to the courtyard with a number of his gentlemen, and had Cortés summoned. Said Cortés to himself: "I don't like the look of this! Please God it means something good!" So he took a dozen Spaniards with him and went out to see what Moctezuma wanted and why he had summoned him, which he was not used to doing. Moctezuma arose, took Cortés by the hand and led him to a room, where he had benches brought for the two of them. Then he said: "I beg you to be gone from this city and country of mine, because the gods are very angry with me for entertaining you here. Ask me what you will and I shall give it to you, because I love you much; and do not think I speak in jest, but very much in earnest. In any case this you must do."

Cortés at once saw what Moctezuma had in mind, for it seemed to him that the other did not receive him with the same expression as before, although Moctezuma did observe all the usual ceremony and courtesy. So, before the interpreters had finished explaining Moctezuma's words, he told one of the twelve Spaniards to alert his companions, because this was a matter of life and death. Then our men recalled the warning of the Tlaxcalans and all saw they would need the help of God and a stout heart to get them out of their predicament.

When the interpreters had finished, Cortés said to Moctezuma: "I have understood what you have told me. Consider now when you would have us leave, and so it shall be done." Moctezuma replied: "I do not wish you to go until you wish; take all the time you think necessary, and then I shall give you two loads of gold, and one to each of your men." Cortés said: "My lord, you already know that I sank my ships as soon as we arrived in your country, so we shall need others in which to return to our own. I should like you, therefore, to have your carpenters cut and shape timbers, for I have men who can build ships, and when they are built we shall go, if you give us what you have promised. This you may tell your gods and your vassals." Moctezuma showed great joy at his words and said: "So be it!" Then he had many carpenters summoned, and Cortés provided certain sailors and craftsmen, and all went to some pine woods and there felled many large trees, which they began to shape.

Moctezuma, who could not have been a suspicious man, believed him. Cortés, on the other hand, called the Spaniards he was sending and said to them: "Moctezuma wants us to leave, because his vassals and the devil have persuaded him. Ships must be built. Go with these Indians, in God's name, and cut plenty of timber. Meanwhile, God Our Lord, on whose business we are, will provide men and help us to save this good country for us. It will be necessary, therefore, for you to move as slowly as possible and only pretend to work, to keep the Indians from suspecting evil, and here we shall do what we must. Go now with God and always keep me informed of what you are doing, and of what the Indians are doing and saying."

95. Cortés and His Men Fearful
of Being Sacrificed

A WEEK after the departure of the men to cut timber, fifteen ships arrived off the coast of Chalchiuhcuecan. The Indians on watch there sent word of it to Moctezuma by messengers, who covered the eighty leagues in four days. Moctezuma was frightened and called Cortés, who was no less frightened, for he was always apprehensive of some popular uprising, or of some whim of the king. When Cortés learned that Moctezuma was coming to the courtyard, he thought they would all be lost if Moctezuma found Spaniards there, so he said to them: "Gentlemen and friends, Moctezuma has summoned me, which is not a good sign after what happened the other day. Be on the alert and keep your chin in the feedbag, in case these Indians are up to some-thing. Commend yourself to God, remember who you are and who these infidels are, abhorred of God, friends of the devil, badly armed and unskilled in war. If we must fight, you will prove by deed and sword the strength of your hearts. So even if we die, we shall triumph, for we shall have been true to our calling and to our Christian duty in the service of God; also to our King as Spaniards, to the honor of Spain, and the defense of our lives."

To this they replied: "We shall do our duty till death, and fear and danger will not stop us, for we hold death cheaper than honor." Thereupon Cortés went to Moctezuma, who said: "My lord captain, know that you now have ships in which you can sail away, so you may go whenever you say." Cortés answered: "Most powerful lord, I shall depart as soon as they are finished." "Eleven ships," said Mocte-zuma, "are at Cempoala, and I shall soon know whether their men have landed, who they are, and how many." "All praise to Jesus Christ!" said Cortés, "and I give many thinks to God for the favors He does me and these gentlemen of my company!"

One of the Spaniards ran to inform his companions, who were filled with joy at the news, praising God and embracing each other. While Cortés and Moctezuma were talking, another courier arrived and announced that 80 horsemen, 800 foot, and 12 guns had been landed, and he showed them a painting of it which represented men, horses, guns, and ships. Moctezuma then rose to his feet, embraced

Cortés, and said: "Now I love you more than ever and wish to come and eat with you." Cortés thanked him on both counts, and they clasped hands and went to Cortés' apartment. Cortés told his men to be quiet, but to stay together and on the alert, and to thank God for the news.

Moctezuma and Cortés ate together, to the great relief of everyone; some thinking they would stay and conquer the kingdom and people, and others believing that those who hated the country would be able to leave it. Some say that Moctezuma was grieved at the news, although he concealed his feelings. One of his captains, noting it, advised him to kill the Spaniards of Cortés, who were few, so they would have fewer of the newcomers to kill, and not to allow them to get together. The newcomers [they said] would not dare to penetrate the country if the others were dead. At this Moctezuma summoned to council many of his lords and captains; he explained the situation to them and told them the captain's opinion. There were different votes in the matter, but in the end it was agreed they should allow the new Spaniards to come to Mexico, in the belief that *The more Moors, the greater the spoils;* also, that in this fashion they could kill more Spaniards and all of them at once; that otherwise, if they should kill only those in the city, the rest would go back to their ships and the gods would be deprived of the desired sacrifice.

After this decision, Moctezuma came daily to see Cortés, accompanied by five hundred gentlemen and lords, and ordered the Spaniards to be served and regaled better than ever, since they were soon to die.

96 *Pánfilo de Narváez*
Against Cortés

DIEGO VELÀZQUEZ was very angry with Cortés, not because he had lost money [in the venture], for he had invested little or none, but because he was losing the profit, as well as his honor. As Lieutenant Governor of Cuba, he complained bitterly that Cortés had not kept him informed, but had sent his report directly to the King of Spain (as if that were a wicked piece of treason!). He was furious when he learned that Cortés had sent Francisco de Montejo and Alonso Hernández de Portocarrero to the King and Council [of Castile], with the King's fifth and present, and he dispatched two armed caravels in pursuit of Cortés' ship. (In one of them was Gonzalo de Guzmán, who later became Lieutenant Governor of Cuba, after the death of Velázquez.) Owing, however, to the delay in getting the caravels ready they did not overtake Cortés' ship, or even sight it. The more Velázquez heard of the good fortune and accomplishments of Cortés, the greater became his wrath, until he could do nothing but try to think up ways to ruin and destroy him.

While Velázquez was nursing these thoughts, his chaplain, Benito Martín, came from Santiago, bringing him letters from the Emperor which appointed him Governor of whatever territory he had explored and occupied in Yucatan. This pleased Velázquez exceedingly, for it gave a pretext for expelling Cortés from Mexico and assured him of the King's favor. So he immediately set about readying a fleet, which consisted of eleven naos and six brigantines, and 900 Spaniards and 80 horses, and he appointed Pánfilo de Narváez Captain-General and Lieutenant Governor [of Yucatan]. To speed the departure of the fleet, Velázquez himself journeyed through the island as far as Guaniguanico, its farthest western point. But just as he was about to return to Santiago, and Pánfilo de Narváez to sail for Mexico, the Licenciado Lucas Vázquez de Ayllón arrived from the Audiencia of Santo Domingo, armed with the authority of the Jeronymite Governors and that of the Licenciado Rodrigo de Figueroa, the Audiencia's juez de residencia and visitador, to forbid Diego Velázquez, under heavy penalties, to send [Pánfilo de Narváez], and to forbid the latter to attack Cortés, which [they said] would be the occasion for killings, civil strife, and many other evils among the Spaniards, and Mexico would be lost to the King, along with all that part of the country that had thus far been conquered and pacified.

Ayllón told Velázquez that if he had a grievance against Cortés, and differences with him over goods and points of honor, it was the Emperor's prerogative to take cognizance of the suit and pass judgment, not Velázquez', who could not preside over his own suit and thus do violence to his opponent. He begged them [Velázquez and Narváez], if they really wished to serve God and the King, to seek new lands to conquer, for there were plenty of them unexplored besides those of Cortés, and for this purpose they had good men and a good fleet.

Neither this demand, nor the authority and person of the Licenciado Ayllón, sufficed to make Diego Velázquez and Narváez give up their expedition against Cortés. Ayllón, seeing them so obstinate and so little mindful of the law, decided to go with Narváez in the ship in which he had come from Santo Domingo, thinking to prevent mischief and put a stop to it better in Mexico, in the absence of Diego Velázquez, and to negotiate between Cortés and Narváez, in case they should fall out.

Meanwhile, Pánfilo embarked at Guaniguanico and anchored his fleet off Vera Cruz. Learning that one hundred and fifty of Cortés' men were there, he sent ashore Juan Ruiz de Guevara, Alonso de Vergara, and a priest, to demand their recognition of his authority as Captain [-General] and Governor. They refused to listen; rather, they seized the three and sent them to Cortés in Mexico for his information. Narváez thereupon landed his men, horses, guns, and arms, and went to Cempoala, where the Indian friends of Cortés, as well as the vassals of Moctezuma, gave him gold, mantles, and provisions, thinking he was one of Cortés' men.

97. Cortés Writes to Narváez

THIS NEW AND GREAT FLEET agitated Cortés more than anyone can believe, that is, before he knew whose it was. On the one hand he was glad that more Spaniards were on the way; on the other he wished they were not so many. If they were coming to his aid, he considered the country won; if against him, lost. If they were from Spain, he thought they would bring good news; if from Cuba, he feared civil war. He thought it unlikely that so many men could come from Spain, and suspected that they were from the island and that Diego Velázquez was with them. After he learned the truth, he had twice as much to worry about as before, because they would snip the thread of his prosperity and cancel the progress he had made in ferreting out the secrets of the country: its mines, its wealth, its forces, and who were friends or enemies of Moctezuma. They would interrupt the settlements that he had begun, the winning of friends, and the conversion of the Indians, which was and should be his principal aim, as well as many other things that concerned the service of God and King, and the profit of our nation.

He was afraid that if he circumvented one difficulty, many others would follow. If he should allow Pánfilo de Narváez, captain of Diego Velázquez' fleet, to reach Mexico, ruin was certain; if he should attack him, he feared the city would rebel and Moctezuma would be freed, and he would risk losing his life, his honor, and his work. The first thing he did was to dispatch two messengers: one to Juan Velázquez de León, whom he had sent to found a settlement in Coatzacoalcos, to inform him of Narváez' arrival and to order him back to Mexico forthwith with his hundred and fifty men. The other he sent to Vera Cruz, to gather full and accurate intelligence of Narváez: what Narváez was after and what he was saying. Juan Velázquez did what Cortés requested, and did not do what Narváez had begged him to do as brother-in-law and kinsman of Diego Velázquez, that is, to come over to his side—an action for which Cortés greatly honored him thereafter.

Twenty Spaniards came from Vera Cruz to Mexico, with word of what Narváez was proclaiming, bringing as prisoners Alonso de Vergara, Juan Ruiz de Guevara, and the priest, who had gone to Vera Cruz to stir up a mutiny among the men of Cortés, pretending they had a decree of the King authorizing them. Next, Cortés sent Fray Bartolomé de Olmedo, a Mercedarian, with two other Spaniards, to offer Narváez his friendship, failing which, to demand of Narváez in the name of the King and of Cortés, as Justicia Mayor of the country, and in the names of the alcaldes and regidores of Vera Cruz, who were in Mexico, that he should enter quietly (that is, if he carried orders of the King or the Council), without doing harm to the country or stirring up a tumult or causing mischief or disturbing the good fortune that the Spaniards were enjoying, or the conversion of the Indians. On the other hand [they were to tell Narváez] that if he did not carry such orders, to leave the country in peace and go back [to Cuba].

This demand, however, Cortés' letters, and those of the council of Vera Cruz were of little avail. Cortés freed the priest whom the men of Vera Cruz had brought, and sent him to Narváez with several very rich gold necklaces and other jewels, and with a letter which said, in short, how pleased Cortés was that Narváez, rather than another [Velázquez], had come with the fleet, because of their ancient friendship; that, if Narváez so wished, they would meet in order to prevent fighting, killing, and disputes among Spaniards and brothers; that, if Narváez did carry orders from the King and would show them to him or to the council of Vera Cruz, they would be obeyed, as was proper; but that if, on the other hand, Narváez carried no such orders, then they might come to some mutually satisfactory agreement. But Narváez, being in such strength, paid no attention to the letters, offers, and demands, because Diego Velázquez was very angry with Cortés.

98. Narváez Replies

PÁNFILO DE NARVÁEZ told the Indians [of Cempoala] that they had been deceived by Cortés, because he, Narváez, was captain and lord of the Spaniards, and not Cortés, who was a scoundrel, as were the servants he had with him in Mexico, and that Narváez had come to chop off his head and drive the others out of the country, after which he would go away himself and leave it free. The Indians, either fickle or frightened, seeing Narváez with his bearded men and his horses, believed him and entered his service, abandoning that of Cortés. Narváez also ingratiated himself with Moctezuma by telling him that Cortés was there against the wishes of the King, that Cortés was a greedy bandit who was stealing his gold and would kill him and seize his kingdom; that, in order to prevent it, Narváez would set him free and restore to him everything those wicked men had taken, and would seize or kill them, or put them in prison. Therefore [he said] Moctezuma should be of good cheer, for they would soon see each other and he would do nothing but restore Moctezuma's kingdom to him and leave the country.

So evil and ugly were these treacheries, and so insulting were the words that Pánfilo said publicly of Cortés and the Spaniards of his company, that the men of his own army did not like them, and many could not hear them in silence, but denounced them, especially

Bernaldino de Santa Clara who, seeing the country so peaceful and happy under Cortés, gave Narváez a good piece of his mind. The Licenciado Ayllón enjoined him repeatedly, on pain of death and confiscation of his goods, to refrain from such speeches and not to go to Mexico, which would give great offense to the Indians, cause unrest among the Spaniards, be a disservice to the Emperor, and an interruption of the evangelization of the Indians. This angered Narváez, and he arrested Ayllón (who was the King's justice, secretary of the Audiencia, and constable), put him on board a ship, and sent him to Diego Velázquez. But Ayllón was too clever for him and, either by bribing the sailors or threatening them with the King's justice, had them return him to his chancellery. There he related to his associates and the governors the troubles he had had with Narváez, which did no little harm to the affairs of Diego Velázquez and improved those of Cortés.

As soon as Narváez had arrested Ayllón, he declared war to the knife (as the saying goes) against Cortés, promising several gold marks to the one who should capture or kill him, Pedro de Alvarado, Gonzalo de Sandoval, and certain other important personages of Cortés' company, while he distributed money and clothing to his own men (which he extracted from the property of others)—which three acts were exceedingly frivolous and boastful. Many of Narváez' men mutinied by command of the Licenciado Ayllón—or perhaps they did so because of Cortés' reputation for wealth and liberality—and Pedro de Villalobos and a Portuguese, with six or seven others, passed over to Cortés; and still others wrote to him, it is said, offering him their persons if he would come for them. It is also said that Cortés read the letters to his men, without revealing the signatures or names of the writers, in which they reported [that Narváez] had called [Cortés' men] traitors and bandits, and threatened them with death and confiscation of goods.

Some say that the [Narváez] men mutinied; others, that Cortés suborned them with letters, gifts, and a load of necklaces and gold ingots which he sent secretly by one of his men to the camp of Pánfilo de Narváez, while he let it be known that he had two hundred Spaniards in Cempoala. This may all be true, for the one was as tepid and careless in his actions as the other was careful and cunning in his. Narváez sent Cortés a reply by the Mercedarian friar, the substance of which was that Cortés should come to Narváez at once, for Narváez wished to show him the Emperor's decrees directing Narváez to take over and hold the country for Diego Velázquez, and that he had already founded a villa of men only, with its alcaldes and regidores. After sending this letter, he dispatched Bernaldino de Quesada and Alonso de Mata to warn Cortés, on pain of death, to leave the country, and to notify [Cortés] of the Emperor's decrees. They, however, did not do so, either because they did not have the decrees with them (and it would have been very foolish to entrust them to anyone) or because they were not given the opportunity, for Cortés had Alonso de Mata arrested for calling himself a royal notary, which he was not, or at least he did not show his title.

99. Cortés Addresses His Men

WHEN CORTÉS saw that his letters and messages were fruitless, although they were passing back and forth daily, and that the King's decrees had never been seen or displayed, he determined to confront Narváez in person, for, as the saying has it, *Chin to chin, honor is respected,* and to pursue the matter by fair means, if possible. For this purpose he sent the Veedor Rodrigo de Albornoz Chico, Juan Velázquez, and Juan del Río with several proposals for Narváez, the most important being: that Cortés and Narváez meet alone, or with equal numbers on both sides; that Narváez allow Cortés to remain in Mexico, while taking his own men and certain noble persons of his company to the conquest of Pánuco, which was at peace, or to some other kingdom, at Cortés' expense and maintenance; or, conversely, that Narváez remain in Mexico and give Cortés four hundred men from his fleet, whom Cortés would add to his force and take on some expedition. The last proposal of Cortés was that Narváez exhibit the King's decrees, which he would obey.

Narváez accepted none of these proposals, save only that they meet, in the company of ten gentlemen on either side, under safe-conduct and oath. Both signed the agreement, but the meeting did not take place, because Rodrigo de Albornoz Chico warned Cortés of Narváez' plot to seize or kill him during the interview. So, while

Cortés was busy with the negotiations, he was made aware of the other's tricks and fraud, or, perhaps, he was told of them by someone who did not hate him.

The negotiations having come to nothing, Cortés decided to go to Narváez, saying to himself: "Something will turn up." But before he went, he spoke to his Spaniards, reminding them of what he had done for them, and they for him. He told them that Diego Velázquez, instead of thanking them for what they had done in the service of God and the Emperor, had sent a rough and stubborn character, Pánfilo de Narváez, to destroy and kill them for going to the aid of the King like good vassals, and for not supporting Narváez, to whom they owed nothing; that Narváez had confiscated their property and given it to others; that he had condemned their bodies to the gallows and their good names to public shame—all this with insults and jeers directed at all of them—things certainly not worthy of a Christian which they, being what they were, would not overlook or let pass without meet punishment. It seemed to Cortés that, although they should leave [punishment] to God, who repays the proud and envious, yet they should not allow others to reap the profits of their sweat and labor, these others who with their hands washed came to suck the blood of their fellows, and who shamelessly raised up friendly Indians against them, and plotted wars worse than the civil wars of Marius and Sulla, or those of Caesar and Pompey, which had disrupted the Roman Empire. So he had decided to go out to meet Narváez on the road and prevent his reaching Mexico, because *A Take-that is better than a Who-is-it-please,* and *It's better to have God on your side than to get up early in the morning* and *A strong heart breaks bad luck,* as had been tested in the crucible during the days [his men] had fought at his side. Moreover, there were many among the men of Narváez who would join them. And this was why he was telling them what he planned to do, so that those who wished to go with him might make their preparations, and those who did not were quite welcome to stay behind and guard Moctezuma and Mexico, for the one thing was as important as the other. He also promised them many gifts if he should return victorious.

His men answered that they would obey his commands, for in truth he had stirred them to great anger with his speech, besides which they feared the pride and blindness of Pánfilo de Narváez, while on the other hand they feared the Indians [of Mexico] who were emboldened by the dissension among the Spaniards and by the action of the coast Indians in joining the newcomers.

100. Cortés Makes a Request of Moctezuma

WHEN CORTÉS found his men to be friendly and in agreement with him, he spoke to Moctezuma so that he might leave with a freer mind; and, to discover what Moctezuma was thinking, he addressed him in some such terms as these:

"My Lord, you are aware of the love I bear you and of my desire to serve you, and of our hope that when we leave you will bestow great favors upon me and my companions. Now I pray you to grant me the great favor of remaining here and of looking after these Spaniards I am leaving with you and entrusting to you, together with the gold and jewels you gave us. I am about to see those who have recently arrived in the ships, and shall tell them I am doing so at your Highness's command; that it is also your command that they do no harm or mischief to your subjects and vassals, and that they are not to enter your lands, but remain on the coast until we are ready to embark and sail away. If, while I am gone, some subject of yours, ill-mannered, or foolish, or brazen, should harm the men that are under your protection, you will tell him to desist."

Moctezuma promised to do so, and told Cortés that if those other Spaniards should prove to be wicked and refuse to obey Cortés, Cortés should inform him of it and he would send warriors to punish them and drive them out of the country; also, if Cortés so desired, he would give him guides who would lead him to the sea always through the lands of Moctezuma, with orders to serve and supply him on the way. Cortés thanked him warmly and gave him a Castilian robe, gave his children some jewels, and many articles of merchandise to the lords who were present at the conversation.

Moctezuma, however, failed to keep his word, either because he had not yet heard from Narváez or because he slyly concealed his feelings, rejoicing to have the Spaniards kill each other, and thinking in this fashion to recover his freedom more surely and placate his gods.

101. Capture of Narváez

CORTÉS WAS SO WELL LOVED by those Spaniards of his that all of them volunteered to go with him, so he was able to choose the ones he wished to take, who numbered two hundred and fifty, including those of Juan Velázquez de León, whom he met on the way. He left the rest, about two hundred, as a guard for Moctezuma and the city, and appointed Pedro de Alvarado their captain. He gave them his guns and the four brigantines he had built to command the lake, and begged them to attend solely to Moctezuma, to keep him from going over to Narváez and from leaving their camp and fort.

Then he departed, with his small force of Spaniards and his eight or nine horses, and with many Indians for their service. At Cholula and Tlaxcala he was well received and lodged. Fifteen leagues, or a little less, before he reached Cempoala, where Narváez was, he met two clerics and Andrés de Duero, his friend and acquaintance, to whom he owed the money he had borrowed for outfitting the fleet. Their mission was to tell him to obey General and Lieutenant Governor Pánfilo de Narváez and surrender the country and his forces; otherwise, Narváez would consider him an enemy and a rebel, and would fight him to the death. If, on the other hand, Cortés would submit, Narváez would give him ships and would let him go freely and safely with all the men he might wish to take along. Cortés replied that he would rather die than abandon the country he had taken and pacified by his own diligence and effort, unless he was ordered to do so by the Emperor; that, if Narváez wished to make war upon him wrongfully, Cortés would know how to defend himself and, if he should win, as he trusted in God he would, he would have no need of the ships; if he died, still less. Therefore, he said, let Narváez show him the royal orders and instructions, for otherwise he would accept no compromise whatever. Since, however, the orders had not been displayed, he took it as evidence that they did not exist.

Such being the case, Cortés begged, ordered, and demanded that Narváez go with God back to Cuba, for otherwise he would seize him and send him in irons to Spain and the Emperor, who would punish him as his rebellion deserved. With this he dismissed Andrés de Duero and sent along with him a notary and many others with his written authority and orders, to demand of Narváez that he go back to his ships and cease his stirring up of the men and the country (which was rapidly preparing to rise) before he caused more deaths and evils; otherwise, Cortés would be with him by Whitsunday, that is, in three days.

Pánfilo mocked at Cortés' order, arrested the man who carried the written authority, and jeered loudly at Cortés with his few men and his fierce threats. He then paraded his forces before Juan Velázquez de León, Juan del Río, and the other Cortés men who had taken part in the negotiations. He counted 80 arquebusiers, 130 crossbowmen, 600 foot, and 80 horse, and said: "How can you defend yourselves if you refuse to do as we wish?" He promised money for the capture of Cortés dead or alive, and Cortés did the same for Pánfilo. Narváez had his infantry maneuver, his horse skirmish, and fired his guns to intimidate the Indians. Moctezuma's governor, frightened by the firing, gave Narváez a present of mantles and gold in the name of his master, and cordially offered Narváez his services. It is said that Narváez, utilizing the Indians who were taking the painting of the review to Moctezuma, sent a fresh message to Moctezuma and the gentlemen of Mexico.

On Whitsunday, hearing that Cortés was in the vicinity, Narváez set out with his eighty horse and six hundred foot to reconnoiter the country, and approached within a league of where Cortés was. Not encountering him, he thought that his spies had lied to him, and he returned to his camp and slept. As a precaution, he posted Gonzalo de Carrasco and Alonso Hurtado as sentries on the road, about a league from Cempoala.

That same feast day Cortés marched more than eighteen leagues, with great hardship to his men. Shortly before arriving [at Narváez' camp], he gave Gonzalo de Sandoval, his chief constable, a written order to arrest Narváez and the alcaldes and regidores, or to kill them if they resisted, and he gave him eighty Spaniards of the company to help him carry it out. Cortés' scouts, who were always a good piece in advance, came upon Narváez' sentries and seized Gonzalo de Carrasco, who revealed the layout of Narváez' camp, men, and guns. Alonso Hurtado escaped and ran as fast as he could to Narváez' quarters, shouting: "To arms! To arms! Cortés is coming!" At the noise the sleepers woke up, but many of them did not believe it. Cortés left his horses in a wood, where he cut pikes and cudgels for the men who were without arms, and led his force into the city [of Cempoala] and the enemy's camp at midnight, having chosen this hour so that he could approach unseen and take the enemy by surprise.

Cortés' advance, however, was not so speedy that it was not announced by the sentry [Hurtado], who had arrived half an hour before, and all the horses had been saddled, some bridled, and the men armed. Cortés entered so silently, however, that he was not perceived, and he shouted "Attack!" while the enemy was sounding the alarm. There were many fireflies about which looked [to the enemy] like the burning matches of arquebuses, and if a single shot had been fired they would have fled. They said to Narváez, who was donning his coat of mail: "Look, sir, Cortés is coming!" "Let him come," he replied; "he is coming to see me." Narváez had stationed his men in four small towers and in their halls and rooms, and he with some hundred Spaniards was in one of them. He had posted at the gate thirteen guns, or, as some say, seventeen, all of brass. Cortés had Gonzalo de Sandoval mount the tower with forty or fifty companions, while he held the gate with twenty others. The rest of the men surrounded the towers to prevent communication between them.

Narváez heard the commotion and, although he was warned and begged to surrender, showed fight, but, as he was leaving the room, he received a pike thrust which cost him an eye. He was then seized and dragged down the steps. When he saw himself in the presence of Cortés he said "Congratulations, my lord Cortés, for capturing me!" To which Cortés replied: "The least deed I have done in this land was to take you!" Whereupon he had the other put in irons and taken to Vera Cruz, where he kept him prisoner for several years. The fight had been very short; within the hour Pánfilo and the chief men of his army were prisoners and the rest had been disarmed. Seventeen of Narváez' men had died, and only two of the Cortés men, killed by a cannon shot. The enemy had neither the time nor the room in which to work their guns, so hustled were they by Cortés, and were able to fire only one, which killed the two men. They had plugged the touchholes with wax to keep out the heavy rain—which gave the vanquished the opportunity to say that Cortés had suborned the gunner and others.

Cortés behaved very mildly on this occasion. He did not heap abuse upon the prisoners and the defeated, or even upon Narváez, who had said a deal of evil about him, although many of the Cortés men would have liked to avenge themselves upon the others. Cortés even allowed Pedro de Malvenda, the major-domo of Narváez and servant of Diego Velázquez, to keep the ships, clothing, and goods of both.

What advantage has one man over another? What had each of these two captains done, said, or thought? Seldom, perhaps never, had so few vanquished so many of their own people, especially since the larger party was fortified, rested, and well armed.

102. Smallpox

THIS WAR cost Diego Velázquez a great deal of money, Pánfilo de Narváez his eye, and the Indians many dead, who died, not of wounds, but of disease. It happened that among the men of Narváez was a Negro sick with the smallpox, and he infected the household in Cempoala where he was quartered; and it spread from one Indian to another, and they, being so numerous and eating and sleeping together, quickly infected the whole country. In most houses all the occupants died, for, since it was their custom to bathe as a cure for all diseases, they bathed for the smallpox and were struck down. They had the custom, or vice, of taking cold baths after hot ones, so a man sick with the smallpox only escaped by a miracle. Those who did survive, having scratched themselves, were left in such a condition that they frightened the others with the many deep pits on their faces, hands, and bodies. And then came famine, not because of a want of bread, but of meal, for the women do nothing but grind maize between two stones and bake it. The women, then, fell sick of the smallpox, bread failed, and many died of hunger. The corpses stank so horribly that no one would bury them; the streets were filled with them; and it is even said that the officials, in order to remedy this situation, pulled the houses down to cover the corpses. The Indians called this sickness *huitzahuatl*, meaning the "great leprosy," and later counted the years from it, as from some famous event. It seems to me that this is how they were repaid for the *bubas* [syphilis] which they gave our men, as I have related elsewhere.

103. Rebellion in Mexico

CORTÉS KNEW ALMOST ALL the men who had come with Narváez. He spoke courteously to them and begged them to forget the past, as he had done, and come with him to Mexico, the richest of Indian towns. He restored their arms, which many had lost, and kept very few as prisoners with Narváez. The cavalry had sallied forth with a mind to fight, but soon surrendered because of what Cortés said and promised them. In short, all of them, who had only come to enjoy possession of the land, were glad to surrender to him and enter his service. Cortés reconstituted the garrison of Vera Cruz and sent the ships of [Narváez'] fleet there. He dispatched two hundred Spaniards to the Río de Garay [the Pánuco], and again sent Juan Velázquez de León to found a settlement at Coatzacoalcos.

Sending on ahead a Spaniard with news of the victory, Cortés at once set out for Mexico, not easy in his mind about the men he had left there because of the messengers Narváez had sent to Moctezuma. The Spaniard who bore the news [of the victory], instead of being rewarded for it, received wounds at the hands of the rebellious Indians. Even though wounded, he made his way back to Cortés to tell him that the people of Mexico had risen in arms, burned the four brigantines, attacked the fort of the Spaniards, knocked down one wall and mined another, fired the munitions, cut off the food supply, and had attacked in such numbers that they would have killed or captured the Spaniards if Moctezuma had not ordered them to cease. Even so, they destroyed the arms and the enclosure, and only slackened [their attack] to please their lord.

This was very sad news for Cortés, turned his pleasure into worry, and made him quicken his pace in order to come to the aid of his friends and companions. Indeed, if he had arrived a little later, he would not have found them alive, but dead or destined for sacrifice. What gave him the greatest hope of their and his survival was that Moctezuma had not fled. He mustered his troops at Tlaxcala and found that he now had one thousand foot and one hundred horse, for he had recalled those he had sent off to make settlements. He did not pause until he reached Texcoco, where he did not see the gentlemen he knew, nor was he received as before; rather, he found the country either deserted or turbulent. While he was at Texcoco a Spaniard came to him sent by Alvarado, to summon him and recount what has been said above, and to urge him to come at once in order to stop the tumult. Along with [Alvarado's] man came an Indian from Moctezuma, who told Cortés that Moctezuma was not to blame for what had happened, and that if Cortés was offended with him he should get over it and go to his old quarters, where Moctezuma and the Spaniards were, safe and sound, and as Cortés had left them.

Cortés and the Spaniards rested [at Texcoco] that night, and the next day, the feast of St. John the Baptist [June 24, 1520], he was in Mexico by dinnertime, with his one hundred horse and one thousand foot, and a multitude of friends from Tlaxcala, Huejotzingo, and Cholula. He saw few people in the streets, none at all to receive him, some broken bridges, and other dismal signs. He went to his quarters, and the men who could not be accommodated there were lodged in the great temple.

Moctezuma came out to receive him, apparently grieved at what his people had done. He made his excuses, and each retired to his own chamber. Pedro de Alvarado and his men were beside themselves with joy at the arrival of Cortés with so many others, for they had almost given themselves up as lost. Greetings were exchanged, and the good news related by the one group was matched by the bad news of the other.

104. Causes of the Uprising

CORTÉS WANTED to get at the root of the rebellion of the Mexicans. He interrogated all the Spaniards together, and some said it was caused by the message sent by Narváez; others, by the desire of the people to drive them out of Mexico, as had been planned, as soon as there were ships in which to sail, for during the fighting they kept shouting "Get out!" Others said it was to liberate Moctezuma, because the Indians said "Free our god and king if you wish to live!" Still others said it was because the Indians wanted to steal the gold, silver, and jewels of the Spaniards, for they heard the Indians say: "Here you shall leave the gold you took from us!" Again, some said it was to keep the Tlaxcalans and other mortal enemies out of Mexico. Many, finally, believed it was because the images of the gods had been cast down and [the Indians] wished to give themselves to the devil.

Any one of these things could have caused the rebellion, let alone all of them together; but the principal one was this: A few days after Cortés had left to encounter Narváez, there was a solemn festival, which the Mexicans wished to celebrate in their traditional fashion. They begged Pedro de Alvarado (who had stayed behind to act as warden and Cortés' lieutenant) to give his permission, so that he would not think they were gathering to massacre the Spaniards. Alvarado consented, with the proviso that they were not to kill men in sacrifice or bear arms. More than six hundred (some say more than a thousand) gentlemen, and even several lords, assembled in the yard of the main temple, where that night they made a great hubbub with their drums, conches, trumpets, and bone fifes, which emit a loud whistle. They were naked, but covered with precious stones, pearls, necklaces, belts, bracelets, jewels of gold, silver, and mother-of-pearl, wearing many rich plumes on their heads. They performed the dance called *macehualixtli,* which means "reward through work" (from *macehaulli,* a farmer).

This dance is like the *netotelixtli* that I have described, in which they spread mats in the temple yard and placed drums upon them. They danced in rings, grasping hands, to the music of the singers, to which they responded. The songs were sacred, not profane, and were sung to praise the god whose feast was being celebrated, to induce him to give them water or grain, health or victory, or to thank him for giving them peace, children, health, and the like. Those who knew the language and these ceremonial rites said that, when the people danced in the temple [on this occasion], they performed very differently from those who danced the *netotelixtli,* in voice, movement of the body, head, arms, and feet, by which they manifest their concepts of good and evil. The Spaniards called this dance an *areyto,* a word they brought from the islands of Cuba and Santo Domingo.

While the Mexican gentlemen were dancing in the temple yard of Huitzilopochtli, Pedro de Alvarado went there, whether of his own notion or following the decision of the rest, I cannot say. Some say he had been warned that the Indian nobles of the city had assembled to plot the mutiny and rebellion which they later carried out; others, that [the Spaniards] went to see them perform this much-praised and famous dance, and, seeing them so rich, they coveted the gold the Indians were wearing, so he [Alvarado] blocked the entrances with ten or twelve Spaniards at each one, himself went in with more than fifty, and cruelly and pitilessly stabbed and killed the Indians, and took what they were wearing. Cortés, who must have felt badly about the affair, dissembled his feelings so as not to irritate the perpetrators, for it happened at a time when he had need of them, either against the Indians, or to put down trouble among his own men.

105. The Mexicans Threaten the Spaniards

AFTER HE HAD LEARNED the causes of the rebellion, Cortés inquired how the enemy had fought. [The Spaniards] replied that as soon as the Indians had risen in arms they attacked with great fury, and fought and besieged the house for ten days without interruption, and did the damage he already knew about. In order not to afford Moctezuma the opportunity of escaping and joining Narváez, as some said [he intended to do], the Spaniards had not dared to leave the house and fight in the streets, but were able only to defend themselves and guard Moctezuma, as Cortés had ordered. Since they were few and the Indians many, and brought in replacements at every moment, the Spaniards not only got tired, but were fainting, and, if Moctezuma had not gone up to the roof at the first alarm and commanded his people to be quiet if they wanted him to live, the Spaniards would all have been dead by this time. They said also that when the news arrived of the victory over Pánfilo de Narváez, Moctezuma commanded the Indians to slacken their attack and stop fighting—not, as rumor had it, out of fear, but so that they might kill all the Spaniards together when Narváez arrived. They changed their minds, however, when they learned that Cortés had brought so many Spaniards and that they would have a great deal more work to do, so they renewed their attack and siege, with greater enthusiasm and daring, from which some gathered that the attack was not made with Moctezuma's consent.

The Spaniards also told of many miracles: that when their water supply failed they dug a hole knee-deep in the courtyard, or a little deeper, and fresh water flowed from it, although the ground was saline; that the Indians had made many attempts to remove the image of our Most Glorious Lady from the altar where Cortés had placed it, but that, whenever they touched it their hands stuck to it and could not be freed for a considerable time, and that when they did get their hands loose the mark remained upon them, so they let the image stand; that on one of the days of the fiercest fighting they loaded their biggest gun, and when they touched a match to it to frighten off the enemy, it would not fire, seeing which, the Indians attacked boldly, yelling horribly, shooting so many darts, arrows, lances, and stones that the house tnd street were covered with them, while the Indians yelled: "Now we shall redeem our king, free our house, and have our revenge!" But in the thickest of the fight the gun went off with a frightful roar, although it had not been newly primed or fired, and, since it was loaded with grape as well as ball, it spat fiercely, killed many, and frightened all. [It was believed] that St. Mary and St. James (he on a white horse) fought for the Spaniards, and the Indians said that the horse wounded and killed as many with its teeth and hooves as the knight [St. James] killed with his sword; that the woman on the altar cast dust in their faces and blinded them, and they, believing themselves blind and not being able to fight, went home, and there were healed; so when they again attacked they said: "If we had not been frightened by the woman and the man on the white horse, your house by this time would be destroyed and you yourselves would be cooked, but not eaten, for you are not fit to eat; we tried your flesh the other day and it tasted bitter, so we shall throw you to the eagles, lions, tigers, and snakes,

which will eat you for us. Nevertheless, if you do not free Moctezuma and leave at once, you will soon be properly killed, cooked with
mole, and eaten by the beasts, since you are not fit for a human
stomach. This we shall do because you dared to seize our Moctezuma
and touch him with your filthy hands—Moctezuma who is our lord
and the god who nourishes us. Why does the earth not swallow you
up, you who steal the goods of others? Let us get on with it, then,
for our gods, whose religion you have defiled, will give you your deserts! And if they do not do so quickly, we ourselves shall kill you
and strip you, as well as those sons of good-for-nothings and cowards of Tlaxcala, your slaves, who shall also have their punishment
for boasting that they will take the wives of their lords and exact
tribute of those to whom they once paid taxes."

Such were the arrogant threats of the Mexicans, and our men, who
were befouling themselves from pure fear, chided them for the utter
nonsense they were saying about Moctezuma and told them that he
was a mortal man, no better than they; that their gods were vain and
their religion false, while ours was true and good, our God just, the
real Creator of all things; that the woman who fought was the
Mother of Christ, God of the Christians; that the man on the white
horse was an Apostle of that same Christ, who had descended from
Heaven to defend that handful of Spaniards and to kill so many
Indians.

106. The Spaniards in Difficulties

CORTÉS SPENT the whole night listening to the above and inspecting
the house, while he made the necessary arrangements [for its de-
fense]. The next morning, to find out how the Indians felt about
his return, he told them to bring out all their merchandise and hold
their regular market, and to be calm. Alvarado, whose conscience
was bothering him, told Cortés to pretend to be angry with him, and
threaten to arrest and punish him for what he had done, thinking
that Moctezuma and the people would be placated, and might even
plead for him.

Cortés ignored the request; on the contrary, some say that he was very angry and called the Indians a lot of dogs, saying there was no point in treating them gently. Then he ordered a noble Mexican gentleman who was present to see that the market was held, regardless. The Mexican understood that they were being insulted and treated little better than animals, and left [presumably] to carry out Cortés orders. What he actually did, however, was to go to the market place and demand their liberty, while he repeated the insults he had heard. In a short while the whole place was in a tumult: some broke the bridges, others called out the citizenry, and all of them together fell upon the Spaniards, surrounded the house, and raised such a hullabaloo that our men could not hear each other talk. The Indians threw so many stones that it seemed to be hailing, and shot so many arrows and darts that the walls and the yard were filled with them and rendered impassable.

Cortés sallied forth on one side and another captain on the other, each with two hundred Spaniards. The Indians attacked them furiously, killing four and wounding many, while losing few of their own, for they took shelter in the houses near by, or behind the bridges and walls. If our men attacked in the streets, the Indians promptly cut the bridges; if they attacked the houses, they were badly hurt by the blocks and stones hurled from the rooftops; if they retreated, they were closely pursued. Their own house was fired in many places; a good part of it was burned, and the fire could not be put out until rooms and walls were pulled down upon it. The Indians could have entered openly through the breach if it had not been for the guns, crossbowmen, and arquebusiers posted there. The fight lasted all that day until nightfall, and even then the Indians did not cease their shouting and attacks. Our men got little sleep that night, but spent it repairing the breaches in the burned and wrecked parts of the house, attending the wounded, who numbered more than eighty, putting the rooms in order, and organizing a defense against the next day's fighting, if it should be necessary.

At daybreak, the Indians attacked more violently and in greater force; so close-packed were they, indeed, that the gunners fired their pieces without aiming. Crossbows, arquebuses, and falconets, fired without interruption, made no impression. A shot would fell ten, fifteen, or even twenty Indians, but the gaps were immediately filled and the Indians seemed to have suffered no damage whatever. Cortés sallied forth with the same number of men as on the first day; he took a few bridges, burned a few houses, and killed many of their defenders; but the Indians were so many that the damage was not seen or felt; and our men were so few and so exhausted with fighting at all hours of the day that they could not defend themselves, much less attack. No Spaniard was killed, but sixty were wounded by stones and arrows, so they had plenty of hurts to attend to that night. Then, in order to protect themselves from damage from the house-tops, the Spaniards built three wooden engines, square, covered, and fitted with wheels for ease in manipulation. Each carried twenty men armed with pikes, arquebuses, crossbows, and a gun. They were to be followed by sappers to demolish houses and walls, and to help move the engine.

107. Death of Moctezuma

WHILE THEY WERE BUILDING the engines, our men did not go out to fight, being busy with their work, and only defended themselves. The enemy, believing that all our men were badly wounded, attacked with all their strength, shouting insults and defiance, and threatening that, if we did not release Moctezuma, we should suffer the cruelest death that ever man suffered. They attacked so vigorously and stub-bornly that Cortés begged Moctezuma to go up to the roof and com-mand his men to cease fighting and go away; so he mounted upon a battlement to speak to them, but no sooner had he begun than so many stones were thrown from below and from the houses opposite that one of them struck him upon the temple and knocked him down. So Moctezuma was killed by his own vassals, who would rather have torn out their eyes than have done so. They did not see him, however, because a Spaniard covered him with a shield to protect his face from the many stones that were being thrown; nor did the Indians believe that he was there, regardless of the signs and shouts of the Spaniards.

Cortés at once told the Indians of Moctezuma's injury and the danger he was in. Some believed him, others not, and all continued to fight stubbornly. Moctezuma lived for three days in great pain, and then died. To prove to the Indians that Moctezuma had died of the blow they had given him, Cortés had him carried out by two Mexican gentlemen, prisoners, who told the truth of the matter to the attackers. Even so, these did not then abandon the combat or the war, as many of our men thought [they would]; on the contrary, they fought more fiercely and with no respect [for the dead]. Weeping bitterly, they withdrew to bury their king at Chapultepec.

So died Moctezumatzin, whom the Indians held to be a god, and who indeed was a very great king, as we have said. It was said that during Lent he had asked to be baptized, but it was put off because it could be done better at Easter, with the solemnity befitting such an exalted Sacrament and such a powerful prince, although it would have been better not to have postponed it. Meanwhile, with the coming of Pánfilo de Narváez, it could not be done, and, after Moctezuma was wounded, it was forgotten in the heat of the battle. It is said of Moctezuma that, although urged many times, he never consented to the killing of a Spaniard or harm to Cortés, whom he loved very much. Others maintain the contrary. Both sides advance good arguments; nevertheless, our Spaniards were never able to learn the truth, because at the time they did not understand the language, and afterward no one was found alive with whom Moctezuma had shared the secret. One thing I can say is that he never spoke ill of the Spaniards, to the great vexation and annoyance of his own people.

The Indians say that he was the best of his line and the greatest king of Mexico. It is a remarkable thing that, when kingdoms are most flourishing and at their height, then it is that they fall into ruin or suffer a change of masters, as we have witnessed with Moctezuma and Atahualpa. Our people lost more by the death of Moctezuma than did the Indians, if you will consider the death and destruction suffered by the former, and the ease and contentment enjoyed by the latter, for now, Moctezuma being dead, they stayed home and elected a new king.

Moctezuma was fond of food, but was not lecherous like the other Indians, although he had many wives. He was generous and openhanded with the Spaniards and, I believe, with his own people. Otherwise, if he had been so merely from policy, and not from nature, it could easily have been detected in his expression, for those who give unwillingly reveal what is in their hearts. It is said that he was wise. In my opinion he was either very wise in disregarding the things [that he had to put up with], or very foolish, in not resenting them. He was as warlike as he was religious, and took part in many wars in person. They say he won nine battles and nine single combats, one by one. He reigned seventeen years and some months.

108. War

AFTER THE DEATH of Moctezuma, Cortés sent word to Moctezuma's nephews and the lords and captains who were carrying on the war, that he wished to speak with them. They came, and Cortés, addressing them from the same rooftop where Moctezuma had met his death, told them that, now Moctezuma was dead, they should put away their arms and busy themselves in the election of a new king, and in the funeral of the old one, which Cortés wished to attend as a friend; that they must know that it was only at the request of Moctezuma he had not destroyed and laid waste their city for its rebelliousness and obstinacy; that, since they no longer had anyone to respect, they should stop fighting and become his friends; otherwise, he would burn their houses and punish them.

They replied that they would not lay down their arms until they were free and avenged; that without his advice they could choose their rightful king, now that the gods had taken their beloved Moctezuma; that, if Cortés wished to dwell with the gods and keep his friend company, he had only to appear and they would kill him; that, if he intended to remain in the city, they preferred war with him to peace; that, if he did not like it, he had two evils to face, for they were not like others, who surrendered at words; and that, now their lord was dead, out of reverence for whom Cortés had not burned their houses, or roasted and eaten *them,* they would kill Cortés if he did not leave. Let him go at once, and afterward they could talk about friendship.

Finding them obdurate, Cortés saw that his game was going badly and that the enemy wanted him to go so that they could catch him between bridges. He still pleaded with them, as much because of the harm he was receiving as for the harm he was doing. But now, seeing that his life and authority depended upon his fists and a stout heart, he sallied forth one morning with the three engines, four guns, more than five hundred Spaniards, and three thousand Tlaxcalans, to attack the enemy and knock down and burn their houses. The engines were drawn up against several large houses near a bridge, and the Spaniards put up ladders so they could climb to the roofs, which were covered with men, and there began to fight. They soon, however, had to retreat to their fort, without having damaged their adversaries at all, with one man dead and many wounded, and the engines broken. At the noise, such a multitude of Indians came charging, and pressed our men so closely, that they did not give them room or time to fire the guns; and the Indians threw so many and such large stones from the roof that they put the engines and the engineers out of action, and soon obliged them to retreat hastily.

Now that they had our men locked up, the Indians recovered the houses and streets they had lost, as well as the great temple, in the tower of which some five hundred nobles fortified themselves, bringing in quantities of supplies, stones, long lances, and flint swords, wide and sharp. In truth, they did more damage with their stones than with any other weapon, and more safely. The tower was strong and high, as I have said, and was so near the fort of our men that it did them a great deal of harm. Cortés, although himself very depressed, encouraged his men, and was always at their head. In order not to be shut in—a thing which his heart would not allow—he took three hundred Spaniards and attacked the tower. He attacked it three or four times in as many days, but was never able to reach the top, so tall was it and defended by so many men, who badly harassed his rear with stones and arrows. His men were thrown down the steps, wounded and defeated, which filled the Indians with pride, and they pursued our men to the very doors of the fort. The Spaniards were getting more disheartened by the hour, and many of them grumbled, at which the spirits of Cortés were as you can imagine.

Now that the Indians had held the tower and won victories, and in words and deeds were fiercer than ever, Cortés decided to make one more assault on it and not return without taking it. He tied his shield to his wounded arm, sallied forth, and surrounded and attacked the tower with many Spaniards, Tlaxcalans, and friends, and, although those above defended it stubbornly and threw three or four Spaniards down the steps, and were supported by many others, he ascended and took it. The Spaniards closed with the Indians at the summit and forced them to jump down to the battlements and platforms that surrounded the tower, a foot or so wide, of which there were three, two fathoms apart, corresponding to the lofts of the chapels. Several Indians, trying to jump from one platform to the next, fell to the bottom and were hurt, and then were stabbed by our men who were waiting below. Several Spaniards embraced their enemies and jumped with them to the platforms, and even from one to the other, until they reached the bottom, where they left not one alive. The fight at the summit lasted three hours, but the Indians were so numerous that they could not all be conquered or killed. Five hundred Indians died like brave men, and if their weapons had been equal [to ours] they would have killed more than they lost, so strong was the place and such was their courage. The image of Our Lady, which could not be removed when the rebellion broke out, could not be found. Cortés set fire to the chapels and to the three other towers, and many idols were consumed. The Indians, however, although they had lost the tower, did not lose their spirit with its loss and the burning of their gods, which hurt them to the heart; rather, they made repeated attacks on the fort of the Spaniards.

109. The Mexicans Refuse a Truce

CORTÉS, in view of the multitude of enemies, their spirit and stubbornness, and the state of his own men, who had had all the fighting they could stomach and wanted to get out, if the Indians would let them, again made offers of a truce to the Mexicans. He reminded them of how many had died without killing anyone, and told them he was requesting a truce so they might recognize their losses and the bad advice they had followed. But they, more obdurate than ever, replied that they wanted no peace with one who had done them so much harm, one who had killed their men and burned their gods; still less did they want a truce, for Cortés had no water or bread or health; that, if they died, they also killed and wounded [their adversaries]; that the Spaniards were not gods or immortals, and could die just as they died; that he should look at all the people on the housetops, in the towers and streets, not to mention as many more inside the houses, and he would realize that the Spaniards would more quickly perish, dying one by one, than the citizens by their thousands and tens of thousands, for, as soon as those he saw were dead, they would be replaced by as many more at once, and after them, more and more. On the other hand [they said], once Cortés and his men were gone, no more Spaniards would come, and those who did not die by the sword would die of wounds and hunger and thirst; and now even if they wished to depart they could not, for all the bridges had been destroyed and the causeways cut, and they had no boats in which to leave by water.

During the course of these arguments, which gave Cortés plenty to think about, night fell, and truly, hunger by itself, and hardship and worry, were consuming the Spaniards, and would have consumed them without further fighting. That night, very late, half the Spaniards armed themselves and sallied forth, and, since the enemy did not fight at such hours, they easily burned three hundred houses on one street, killing all they found within. Near the fort they burned the houses from the roofs of which they had been badly hurt. The rest of the Spaniards repaired the engines and the fort. Their sally having been successful, at daybreak they returned to the street and bridge where their engines had been broken and, no longer setting much value on honor, because their lives were at stake, in the face of great resistance they took many houses and rooftops and towers, all of which they burned, taking at the same time four of the eight bridges along the causeway, in spite of their walls of earth and adobes, which were so strong that the guns could hardly knock them down. They filled the channels with those same adobes and earth, and with stones and timbers from the demolished houses, posted a guard over the captured places, and returned to the fort with wounds a-plenty, fatigued and gloomy, because they had lost more blood and spirit than they had won ground.

Early the next day they set out again to secure a passage to the land, filling the remaining four channels of the causeway, over which twenty horsemen galloped, driving the enemy before them. While Cortés was occupied in filling the channels and leveling the bad spots for the horses, a messenger came to tell him that a number of lords and captains wished to talk to him about peace, and that he should go to them with the *tlamacazque* (one of the important priests, a prisoner) to consider its terms. The *tlamacazque* did not return, because it was all a trick, either to discover the condition of our men, or to release the priest, or to put our men off their guard.

It was now time to eat, but Cortés had hardly sat down at the table when several Tlaxcalans ran in shouting that the enemy was advancing, had recaptured the bridges and killed most of the Spanish guards. Cortés at once gathered up the horse that were most ready, and a few foot, broke through the ranks of the numerous adversaries and pursued them to the mainland. Upon their return, the foot being wounded and tired with fighting and guarding the causeway, they could not stand against the dash and charge of the multitude of the enemy, who so filled the causeway that our men were scarcely able to make it back to their quarters. Not only that, but there were many canoes in the water whose occupants stoned and speared our men with great courage, wounding Cortés very badly in one knee with two stones. The news spread at once through the city that he had been killed, which saddened our men not a little and filled the Indians with jubilation; but he, although wounded, cheered on his men and struck the enemy. At the last bridge two horses fell, one of which became unmanageable and blocked the way for the rest. Cortés turned and attacked the Indians, clearing a small space, so that all the horsemen were able to pass, although the last one had to jump for it, which he did with great difficulty and danger, and it was a wonder that he was not taken, for he was showered with stones and did not get back to the fort until very late. After eating, Cortés sent several men out to guard the causeway and bridges, and to keep the Indians from recapturing them and from attacking the fort at night, for the Indians were very proud of their success that day, although, as I have said before, they were not in the habit of fighting at night.

110. Cortés Abandons Mexico

CORTÉS, seeing that the affair was now hopeless, spoke to the Spaniards about escaping, and all of them were very glad to hear it, for hardly one of them was unwounded. Although they had the courage to die, still they were afraid they would be killed if they did stay, for the Indians were so numerous that, even though the Spaniards slaughtered them like sheep, there were not enough Spaniards to do it. Our men were so short of bread that they dared not eat their fill; they lacked powder; and their fort was so riddled that not a few were kept busy guarding [the breaches]. All these considerations sufficed to induce them to abandon Mexico and save their own lives, although, on the other hand, they did not relish the notion of turning their backs to the enemy, for the very stones rise up against him who flies. Especially did they dread the prospect of crossing the gaps in the causeway, from which the bridges had been removed, so they were caught between the devil, on the one side, and the deep blue sea, on the other.*

They all agreed to go, and to go at once, that very night, which was "Botello's night." This Botello pretended to be an astrologer (some say a necromancer), who had foretold many days before that if they left Mexico at a certain hour of the night, that very hour, they would save themselves; otherwise, not. Whether they believed him or no, they all decided to go that night. To cross the breaches in the causeway they constructed a movable bridge. It is most credible that they all agreed to go, and not as some say, to wit, that Cortés left secretly and that more than two hundred Spaniards were abandoned in the yard and fort, unaware of his departure, and that these men were later killed, sacrificed, and eaten by the Mexicans, for they could not escape from the city, much less from a single house. Cortés says that they demanded it [the retreat?] of him.

Cortés summoned his chamberlain, Juan de Guzmán, and ordered him to open a room where he kept the gold, silver, jewels, precious stones, featherwork, and rich mantles, so that the treasurers and officers of the King might set aside the royal fifth, this in the presence of the alcaldes and regidores, and he gave them a mare of his and men to transport and guard the treasure. He also told his men that each one might take what he wished of the treasure, for he was

---

* "Así que por un lado les cercaban duelos y por el otro quebrantos." This ancient figure defies close translation. Cervantes uses it in the first chapter of *Don Quixote de la Mancha*, where Don Quixote is said to have dined on *duelos y quebrantos* on Saturdays, meaning odds and ends, or leftovers. See the long note on *duelos y quebrantos* in Schevill and Bonilla's edition of *Don Quixote* (Madrid, 1928), 4 vols., chap. I, p. 4.

making them a present of it. The Narváez men, hungry for it, loaded themselves down with as much as they could carry. This cost them dearly, for during the retreat they could not fight or move because of the weight, so the Indians killed many of them and dragged them away and ate them. The mounted men took some of the treasure on the cruppers of their horses. In a word, all took something, for the treasure was worth more than seven hundred thousand ducats. The only trouble was that it consisted of jewels and large pieces, which made a very bulky mass. The one who took the least came off best, and saved himself because he was unencumbered. Some say that a large quantity of gold and other things was left behind, but I do not believe it, for the Tlaxcalans and other Indians sacked the place and removed everything.

Cortés ordered certain of his men to take charge of a son and two daughters of Moctezuma, Cacama and his brother, and many great lords whom he held as prisoners. He ordered forty men to carry the portable bridge, and the Indian friends the guns and the small amount of maize that remained. He put Gonzalo de Sandoval and Antonio de Quiñones at the head of the column, Pedro de Alvarado at the rear, and he himself, with about a hundred Spaniards, covered all parts. In this order they left their house at the stroke of midnight, in a heavy fog, very silently, and Cortés prayed to God to get them alive out of that danger and out of the city. Cortés left by the Tacuba causeway, the same by which he had entered, and all followed him. They passed the first channel by means of the portable bridge, but the many sentries and guards of the temple and city immediately sounded the alarm on their conches, shouting that the Christians were leaving; and in a trice, since they were not impeded by armor or clothing, all the people poured out in pursuit of the Spaniards, screaming at the top of their voices: "Death to the wicked men who have done us so much harm!" So when Cortés tried to place the bridge across the second channel, many Indians came up to prevent it, fighting; but finally he did so well that he got it placed and crossed over it with five horse and one hundred foot, and with them he spurred on to the mainland, swimming the channels and breaks in the causeway, for by this time the portable bridge was a ruin. There he left the foot under the command of Juan Jaramillo, and returned with the five horse to bring out the rest and urge them forward. When he reached them, although many were fighting stoutly, he found a number of them dead. The gold was lost, the baggage, the guns, and the prisoners; in short, he found no two things or men together, or as he had brought them out of the fort. He gathered up as many as he could and sent them on ahead of him, and left Pedro de Alvarado to guard and pick up those who remained. Alvarado, however, could not stand against the enemy's charges and, in view of the slaughter of his companions, he saw that he could not escape if he delayed, so he followed Cortés, lance in hand, making his way over the dead and fallen Spaniards, whose groans filled his ears. He reached the last channel and vaulted over it with his lance, a feat that amazed the Indians and even the Spaniards, for it was a prodigious leap which others were unable to make, although they tried and were drowned.

At this point Cortés stopped and even sat down, not to rest, but to mourn over the dead and those still living, and to consider the heavy blow that fate had dealt him in the loss of so many friends, such treasures, such authority, and such a great city and kingdom. Not only did he bemoan his present misfortune, but feared those to come, because all his men were wounded and he knew not what way to turn, and because he was not sure of finding a refuge in Tlaxcala, or friends. Who, indeed, would not weep at the death and ruin of those who had entered in such triumph, pomp, and rejoicing? To prevent the loss of those who remained he marched and fought his way to Tacuba, which is on dry land beyond the causeway. In the rout of this sad night of July 1, 1520, 450 Spaniards died, 4,000 Indian friends, 46 horses, and, I believe, all the prisoners. Some say more, some less, but this is the truest number.

If the retreat had occurred in daylight perhaps fewer would have died and there would have been less confusion, but, since it happened at night and in the fog, it was an affair of many shouts, wailings, howling, and frightfulness, as the victorious Indians invoked their gods, insulted the fallen, and killed those who defended themselves. Our men, beaten, cursed their disastrous luck, the hour, and him who had got them into this trouble. Some called upon God, others upon St. Mary, and still others cried "Help, help, I'm drowning!" I cannot say whether as many died in the water as on the land, trying to swim or jump over the breaches in the causeway, or were thrown into the water by the Indians. It is said that when a Spaniard fell into the water an Indian fell with him and, the Indians being good swimmers, they carried them to their canoes, or wherever, or slit open their bellies.

Many Indians fought from canoes along the causeway, shooting at random and striking everybody, although they could distinguish somewhat the dress of their own people, which was like a masquerade costume. There were so many Indians on the causeway that they knocked each other into the water or to the ground, doing more damage to themselves than our men did to them; besides, if they had not stopped to strip the fallen Spaniards they would have left few alive, or none. Among our men, those who were most encumbered with clothing, gold, and jewels were the first to die, and those were saved who carried the least and forged ahead fearlessly. So those who died, died rich, and their gold killed them.

After the Spaniards had passed the causeway, the Indians did not pursue them, either because they were satisfied with what they had done or they did not dare fight in the open or they stopped to mourn the death of Moctezuma's children, for up to that time they had not recognized them or known they had been killed. The Indians wailed and made a great lamentation for them, and tore their hair for having killed them.

111. Battle of Otumba

When our men reached Tacuba, the people there did not know how beaten and broken they were, and our men milled about in the square because they did not know where to turn. Cortés rode in the rear and urged his men to make for the open country, before the people of the town should arm themselves and join the Mexicans. These, having ceased their mourning, were coming in pursuit, forty thousand strong. Cortés took the lead, sent on ahead the Indian friends who were left, and set out over some cultivated land, fighting his way to a hill, where there was a tower and temple (now, to commemorate the event, called Our Lady of Remedies). Some Spanish stragglers and many Indians were killed before he could reach the top; he lost a great deal of the gold that he still carried, and was hard put to it to free himself from the multitude of enemies, because none of the twenty-four remaining horses could run, so tired and hungry were they, nor could the Spaniards lift their arms or feet, from hunger, thirst, fatigue, and fighting, for they had not stopped or eaten all that day and night.

The Spaniards fortified themselves in the temple, which had fairly large living quarters. They drank, but ate nothing or very little, and waited to see what all those Indians would do who surrounded them as in a siege, shouting and attacking. Meanwhile, the Spaniards had nothing to eat—an enemy worse than the Indians. They built many fires with the wood used in the sacrifices, and toward midnight departed unperceived, marching blindly, since they did not know their way, until a Tlaxcalan said that he would lead them to his country, unless the Mexicans stopped them. So they set out.

Cortés put his men in order, placing in the middle the wounded and what clothing there was, and distributing the unwounded and the horse between the van and rear. Their movement was not so quiet, however, that they were not heard by the lookouts near by, who, upon perceiving them, gave the alarm at once, at which many men came in pursuit, but followed them only until daylight. Five of the mounted men who were on ahead scouting encountered several squadrons of Indians lying in wait to rob the Spaniards, but the Indians fled, thinking that the main body of our men was coming. They halted, however, when they saw how few they were, others joined them, and they pursued the Spaniards for three leagues, when our men took a hill surmounted by another temple with a good tower and quarters, where they were able to take shelter that night, but not to eat. At dawn the Indians made a surprise attack, but the scare was worse than the damage.

The Spaniards marched to a large town, the road to which was so rough that our horse could do little harm to the Indians, and they not very much to our men. The people of the town, frightened, fled to another, so our troops were able to stay there that night and the next, recuperating and treating the wounded men and horses. They also found some provisions and took some with them, but not many, there being no one to carry them. When they left they were pursued by an infinity of the enemy, who attacked fiercely and harassed them.

Their Tlaxcalan guide, as it turned out, was unfamiliar with the way, and they got lost, but they finally came to a hamlet of a few houses, where they slept that night. The next morning they continued their march under constant attack by the enemy, who molested them all that day. Cortés was wounded by a stone from a sling, so badly that he fainted, either because the fragments were not properly removed, or because of the excessive hardships he had suffered. He went to a deserted village to treat his wound, but was soon obliged to bring away all his men to prevent their being surrounded, whereupon they were so fiercely assailed by a multitude of Indians that five Spaniards and four horses were wounded, one of which died and was eaten, they say, down to the very hair and bone. The Spaniards considered this a good supper, although it was insufficient for all of them, because there was not a Spaniard who was not perishing of hunger. I shall pass over their hardships and wounds, either one of which circumstances would have been enough to finish them; but our Spanish nation can suffer hunger longer than any other, and more than all, these men of Cortés, who were not given time to gather even herbs for coarse food.

When he left the hamlet early the next day, Cortés, fearing the many Indians who appeared, ordered the horsemen to take up behind them those who were most badly wounded and suffering, and told those who were not so badly off to cling to the tails and stirrups, or to make crutches and canes to help them walk, unless they wanted to give the enemy a good dinner. The warning was timely, in view of what happened later, and there were even Spaniards who carried others on their backs, and so saved them. They had marched a league across a plain when they were attacked by a multitude that covered the country and surrounded them. The Indians fought so fiercely that our men thought that day would be their last, for the Indians now dared fight the Spaniards breast to breast and drag them away, either because of their great spirit, or because our men, worn out by hardship, hunger, and wounds, were lacking in it. Indeed, it was a great pity to see them carry off the Spaniards and to hear the things they said to them.

Cortés was riding from one spot to another cheering his men. He plainly saw the strait they were in, so he commended himself to God and to his advocate, St. Peter, and charged into the thick of the enemy's ranks. He broke through to the man who was bearing the royal standard of Mexico, struck him twice with his lance, and felled and killed him. When the Indians saw their standard and its bearer fall, they dropped their banners to the ground and fled, for such is their custom in war when their general is killed and their standard knocked down. Our men took heart at this and our horse pursued the enemy, slaying an infinity of them, so many, it was said, that I do not venture to guess the exact number, but it is affirmed that there were two hundred thousand Indians in the field at Otumba, where the battle took place.

Never had there been a more notable feat of arms in the Indies since their discovery, and all the Spaniards who that day saw Hernán Cortés in action swear that never did man fight as he did, or lead his troops, and that he alone in his own person saved them all.

112. Tlaxcala Receives the Spaniards

AFTER THIS SUCCESS, Cortés and his Spaniards, weary of killing Indians, spent that night in a house on the plain, within sight of the mountains of Tlaxcala, which cheered them not a little, although on the other hand they wondered whether men as warlike as the Tlaxcalans would be their friends at such a time, for the unlucky and defeated man who flies finds nothing in his favor: everything turns out badly for him, or the opposite of what he wishes. That night Cortés acted as sentry for his companions, not so much because he was in better health or less fatigued than they, but because he always wished to share in their hardships equally, just as the harm and losses they suffered were common to all.

At daybreak they set out straight for the mountains and province of Tlaxcala, passing a very good spring where they refreshed themselves, which, according to their Indian friends, was the dividing point between Mexicans and Tlaxcalans. They went to Hueyotlipan, a Tlaxcalan town of four thousand, where they were very well received and provided for, and spent three days there resting and recuperating. Some of the townspeople refused to give them anything unless they were paid for it, but most of them treated the Spaniards very well. Maxixca, Xicoténcatl, Acxotécatl, and many other lords of Tlaxcala and Huejotzingo came there with fifty thousand warriors who, having heard of the revolt, were on their way to Mexico to relieve the Spaniards, but had not heard of the retreat or the damage and losses suffered. Others say that, hearing how broken the Spaniards were and how they were in retreat, they came out to console them and invite them to Tlaxcala in the name of the republic. In short, they showed grief at seeing the Spaniards in such a state, and pleasure at finding them there. They even wept as they said: "We warned you that the Mexicans are wicked and treacherous, but you did not believe us. We are sorry about your trouble and disaster, and, if you wish, we shall go to Mexico and avenge this wrong and those of the past, the deaths of your Christians and our citizens; otherwise, come with us and we shall heal you in our houses."

Cortés was overjoyed to find this unexpected help and friendship among such good warriors. He thanked them warmly for coming and for their good will, gave them such jewels as he had left, and told them that a time would come when he would use them against the Mexicans, but that at the moment what was needed was care of the sick. The Tlaxcalan lords begged him, since he did not wish to return to Mexico, to let them go out and fight the Culhúans, many of whom, it was said, were about, more for robbery than anything else. Cortés gave them a few Spaniards who were either well or only slightly wounded, with whom they fought and killed many, and from that time on the enemy did not appear. Then the Tlaxcalans set out happy and victorious for their city, and our men followed after.

On the way, it is said, some twenty thousand men and women came to meet them, bringing them food, although I think most of them came to stare, such was the love they bore our men, or to hear word of their own people who had gone to Mexico, few of whom had returned. Our men were welcomed and well treated at Tlaxcala; Maxixca gave his house and bed to Cortés, while the rest of the Spaniards were lodged by the gentlemen and nobles of the city. They even pressed gifts upon our men which were the more enjoyed the more battered our men were, for I believe they had not slept in beds for a fortnight. Great was their debt to the Tlaxcalans for their loyalty and aid, especially to Maxixca, who had thrown Xicoténcatl down the stairs of the great temple for advising his people to slay

the Spaniards and appease the Mexicans. [On that occasion] Maxixca had made two speeches, one to the men and one to the women,
saying they had not eaten salt or worn cotton for many years until
the Spaniards had become their friends. The Tlaxcalans were very
proud of this [friendship], as well as of the resistance and battle
they had offered Cortés at Teocacingo. And so it is now that, when
they celebrate a fiesta, or receive a viceroy, some sixty or seventy
thousand of them sally forth to stage a mock battle such as they had
fought against him.

113. The Soldiers' Demand

AT THE TIME Cortés departed from Tlaxcala for Mexico to see Moctezuma, he had left behind undistributed gold to the value of twenty
thousand pesos, after deducting the King's fifth and sending it to
Spain by the hands of Montejo and Portocarrero—this according to
the agreement he had made with his companions. He had also left
in Tlaxcala the mantles and featherwork, so as not to be burdened
and embarrassed needlessly. A further reason was to discover what
kind of friends the Tlaxcalans were. Moreover, if he should not
need the money in Mexico, it could be sent to Vera Cruz for distribution among the Spaniards who had stayed there as guards and settlers, for it was just to give them their share. When he returned [to
Mexico] after his victory over Narváez, he wrote the commandant
[of Vera Cruz] to send for the clothing and gold, and distribute it
among the settlers, to each according to his merit. The commandant
sent fifty Spaniards for it with five horses, and they, upon their return with all the clothing and gold, were captured and killed by the
Culhúans, who, upon the arrival of Pánfilo, and flattered by his
promises, had risen and gone into banditry.

Cortés felt keenly the loss of so many men and the gold, and, fearing that some similar misfortune had befallen the Spaniards at Vera
Cruz, he at once sent messengers there, who returned and reported
that all were safe and well, and that the neighboring Indians were
secure and peaceable, a piece of news that greatly pleased Cortés,
and pleased still more his men who wished to go to Vera Cruz, only

Cortés would not permit it. For this reason they growled and grumbled against him, saying: "What does Cortés think he is doing? Why does he want to keep us here to die the evil death? What has he got against us that he won't let us go? Our heads are broken, our bodies are rotting and covered with wounds and sores, bloodless, weak, and naked. We are in a strange land, poor, sick, surrounded by enemies, and without hope of rising from the spot where we fall. We would be fools and idiots if we should let ourselves in for another risk like the past one. Unlike him, we do not wish to die a fool's death, for he, in his insatiable thirst for glory and authority, thinks nothing of dying himself, and still less of our death. He does not consider the fact that he is without men, guns, arms, and horses (which bear the brunt of this war), and has no provisions, which is the worst lack of all. He is wrong and very wrong to trust these men of Tlaxcala who, like all Indians, are frivolous, fickle, and fond of novelty, who very likely love the Mexicans more than they love the Spaniards, and who, although they dissemble and temporize with him, will, as soon as they see a Mexican army coming against them, deliver us up alive to be eaten and sacrificed, for true it is that a friendship between peoples of different religions, dress, and speech never endures."

Having given vent to these complaints, they made a formal demand on Cortés, in the name of the King and of them all, to the effect that he should forthwith abandon the place, without delay or excuse, and go to Vera Cruz before the enemy could cut the road, block the passes, seize the provisions, and leave them isolated and betrayed, for at Vera Cruz he would find much better means to rehabilitate himself and turn back to Mexico, or, if necessary, to sail away.

Cortés was somewhat disturbed and perplexed by their demand and decision, and realized that it was all for the purpose of getting him out of Tlaxcala and doing with him afterward what they wished, and, since all this was very far from his purpose, he answered them thus:

"I, GENTLEMEN, would gladly obey you if it were in your interest, for there is not one of you, let alone all of you together, for whom I would not stake my life and fortune in case of need, for I am obligated to you by considerations which, unless I were an ingrate, I shall never forget. And do not think that if I fail to accede to your insistent demand I am depreciating or scorning your authority; on the contrary, by refusing I shall exalt it and give it greater renown, because as soon as we should leave it would end, but, if we stay, it will not only be conserved, but increased. What nation of those which have ruled the world has not once been defeated? What famous captain, I say, ever went home because he had lost a battle or had been driven out of some town? Not one, certainly, for if he had not persevered he would not have conquered or triumphed. He who retreats seems to be running away, and all jeer at him and chase him; but he who turns a bold face to the enemy stays where he is, and is favored and feared by all. If we go these friends of ours will think we do so out of cowardice, our enemies will think we are afraid of them, and so will not fear us, which would be a very heavy blow to our reputation. Is there one among you who would not take it as an insult to be told he had turned tail? Well, the more there are of us the greater would be our shame. I marvel at the stoutness of your unconquerable hearts in battle, for you are commonly as greedy for a fight when you have it not, as you are tumultuous when you are in it. And now that you are offered a just and praiseworthy war, why, you reject and fear it! A very strange thing for Spaniards to do, and very contrary to your character! By chance is he who summons and invites you to undertake it one of those who boast of their coat of mail and never don it? Never before in these Indies of the New World have Spaniards been seen to turn back through fear, no, not even from hunger and wounds. Do you want it said: 'Cortés and his men retreated when they were safe, well fed, and in no danger?' God forbid!

"The outcome of a war depends much upon fame, and how can you win greater fame than by remaining here in Tlaxcala in defiance of your enemies, declaring war against them, and seeing them afraid to come and molest you? You must know, indeed, that you are safer and stronger here than away from here, and that in Tlaxcala you enjoy security, strength, and honor, in addition to which you have all necessary and proper medicines for your recovery and health, and many other comforts by which you are improving daily, and which I shall not mention. You would not have fared better in the land of your birth.

"I shall call back the men from Coatzacoalcos and Almería, and with them we shall be many. Even if they do not come we shall still be more than enough, for we were fewer when we came to this country and had no friends. You are well aware that it is not numbers that count in a fight, but spirit. Victories are not won by the many, but by the valiant. Why, I have seen one of this company, like another Jonathan, put to flight a whole army, and many of you singly defeat a thousand or ten thousand Indians, as David did among the Philistines. We shall soon have horses from the islands, and we shall bring up guns and arms from Vera Cruz, where there are plenty and near at hand. Have no fear or worry about provisions, for I shall give you a great abundance, especially since they follow him who masters the country, as we shall do with our horse. With respect to the people of this city, you have my word that they will be loyal to you, and good and constant friends, as they have promised and sworn to be. If they had wished otherwise, what greater opportunity could they have had than in these past days, when we were lying sick in their own beds? These people will not only help you as friends, but will be your servants, for they prefer slavery among us to subjection among the Mexicans, such is the hatred they have for them, and such is the love they bear you. To prove to you that this is so, I shall test them and test you in an expedition against the people of Tepeaca, who killed twelve Spaniards in days past. If the sortie turns out badly, I shall do as you request; if it turns out well, you will do what I beg of you."

With this speech and reply of Cortés, his men gave up the notion they had of abandoning Tlaxcala and retreating to Vera Cruz, and said they would do everything he commanded. The reason [for their decision] was quite likely the hope he had given them [for action] after the Tepeaca campaign, or, still more likely, the fact that a Spaniard never says "no" to war, which for him would be a dishonor and a disgrace.

CORTÉS WAS THUS relieved of the anxiety that had been bothering him, and truly, if he had done what his companions wished, he would never have regained Mexico and they would have been killed on the way [to Vera Cruz], for there were some very bad spots to be passed. Even if they had passed them, they would not have stopped at Vera Cruz, but gone on to the islands, as was their intent, and thus Mexico would have been really lost, and Cortés would have been ruined and brought low. Cortés, who understood this very well, had the wisdom and strength [to meet the situation], as we have said. He recovered from his wounds, and his companions from theirs. Some Spaniards died from having neglected their wounds when they occurred, leaving them dirty or unbandaged, or perhaps they did so from weakness and fatigue, as the surgeons said. Some were left lame and others with one arm, a great pity. But most of them recovered, and so, within twenty days of their arrival, Cortés declared war on Tepeaca, a large town at no great distance, because its people had slain twelve Spaniards on their way from Vera Cruz to Mexico; also because they belonged to the league of Culhúa and with the aid of the Mexicans had damaged the land of Tlaxcala, according to Xicoténcatl.

Cortés invited Maxixca and the other lords to go with him. They brought it up before the republic, it was agreed to, and they gave him more than forty thousand warriors, many *tamemes* as bearers, and food and other supplies. With this force, then, and with the horses and men that were able to march, Cortés went to Tepeaca and admonished the Tepeacans, in satisfaction for the twelve Spaniards they had slain, to be his friends and subjects of the Emperor, and never again to receive in their houses or country any Mexicans or men of Culhúa. They replied that if they had killed any Spaniards, they had done so with just cause in time of war, for the Spaniards had tried to force their way through the country without permission; moreover, that the people of Culhúa and Mexico were their friends and lords, whom they would receive at any time; that they had no desire to be friends of, or to obey, one whom they did not recognize; that Cortés, therefore, should return at once to Tlaxcala, if he wished to live.

Cortés urged them many times to accept peace, and, when they refused, waged war upon them in good earnest. The Tepeacans and their Culhúan friends fought fiercely; they occupied the strong gates and denied entrance to the Spaniards, and, since they were numerous and had brave men among them, fought very well and often; but in the end they were defeated and died, without having killed a single Spaniard, although a good many Tlaxcalans lost their lives.

The lords and governors of Tepeaca, seeing that neither their forces nor those of the Mexicans prevailed against the Spaniards, surrendered to Cortés as vassals of the Emperor, and he stipulated that they expel the Mexicans from every part of the country and that they allow him to punish as he pleased those who had killed the Spaniards. So the inhabitants of all the towns that had had a part in the killing of the twelve Spaniards were enslaved by Cortés, who set aside the King's fifth. Others say that Cortés took them all without further ado and punished them: for killing the Spaniards; for being sodomites, idolaters, and eaters of human flesh; and for rebellion—all this to intimidate the others. Indeed, if he had not treated them in this fashion, they, being numerous, would have risen. However it was, he made slaves of them all and, within a little more than twenty days, he had subjected and pacified the province, which is very large. He expelled the Mexicans from it and cast down its idols, and its lords tendered their obedience. For greater security he founded a villa there which he named Segura de la Frontera, and appointed a council to hold it, so that Spaniards and Indians might safely come and go over the road from Vera Cruz to Mexico which passes by there. In this war he was aided by the people of Tlaxcala, Huejotzingo, and Cholula, who did their part like true friends and told him they would do the same against Mexico, or even better. With this victory the Spaniards recovered their spirit and won great fame in that whole region, which had considered them as good as dead.

116. Huaquechula Submits

WHILE CORTÉS was in Segura messengers came to him from the lord of Huaquechula, to inform him secretly that the lord would surrender himself and all his vassals to him, if he would liberate them from their servitude to the Culhúans, who not only devoured their estates but took their wives and committed other outrages as well; also, that the [Mexican] captains and many soldiers were quartered in the city and its villages and vicinity; that in Mexinca, which was close by, 30,000 more were stationed to interdict Cortés' entrance; and that if Cortés would order him to go, or would send him Spaniards, he, with their help, would take the Mexican captains with his bare hands.

Cortés was delighted to receive this message, and truly it was something to rejoice about, because his men were beginning to gain more ground and reputation than they had thought possible a short while before. So he praised the Lord, rewarded the messengers, gave them more than 300 Spanish foot, 13 horse, and 30,000 Tlaxcalans and other Indian friends from his army, and sent them off. They went to Cholula, eight leagues from Segura, but while they were marching through the territory of Huejotzingo one of the people there told the Spaniards that they had been betrayed and that Huaquechula and Huejotzingo had made an agreement to lead them over this route and kill them in the former town, this to please the Culhúans, whose allies and friends they had recently become. Andrés de Tapia, Diego de Ordaz, and Cristóbal de Olid, captains, acting either from fear or from failure to understand the matter more fully, seized the messengers from Huaquechula and the captains and nobles of Huejotzingo, and returned to Cholula. From Cholula they sent the prisoners to Cortés in the charge of Domingo García de Alburquerque, together with a letter explaining the affair and telling Cortés how terrified they all were.

Cortés read the letter, spoke to the prisoners and interrogated them, and discovered that his captains had misunderstood, or had been deceived by whoever had informed them. The truth of the matter is that the arrangement [between Cholula and Huejotzingo], as reported by the messengers, was to bring our men secretly into Huaquechula and kill the Culhúans. So Cortés released the captains and messengers, who were resentful, and apologized to them, and then went with them to forestall a disaster among his companions; also, because they had begged him to come. On the first day he got as far as Cholula, and on the second reached Huejotzingo, where he arranged with the messengers how and where he was to enter Huaquechula, the citizens of which were to lock the doors of the [Mexican] captains' quarters, the better and more quickly to capture or kill them. The messengers left that evening and did what they had promised, slipping past the sentries, surrounding the captains, and fighting the rest.

Cortés set out an hour before daybreak, and by ten o'clock was in contact with the enemy. Just before he entered the city many citizens came out to meet him, bringing more than forty Culhúan prisoners as proof that they had kept their word, and led him to a large house, in which the captains were besieged by three thousand townspeople, who had them surrounded and in dire straits. At the arrival of Cortés, they charged, with such fury and in such numbers that neither Cortés nor the Spaniards could prevent their killing almost all the captains. Many of the remaining Culhúans died before he came, and the rest fled to the protection of their garrison. Three thousand of these came to the rescue of their captains and set fire to the city while the citizens were occupied and drunk with fighting and killing. When Cortés learned of it, he attacked [the Culhúans] and broke their ranks with his cavalry, forcing them back to a very high and steep hill. With the labor of climbing it neither they nor our men were able to move, two horses foundered and one died, and many of the enemy fell to the ground suffocated by the heat, without any wounds at all. Our friends soon came up and renewed the battle, and in a very short time the field was empty of living men and covered with dead.

After this slaughter, the Culhúans abandoned their quarters, which our men then burned and sacked. It was astonishing to see their luxury and the quantity of provisions stored in them, and how the Culhúans were decked out with gold, silver, and feathers. Their lances were longer than pikes, and with them they thought to kill the horses, and in truth, if they had known how to use them, they could well have done so. Cortés had in his camp that day more than one hundred thousand armed men, and the speed with which they assembled was as remarkable as their numbers.

Huaquechula is a town of five thousand citizens or more, situated on a plain between two rivers, which flow in deep canyons and make it impossible to approach [the town] except in a few places, and these are so rough that a horse can hardly negotiate them. The wall is of stone and mortar, wide, and four fathoms high, with battlements for its defense, and only four gates, narrow, long, and protected by three folds in the wall, and many stones piled everywhere for throwing, so that the Culhúans could have held it with a small force if they had been warned. To one side of the town are very many rough hills; to the other, a wide plain and cultivated fields. In its jurisdiction and vicinity it has an equal number of people.

Cortés spent three days in Huaquechula, to which messengers came from Izúcar, four leagues distant on the slope of the volcano called Popocatépetl. They came to offer their submission and to inform him that inasmuch as their lord had gone off with the Culhúans, they wished him to consent to the election of their lord's brother, who was very fond of Cortés and a great friend of the Spaniards. Cortés received them in the name of the Emperor and gave them permission to elect the lord of their choice, after which he departed.

117. Capture of Izúcar

WHILE CORTÉS was still at Huaquechula, he was told that there were Culhúans at Izúcar, four leagues away, who were threatening him and hurting his friends, so he went there, forced an entrance, and expelled the enemy, some of whom escaped through the gate, others over the walls. He pursued them for a league and a half and took many. In short, of the garrison of 6,000, few escaped. Some died at his hands and many were drowned in the river that flows past the town, the bridge having been cut for its defense. Of our forces, the horse entered quickly, but the foot were much delayed. Cortés now had 120,000 fighting men and more, who, learning of his fame and victories, flocked to his standard from many cities and provinces.

Izúcar is a trading town, dealing principally in fruits and cotton. It has 3,000 houses, good streets, 100 temples with their towers, and a fortress upon a low hill The rest of the town lies upon a plain. It has deep ravines around it cut by the river. A stone wall, its battlements heaped up with large round stones [for throwing], crossed the ravines and encircled the town. Close by is a good valley, round and fertile, watered by ditches dug by hand. The town was deserted, because the people, thinking to recover it [later], had all sought refuge in the highest and roughest parts of the neighboring mountains.

The Indian friends of Cortés took what they could find, while he burned the idols and even the temples.

Cortés released two prisoners and sent them to summon the lord and citizens, giving his word that they would not be harmed. Three days later, certain nobles, trusting to his safe-conduct and the Spaniards' reputation for not molesting those who surrender (also, because they wanted to come home), gave themselves up. Cortés pardoned and received them, freed the prisoners, and within a few days Izúcar was as populous as before. The only one to refuse his offer was the lord, either because he was afraid or because he was a kinsman of the lord of Mexico, a circumstance that gave rise to a dispute between the people of Izúcar and those of Huaquechula, over who should be elected in his place. Those of Izúcar wanted as lord the bastard son of a lord whom Moctezuma had put to death; the others said it should be the grandson of the absent lord, who was himself son of the lord of Huaquechula. Cortés finally interposed his authority, and, rejecting the bastard, they agreed upon the lord's grandson, as being legitimate and besides a close kinsman of Moctezuma on the female side. It is the custom in that country, as will be explained elsewhere, for a man to be succeeded by a son he has by the female kin of the kings of Mexico, even though he may have other and older sons. The present one being merely a boy of ten, Cortés ordered him to be reared under the guardianship of two gentlemen from Izúcar and one from Huaquechula.

While Cortés was occupied in settling this difference and pacifying the country, he was visited by ambassadors from eight towns of the province of Claoxtomacan, forty leagues distant, with an offer of men and their own submission, saying they had not killed any Spaniards or taken up arms against them. Such, indeed, was now the fame of Cortés that it spread over many lands, and all held him to be more than man, and many ambassadorial parties hastened to visit him; but, since they did not come from such a great distance as this one, they will not be described.

Now they attack the house where Moctezuma is.

ycq̄tla ti tetzavitl
yn mal ques.

The Marqués burns the temple of the idols.

The Spaniards attack the temple at Tepotzotlán and defeat the defenders.

Cortés receives the Tlaxcalan lord Citlalpopoca.

Cortés attacks Acatzingo.

quauhq̃cholan.

Cortés takes Huaquechula.

The cities of Tepatepec, Xochimilco, Coyoacán, Tacuba taken.

The battle in the main square of Tenochtitlán, June 16, 1521.

AFTER THESE EVENTS, Cortés returned to Segura, and each Indian to his own house, save those he had brought from Tlaxcala. From Segura he dispatched one of his servants to Vera Cruz. In order not to delay the campaign against Mexico, now that things were going so well with him, he ordered him to take four of Pánfilo's ships, which were anchored at Vera Cruz, and sail with them to Santo Domingo to get men, horses, swords, crossbows, guns, powder, and munitions; clothing, linen, shoes, and many other things. He wrote to the Licenciado Rodrigo de Figueroa and the Audiencia, giving an account of himself and events since his expulsion from Mexico, and begging their prompt assistance and support, so that his servant might quickly return with their favorable reply.

He also sent twenty horse, two hundred foot, and many Indian friends against Zacatami and Xalacingo, which were subject to Mexico and situated on the Vera Cruz–Mexico road, and which for some days had been under arms and had killed several Spaniards who were passing through. The men went there, made their protests, gave warning, fought, and, although they were moderate, there was killing, burning, and sacking. Several lords and nobles from the two towns came to see Cortés, induced thereto as much by force as by invitation, and offered their submission, begging his forgiveness, and promising never again to take up arms against the Spaniards. He pardoned them and sent them away as friends, whereupon the army returned.

Cortés wished to celebrate Christmas, now only twelve days off, in Tlaxcala, so he left a captain and sixty men in the new villa of Segura de la Frontera to guard the pass. Further to discourage the neighboring towns, he sent his whole army on ahead and went himself to spend the night at Colunán, with twenty horse. Colunán was a friendly town, very desirous of seeing him and using his authority to elect many lords and captains, to replace those who had died of the smallpox. He spent three days there, during which the new lords were proclaimed, who afterward proved to be good friends of his. The next day he arrived at Tlaxcala, six leagues distant, and was received in triumph. And true it is that he had waged a campaign worthy of a triumph.

Meanwhile, his great friend Maxixca had died of the smallpox introduced by the Negro of Pánfilo de Narváez, and Cortés wore mourning for him in the Spanish fashion. Maxixca had left sons, the eldest of whom, a lad of twelve, was named by Cortés lord of his father's state—this at the request of the republic. No small glory was it to give and remove dominions, and to be held in such respect that no one, without his permission and pleasure, would dare accept an inheritance or state. Cortés saw to it that the arms of all his men were kept in order; he pushed the construction of the brigantines, for the timber had been cut for them before he had left for Tepeaca; and he sent to Vera Cruz for sails, rigging, nails, ropes, and the other gear from the ships he had scuttled. Having no tar, which is not known or used in that country, he sent several sailors to make it in the mountains near the city.

119. Preparations for the Assault on Mexico

THE REPUTATION and prosperity of Cortés, at the time he held Moctezuma in his power, and after his victory over Pánfilo de Narváez, were such that the Spaniards in Cuba, Santo Domingo, and the other islands flocked to him by twenties, making their way as best they could, although many lost their lives on the way, killed by the people of Tepeaca and Xalacingo, as has been related; other Indians, seeing them in such small groups and Cortés driven from Mexico, made bold to attack them. And yet, so many [Spaniards] reached Tlaxcala that Cortés found his army greatly strengthened and was encouraged to press the war.

Cortés was unable to have spies in Mexico, because the Tlaxcalans would immediately be recognized by their pierced lower lips and ears, as well as by other marks. Besides, the Mexicans kept a careful watch, so Cortés could not learn how things were in the city as fully as he would have liked, in view of his necessary preparations. The only thing he discovered was told him by a Culhúan captain who had been captured at Huaquechula, which was that upon the death of Moctezuma, his nephew Cuitlahuac, lord of Ixtapalapa, had been elected lord of Mexico. Cuitlahuac was an astute and valiant man, who had fought Cortés and driven him from Mexico. He had since strengthened the city with caves and walls and many kinds of arms, especially with some very long lances, like those found in the quarters of the Culhúan garrisons at Huaquechula and Tepeaca, used for attacking horses. He had remitted the tributes and taxes for a year, or for the duration of the war, of all subject lords and towns, provided they would kill Spaniards or expel them from their territories, an action which won him great credit among his vassals and inspired them to resist the Spaniards and even to attack them. The device of the lances was not a bad one, if those who were to wield them had been skillful enough to lie in wait for the horses and wound them.

What the prisoner told him was all true, save that Cuitlahuac had died of the smallpox and Cuauhtémoc now ruled, a nephew of Moctezuma and not, as some say, his brother. He was a brave and warlike man, as we shall relate, who sent messengers throughout the country, some to remit tributes, others to give and promise great things to those who would follow him and not Cortés, for it was a just thing to help their own people rather than strangers, and to defend their ancient religion rather than accept that of the Christians, who wanted to take over the whole country and, not satisfied with this, would make slaves of its people, or kill them, as he knew on good authority. Cuauhtémoc aroused the Indians to a high pitch with these messages, and some sent him aid and others took up arms. A great many, however, paid him no heed and either supported our men and the Tlaxcalans, or did nothing—this from fear of Cortés and his reputation, or from hatred of the Mexicans. In view of the situation, Cortés determined to undertake the war and the march against Mexico at once, before his Indian followers and his Spaniards should grow cold, for they, with the successful campaigns against Tepeaca and other provinces, no longer remembered [their desire to return to] the islands—such is the power of success.

Cortés reviewed his troops the second day after Christmas and counted 40 horse and 540 foot, 80 of whom were armed with crossbows or arquebuses, and nine guns, for which, however, he had little powder. He divided the horse into four squadrons of ten, and the foot into nine companies of 60. He appointed the captains and officers of the army, assembled them all, and addressed them.

"My brothers, I give many thanks to Jesus Christ to see you now cured of your wounds and free from sickness. I am glad to find you armed and eager to return to Mexico to avenge the deaths of our comrades and recover that great city. This, I trust in God, we shall soon do, because we have with us Tlaxcala and many other provinces, and because you are who you are, and the enemies the same as they have been, and we shall do so for the Christian Faith that we shall proclaim. The Tlaxcalans and the others who have always been with us are ready and armed for this war, because they are as strong for defeating and subjugating the Mexicans as we are. Not only is their honor at stake, but their lives and liberty as well, because if we should be defeated they would be ruined and reduced to slavery, for the Culhúans hate them worse than they hate us, for receiving us in their country. For this reason the Tlaxcalans will never forsake us and will intelligently strive to serve and provide for us, and will even urge their neighbors to do likewise. And truly they are performing as well and as loyally as they promised me at the beginning, as I assured you they would. They have under arms some hundred thousand men to send with us, and a large number of *tamemes* to carry our provisions, guns, and baggage. You are the same men you have always been, and while I have been your captain have won many battles against one or two hundred thousand enemies, taken by storm many strong cities, and reduced great provinces, when you were fewer than you are now. And even when we invaded this country you were not more numerous, nor at the present time do we need men, because we have many friends, and even if we did not have them, you are such that without them you would conquer this whole land, God giving us health, for Spaniards dare face the greatest peril, consider fighting their glory, and have the habit of winning.

"Your enemies are not greater or better than they have been, as they proved at Tepeaca and Huaquechula, Izúcar and Xalacingo, although they now have a different lord and captain. He, however, no matter what he has done, has not been able to take away from us the places and towns we have taken from him; rather, there in Mexico he fears our coming and our good fortune, because, as all his men think, we shall be masters of that great city of Tenochtitlán. If we should fail to take it, and if Cuauhtémoc should inherit the kingdom, the death of Moctezuma would be held against us, and the rest [of our achievements] would do little to further our purpose; besides, our victories would be hollow if we did not avenge our comrades and friends. The principal reason for our coming to these parts is to glorify and preach the Faith of Jesus Christ, even though at the same time it brings us honor and profit, which infrequently come in the same package. We cast down their idols, put a stop to their sacrificing and eating of men, and began to convert the Indians during the few days we were in Mexico. It is not fitting that we abandon all the good that we began, rather, we should go wherever our Faith and the sins of our enemies call us. They, indeed, deserve a great whipping and punishment, because, if you remember, the people of the city, not satisfied with killing an infinite number of men, women, and children in sacrifices to their gods (devils, rather), eat them afterward, a cruel thing, abhorrent to God and punished by Him, and one which all good men, especially Christians, abominate, forbid, and chastize. Moreover, without penalty or shame, they commit that accursed sin because of which the five cities, along with Sodom, were burned and destroyed. Well, then, what greater or better reward could one desire here on earth than to uproot these evils and plant the Faith among such cruel men, by proclaiming the Holy Gospel? Let us go, then, and serve God, honor our nation, magnify our King, and enrich ourselves, for the conquest of Mexico is all these things. Tomorrow, with the help of God, we shall begin."

All the Spaniards acclaimed his words in one voice, saying they would not fail. They were so enthusiastic, indeed, that they wished to depart forthwith, either because such is the Spanish character or because they were attracted by the power and riches of the city which they had enjoyed for eight months.

Thereupon Cortés announced by crier certain rules of war which he had written concerning the good government and order of the army. Among others were these:

No one might blaspheme the Holy Name of God.

No Spaniard might quarrel with another.

No one might wager his arms or horse.

No one might force a woman.

No one might take the Indians' clothing, do violence to them, or put [their towns] to the sack, without Cortés' permission and the consent of the council.

No one might insult friendly Indians warriors, or use the *tamemes* as gifts.

In addition, he fixed the charges for horseshoes and clothing because of the excessive prices demanded.

121. Cortés to the Tlaxcalans

ON THE FOLLOWING DAY Cortés summoned all the lords, captains, and nobles of Tlaxcala, Huejotzingo, Cholula, Chalco, and the other towns roundabout, and, speaking through his interpreters, addressed them as follows:

"My lords and friends: You already know about the course and the campaign I am undertaking. Tomorrow, please God, I shall depart for the war and the siege of Mexico, and I shall invade the country of my enemies and yours. What I beg of you in the presence of all is that you be faithful and constant to the friendship and agreement we have made, as you have been before, and as I proclaim and trust you to be. Now, I cannot end this war as quickly as I plan, and as you desire, without having on the lake of Mexico the brigantines that are being built here, so I beg of you as a favor to treat with your customary love the Spaniards I am leaving here to build them, and to give them whatever they ask for themselves and their task. For my part I promise to deliver you from the yoke of servitude that the Culhúans have placed on your necks, and to persuade the Emperor to reward you with many and rich gifts."

All the Indians present indicated their pleasure, and in a few words their lords replied that not only would they do what Cortés requested but that when the brigantines were finished they would carry them to [the lake of] Mexico and all would go with him to the war.

122. Cortés Takes Texcoco

ON THE DAY of the Holy Innocents Cortés left Tlaxcala with his Spaniards in good order. The departure was a thing to see, because he was accompanied by more than eighty thousand men, most of them armed and wearing the feathers that gave their army a splendid appearance. Cortés however, did not want to bring them all, but to have them wait for the completion of the brigantines and the encirclement of Mexico. He was also concerned over the problem of feeding them, because he thought it would be difficult to maintain such a multitude on the road and in enemy territory. He did, however, take along twenty thousand, in addition to those he needed for hauling the guns and carrying provisions and baggage. That night he slept at Texmelucan, six leagues distant, a town in the jurisdiction of Huejotzingo, in which the lords of the province received him very well. He spent the next night at a place four leagues farther on, in the territory of Mexico, on a mountain, where, if it had not been for the abundance of firewood, the Indians would have perished with the cold; even so, they and the Spaniards suffered considerably. At daybreak he began to ascend the pass, sending on ahead a scouting party of four foot and four horse, who found the road covered and blocked by recently felled trees. In the hope, however, that it would be better farther on (also because they wanted to bring back a good report), they continued until they could no longer proceed, and returned to announce that the road was impassable because of the many thick pines, cypresses, and other trees, which the horses could by no means penetrate. Cortés asked them if they had seen any men, and they answered, none, so he advanced with all his horse and some foot, and ordered the rest to follow quickly with the whole army and all the guns. Meanwhile, he took a thousand Indians and began to remove the trees from the road, and, as the others came up, they cleared away the branches and trunks, so that the guns and horses got through without danger or harm, although at the cost of considerable hardship. And certainly, if the enemy had been present they would not have passed, or, if they had, it would have meant the loss of many men and horses, for the way was very rough and through a thick forest. But the enemy, in the belief that our men could not get

243

through, had contented themselves with blocking the road, and had taken up positions on the passes lower down. Cortés chose the most difficult route, either because he guessed what the enemy was thinking or perhaps because someone had informed him the enemy was not there.

Once beyond the pass, our men caught sight of the lakes and gave thanks to God, swearing they would not turn back until they had taken Mexico or died in the attempt. They paused a while so that they might all descend to the plain together, for the enemy was already sending up many smoke signals, and was beginning to shout at them and arouse the whole country. [The enemy] had already recalled the men who were guarding the approaches and, thinking to catch the Spaniards between bridges, they posted a large company at them. But Cortés sent forward twenty of his mounted troops, who lanced and broke through the enemy. The rest of the Spaniards soon came up, killed several, and cleared the road. They safely reached Coatepec, in the jurisdiction of Texcoco, where they spent the night. The town was deserted, but near by were more than one hundred thousand warriors of Culhúa, sent against ours by the lords of Mexico and Texcoco. Cortés ordered out a mounted patrol of ten [to reconnoiter] and alerted his men, but the enemy remained quiet.

The next morning Cortés departed for Texcoco, three leagues distant, but had not gone far when he was met by four Indian nobles of that town, bearing a banner mounted in a bar of gold, which weighed all of four marks, a sign of peace, and told him that their lord Coanacoxtzin had sent them to beg him not to damage their country, and to invite him to quarter his whole army in their city, where they would be well looked after. Cortés, even though he thought it was all a trick, was pleased with the embassy. He saluted the one man he knew and answered that he had no intention of harming them; on the contrary, he would receive as friends the lord and all of them, provided they restored what they had taken from the forty-five Spaniards and three hundred Tlaxcalans they had killed some time since. He would also pardon them the killings, since death has no remedy. They said that Moctezuma had ordered the killing and had taken the spoils, and that the city was not to blame. So saying, they turned back.

Cortés went on to Coatlinchán and Huejutla, which are, so to speak, suburbs of Texcoco, and there he and all his men were well provided for. He cast down their idols and went directly to the city, taking quarters in several large houses, where all the Spaniards and many of his friends were accommodated; but, since he had not observed any women and children, he suspected treachery and prepared [for trouble], and had it announced that none of his men, on pain of death, should venture outside. The Spaniards fortified their quarters, and in the afternoon several of them mounted to the roof and looked over the city, which is as large as Mexico, and noticed that the people were abandoning it and removing their belongings, some to the woods, others over the water. It was a remarkable spectacle to see the swarm of twenty thousand or more canoes milling about, filled with people and clothing. Cortés tried to put a stop to it, but night came on and he could not. He would also have liked to arrest the lord, but the lord had been the first to leave for Mexico. Cortés then summoned the Texcocans and told them that, inasmuch as Coanacoxtzin had gone over to the enemy and had murdered Cucuzca, his brother and lord, in his ambition to reign (persuaded thereto by Cuauhtémoc, the mortal enemy of the Spaniards), Cortés was naming Don Fernando, the son of their beloved lord Nezahualpiltzin, their king. Thereupon the Texcocans began to return to see their new lord and to reoccupy the city, which in a short time was as populous as before. They were not molested by the Spaniards, so they served them in everything they were commanded to do. Don Fernando, who had learned our language and taken the name of Cortés (who had acted as his godfather), proved to be a faithful friend of the Spaniards.

A few days later, the people of Coatlinchán, Huejutla, and Atengo came to offer their submission and beg forgiveness for any errors they might have committed. Cortés received and pardoned them, and made a pact by which they should go home to their wives, children, and estates, for they had run away to the mountains and to Mexico. Cuauhtémoc, Coanacoxtzin, and the other lords of Culhúa sent messengers to reprimand these three towns for submitting to the Christians, but the messengers were seized and brought to Cortés, who learned from them how things were in Mexico, and then sent them back to beg their lords to accept his peace and friendship; but it did him little good, for they were bent on war.

At that time certain followers of Diego Velázquez were going about among the men to stir them up to mutiny against Cortés and ruin him, after which they would return to Cuba. Cortés learned of it, had them arrested, and took their statements. Then acting on their confessions, he condemned to death as a mutineer one Antonio de Zamora and executed the sentence, whereupon the mutiny and its suppression ended.

123. Action at Ixtapalapa

CORTÉS STAYED A WEEK at Texcoco, fortifying his quarters (since he could not fortify the whole city because of its great size), and storing up provisions against a possible siege by the enemy. Then, seeing they did not attack, he took 15 horse and 200 foot, armed with 10 arquebuses and 30 crossbows, and some 5,000 friends, and marched along the shore of the lake straight to Ixtapalapa, about five leagues away. The inhabitants were warned by smoke signals, sent up from watchtowers by the Culhúan garrison, that the Spaniards were descending upon them, so they placed their clothing, women, and children in the houses that were built over the water and launched a large fleet of canoes. Many of them, organized in squadrons and well armed after their fashion, advanced two leagues. They did not stage a pitched battle, but skirmished and retreated to the town, thinking to trap and kill their enemies there. The Spaniards followed them in helter-skelter (which is what the others wanted them to do), and fought stubbornly until they drove the citizens into the water, where many were drowned. Since, however, they were good swimmers and had canoes to pick them up, not so many died as was believed at the time. Still, the Tlaxcalans killed more than 6,000, and if they had not been interrupted by darkness, they would have killed many more.

The Spaniards took some booty, fired many houses, and were beginning to set up their quarters, when Cortés ordered them to quit the place at once, although it was late, for the townspeople had breached the causeway, and so much water came in that it covered everything. And certainly, if they had spent the night there, not a man would have escaped drowning. Even though they got out as fast as they could, it was nine o'clock by the time they had all left, and even then they had to dash through the water, in which they lost all their booty and several Tlaxcalans were drowned. After this mishap, they suffered badly from the cold that night, for they were soaked; also from hunger, because they had not been able to bring out any provisions. The Mexicans, who were aware of all this, attacked in the morning, so the Spaniards were forced to retreat to Texcoco, beating off the enemy who pressed them by land, and others who attacked from the water. These last could not be hurt, because they took to their boats; nor did the Spaniards dare break into the ranks of the many land troops. In this fashion they made it as far as Texcoco, suffering greatly from fatigue and hunger. Many of our Indian friends were killed, and one Spaniard, who, I believe, was the first to die in the field.

Cortés was apprehensive that night, thinking that this engagement had given the enemy much encouragement, while it frightened the others, who feared that our men might surrender. The next morning, however, messengers came from Otumba (where Cortés had won the great battle) and from four other cities five or six leagues from Texcoco, to ask his pardon for their past hostilities, to offer their services, and to beg his help against the Culhúans, who had threatened and maltreated them, as indeed they did all those who submitted to them. Cortés praised and thanked them, but said that if they did not bring him all the messengers from Mexico he would neither pardon nor receive them. After the Otumbans had left, Cortés was told that the people of the province of Chalco wished to be his friends and to submit to him, but were prevented from doing so by the Culhúan garrison there. Cortés immediately dispatched Gonzalo de Sandoval with twenty horse and two hundred foot, to take Chalco and expel the Culhúans.

He also sent letters to Vera Cruz, for he had had no word of the Spaniards there for a long time, since the road was held by the enemy. Sandoval set out with his company; but first he took measures to secure the letters and messengers of Cortés [who were being dispatched to Vera Cruz]. Then he made shift to see that the Tlaxcalans should get home in safety with the clothing they had taken, after which he planned to join the people of Chalco. But as soon as he was separated from [the Tlaxcalans] they were assailed by the enemy, who killed some and stole a good part of their booty. When Sandoval learned of this, he quickly went to their relief, and put to flight and pursued the enemy, so [the Tlaxcalans] were able to go to Tlaxcala and Vera Cruz.

Sandoval immediately joined forces with the men of Chalco, who, having learned of his approach, were armed and waiting for him. Together they attacked the Culhúans, who fought stoutly, but in the end were defeated with considerable loss, and their camps were sacked and burned. Sandoval returned to Texcoco, bringing with him several sons of the lord of Chalco, who gave Cortés some four hundred pesos in bits of gold and, weeping, excused themselves, saying that their father, just before his death, had commanded them to submit to Cortés. He comforted them, thanked them for their good wishes, confirmed them in their rank, and had Sandoval himself escort them home.

124. Sacrifice of Spaniards at Texcoco

THE POWER AND REPUTATION of Cortés were increasing so much every day that he was joined by all those not of the party of Culhúa, and even by many who were. So it was that two days after he had made Don Fernando lord of Texcoco, the lords of Huejutla and Coatlinchán (who were already his friends) brought him the intelligence that the Mexicans were coming to attack [Huejutla] in force, and [they asked him] whether they should take their children and goods to the mountains, or whether they should bring them to him —such was their fear. He reassured them and begged them to stay at home and not to be afraid, but to be on their guard and keep a lookout, for he was glad the enemy was coming; therefore, they should keep him informed and they would see how he would punish the Culhúans.

The enemy, however, did not descend upon Huejutla, as had been reported, but fell upon the Tlaxcalan *tamemes* who were bringing supplies to the Spaniards. Cortés met them with two guns, twelve horse, two hundred foot, and many Tlaxcalans. He fought them without, however, killing many, for they took to the water, but he did burn several towns where the Mexicans had taken refuge, and returned to Texcoco. The following day [representatives of] three of the largest towns of the region came to him to ask his pardon and beg him not to destroy their towns, saying they would never again give shelter to a Culhúan. The Mexicans punished them for this embassy, and later many came to Cortés with their heads broken, seeking revenge. The men of Chalco also asked for help, because the Mexicans were destroying them; but Cortés, who was about to send for the brigantines, had to refuse them. Instead, he referred them to the men of Tlaxcala, Huejotzingo, Cholula, and Huaquechula, and to other friends, assuring them he would soon come himself. They, however, were not at all happy at the prospect of help from these provinces, but wanted only Spanish help and sent more messages demanding it.

While this was going on, some Tlaxcalans arrived to tell Cortés that the brigantines were ready, and to inquire whether he needed help, because shortly before they had observed more smoke signals and signs of war than ever. He sent them to join the men of Chalco and begged them to tell the lords and captains [of Chalco] to forget the past, to make friends with [the Tlaxcalans] and help them against the Mexicans, by which they would be doing him a very great favor. So from that time on they were very good friends and helped each other.

A Spaniard also arrived from Vera Cruz, with the tidings that some 30 Spaniards, not counting the crew of the nao, had landed there, bringing 8 horses, a great deal of powder, and many crossbows and arquebuses, which filled our men with joy. Cortés at once sent Sandoval to Tlaxcala with 200 foot and 15 horse, to fetch the brigantines. He ordered him to destroy on the way the town [Calpulalpan] that had seized 300 Tlaxcalans, 45 Spaniards, and 5 horses during the encirclement of Mexico. This town was subject to Texcoco and was situated on the border of Tlaxcala. He would have liked to punish the Texcocans for the same offense, save that it was not the time or the place for it. The Texcocans, indeed, deserved a greater punishment than the others, because they had sacrificed and eaten [their victims], and sprinkled their blood over the walls, even indicating that it was Spanish blood. They had also flayed the horses, tanned the hides, with the hair and shoes still in place, and hung them up in the great temple as a memento, next to the clothing of the Spaniards.

Sandoval went to this town, determined to attack and destroy it, not only because Cortés had ordered him to do so, but because, a little before arriving there, he read a message scrawled in charcoal on the wall of a house: "Here the luckless Juan Juste was imprisoned." Juste was one of the five horsemen. The inhabitants of the place, although they were many, abandoned it and fled when they saw the Spaniards upon them. The Spaniards pursued them, killed a number, and took a good many prisoners, especially the children and women who could not run; these threw themselves upon the mercy of our men and gave themselves up as slaves.

Seeing how feeble was the resistance, and how the women were weeping for their husbands, the Spaniards took pity on them, and neither killed the men nor destroyed the town; rather, they summoned the men and pardoned them on their promise of service and loyalty. Thus the deaths of the forty-five Spaniards were avenged. The Indians were asked how it was that they were able to take so many Spaniards without a struggle and without allowing a single one to escape. They answered that they had set an ambush of many men on a hillside above a defile, where the road was narrow, and had attacked from the rear. Since the Spaniards were marching in single file, leading the horses by their halters, they could not wheel or make use of their swords, so the Indians took them all and sent them to Texcoco, where, as I have said, they were sacrificed in revenge for the imprisonment of Cacama.

125. The Tlaxcalans Carry the Brigantines

NOW THAT HE HAD REDUCED and punished those who had captured the Spaniards, Sandoval set out for Tlaxcala, and at the border of that province came upon the brigantines, the planking and fittings for which were being carried on the backs of 8,000 men, who were escorted by 20,000 soldiers, with 2,000 more bringing provisions and supplying services. When Sandoval arrived, the Spanish carpenters asked him whether, since they were now entering enemy territory, it would not be better to put the rigging in the van and the planking in the rear, this being the heavier and more cumbersome. All approved of the suggestion except Chichimecatecatl, a noble lord and courageous man, captain of the 10,000 men of the van, in charge of the planking. He took it as an insult that he should be shifted from the front to the rear, and said some pretty things about it, but in the end he had to make the change. Teuctepil, Ayotecatl, and the other captains, noble lords also, took over the van with their 10,000. The *tamemes* and those who were carrying the planking and gear of the brigantines were placed in the middle. A hundred Spanish foot and eight horse took the lead, and Sandoval, with the rest of the Spaniards and seven horse, brought up the rear. If Chichimecatecatl was angry at the beginning, he was furious when the Spaniards did not stay with him, for he said they did not think him valiant or loyal.

The squadrons having been arranged as you have heard, they set out for Texcoco, to the accompaniment of the greatest yelling, whistling, and whinnying in the world, and shouting: "Christians! Christians! Tlaxcala! Tlaxcala and Spain!" On the fourth day they entered Texcoco in order, to the sound of many drums, conches, and other musical instruments. They had donned feathers and clean mantles for the occasion, and truly it was a gay entrance, for they were fine men and made a fine appearance. There were so many of them that it took six hours, this without breaking their line, which extended over two leagues of road. Cortés came out to greet them; he thanked the lords and found good lodging for all the men.

126. Cortés Reconnoiters Mexico

THEY RESTED for four days, after which Cortés ordered the carpenters to assemble and ready the brigantines without delay, and he ordered a ditch dug meanwhile by which to launch them in the lake without risk of damage. [The Tlaxcalans] were very anxious to encounter the Mexicans, so Cortés sallied forth with them, and with

25 horse, 300 Spanish foot (including 50 arquebusiers and crossbow-men), and six guns. After a march of four leagues they came upon a large body of the enemy, whose ranks were broken by the cavalry, whereupon the foot advanced and put them to flight. The Tlaxcalans joined in the pursuit and killed all they could. The hour being late, the Spaniards went no farther, but pitched camp in the field, sleeping that night under careful guard, for there were many Culhúans about. At daybreak they took the road to Xaltocan, but Cortés did not make his route public, for he feared that the many Texcocans who were with him might inform the enemy of it.

They reached Xaltocan, a town built over the water, having on the land side many deep and wide ditches filled with water, which the horses could not pass. The townspeople shouted and mocked at them, seeing them floundering among the ditches, while they hurled arrows and stones. The Spanish foot, jumping and advancing as best they could, got past the ditches, attacked the town, and entered it, although not without difficulty. They drove the citizens out at sword's point and burned a good part of the houses. They did not stop there, but spent the night a league farther on. (The device of Xaltocan is a toad.) The next night they slept at Cuauhtitlán, a large town, but deserted. The next day they passed through Tenayuca and Atzca-potzalco without opposition, and reached Tacuba, which had been strengthened with men and ditches. It put up some resistance, but they entered, killed many, and drove the rest out. Night coming on, they retired in time to a large house. In the morning they put the town to the sack and burned nearly all of it, in revenge for the Span-iards who had been killed there during the retreat from Mexico. During the next six days, not one day passed without a skirmish with the enemy, and some days there was such a hubbub and shouting (a custom among the Mexicans) that it was a frightful thing to hear.

The Tlaxcalans, who wanted nothing better than to close with the Culhúans, fought marvelously well, and, since their opponents were brave, it was something to see, especially when they defied each other man to man, or group to group, making such long speeches, and shouting such threats and insults at each other, that those who under-stood them died of laughter. The Mexicans came out along the causeway to fight and, thinking to catch the Spaniards upon it, pre-tended to fly. At other times they invited them to enter the city, saying: "Come in, men, and have a good time!" Some said: "Here you will die, as you did before!" Others: "Go home, for there is no longer a Moctezuma to do your bidding!" While these exchanges were going on, one day Cortés approached a raised drawbridge, made signs that he wished to speak, and said: "If your lord is here I should like to speak with him." They answered: "Everyone you see here is a lord; say what you wish." Since he [Cuauhtémoc] was not there, Cortés said no more, while they shouted insults at him. At this point a Spaniard told them they were surrounded and would die of hunger unless they yielded. They answered that they had plenty of bread and that, even if it should give out, they would have Spaniards and Tlaxcalans to eat. Whereupon they threw over some maize cakes and said: "Eat if you are hungry, for we are not, thanks be to our gods! And now get out, or you shall die!" After which they began again to shout and fight.

Cortés, seeing that he would not be able to speak with Cuauhtémoc, and that all the towns were deserted, turned back to Texcoco by the same road by which he had come. The enemy, thinking he did so from fear, gathered in large numbers to attack him, and did so with great spirit. Cortés, thinking to punish them for their folly, one day sent forward his whole army and the Spanish infantry, but with only five horse, while he put six horse in ambush on one side of the road, five on the other, and three in another place, and concealed himself with the rest among some trees. The enemy, seeing no horses, attacked in great disorder. Cortés, as soon as they had passed, shouted: "St. James and at them! St. Peter and at them!"—which was the signal for the horse to attack. This they did, from both sides and from the rear, lancing the enemy at will. They put them to flight at the first charge, pursued them for two leagues over the plain, and killed a great many.

With this victory behind them, they went on to Acolman, two leagues from Texcoco, and slept there. The enemy had been so badly battered in the ambush that they did not appear for many days. The lords of Tlaxcala asked permission to go home, and went, very proud and full of victory, while their men were rich from the quantity of salt and clothing they had taken on their journey around the lake.

127. Action at Yecapixtla

THE MEXICANS, seeing how badly things were going for them with the Spaniards, descended upon Chalco, a very important province on the road to Tlaxcala and Vera Cruz. The people of Chalco appealed for help to Huejotzingo and Huaquechula, and asked Cortés to send them some Spaniards. He sent them three hundred foot and fifteen horse, under Gonzalo de Sandoval. Upon arrival, Sandoval mounted an expedition against Oaxtepec, where a Culhúan garrison was stationed which was causing them trouble. The men of the garrison advanced to meet him and fought, but they could not withstand the fury of the horses and the slashing swords, and took refuge in the town. Ours followed them in, killed many, and drove out the citizens, who, not having wives or goods to defend, did not stay. The Spaniards ate, and fed their horses, and the friends ransacked the houses for clothing. While our men were thus occupied, they heard the noise and shouts of the enemy in the streets and square of the town. They dashed out and expelled the enemy again at the point of the lance, and pursued them a good league, slaughtering a large number.

Our men remained there for two days and then marched against Yecapixtla, where more men of Mexico were stationed. These were admonished to submit peacefully, but they, being in a high and strong place—one which, moreover, was difficult for horses—refused to listen; rather, they hurled stones and darts, and threatened those of Chalco. Our Indian friends, though numerous, did not dare attack, so the Spaniards, shouting "St. James!" made the assault on the town and took it, despite its strength and defenses, although it is true that many of them were wounded by darts and stones. The men of Chalco and allies followed them in and did a great butchery among the Culhúans and citizens, many of whom cast themselves off a cliff into the river that flows by there. In short, few escaped with their lives. Such was the renowned victory of Yecapixtla. Our men suffered severely from thirst that day, as much from the heat and fatigue as from the fact that the river ran red with blood and the water could not be drunk for a considerable while, and there was no other source.

Sandoval returned to Texcoco, and the others to their several abodes. In Mexico there was great lamentation over the loss of so many men and such a strong place, and a fresh army was sent against Chalco, under orders to attack before the Spaniards should get wind of it. This army obeyed the orders of Cuauhtémoc with such speed that its opponents were not given the opportunity to await help from Cortés, help which they had begged and expected. Nevertheless, the men of Chalco all assembled and awaited the battle, which they won handsomely with the help of their neighbors. They killed many Mexicans and captured forty, among them a captain, and drove the enemy out of their country. This victory was considered all the greater because it was unexpected. Gonzalo de Sandoval had set out for Chalco with the same Spaniards as at first, marching quickly so as to arrive before the battle; but it was over and won by the time he got there, so he returned to Texcoco with the forty prisoners.

These successes at Chalco cleared and secured the road between Mexico and Vera Cruz. The Spaniards that I have mentioned soon arrived, bringing horses, many crossbows and arquebuses, and a great deal of powder and ball, as well as many other things from Spain, from which our army received a pleasure commensurate with its need. [The new men] brought word also that other naos had arrived there with men and horses.

128. Our Men Take Two Dangerous Heights

CORTÉS INTERROGATED Sandoval's forty prisoners about affairs in Mexico and about Cuauhtémoc, and learned from them [the Mexicans'] determination to defend themselves and refuse the friendship of the Christians. It now seemed to Cortés that the war promised to be protracted and difficult, and hence that peace would be preferable to war, so, in order to gain time and not expose himself to daily risks, he begged [the prisoners] to go to Mexico and propose a cessation of hostilities to Cuauhtémoc, and assure him that Cortés had no desire to kill and destroy, although he had the means to do so. But they did not dare to carry this message, knowing the hatred that their lord had for Cortés. He however, urged them so strongly that two of them consented to go. They asked him for letters, not because the letters could be read, but for their credit and security. Cortés gave the letters and an escort of five horse; but nothing came of it, for he never received a reply; rather, the more he argued for peace, the more stubbornly the enemy refused to listen, thinking he was acting from weakness. In this belief more than fifty thousand of them marched against Chalco, to take him in the rear.

The people of that province advised Cortés of it and asked him for Spanish support, at the same time sending him a painted cotton cloth representing the towns and [the numbers of] men who were advancing against them, and the routes they were taking. Cortés answered that he would come in person within ten days, but not sooner, because he had to celebrate the Good Friday and Easter of his God. They were discouraged by his reply, but they waited, and on the third day after Easter messengers came to him urging him to make haste, for the enemy was already in their land.

Meanwhile, the towns of Tuxpan, Mexicalcingo, and Nautla had submitted, together with certain neighbors of theirs. They said they had never slain a Spaniard, and they brought a present of clothing. Cortés received [their ambassadors], treated them cordially, and quickly dismissed them, because he was about to leave for Chalco. He soon did so, with 30 horse and 300 foot, over whom he put Gonzalo de Sandoval as captain. He brought along some 20,000 friends from Tlaxcala and Texcoco. He slept at Tlamanalco, where, since it was on the frontier of Mexico, the men of Chalco kept a garrison.

The next day more than 40,000 others joined him, and on the following he learned that the enemy was in the field awaiting him. He heard Mass and set out to meet them, and at two o'clock in the afternoon came to a very high and rugged rock, upon the summit of which was an infinity of women and children, and at its rear were many warriors. These, upon sighting the Spanish forces, sent up smoke signals, and the women on the summit set up such a howling that it was marvelous to hear. The men at the foot began to shoot darts, stones, and arrows, with which they did some damage to those who approached too near, and these had to withdraw with broken heads. To storm such a strong point would have been madness; to retreat would have looked like cowardice; so, not to appear lacking in spirit, and to learn whether [the enemy] would yield from fear or hunger, Cortés attacked the rock on three sides.

Cristóbal del Corral, an ensign, with 70 Spaniards from the guard of Cortés, attacked the roughest side; Juan Rodríguez de Villafuerte, with 50 men, the second; and Francisco Verdugo, also with 50, the third. All were armed with swords and crossbows, or arquebuses. A little later a bugle was blown, and Andrés de Monjaraz and Martín de Ircio, each a captain over 50 Spaniards, followed them, and then Cortés with the rest. They carried two sides of the rock but had to retreat, badly mauled, for they could not hold their positions, even by clinging with hands and feet; much less could they fight and climb, so rough was the ascent. Two Spaniards died and more than 20 were wounded, all of the latter struck with splinters of stones thrown from above and shattered; and if the Indians had been at all clever not a Spaniard would have escaped unwounded.

By this time our men had abandoned the rock and were scrambling about to fortify themselves, for so many Indians had come to the relief of the besieged that they covered the field, and they looked as if they wanted to fight. So Cortés and the cavalry, who were on foot, mounted again, charged, and drove the enemy off with their lances. In the pursuit they sighted another rock, not so strong as the first and manned by a smaller force, but surrounded by many villages. Cortés took all his men there to spend the night, thinking to recover the reputation he had lost by day; also to drink, for they had not found any water during the whole march. That night the men on the [first] rock made a very great racket with horns, drums, and shouting.

In the morning the Spaniards examined the strong and weak points of the rock, and found it everywhere difficult to storm and take. It was, however, commanded by two hills near by which were defended by armed men. Cortés, who thought to take these two hills, told all his men to follow him, and began the ascent. Their defenders, thinking the Spaniards were going to attack the rock, abandoned their position and went to its relief. When Cortés saw their confusion, he sent a captain with fifty men to take the more rugged and nearer hill. These took one face of it and made it to the top, where they discharged their crossbows and arquebuses, which frightened rather than harmed the Indians, who at once threw their arms to the ground as a sign of surrender and gave themselves up. Cortés showed them a pleasant face and ordered that they were not to be harmed, and they, seeing such gentleness, sent word to the men on the rock to yield to the Spaniards, who were such kindly men and who, besides, were equipped with wings to climb wherever they wished. For these reasons, or for lack of water, or because they wanted to go home in safety, the men of the rock came at once to surrender to Cortés and ask pardon for having killed the two Spaniards. He willingly granted it, greatly pleased that those who had had victory in their grasp should yield, and this gave him a great name among the people of the region.

129. Battle at Xochimilco

CORTÉS SPENT TWO DAYS there, sent the wounded back to Texcoco, and departed for Oaxtepec, where there was a large garrison of Culhúans. He stopped that night, with all his army, at a stone pleasure house. It had a garden a square league in extent, enclosed by a wall and watered by a pretty stream that flowed through the middle. The people of the place fled at daybreak and our men pursued them as far as Xilotepec, which had not been warned. They entered, killed a few men, and seized many women, children, and old people who could not run away. Cortés waited there two days to see if its lord would return, but, since he did not, fired the town. While he was there, Yautepec submitted. From Xilotepec Cortés went to [Oaxtepec and then to] Cuernavaca, a large town, strong and surrounded by deep ravines. Horses could enter it only in two places, which, however, were protected by drawbridges, so the cavalry had to make a detour of a league and a half, in great hardship and danger.

Our men were so close that they could talk with the townspeople, and [both sides] hurled rocks and arrows at each other. Cortés offered them peace; they answered with war. While these exchanges were taking a place, a Tlaxcalan passed a ravine by a secret but dangerous crossing without being detected. Four Spaniards followed him and then many others. They penetrated the town, where the inhabitants were occupied with fighting Cortés, and forced them to fly at sword's point. Dismayed at seeing their town entered, a thing they considered impossible, they fled to the mountains, and by the time [Cortés'] army arrived most of the town had been burned. In the afternoon its lord came with several nobles to surrender, offering his person and his goods for service against the Mexicans.

From Cuernavaca Cortés marched to a place in a deserted and waterless country, where the army had a bad time from thirst and fatigue. The following day they advanced to Xochimilco, a very pretty town on the fresh-water lake. Its citizens and the numerous Mexicans raised the bridges, cut the ditches, and set about defending it, thinking they could do so, they being many and the place strong. Cortés put his men in order, dismounted the cavalry, and advanced with some of his companions to see whether they might not take the first barrier. They pressed the enemy so closely with their arque-buses and crossbows that the enemy, though numerous, broke and fled, badly mauled. When they had gone, the Spaniards dashed into the water, passed over it, and in half an hour's fighting had taken the principal and strongest bridge of the city. Its defenders took to their canoes and fought until night, some asking for peace, others for war; but it was all a stratagem to give them time to collect their clothing and wait for help from Mexico, which is only four leagues distant, and to cut the causeway by which our men had entered. At first Cortés did not understand why some demanded peace and others not, but he soon divined the reason, and with his cavalry fell upon those who were breaching the causeway and routed them. They fled, and he pursued them over the field, lancing many.

They were so brave that they gave our men a rough time, because many of them, armed only with sword and shield, would wait for a horse and attack its rider; and if it had not been for a Tlaxcalan they would have taken Cortés that day, for his horse had fallen from fatigue, having been fighting a great while. The foot came up at this point and put the enemy to flight. Two Spaniards who had stayed behind in the city to loot were killed. Our men did not pursue the enemy, but returned to the town to rest and fill the broken places in the causeway with stones and adobes.

When word of this action was brought to Mexico, Cuauhtémoc sent a large force by land and some two thousand canoes by water, these manned by twelve thousand, thinking to take the Spaniards with their bare hands at Xochimilco. Cortés mounted to the top of a tower to observe the enemy, to see what order they were in, and how they might attack the city. He marveled at the number of canoes and men covering land and water. He posted the Spaniards for the protection and defense of the town and causeway, dividing them into three groups, with orders to assemble upon a certain hill (which he pointed out to them) half a league away, when he had broken the ranks of the enemy. He himself set forth with the horse and six hundred Tlaxcalans. The Mexican captains were in the van, brandishing their swords and shouting: "Spaniards, here we shall kill you with your own weapons!" Others said: "Moctezuma is dead, and we have no one to fear when we eat you alive!" Still others threatened the Tlaxcalans. In short, they all screamed insults at our men, and shouting "Mexico, Mexico! Tenochtitlán, Tenochtitlán!" advanced with great speed. Cortés charged them with the horse, and each squadron of Tlaxcalans did the same on their part, and he routed the enemy at the point of the lance. They soon reformed, however, and he, seeing their discipline, spirit, and great numbers, broke through their ranks again, killed a few, and then retired to the hill he had indicated. But the enemy had occupied it meanwhile, so he ordered his men to climb up at the rear, while he rode around the base. The enemy at the summit fled at the approach of our men, but were met by the horse, at whose feet some five hundred of them died in a short time.

Cortés rested there briefly, while he sent for a hundred more Spaniards. When they arrived, he attacked another large body of Mexicans, who were following [the first]. He routed them also and retired to the town, because they were attacking him fiercely by land and water; but with the arrival [of the hundred] they retreated. The Spanish defenders killed many of their adversaries and recaptured two swords. They were still in danger, because the Mexican captains were pressing them and their crossbow bolts and ammunition had given out. These [new enemies] had hardly left when others came in by the causeway, yelling at the top of their voices. Our men met them and found them to be many but terror-stricken, so our horse charged and drove a very large number into the water, and the rest were forced off the causeway.

Cortés had the whole city burned, except that part where he and his men were quartered. There he spent three days, not one of which was free from fighting. On the fourth day he left and went to Coyoacán, two leagues away, under assault by the men of Xochimilco, whom he punished. He found Coyoacán deserted, as were the other towns on the lake, but, since he planned to lay siege to Mexico from that direction, he stayed there two days, casting down idols, surveying a site for his camp, and locating a place where the brigantines could be sheltered. He also made a reconnaissance of Mexico with two hundred Spanish foot and five horse, and attacked a barricade which, although it was stoutly defended, he took, but at the price of many wounded. He then set out on his march back to Texcoco, because he had completed his circuit of the lake and his survey of the lay of the land. He had several more brushes with the Culhúans, in which many Indians died on both sides; but the principal part of it has been described.

130. Ditch for Launching the Brigantines

WHEN CORTÉS ARRIVED at Texcoco he found there a number of Spaniards newly come to join him in the war, the beginning of which had won him great renown. They brought many arms and horses, and said that all the men in the islands were eager to serve him, save that Diego Velázquez had stopped many of them. Cortés did these men every honor and gave them of what he had. The people of many towns also came to offer their services, some out of fear of being destroyed, others from hatred of the Mexicans. In this fashion Cortés increased his forces by a good number of Spaniards and a very great abundance of Indians.

The captain in command at Segura de la Frontera sent Cortés a letter he had received from a certain Spaniard, which said in substance: "Noble lords, I have written you two or three times and have received no reply; nor do I expect one now. The Culhúans are in this country [of Chinantla] waging war and doing evil. They have attacked us; we have vanquished them. This province wishes to see Cortés and submit to him. It has need of Spaniards. Send thirty."

Cortés did not send the thirty Spaniards requested, because he was about to besiege Mexico; but he did answer and thank him, and gave him the hope that they would soon see each other. This Spaniard was one of those Cortés had sent to Chinantla the year before, to ferret out the secrets of the country, discover gold, and do some trading. The lord of that province had made him a captain against the Culhúans, his enemies, who, since the death of Moctezuma, had been making war upon him for harboring Spaniards. He, however, had always won through the skill and daring of this Spaniard, who, when he learned there were Spaniards in Tepeaca, had written several times, as his letter stated, but none of his letters save this one had been delivered. Our men were overjoyed to hear that the Spaniards [who had been sent to Chinantla] were still alive and that that province was on our side, and they thanked God for it. Indeed, they could talk of nothing else but the escape of this man, because at the time of the retreat from Mexico the Indians had killed all the others who had been sent to explore for mines and to trade.

Cortés pushed his preparations for the siege, accumulating supplies, fabricating equipment for scaling and attacking, and storing provisions. He speeded up the completion of the brigantines and dug a ditch for launching them in the lake. This ditch was a quarter of a league long, more than twelve feet wide, and two fathoms deep at the shallowest part. This depth was necessary to take the flow of water from the lake, and the width to accommodate the brigantines. It was lined throughout with planks and topped by a wall. It followed an irrigation ditch of the Indians. In took fifty days to complete, and on each of the fifty days some four hundred thousand men of Texcoco and its territory worked upon it—a memorable achievement. The brigantines were calked with tow and cotton, and from lack of tallow and oil (I have already mentioned the manufacture of tar) they were sealed, according to some, with human fat (not that men were killed for this purpose) taken from those who were killed in war. This was a cruel thing to do, repulsive to the Spaniards, but the Indians, who were inured to sacrifice, were cruel and cut open the bodies and extracted the fat.

As soon as the brigantines were launched, Cortés held a review. He counted 900 Spaniards: 86 of them mounted, 118 armed with crossbows and arquebuses, and the rest with pikes, shields, and halberds, besides the swords and daggers that they all carried. They also had several corselets, and many cuirasses and leather jackets. He counted, besides, three heavy guns of cast iron and 15 small bronze pieces, ten hundredweight of powder and plenty of shot. Such were the army, the weapons, and the munitions of Spain with which Cortés undertook the siege of Mexico, the greatest and strongest city of the Indies and the New World. He had the crier read again the rules of war, and begged everyone to observe them. Then, pointing to the brigantines in the ditch, he said:

"My brothers and comrades, you now see these brigantines finished and ready for action, and you know how much work they have cost us, and how much sweat they have cost our friends. A very great part of the hope I have to take Mexico lies in them, because with them we shall either quickly burn all the canoes of the city, or seal them up in the canals. In this we shall do the enemy as much harm as the land forces can do, because the enemy can no more live without canoes than without eating. To help us in the siege of Mexico we have a hundred thousand friends who, as you know, are the most valiant and skillful men in these parts. You will not suffer from want of food, which they have abundantly provided. Your duty will be to fight as you are accustomed to fight, and to pray God for health and victory, for this war is His."

131. Cortés' Army at the Siege

THE FOLLOWING DAY Cortés sent messengers to the provinces of Tlaxcala, Huejotzingo, Cholula, Chalco, and to others, summoning them to bring all their men within ten days to Texcoco, with their arms and the rest of the equipment necessary for the siege of Mexico, for the brigantines were now finished, and everything else was ready, the Spaniards being so anxious to descend upon the city that they could not wait a single hour longer than the appointed term. The Indians came immediately, as they had been commanded, lest the siege begin in their absence. More than sixty thousand entered [Texcoco] in formation, the finest-looking men you could wish to see, and the best armed after their fashion. Cortés went forth to meet them and lodged them very well.

On the second day after Whitsunday, all the Spanish troops were paraded in the square, and Cortés appointed three captains as their field commanders, among whom he divided the whole army. To Pedro de Alvarado he gave 30 horse, 170 foot, three guns, and more than 30,000 Indians, with quarters at Tacuba. He gave Cristóbal de Olid 33 horse, 180 foot, two guns, and nearly 30,000 Indians, with quarters at Coyoacán. He gave Gonzalo de Sandoval, the third field commander, 23 horse, 160 foot, two guns, and more than 40,000 Indians from Chalco, Cholula, Huejotzingo, and other places, with orders to destroy Ixtapalapa, and then to pitch his camp wherever he thought best.

Cortés armed each brigantine with one gun, six arquebuses or crossbows, and 23 Spaniards, most of whom were skilled in things of the sea. He appointed captains and inspectors for them, and named himself commander of the fleet, at which some of his land forces grumbled, in the belief that they ran the greater risk, and they demanded that he take command of the land forces, not the fleet. But Cortés paid no heed to their demand: this for several reasons: one, it was more dangerous to fight on the water, and two, it was more urgent to supervise the brigantines and the naval action (in which they had had no experience) than the land fighting (in which they had often been engaged).

Alvarado and Cristóbal de Olid set out on the tenth of May and spent that night at Acolman, where they quarreled fiercely over their lodgings, and, if Cortés had not sent a man to calm them down that very night, there would have been a bad row and even bloodshed. The next night they slept at Xilotepec, which was deserted. The third day, very early, they entered Tacuba, which was also deserted, like all the towns on the shore of the lake. They took quarters in the lord's houses, while the Tlaxcalans made a raid into Mexico by the causeway and fought with the enemy until darkness stopped them.

The next day, the thirteenth of May, Cristóbal de Olid, following Cortés' instructions, went to Chapultepec, broke the pipes at the spring and cut off Mexico's water supply, in the face of strong resistance by land and water. The Mexicans were badly hurt by the loss of the spring, which, as has been related elsewhere, supplied the city. Pedro de Alvarado busied himself in repairing the bad places in the causeway for the horses, mending the bridges, and filling the breaches. This work occupied his men for three days, and, since they were attacked by the enemy, several of them were wounded and a good many Indian friends were killed, although they did take certain bridges and barricades.

Alvarado remained in Tacuba with his troops, and Cristóbal de Olid went to Coyoacán with his, according to Cortés' instructions. They made themselves strong in the houses of the lords of those cities, and every day they either skirmished with the enemy or joined forces to scour the countryside for maize, fruit, and other provisions from towns in the mountains. In these activities they spent a whole week.

132. Victory of the Brigantines

KING CUAUHTÉMOC, as soon as he learned that Cortés had launched the brigantines and had gathered such a great force for the siege of Mexico, conferred with the lords and captains of his kingdom, to seek a remedy. Some, confident of the many men and strength of the city, urged war; others, concerned with the public welfare, counseled peace, giving it as their opinion that the captured Spaniards should not be sacrificed but kept against the time when they should need friends. Still others said that the gods should be consulted. The king, who was inclined more toward peace than war, said he would speak with his idols and bring back their opinion. In truth, he would have liked to come to an understanding with Cortés, fearing what, in fact, happened later; but, seeing his people so determined, he sacrificed to the gods of war four Spaniards whom he was keeping alive in cages, and, according to some, four thousand other persons. In my opinion, these, although many, were fewer. He spoke with the devil in the person of Huitzilopochtli, who told him to have no fear of the Spaniards, for they were few; nor should he fear those others who were with Cortés, for they would not last out the siege; that, therefore, Cuauhtémoc should attack and await them without any misgiving whatever, for he [Huitzilopochtli] would help him destroy his enemies.

Thus counseled by the devil, Cuauhtémoc forthwith ordered the bridges removed, the barricades raised, the city guarded, and five thousand canoes armed. Such was his determination, and such his preparation, when Cristóbal de Olid and Pedro de Alvarado came to take the bridges and cut off the water supply of Mexico. He did not greatly fear them; rather, he threatened them from the city, saying that the gods would be pleased with their sacrifice, and the snakes would have their fill of blood, and the tigers their fill of Christian flesh, now that they had taken a liking to it. He also addressed the Tlaxcalans in these words:

"Ah, you cuckolds, slaves, and traitors to your gods and king! You will repent of what you are doing against your lords! For here you will die the evil death, either from hunger or our knives! Or we shall take and eat you in the greatest sacrifice and banquet ever celebrated in this country! And as a sign and reminder of it we are here tossing you the arms and legs of your own men, who were sacrificed for victory! Later we shall invade your country, raze your houses, and leave not a trace of your people!"

The Tlaxcalans laughed heartily at his threats and replied that he would do better by submitting to Cortés than by resisting him; by fighting rather than boasting; by holding his tongue rather than insulting his betters; that, if he wanted anything, he should take the field, where he would certainly see the end of his knavery, his rule, and even his life.

These and similar speeches and challenges exchanged between the Indians were something to hear. Cortés, who was kept informed of this and of daily events, sent Gonzalo de Sandoval forward to take Ixtapalapa, and himself embarked for the same place. Sandoval attacked one side of the town, and the citizens, either from fear or a desire to take refuge in Mexico, left by the other and took to their canoes. Our men entered the town and burned it.

Cortés, about this time, approached [in the brigantines] a high rock, strong and surrounded by water, defended by many Culhúans, who, as soon as they saw the brigantines sailing toward them, sent up smoke signals and, as the Spaniards drew near, began to yell and shoot many arrows and stones at them. Cortés landed with about one hundred and fifty companions, forced the barricades which had been erected for its defense, and gained the summit, although with considerable difficulty. There he fought so well that he left not a man alive, only the women and children. Although twenty-five Spaniards were wounded, it was a very fine victory, not only because the place was strong, but because of the slaughter of the enemy and the scare it gave [the others]. By this time so many smoke signals and fires were seen about the lake and in the mountains that the whole country seemed to be burning. In the city, the Mexicans, hearing that the brigantines were coming, took to their canoes. Certain gentlemen manned five hundred of the best and advanced to engage the brigantines, thinking either to defeat them or at least to learn what these famous vessels were like.

Cortés embarked with his spoils [from the rock] and commanded his men to remain together and keep quiet, the better to defend themselves or, by convincing the enemy that they were acting from fear, to induce the enemy to attack and face destruction. The five hundred canoes advanced with great speed, but halted at an arquebus shot from the brigantines to await the arrival of the rest of the fleet, [their crews] being too small and too tired to give battle. Little by little, so many canoes came out that they covered the lake, with such a yelling, beating of drums, and blowing of conches and other horns that [the crews] could not understand each other, while they repeated the same insults and threats they had offered the other Spaniards and Tlaxcalans. But while the two fleets were confronted and ready to do battle, a wind came up in the poop of the brigantines, so favorable and timely that it seemed a miracle. Then Cortés, praising God, ordered his captains to attack together at the same time, and not to stop until they had their adversaries bottled up in Mexico, since Our Lord had been pleased to give them a wind for victory. And [he admonished them] to consider how much was at stake in winning this first battle and making the canoes dread the brigantines. At his words they closed with the canoes, which had already begun to fly before the contrary wind, and [the brigantines] had such a start that they wrecked some of the canoes and sank others, while [the crews] that were overtaken and attempted to defend themselves were killed. [The brigantines] did not encounter as much resistance as had been anticipated, so they soon routed the canoes, pursued them for two leagues, and shut them up in the city. Some lords were captured, and many gentlemen and others. It could not be learned how many had died, but the lake was red with blood.

This notable victory was the key to the war, for our forces now commanded the lake, and the enemy was disheartened and ruined. They might not have suffered such losses if they had not been so numerous, for they got in each other's way; nor would they have been so quickly defeated but for the weather. Alvarado and Cristóbal de Olid, seeing the rout, destruction, and pursuit of the canoes by the brigantines of Cortés, advanced over the causeway with their troops. They attacked and took certain bridges and barricades in the face of heavy resistance, and with the help of the brigantines they pursued the enemy for a league, forcing them to leap into the water on the side away from the brigantines. Which done, they retired, but Cortés continued and, not encountering any canoes, made a landing with thirty men on the Ixtapalapa causeway, where he attacked the two small towers [at Xoloc] where Moctezuma had first received him. (They were full of idols and surrounded by low stone walls.) Cortés took them, but with great danger and difficulty, for they were stoutly held by numerous defenders. He then had three guns brought up to frighten off the enemy, who covered the causeway, very belligerent and stubborn. He fired one salvo, which did a good deal of damage, but, since the rest of the powder had been burned through the carelessness of a soldier, and the sun had set, both sides ceased fighting. Cortés, although he had planned something different with his captains, remained there that night. He sent to Gonzalo de Sandoval's camp for more powder, and for fifty foot of his guard and half the men at Coyoacán.

133. The Siege

CORTÉS SPENT the night [in the towers] in considerable anxiety, because he had only a hundred companions with him, those in the brigantines being necessary [to man them]. Toward midnight a large number of the enemy attacked, in canoes and along the causeway, with frightful yells and showers of arrows. But the noise was greater than the damage, for this was a new thing for the Indians, who were not in the habit of fighting at such an hour. Some say they retreated because of the fire from the brigantines. At daybreak eight horse and some eighty foot from the forces of Cristóbal de Olid arrived, and the Mexicans at once attacked the towers by land and water, with their usual yelling and howling. Cortés met them and drove them along the causeway, taking a bridge and its barricade. He did much damage to the enemy with his guns and horse, and pursued them as far as the first houses of the city, where he held them. Meanwhile, since he was being hurt and many men wounded by the canoes, he cut a gap in the causeway next to his camp in order to allow four brigantines to pass through, and they, after several assaults, drove the canoes in among the houses, and so he took command of both lakes.

The next day Gonzalo de Sandoval left Ixtapalapa for Coyoacán, and on the way took and destroyed a small city on the lake, the people of which had attacked him. Cortés sent him two brigantines, to be used as a bridge over a gap in the causeway cut by the enemy. Sandoval left his men with Cristóbal de Olid and joined Cortés with ten horse. When he found Cortés embroiled with the Mexicans, he dismounted to fight, and was struck in the foot by an arrow. Many other Spaniards were wounded that day, but the enemy paid dearly for it, being treated so roughly that thenceforth they displayed more fear and less than their customary pride.

With these exploits behind him, Cortés was now able to place and arrange his forces and quarters as he pleased, and to provide himself with bread and many other necessities. This occupied him for six days, none without its skirmish. The brigantines were able to navigate the canals about the city, which was a very profitable thing to do, for they penetrated deeply into the city and burned many houses in the outlying districts. Cortés now had the city hemmed in on four sides, although at first he had planned on three. His station was between two towers [at Xoloc] on the causeway that separates the lakes. Pedro de Alvarado was in Tacuba, Cristóbal de Olid in Coyoacán, and Gonzalo de Sandoval was, I believe, in Xaltocan, because Alvarado and others had said that the Mexicans, if they should be pressed, would leave by the causeway that passes by there.

Cortés would not have been averse to allowing the enemy to escape, especially from such a strong place [as Mexico], because he would have a greater advantage over his adversaries on land than on the water, and in any other town than that one. Also, according to the proverb, *If your enemy runs away, build him a silver bridge.* On the other hand, he feared that the enemy might be able to leave stores of food, men, and arms here and there in the country.

134. First Action in the City

ONE DAY Cortés decided to follow the causeway into Mexico and take what he could of the city; also, to see how the spirit of the people was holding up. He sent word to Pedro de Alvarado and Gonzalo de Sandoval to attack from their positions, and he told Cristóbal de Olid to send him some foot and horse, and with the rest of his troops to guard the entrance of the Coyoacán causeway and prevent the allied and subject cities of Xochimilco, Ixtapalapa, Churubusco, Mexicalcingo, Cuitlahuac, and others from moving against his rear. He ordered the brigantines to sail alongside the causeway and protect both his flanks. He left his quarters very early that morning with more than two hundred Spaniards and some eighty thousand friends. He had not proceeded far, however, when he encountered the enemy, well armed, defending a break in the causeway. The break was about a lance's length across and equally deep. He attacked, and the enemy stood him off for a good while, fighting from behind a barricade; but he finally took the position and chased them to the entrance of the city. A tower stood at this point, and at its base was a large drawbridge spanning a swift current. The drawbridge was raised and was defended by a strong barricade. It was so difficult to storm and dangerous to pass that the mere sight of it was frightening, and the enemy was shooting so many stones and arrows that our men could not approach. Cortés attacked it nevertheless, and by bringing up two brigantines on either side, he took it with less trouble and danger than he had thought; indeed, he could not have done so without them. The enemy then began to abandon the barricade, at which the men of the brigantines leaped ashore, and the army crossed the gap, walking [over the brigantines] and swimming. The gap was then closed with stones and adobes by the men of Tlaxcala, Huejotzingo, and Texcoco.

The Spaniards proceeded and took another barricade in the principal and widest street of the city, and, since it had no canal, they passed it easily. The enemy retreated to another bridge, which was also raised, with only a single plank left in place. It, however, could not hold all of them, so the rest swam over as fast as they could to reach a place of safety. They then removed the plank and took up the defense. Our men arrived and halted, because they could not cross without jumping into the water, a dangerous thing to attempt without the brigantines. Meanwhile, the enemy fought with great spirit, from the street, the barricade, and the rooftops, and did considerable damage, so Cortés had two guns trained on the street and had the crossbows and arquebuses play on it continuously. The people of the city were badly hurt by the fire and lost some of the braggadocio they had displayed at first. Our men recognized this, and several of them jumped into the water and swam across. When the enemy saw what was happening, they abandoned the rooftops and the barricade which they had defended for two hours, and fled. The army then crossed, and Cortés at once put the Indians to work filling the gap with the materials from the barricade and other things. The Spaniards and a few friends went on ahead, and at a distance of two crossbow shots came upon another bridge, without a barricade, leading into one of the principal squares of the city. Here they placed a gun, with which they did a good deal of mischief among the men in the square, but they did not dare to enter because of its many defenders. They finally decided to risk it, and at their approach the enemy fled, every man for himself, although most of them took refuge in the great temple, where the Spaniards and friends followed them and soon drove them out, so terrified that they acted quite madly, climbing up to the towers, overturning the idols, and wandering aimlessly about the temple yard.

Cuauhtémoc severely reprimanded his men for flying in this fashion, whereupon they came to their senses, recognized their cowardice, and, not seeing any horses, turned upon the Spaniards, drove them from the towers and from the whole compass of the temple, and put them prettily to flight. Cortés and the other captains stopped the rout and made their men face the enemy under the portals of the temple yard, reproaching them for their disgraceful conduct. In the end, however, they could not stay in the face of the danger and the heavy attack of the enemy, so they retreated to the square, where they tried to reform their ranks, but were driven out of it also. They even abandoned the gun I have mentioned, not being able to stand against the fury and strength of the enemy. At this juncture three mounted troopers came up and charged into the square, lancing Indians. When the citizens saw the horses they took to their heels, while our men plucked up courage and turned upon the enemy with such violence that they retook the great temple. Five Spaniards climbed up to the chapels, where they killed some ten or twelve Mexicans who had barricaded themselves there.

Six more horsemen arrived and joined the first three, and among them they set an ambush, in which they killed more than thirty Mexicans. It was now getting late, and Cortés, seeing that his men were tiring, gave the signal to withdraw, at which such a multitude of the enemy came charging that, if it had not been for the horse, a great many of the Spaniards would have been endangered, because the enemy fought like mad dogs, with no fear whatever. Even the horse would not have saved the situation if Cortés had not had the foresight to level the bad spots in the street and causeway. In short, everyone ran away and everyone fought well. Such is war. Our men burned a few houses along that street, so that the next time they would not be so badly hurt by stones thrown from the rooftops. Gonzalo de Sandoval and Pedro de Alvarado also did very well at their stations.

135. Demolition and Burning

DURING THIS WHILE Don Fernando of Texcoco was making a tour of his province to persuade his people to accept the service and friendship of Cortés. This, indeed, was his purpose in remaining there. Owing to his skill, or perhaps to the success of the Spaniards, he brought in almost the whole province of Acolhuacán, of which Texcoco is the capital, but only six of his brothers, of whom he had more than a hundred, as will be explained later on. One of them, named Ixtlilxóchitl, a valiant youth of about twenty-four, he made a captain and sent him to the siege with some forty thousand warriors, very well equipped and armed. Cortés received him joyfully and thanked him for his good will and deed. Cortés took thirty thousand of them for his own camp and distributed the others among the garrisons. The Mexicans were badly hurt by the aid and favor that Don Fernando rendered Cortés, not only because he deprived them of it, but because among his men were kinsmen, brothers, and even fathers of many who were in the city with Cuauhtémoc.

Two days after the arrival of Ixtlilxóchitl, some of the men of Xochimilco and certain mountain people who speak the language called Otomí came to offer their submission to Cortés and beg his forgiveness for having been so long about it, while they offered him men and provisions for the siege. Cortés was very pleased with their coming and with their offer, because with them at his back his men at Coyoacán would be safe. So he greeted the ambassadors cordially and told them that within three days he would invest the city; that, therefore, they should appear at that time, for in their actions he would know whether or not they were his friends, and then he dismissed them. They promised to come, and they kept their word.

Cortés then dispatched three brigantines to Sandoval and three others to Pedro de Alvarado, to cut the Mexicans off from the land and prevent their using canoes to bring in water, fruits, and maize, as well as other provisions; also, so that [the brigantines] might cover his flanks and help the Spaniards during any attacks on the city along the causeways, for he had learned how valuable the vessels were at the bridges. Their captains made raids by night and day along the shores against the towns on the lake, taking many canoes loaded with men and supplies, and not permitting any to enter the city.

On the day appointed for the assault, Cortés heard Mass, issued instructions to his captains, and left his quarters, with twenty horse, three hundred foot, a great multitude of friends, and two or three guns. He soon encountered the enemy, who, not having been molested for three or four days, had reopened at their leisure the channels that our men had filled; they had erected better barricades than before and were awaiting [the assault] with their customary howling. When, however, they espied the brigantines on both sides of the causeway, they slackened their defense. Our men saw at once the damage they were inflicting; they jumped ashore from the brigantines, took the barricade and bridge, and charged after the enemy, who soon fortified themselves at the next bridge. This one was also soon taken by our men, although with considerable effort, and they chased the enemy to the next. And so, from bridge to bridge, they drove them from the causeway and street, and even from the square.

Cortés advanced with some ten thousand Indians, sealing up all the breaches with adobes, stones, and lumber, and leveling the bad spots. There was so much work to do that all the ten thousand were kept at it until evening. Meanwhile, the Spaniards and friends skirmished with the men of the city, of whom they killed many from ambush. The mounted troops also rode the streets (those without gaps or bridges) for a while, lancing the citizens and shutting them up in their houses and temples.

What our Indians did and said that day to those of the city was a notable thing: sometimes they defied them; sometimes they invited them to dine, exhibiting legs and arms and other parts of human bodies, and saying: "This is your own flesh, which we shall have for dinner tonight and for breakfast tomorrow, after which we shall come for more. But don't run away on that account, for you are valiant men, and it is better to die fighting than to starve to death." At which each shouted the name of his city and set fire to the houses. The Mexicans were greatly disheartened at seeing themselves so tormented by the Spaniards, but felt even worse at being insulted by their vassals and hearing at their doorsteps shouts of "Victory, victory! Tlaxcala! Chalco! Texcoco! Xochimilco!" and the like, which vexed them more than seeing their flesh eaten, because they also ate the flesh of those they killed.

Cortés, seeing the Mexicans so stubbornly resolved to defend themselves to the death, realized two things: one, that he would recover few or none of the treasures he had seen and taken in the time of Moctezuma; two, that they were forcing him to destroy them utterly. Both these things grieved him, especially the latter, and he pondered how he could terrify them into recognizing their error and the evil they would suffer. For this purpose he demolished many houses and burned their idols; he also burned the big houses near at hand where he had been lodged the first time. There was not a

Spaniard, especially among those who had seen these houses before, who did not regret the destruction of such magnificent buildings. Nevertheless, since it greatly hurt the citizens, they let them burn. Never did the Mexicans, or any man of that country, think that any human force, let alone that small number of Spaniards, could take their city and burn the principal part of it. While the fire was raging, Cortés gathered his men and retired to his quarters.

The enemy would have liked to extinguish the fire, but could not. When they saw their adversaries withdrawing, they charged with great violence, screaming, and killing the stragglers who had loaded themselves down with booty. The troops, now able to ride the streets and causeway, stopped them with lances, and so, before night fell, our men were in their fort and the enemy in their houses, the latter sad, the former tired. Great was the slaughter that day, but greater was the burning of the houses, for, besides those mentioned, the brigantines burned many others along the canals. The other captains also attacked from their positions, but, since their object was merely to divert the enemy, there is little to say about it.

136. Activities of Cuauhtémoc and Cortés

VERY EARLY the next day Cortés heard Mass and returned to the city, with the same men in the same order, to give the enemy no time to repair the bridges and build barricades. But in spite of his early start he was too late, because the people of the city had not slept, but as soon as their enemy had gone they took shovels and picks and reopened the breaches that had been filled, and built barricades with the materials extracted, and soon they were as strong as before. In this work many fainted from fatigue, and very many perished from loss of sleep and hunger, but they could not do otherwise, for Cuauhtémoc was present. Cortés attacked two bridges and their barricades, and, although they were stubbornly defended, took them. The battle lasted from eight o'clock in the morning until one in the afternoon, and a large number [of Indians] died from the excessive effort and fatigue. All the powder and ball for the arquebuses was used up, and all the bolts and ammunition for the crossbows. Our men were hard put to it that day to take and fill these two breaches.

When they withdrew they received some damage also, because the enemy charged as if our men had been routed. They fought with such blind enthusiasm, indeed, that they did not notice the ambushes our horse set for them, in which many of those in the front ranks, who must have been the most courageous, died; but even with this setback they did not halt until their adversaries had been driven from the city. Pedro de Alvarado that day took two bridges on his causeway [of Tacuba], burned several houses with the help of the three brigantines, and killed a number of the enemy.

Some Spaniards blamed Cortés for not moving his quarters forward as he gained ground, and they had weighty arguments in their favor, because every day he had the same work to do, or even greater, in retaking the bridges and refilling the breaches. The risks they ran in this were great and notorious, because every time they retook a bridge they had to jump into the water, and some could not swim, while others did not dare or wish to do so, for the enemy, with knives and lance thrusts, prevented them from landing, and they had to turn back wounded or drowning. Others said that, even though Cortés did not advance his quarters, he should have held the bridges with a sufficient guard. He, however, who knew all this perfectly well, had a better argument on his side, for it was certain that if he removed his quarters to the square, the enemy could hem him in, the city being great and its citizens numerous, and thus the besieger would become the besieged, and every hour of the day and night he would be harassed and violently attacked; nor would he have been able to resist or even to eat if he lost command of the causeway. To guard the bridges would have been impossible, or at least doubtful, for two reasons: one, because the Spaniards were too few and, being tired from the day's work, would not have been able to combat the enemy by night; two, if he should entrust them to the Indians, their defense would have been uncertain, and their loss and the defeat [of the Indians] certain, from which great harm would ensue. So it was that for these reasons, as well as for his trust in the courage of his Spaniards, who would follow him in defeat or victory, he took his own counsel and not that of others.

137. Cortés Has Two Hundred Thousand Men at the Siege

THE PEOPLE OF CHALCO were such loyal friends of the Spaniards, or such bitter enemies of the Mexicans, that they summoned many towns and declared war on Ixtapalapa, Mexicalcingo, Cuitlahuac, Churubusco, Culhuacán, and the other towns of the fresh-water lake which had not submitted to Cortés, although they had not molested him since he had begun the siege of Mexico. For this reason, or because they saw the Spaniards victorious over the Mexicans, ambassadors from all these places came to offer Cortés their submission, to ask his pardon for their past offenses, and to beg his protection against the people of Chalco. He promised to do so and assured them they would not be molested again, and that he had never been angry with them, but with the Mexicans. And then, to learn whether their embassy was true or false, he informed them that he would not raise the siege until he had taken the city, in war or peace. He begged them to help him with their canoes, of which they had a great many, and with all the men the canoes could carry; also, to lend him men to build shelters for the Spaniards who did not have them, for it was now the season of heavy rains.

They gave their word, and so many men came from these towns and built so many huts along the causeway between the towers, where the camp was, that the Spaniards and the two thousand Indians who were serving them were easily accommodated. The rest slept in Coyoacán, which was only a league and a half distant. They also supplied the camp with bread, fish, and a great abundance of cherries, of which there are so many in those parts that there would have been enough for twice the population of the whole country. (These cherries yield two crops a year and are somewhat different from ours.) Not a single town now remained in that area which had not submitted to Cortés, and the people mingled freely with the Spaniards. They all came to our camps: some to serve, others to steal, and many to gape. Altogether, I believe, there were two hundred thousand men present at the siege of Mexico. It was a notable thing to be captain of such a host, but the skill and cleverness of

Cortés in managing and ruling it for such a long time without mutiny or disturbance were more notable still.

Cortés wished to take and level the street and causeway of Tacuba (which was the most important of them, having seven bridges), so that he might communicate freely with Pedro de Alvarado, by which time he thought everything would be [as good as] finished. For this purpose he summoned the men and canoes from Ixtapalapa and the other towns on the fresh-water lake. Three thousand [canoes] came at once, fifteen hundred of which, with four brigantines, he put into one lake, and the other fifteen hundred, with three brigantines, into the other, with orders to penetrate the city, burn houses, and do all the damage they could. He ordered the [three] garrisons to attack from their positions, and take and destroy as much [of the city] as possible, while Cortés himself set out over the Tacuba causeway with eighty thousand men. He took three of its bridges and filled the breaches, leaving the rest for the next day, when he set out by the same route, with the same forces in the same order. He took a large part of the city, but Cuauhtémoc made no sign of peace. Cortés was amazed at this, and even regretful, as much for the harm he was suffering as for that he was inflicting.

138. Pedro de Alvarado
Improves His Position

PEDRO DE ALVARADO wished to remove his camp to the square of Tlatelolco, because his task of guarding with his foot and horse the bridges he took was difficult and dangerous, his camp being three-quarters of a league distant. He also wanted to make a name for himself as captain, besides which the men of his company were importuning him, saying it would be an insult if Cortés or anyone else should occupy the square before them, they being the closest to it. So he decided to take the remaining gaps in the [Tacuba] causeway and penetrate to the square. He took all the men of his garrison and advanced to a breach some 60 paces across, which had been widened, and deepened to two fathoms, to prevent his passage.

He attacked it and, with the help of the brigantines, crossed the breach and took it. Leaving some of his men behind with orders to seal it, he pressed forward with about fifty Spaniards; but, when the men of the city saw how few they were and saw that the horse could not cross, they turned upon him so suddenly and boldly that they forced him to fly and jump blindly into the water. They killed many of our Indians and captured four Spaniards, whom they sacrificed and devoured at once and in the sight of all.

Thus Alvarado was cured of his madness in not believing Cortés, who had always told him never to advance without first securing his way of retreat. Those who had advised him [to attack] paid with their lives. Cortés regretted their loss; indeed, the same thing would have happened to him if he had believed those who had urged him to go on to the market place. But he was better advised, for by this time each house was an island, the causeways had been cut in many places, and the rooftops were piled with stones, for Cuauhtémoc had recourse to these and many other such measures. Cortés went to Alvarado's new camp to reprimand him for his action and advise him what he was to do; but when he found him far advanced into the city and saw the many places he had taken, he did not scold, but praised him. Then he conferred with Alvarado about many things regarding the conclusion of the siege and returned to his quarters.

139. The Mexicans Celebrate a Victory

CORTÉS PUT OFF removing his camp to the square, although he entered the city daily (or commanded others to enter), to engage the citizens, for the reasons just given, and to see whether Cuauhtémoc was ready to yield. Another reason was that the removal would be very risky, for the enemy were very close and very strong. But all the Spaniards, including the King's treasurer [Alderete], in view of his decision and past losses, begged and demanded that he enter the square. He replied that, although they spoke like brave men, they should consider the matter carefully, for the enemy were strong and determined to die defending themselves. They argued to such effect, however, that he had finally to yield, and he set the next day for the attack. He wrote Gonzalo de Sandoval and Pedro de Alvarado their instructions, which were, in brief: that Sandoval was to pack up all the baggage of his garrison, as if he were breaking camp; then he was to station ten horse on the causeway, concealing them behind houses, to induce the enemy to come out, in the belief that he was retreating, whereupon [the horse] would lance them; that Sandoval was to join Pedro de Alvarado with ten horse, one hundred foot, and the brigantines, leave his men there, take the other three brigantines and capture the breach where Pedro de Alvarado's men had been routed. Once the breach had been secured, he was to seal it very well before advancing, and, if he did advance, he was not to go far, or take a single breach without sealing it tight and leveling it. As for Alvarado, he was to penetrate the city as far as he could, with the 80 foot that would be sent to him.

Cortés also gave orders for the seven other brigantines to lead the 3,000 canoes into the two lakes, as they had done before. He divided the men of his own camp into three companies, corresponding to the three streets that led into the square. The treasurer and auditor entered one of them with 70 Spaniards, 20,000 Indians, eight horse, 12 sappers, and many pioneers for filling the canals, leveling the breaches, and demolishing the houses. He dispatched Jorge de Alvarado and Andrés de Tapia by the second street, with 80 Spaniards and more than 10,000 Indians, and posted two guns and eight horse at its mouth. Cortés entered by the third street, with a large number of friends and 100 Spanish troops, of whom 25 were crossbowmen and arquebusiers. He ordered the eight horsemen who were with him to stay where they were and not to follow him in without orders.

In this fashion all entered simultaneously, each squadron from its own position, and they did wonders, knocking over men and barricades, and taking bridges. They approached the market place, and so many of our Indian friends charged in that they entered the houses openly and robbed them, and, as things were going that day, it looked as though everything would soon be over. Cortés told them to go no farther, for they had done enough, lest they should get a setback, and to inspect the breaches they had won and make sure they were well sealed, for everything depended on it. But the men who were with the treasurer, following up their victory, left behind them a breach badly sealed, about twelve paces wide and two fathoms deep.

Cortés went there as soon as he had been told of it, to repair the damage; but he had no sooner arrived than he saw his men in flight and jumping into the water to escape their pursuers, who jumped in after them. Many canoes came up also and captured alive a number of our friends and even some Spaniards. But all Cortés and his fifteen companions could do was to give a hand to those in the water, some of whom escaped wounded and others half-drowned, and many of whom had lost their weapons. A large force of the enemy charged and surrounded them. Cortés and his companions, absorbed in rescuing the men in the water and in caring for those they had rescued, did not realize the danger they were in, and Cortés was seized by several Mexicans and would have been carried off if it had not been for Francisco [Cristóbal] de Olea, his servant, who with one stroke cut off the hand of the man who had seized Cortés, only to be immediately killed himself by the enemy, so he died to save his master's life.

Antonio de Quiñones, captain of the guard, came up at this moment, took Cortés by the arm and dragged him away from the enemy, with whom [Cortés] was struggling mightily. At the rumor that Cortés had been taken, the Spaniards rushed into the breach and a horseman cleared a small space, but he received a lance thrust in the throat which forced him to turn back. The fight was deadlocked for a while, until Cortés mounted a horse that had been brought for him; but, not being able to operate effectively, he gathered up his Spaniards and abandoned that bad spot, retreating by way of the street of Tacuba, which was wide and good. [Cristóbal] de Guzmán died in his attempt to give Cortés a horse, and his death was mourned by all, because he was an honorable and valiant man. The action was so confused that two mares fell into the water, one of which was rescued, the other killed by the Indians, as they had killed Guzmán's horse.

While the treasurer and his men were attacking a barricade, the Indians tossed them the heads of three Spaniards, saying they would do the same with them if the siege was not lifted. At this, and in view of the havoc I have described, they little by little withdrew. Then the priests mounted up into the temples of Tlatelolco, lit braziers, and sent up clouds of incense to celebrate their victory. They stripped the captured Spaniards, who numbered about forty, opened their breasts and tore out their hearts as an offering to the idols, and sprinkled the blood about. Our men would have liked to take revenge for that piece of cruelty, which they could not prevent, but they had enough to do to save themselves, so closely were they pressed by the enemy, who no longer feared horses or swords.

Forty Spaniards were taken and sacrificed that day; Cortés was struck in one leg, and thirty others were wounded, while more than two thousand of our Indian friends died. Many of our canoes were lost, and the brigantines barely escaped. The captain and sailing master of one were wounded, and the captain died of his wounds a week later. On that same day four of Alvarado's Spaniards also died in the fight.

This was a melancholy day for our Spaniards and their friends, and the night was spent in mourning. The Mexicans celebrated that afternoon and night with great bonfires, with the blowing of many trumpets and the beating of drums, with dancing, feasting, and drinking. They cleared the streets and breaches, [and restored them] as they had been before. They set watches in the towers, and sentinels near our camps. Then early the next morning the king paraded the heads of two Christians and two horses throughout the region, as a token of his victory, while he begged [the people] to abandon the friendship of the Spaniards, and promised to finish off those who remained and free the whole country from war. For this reason, certain provinces were emboldened to take up arms against the friends and allies of the Spaniards, as Malinalco and Cuixco did against Cuernavaca. Their action was noised about the country, and our men became fearful of rebellion among our friends and mutiny in our army; but God willed otherwise. The next day Cortés made a sally with his men, to show that he was not afraid, but he turned back at the first bridge.

140. Conquest of Malinalco, Matalcingo, and Other Towns

TWO DAYS AFTER the defeat, the men of Cuernavaca, who had for some time past been our friends, came to the quarters of Cortés to tell him that the people of Malinalco and Cuixco were attacking them and destroying their fields and orchards, and were threatening to attack him after they had won; therefore, that he should send Spaniards to help them. Cortés, who was in greater need of help himself than of helping, promised them Spaniards, as much to keep up his credit as to quiet their insistence. In this he was opposed by certain Spaniards, who did not like the idea of taking men from the army. Nevertheless, he sent eighty foot and ten horse, under the command of Andrés de Tapia, whom he urged to make the raid brief. He allowed [Tapia] ten days for the journey going and coming. Andrés de Tapia joined the men of Cuernavaca and came upon the enemy at a small village near Malinalco. He attacked them in the open, routed them, and pursued them to the city, which is a large town, well-watered, situated on a very high hill, which the horse could not negotiate. He laid waste the plain and turned back. This successful raid liberated our friends and frightened our enemies, who had gone beyond themselves in the belief that the Spaniards were about finished.

Two days after Andrés de Tapia's return from Cuernavaca, some sixteen messengers of the Otomí language came to [Cortés] to complain of the lords of the province of Matalcingo, their neighbors, who were waging war upon them and who had burned a town and carried off its inhabitants. For this reason [the Otomí] were coming to Mexico to fight beside the Spaniards, and drive out the people and kill them; or at least to force them beyond the barricades. They urged [Cortés] to take prompt action, for they were many and were only twelve leagues distant. Cortés believed them, because a few days previously, during the battle, the Mexicans had threatened him with [these same men of] Matalcingo. So he sent Gonzalo de Sandoval to them with eighteen horse and 100 foot, and many of the mountain people who for some days past had been helping him in the siege. Cortés was persuaded to do so, as much to keep from showing weakness before friends and enemies as to help the Otomí, for he was well aware of the risk, not only to those who went but to those who stayed, and of the complaints of his own men.

Sandoval departed, spent two nights in the devastated Otomí territory, and came to a river which was being crossed by the enemy, who were loaded down with the spoils they had taken from a town they had just burned. When they caught sight of the Spaniards and the horses, they fled, abandoning a good part of their booty. They crossed another river and halted on a plain, where Sandoval followed them. He found along the road bundles of clothing, loads of maize, and roasted babies. He charged with his horse, after which his foot came up and routed the enemy. He pursued them and shut them up in Matalcingo, which was three leagues distant. In the pursuit two thousand died. The city threw up defenses in order to gain time for the women, children, and clothing to be taken to a very high hill, where there was a kind of fortress. At this juncture, our friends, numbering as many as seventy thousand, arrived; they entered the town, expelled the inhabitants, put it to the sack, and burned it. In this they spent the night. The defeated took refuge on the hill I have mentioned, where they set up an incredible howling and weeping, beating of drums and blowing of horns, until midnight, when they all left.

At daybreak Sandoval ordered out his whole army and went to the hill, but found no trace of the enemy. He then attacked a town which had been involved in the fighting, but its lord laid down his arms, opened the gates, submitted, and promised to bring in peace the people of Matalcingo, Malinalco, and Cuixco. He kept his word, for he spoke to them at once and brought them to Cortés, who pardoned them, and they served him well in the siege, much to the chagrin of Cuauhtémoc.

141. Cortés Decides to Destroy Mexico

CHICHIMECATECATL, the Tlaxcalan who had transported the frames of the brigantines, and who had been with Pedro de Alvarado since the beginning of the siege, seeing that the Spaniards were no longer fighting as was their habit, made a raid into the city with only the men from his province, something which had not been done before. He attacked a bridge with a great shouting and, invoking his ancestors and his city, won it. He left four hundred bowmen at the bridge and pursued the enemy, who had retreated in the expectation of taking him on his way out. They did turn upon him, and a very pretty skirmish ensued, in which both sides fought stoutly with equal arms, shouting defiance at each other. Both sides lost many dead and wounded, upon whom all dined well! The enemy charged in to cut off his passage of the breach, but he crossed it in safety, thanks to his four hundred bowmen, who stopped his adversaries and knocked some of the bravado out of them.

The Mexicans were humiliated by this raid and astonished at the daring of the Tlaxcalans, and even the Spaniards were amazed at their tactics and skill.

The Mexicans attributed our lack of activity to cowardice or sickness, or perhaps to hunger, and so, during the early morning watch they made a sharp attack on Alvarado's camp. The sentries heard them coming, sounded the alarm, and the foot and horse sallied forth and put the enemy to flight at the point of the lance. Many were drowned, many wounded, and all were taught a lesson. After this episode the Mexicans indicated that they wanted to speak with Cortés, who went to an open bridge to hear what they had to say. In one breath they asked for a truce, in the next for peace; but they always insisted that the Spaniards leave the country. Their purpose was to discover what spirits our men were in, and to use the days of the truce to replenish their supplies, for they had never abandoned their resolution to die in the defense of their country and their religion. Cortés replied that a truce would be of no advantage to either of them, but that he would not stand in the way of peace, which was good at all times, even though he was the besieger and had plenty of food; that they should consider how badly they needed peace, before their bread gave out and they died of hunger. While he was talking with the interpreter, an old man mounted a barricade in the sight of everyone, took bread and other things from his wallet, and ate them, giving [Cortés] to understand that he was not in want, and so ended the conversation.

Cortés was beginning to feel that the siege was too long drawn out, since he had not been able to take Mexico in fifty days of it; and he wondered at the endurance of the enemy, in skirmish and combat, and at their determination not to accept peace, for he knew how many thousands of them had died at the hands of their adversaries, and how many from hunger and disease. He begged them to accept his friendship, for otherwise he would kill them all, since he had them surrounded on land and water, and they could not bring in fruit, bread, or water, and would have to eat each other. They replied that the Spaniards would be the first to die; that the more they were threatened, the stronger would be their resistance, and the more tricks and stratagems they would employ. Indeed, they had covered the square and many streets with great stones, to stop the horses, and had built walls across other streets, to keep out the Spaniards.

Cortés was reluctant to destroy such a beautiful city, but he then determined to raze all the houses on the streets he should take, and fill the canals with [the débris]. He told his captains of his decision, and they all approved of it, although it did seem to be a long and arduous task. He also informed the Indian lords of the army, who were delighted at the news, and at once brought in many farmers armed with digging sticks, which they used for spades and hoes. In this they spent four days. Now that Cortés had a corps of pioneers, he put his men in order and mounted an attack on the street that led into the main square. The people came out and made a false bid for peace, but he stopped them and asked for their king. They replied that he had been summoned. Cortés waited an hour, at the end of which they showered him with stones, arrows, darts, and insults. The Spaniards then charged, took a high barricade, and penetrated into the square. They removed the stones that impeded the horses and sealed the canal so thoroughly that it was never opened again. They demolished all the houses, cleared and opened the entrance [to the square], and returned to camp.

Our men spent the next six days continuously at this kind of thing, without receiving much damage, except that on the last day two horses were wounded. The following day Cortés set an ambush. He summoned Gonzalo de Sandoval and told him to bring thirty of his and Alvarado's horse and group them with twenty-five of his own. He sent two brigantines on ahead with the foot, while he, with thirty horse, concealed himself in one of the great houses on the square. The Spaniards attacked the people of the city in many places and then retired. As they passed the great house they fired an arquebus, which was the signal for the [horse] to emerge from their ambush. The enemy were pursuing our men so furiously and with such shouting that they went considerably beyond this point, whereupon Cortés galloped out with his thirty horse, shouting "St. Peter and at them! St. James and at them!" and played havoc with the enemy, killing some, knocking down others, and cutting off many, who fell into the hands of our Indian friends. In this ambush, without counting their losses in the [previous] fighting, five hundred Mexicans died and many others were captured. Our Indian friends had a good dinner that night, for they could never be persuaded to give up the eating of human flesh. Some of our Spaniards climbed up to a shrine and found there gold articles to the value of fifteen hundred castellanos.

This exploit filled the Mexicans with such terror that they no longer shouted and threatened as they had been doing; nor, from that moment on, did they wait in the square for our men to retire, for fear of another such [disaster]. In short, this made it possible for us to take Mexico more quickly.

142. Fortitude of the Mexicans

TWO MEXICANS, men of no great importance, came to Cortés' camp one night, driven by hunger. They said their neighbors were terror-stricken and were dying of hunger and disease; that they piled up the dead in their houses to conceal them and went out by night to fish between the houses, where the brigantines could not catch them, and to search for wood, and gather herbs and roots to eat. Cortés wanted to know the whole of the story, so he had the brigantines cruise about the city, while he, with some fifteen horse, a hundred Spanish foot, and many friends, sallied forth before daybreak and concealed himself behind some houses, posting lookouts to warn him, by a certain signal, when they saw people approaching. Some did appear at dawn, looking for food. The signal was given, and Cortés rode out and slaughtered many of them, mostly women and children and unarmed men. Eight hundred died there. The brigantines captured many men and canoes that were out fishing. The Mexican lookouts heard the noise [and gave the alarm], but the citizens, terrified at seeing Spaniards about at such an unusual hour, feared another ambush and did not resist.

The following day, which was the eve of the feast of St. James [July 25], Cortés made his customary raid into the city, advanced along the street of Tacuba, and burned the houses of Cuauhtémoc, which were large, strong, and surrounded by water. By this time three-fourths of the city had fallen, and one could go in safety from the camp of Cortés to that of Alvarado. While the houses in the captured parts were being demolished and burned, the Mexicans said to the Tlaxcalans "Hurry! Burn and destroy these houses, for you will build them again, whether you like it or not, at your own cost and by your own hands. If we win, you shall do it for us; if we lose, for the Spaniards."

Four days later, Cortés attacked from his side, and Alvarado from his. The latter did all he could to take the two towers of Tlatelolco, in order to box in the enemy, as his captain was doing. He did so well, indeed, that he took them, although he lost three horses. The next day the cavalry were in the square, while the enemy looked on from the rooftops. As they rode through the city they found dead bodies heaped up in the houses and streets, and floating in the water. They also saw a great deal of gnawed bark and roots, and men who were so emaciated that the Spaniards were filled with pity for them. Cortés proposed a truce, but they, although their bodies were starved, were strong of heart and told him he should not expect to get any spoils from them, because they intended to burn whatever they had left, or throw it into the water, where it would never be found, and that if a single one of them survived, he would die fighting.

Our powder had been used up, although there were plenty of [crossbow] bolts and pikes, which were replenished every day. So, in order to damage, or at least to frighten, the enemy, a catapult was built and placed in the square, and our Indian friends trained it upon those of the city. But our carpenters lacked the skill to finish it, so it failed. The Spaniards concealed their disappointment [on the pretext] that they did not want to do more damage than they had done already. While the catapult was under construction, a matter of four days, our men did not enter the city, and, when they did go in, they found the streets crowded with women, children, old men, and other miserable creatures, overcome with hunger and sickness. Cortés ordered his men not to harm the poor wretches. The nobles and those in good health were on the rooftops, dressed in mantles, but without arms, a novel and surprising thing. I believe they were celebrating some festival. Cortés asked them to submit peacefully; they answered with dissimulation.

The next day Cortés told Pedro de Alvarado to attack a district of about a thousand houses, which had not yet been taken, while he would advance from the opposite side. Its inhabitants defended themselves very well for a good while, but in the end they fled, not being able to stand before the fury and pressure of their attackers. Our men took the whole district and killed twelve thousand citizens. The heavy mortality was caused by the cruelty of our Indian friends, who would spare the life of no Mexican, no matter how they were reprimanded for it. [The people] were so crowded after the loss of this district that there was hardly room for them to stand in the remaining houses, and the streets were so covered with dead bodies that one had to walk over corpses. Cortés wanted to find out how much of the city was yet to be taken, so he mounted a tower, looked, and estimated it to be about an eighth. The next day he again attacked the remnant, but ordered his men to kill only those who resisted.

The Mexicans, bewailing their ill luck, begged the Spaniards to kill them and have done with it, but certain gentlemen urgently summoned Cortés, who hurried to them, thinking they might be seeking an arrangement. He stood at the edge of a breach, and they said to him: "Ah, Captain Cortés, since you are a child of the Sun, why do you not persuade him to finish us? O Sun, who can make the circuit of the earth in the short space of a day and a night, kill us now and relieve us of this long and dreadful penance, for we desire to rest with Quetzalcoatl, who awaits us." Then they wept and invoked their gods with loud cries. Cortés answered with whatever came to his mind, but could not persuade them. Our Spaniards were struck with pity.

143. Capture of Cuauhtémoc

CORTÉS, seeing them in such dire and evil straits, wanted to find out whether they would submit, so he spoke with an uncle of Don Fernando of Texcoco, who was still wounded, and begged him to see his king and arrange a peace. This gentlemen refused at first, knowing the resolution of Cuauhtémoc, but finally consented as a matter of honor and goodness of heart. The next day, Cortés entered the city with his men, sending him on ahead with several Spaniards. The guards in the streets received and greeted him with the respect due his rank, and he went at once to the king and delivered his message, at which Cuauhtémoc flew into a rage and ordered him to be sacrificed, and the answer he sent back was in the form of flights of arrows, showers of stones, lance thrusts, and howls [to the effect] that they preferred death to peace. They fought hard that day, killed and wounded many men, and even killed a horse with a sickle a Mexican had fashioned out of a Spanish sword; but, although they killed many, many of them died also.

Cortés entered the city again the next day, not to fight, but in the hope that the enemy would surrender. They, however, had no such thought. He approached a barricade and spoke from horseback with certain gentlemen he knew. He said that he could easily finish them in a short while, but that out of compassion and love he refrained from doing so; that they should persuade their lord to allow them to submit, and they would be well received and treated, and given something to eat. With these and other words he had them in tears. They answered that they were well aware of their error and felt badly enough about the harm they had suffered and their ruin. They told him, however, that they had to obey their king and their gods, who had so willed; that, nevertheless, he should wait and they would speak with their lord Cuauhtémoc. At this they departed, but returned after a little while, saying that it was too late in the day for their lord to come, but that doubtless he would appear at dinnertime the next day to talk of peace.

Cortés went back to his camp very happy, thinking that [between the two of them] they would reach an agreement, so he ordered a dais set up in the square for the next day, after the custom of the Mexican lords, and food prepared; and he, accompanied by many Spaniards, all well-armed, went there. The king, however, failed to appear, excusing himself because of illness; but he did sent five very noble lords to make an arrangement. Cortés was disappointed at the king's absence, but was glad to see these gentlemen, with whose intervention he might make peace. They ate and drank like hungry and thirsty men, took some refreshment, and promised to return, as Cortés had begged them to do, warning them that in the absence of the king no treaty could be considered. They reappeared two hours later, bringing a present of some very fine cotton mantles, but told Cortés that their king would not come in any circumstances, being fearful and humiliated. It was now night, so they left, but came again the next day to summon Cortés to the market place, for Cuauhtémoc wished to speak with him. Cortés waited there for more than two hours, but the king did not appear.

It was now evident that he was being mocked, so Cortés sent Sandoval with the brigantines to attack from one direction, while he, from the other, attacked the streets and barricades where the enemy was fortified. Encountering little resistance, for the enemy had neither stones nor arrows, he went in and did as he pleased. The number of dead and prisoners that day exceeded forty thousand, and the Spaniards had more work to do in preventing their friends from killing, than they had in fighting. They did not, however, interfere with the looting. The wailing of women and children was piteous, and so frightful was the stench of the dead bodies that our men soon retired. Cortés made up his mind to finish the war that night. Cuauhtémoc resolved to escape, and for this purpose he embarked in a canoe of twenty paddles. Early the next morning Cortés took his men and four guns and went to the narrow place where the enemy was confined. He told Pedro de Alvarado to remain quiet until he heard an arquebus shot; Sandoval, to take the brigantines to a lagoon among the houses where all the Mexican canoes were kept, and there to seek out the king, but not to kill him. He ordered the rest of his men to drive the enemy toward the brigantines. Then he climbed a tower and asked for the king. Xihuacoa, the governor and captain-general, spoke to him, but had not the authority to agree to a surrender. Meanwhile, a great throng of people, mainly old men, children, and women, came out; but there so many of them, and they were in so great a hurry, that they pushed each other into the water, where many drowned.

Cortés begged his Indian lords not to kill these poor wretches, for they were giving themselves up; but the temptation was too great, and some fifteen thousand were killed and sacrificed. Then very loud cries arose from the common people of the city, for their lord had fled and they had no place to go, nor did they know of any, so they all tried to get into the canoes, but there was not room for them and they fell into the water and perished, although many escaped by swimming. The warriors were backed up against the walls of the rooftops, pretending to be unaware of their ruin. The Mexican nobles and many others were in canoes with the king. Cortés fired the arquebus as a signal for Pedro de Alvarado to attack, and the guns opened fire on the narrow place where the enemy was confined. Cortés pressed them so closely that in a little while he took it, and now there was nothing left to take. The brigantines broke up the flotilla of canoes, none of which put up any resistance; rather, they all fled as best they could, and the royal standard was lowered.

Garcí Holguín, captain of a brigantine, set out in pursuit of a canoe of twenty paddles, loaded down with men. A prisoner he had with him said that those were the king's men, and that the king might well be among them. Holguín overtook it, but avoided a collision, and aimed his three crossbows. Then Cuauhtémoc stood up in the stern and prepared to fight; but, when he saw the crossbows readied, the swords bared, and the great advantage enjoyed by the brigantine, he made a sign that he was the lord and gave himself up.

Garcí Holguín, overjoyed at his great prize, brought Cuauhtémoc to Cortés, who received him with royal honors, saluted him cordially, and had him brought near, whereupon Cuauhtémoc touched Cortés' dagger and said: "I have done everything in my power to defend myself and my people, and everything that it was my duty to do, to avoid the pass in which I now find myself. You may do with me whatever you wish, so kill me, for that will be best."

Cortés comforted Cuauhtémoc with kind words and the hope of life and authority. He then took him up to a rooftop and begged him to command his men to yield. Cuauhtémoc did so, and they, who numbered some seventy thousand dropped their arms at the sight of him.

144. Fall of Mexico

IN THE MANNER that you have heard, Hernán Cortés took Mexico-Tenochtitlán, Tuesday, the thirteenth of August, the day of St. Hippolytus, in the year 1521. In commemoration of this great event and victory, the people of the city celebrate the day every year, with a festival and processions, in which they carry the standard he won.

The siege had lasted three months. In it Cortés had 200,000 Indian friends, 900 Spaniards, 80 horses, 16 pieces of artillery, 13 brigantines, and 6,000 canoes. He lost about 50 Spaniards killed, six horses, and not many Indian friends. The enemy lost 100,000 men, or many more, according to others, but I am not including those who died of hunger and the pestilence. All the lords, gentlemen, and nobles took part in the defense, and thus many people of rank died. [The defenders] were numerous; they suffered from hunger and had to drink salt water; they slept among the dead and lived in a perpetual stench, for which reasons they sickened or were struck down by the pestilence, in which an infinite number died. From these circumstances one can appreciate their constancy and fortitude in holding to their resolution, for, although they were reduced to the extremity of eating twigs and bark and drinking salt water, they never sued for peace.

Toward the end they would have liked to do so, but Cuauhtémoc would not have it, because at the beginning they, against his will and counsel, had refused it. In order not to show signs of weakness before the enemy, even though they should all die, the bodies were concealed in the houses. Thus it is evident that, although the Mexicans did eat human flesh, they did not eat that of their own people, for, if they had done so, they would not have died of starvation. The Mexican women won great praise for themselves, not only because they stood by their husbands and fathers, but nursed the sick, treated the wounded, made slings and missiles, and fought from the housetops, throwing stones as effectively as the men.

The city was put to the sack, the Spaniards seizing the gold, silver, and featherwork; the Indians, the clothing and other spoils. Cortés had great fires lighted in the streets to celebrate, and to get rid of the suffocating stench. He had the dead buried as best he could, and he branded with the King's iron many men and women as slaves; the rest he set free. He had the brigantines hauled up on land and set a guard of fifty men over them, commanded by Villafuerte, to keep the Indians from burning them. In these activities he spent four days, after which he retired to Coyoacán, where he thanked the lords and friendly towns for their help, promised to reward them, and told all who wished, to go with God, for at the moment there was no more fighting to do, but he would summon them if need arose. At this they all departed, rich and very happy at having destroyed Mexico, at being friends of the Spaniards, and in favor with Cortés.

145. Portents Presaging the Fall

A LITTLE WHILE before Hernán Cortés came to New Spain, a great illumination appeared for many nights above the sea at the spot where he landed; it began two hours before dawn, mounted to the sky, and then vanished. At the same time the people of Mexico observed flames toward the east, that is, toward Vera Cruz, and a thick cloud of smoke that seemed to reach the sky, badly frightening them. They also saw armed men fighting in the air, a novel and marvelous thing for them, which gave them a good deal to think and worry about, for there was talk among them of white and bearded men who would come to take the country during the life of Moctezuma. The lords of Texcoco and Tacuba were greatly disturbed [by these signs], saying that the arms of those men in the air were like the sword of Moctezuma, and their dress like his dress. Moctezuma had great difficulty in placating them, alleging that the garments and arms were those of his ancestors. To convince them of this, he invited them to try to break his sword, and, when they failed, lacking the strength or knowledge, they were astonished and quieted.

The truth seems to be that some men from the coast had brought to Moctezuma a chest containing clothing, this sword, a few small gold rings, and other things of ours, which they had found on the beach, cast up by a storm. Others say that the disturbance of the two lords was owing to the garments and the sword that Cortés had sent to Moctezuma by the hand of Teudilli, which resembled the dress and arms of the men who had been seen fighting in the air. However it was, they were convinced that they would be ruined with the arrival of men thus dressed and armed.

The very year in which Cortés arrived at Mexico, a *malli* (that is, a prisoner of war destined for sacrifice), who was bewailing his ill fortune and death, and calling upon God in heaven, saw a vision which told him not to fear death, because God, to whom he had commended himself, would have mercy on him; that he should tell the priests and ministers of the idols that sacrifice and the sprinkling of human blood would soon cease, because those who were to stop it and seize the country were at hand. They sacrificed him in [the square of] Tlatelolco, where the gibbet of Mexico now stands, but his words and his vision (which they called a wind from heaven) were remembered; and when later they saw angels painted with wings and diadems, they said these resembled the vision that had spoken to the *malli*.

Also, in the year '20, near Mexico, the earth burst open and a stream of water gushed out, with many fishes in it. The Mexicans then said that Moctezuma, who was returning very proud of his victory at Soconusco, told the lord of Coyoacán that Mexico was safe and strong, and that no one could prevail against him. "Do not be so certain, good king," said the lord, "for one force can overthrow another." Moctezuma was furious at this reply and regarded the lord with disfavor. Later, however, when Cortés had both of them in his power, these prophetic words were recalled.

146. Torture of Cuauhtémoc

THE GOLD that our men had taken in Mexico was not all recovered; nor was a trace of Moctezuma's famous treasure ever found. The Spaniards were much annoyed at this, for they had thought, once Mexico had been taken, to find a great hoard, or at least as much as they had lost in the retreat. Cortés marveled that no Indian led him to any store of gold or silver, while the soldiers pressed the citizens to bring forth their money. The King's officers also wanted to uncover gold, silver, pearls, precious stones, and jewels, in order to assemble a great fifth for the King; but they were never able to persuade any Mexican to reveal anything, although all agreed that the treasure of the gods and kings was very rich. So it was decided to put Cuauhtémoc and one of his gentlemen to the torture. The latter showed such great fortitude that, although he died in the fire, he answered none of the questions put to him, either because he did not know the answers, or because he was faithful to his trust. While he was being tortured he kept his eyes on the king, in the hope that the king would be moved to pity and give him leave to tell what he knew, or perhaps would be moved to reveal it himself. But Cuauhtémoc looked at him fiercely and spoke to him with contempt, calling him weak and cowardly, and saying: "Am I by chance in some feast or bath?" Cortés stopped the torture of Cuauhtémoc, either because he thought it degrading and cruel, or because [Cuauhtémoc] had told him that, ten days before his capture, the devil had informed him he was going to be defeated, so he had thrown the [captured] guns, his gold and silver, precious stones, pearls, and rich jewels into the water.

In his residencia Cortés was charged with the crime of putting a great king to death in this shameful fashion, and with doing so from avarice and cruelty.* Cortés defended himself by saying that he had acted at the request of Julián de Alderete, the King's treasurer; also, to bring the truth to light, for everyone was saying that he had kept all the treasure of Moctezuma for himself and had not wanted to torture [Cuauhtémoc], lest this fact be laid bare. Many, acting on Cuauhtémoc's words, sought the treasure in the lake and on land, but it was never found. And truly it was a remarkable thing that he could have hidden such a quantity of gold and silver and not reveal it.

---

* Cuauhtémoc did not die under torture, but was hanged four years later, during the Honduras expedition, for allegedly plotting a rebellion against Cortés. See below, chap. 179.

147. King's Fifth of the Spoils

THE SPOILS OF MEXICO were melted down and came to 130,000 castellanos, which were distributed [among the men] according to their service and merit. The King's fifth amounted to 26,000 castellanos, not including many slaves, articles of featherwork, fans, cotton and feather mantles; shields of wickerwork covered with tiger skins and lined with feathers, with bosses and rims of gold; many pearls, some as large as hazelnuts, but most of them somewhat blackened, because the shells had been burned to extract the pearls and meat. The Emperor was also given many precious stones, among them a fine emerald as big as the palm of one's hand, square, pointed like a pyramid; a great table service of gold and silver, cups, pitchers, plates, bowls, and pots, as well as some cast pieces in the form of birds, fishes, animals, and others in the form of fruits and flowers, and all of them so lifelike that they were well worth seeing. He was also given many coronets, earrings, finger rings, lip rings, and other jewels for men and women, and several idols and blow-guns of gold and silver, the whole of which was worth 150,000 ducats, although others say twice as much.

Besides this, he was sent a number of masks made of mosaic in small stones, with golden ears, and bone teeth protruding beyond their lips; many priestly robes, frontals, palliums, and other temple ornaments, of feathers, cotton, and rabbit skins; also, some giant bones found in Coyoacán, and three tigers, one of which broke loose on shipboard and scratched six or seven men, killed two of them, and then jumped into the sea. A second tiger was killed to prevent another such accident. The Emperor was sent still other things, but this is the main part of them. Many sent money home to their kin; Cortés, 4,000 ducats to his parents by the hand of Juan de Rivera, his secretary. The treasure was transported by Alonso de Avila and Antonio de Quiñones, attorneys for Mexico, in three caravels; but the two caravels that had the gold on board were seized by the French pirate Florin, this side of the Azores. He also took another ship inbound from the Indies, with 72,000 ducats, 600 marks of pearls and mother-of-pearl, and 2,000 arrobas of sugar.

The city council [of Mexico] wrote to the Emperor praising Cortés, while he pleaded for confirmation of the encomiendas of the conquistadores, and begged the Emperor to send over a learned and studious person to see the great and marvelous land he had con-quered, which he hoped the Emperor would see fit to call New Spain. Moreover, [he begged the Emperor] to send bishops, secular priests, and friars, to take charge of the conversion of the Indians; and farmers, with herds, plants, and seeds; and not to allow turncoats [i.e., Moslem and Jewish converts], physicians, or lawyers to go there.

THE DESTRUCTION OF MEXICO filled everyone with astonishment and dread, for it was the greatest and strongest city in all those parts, as well as the most powerful in its dominion and wealth. For this reason not only did its subjects submit to Cortés, but its enemies also, to avoid a war and the fate of Cuauhtémoc. Many ambassadors, therefore, came to Coyoacán from large, diverse, and distant provinces, some of which, it is said, were three hundred leagues away. The king of Michoacán, called the Cazonci, an ancient and natural enemy of the Mexicans, and himself a very great lord, sent ambassadors to Cortés, congratulating him upon his victory and offering friendship. Cortés received them cordially and kept them with him for four days. He had the cavalry maneuver for them, to give something to talk about in their country, and gave them trinkets, two Spaniards to go with them and see their country and to pick up an interpreter for the south coast, and then dismissed them.

These ambassadors told their king so many things about the Spaniards that he had a mind to come and see them, but his advisers spoke gainst it, so he sent his brother in his place, with a thousand servants and many gentlemen. Cortés received [the brother] with the courtesy due his rank and took him to see the brigantines and the ruins of Mexico. The Spanish foot drilled for him and discharged their arquebuses and crossbows, the artillery fired at a target in a tower, and the cavalry maneuvered and skirmished with lances. He was amazed by these things, and by the beards and dress of the men. He left after four days, with much to tell his brother the king.

Thus assured of the good will of King Cazonci, Cortés sent Cristóbal de Olid, with 40 horse and 100 Spanish foot, to found a colony at Tzintzuntzan. Cazonci was happy to have them settle there and gave them a quantity of feather and cotton clothing, 5,000 pesos in base gold (mixed with silver), and 1,000 marks of an amalgam of silver and copper, all of which consisted of articles for the dressing table and personal ornaments. Then he offered himself and his country to the King of Castile, as Cortés had requested.

The principal city and capital of Michoacán is Tzintzuntzan, which is a little more than 40 leagues from Mexico, situated at the base of the mountains on the shore of a fresh-water lake, which is as large as that of Mexico and abounds with excellent fish. Besides this lake there are many others in that kingdom, also full of fish, which gives the country its name of Michoacán, meaning "land of fish." There are also many springs, some of which are so hot that they will scald one's hand. These are used as baths. The country has a very mild climate, with gentle winds, and is so healthful that the sick from many parts go there to be healed. It yields an abundance of grain, fruit, and greenstuff. Game is plentiful. A great deal of wax and cotton is produced. The men are better-looking than their neighbors, strong and enduring in work. They are great bowmen and excellent marksmen, especially those called Teuchichimecas, who are subject to, or near, that kingdom. If one of them should miss a shot at a piece of game, he will don a woman's skirt, called a *cueitl*. [The men of Michoacán] are warlike and skillful; they had always been at war with the Mexicans and never, or very rarely, had lost a battle.

There are many mines of silver and base gold in this kingdom. In the year 1525 the richest silver mine thus far seen in New Spain was discovered, and because of its value the royal officers seized it for the King, not without injury to its discoverer. But it was God's will that the mine should be lost or soon exhausted, and so the discoverer lost his mine, the King his fifth, and both suffered a loss of reputation.

There are also good deposits of salt, a great deal of the black stone [obsidian] used in the fabrication of knives, and some very fine jet. Good cochineal is produced. The Spaniards have planted mulberry trees for silk, sown wheat, and bred cattle. Everything yields well. Francisco de Terrazas, for example, harvested six hundred fanegas of wheat from four he had sown.

149. Gonzalo de Sandoval Conquers Tuxtepec and Coatzacoalcos

AT THE TIME that Mexico rebelled and drove out the Spaniards, all the towns allied with it rebelled also and killed the Spaniards who were in their country exploring for mines and other things. The siege of Mexico, however, had prevented their punishment. The principal culprits were Huatusco [Vera Cruz], Tuxtepec, and other towns on the [north] coast, so, toward the end of October of the year '21 Cortés sent Gonzalo de Sandoval from Coyoacán with 200 Spanish foot, 35 horse, and a reasonable number of friends, including several Mexican lords. Upon Sandoval's arrival at Huatusco, the whole of that country submitted to him. He founded a colony at Tuxtepec, 25 leagues from Mexico, and named it Medellín, by command and in honor of Cortés, for such is the name of his birthplace. From Tuxtepec, Sandoval went to Coatzacoalcos to found a colony, in the belief that the people of the river were friendly to Cortés, as they had promised to be when Diego de Ordaz went there while Moctezuma was still alive.

Sandoval did not, however, get either a good reception or friendship. He told the people that he was there in the name of Cortés and inquired whether they were in need of anything. They replied that they needed neither his men nor his friendship, and told him to go with God. He asked to be heard, and begged them [to accept his friendship], with peace and the Christian religion, but they refused. They not only refused, but armed themselves and threatened him with death. Sandoval had no desire to fight, but, having no choice, he made a night attack on a village and there captured its lady, which made it possible for our men to reach the river without opposition, occupy its banks, and seize Coatzacoalcos.

Sandoval founded the town of Espíritu Santo four leagues from the sea because there was no good site nearer. He induced Quechula, Cihuatlán, Quetzaltepec, and Tabasco to accept his friendship (although they rebelled later), and a number of other towns, which he gave in encomienda to the settlers of Espíritu Santo, acting with the written authority of Cortés.

During this same period Oaxaca was conquered, together with a great part of the province of Mixteca, because they had been making war upon the Tepeacans and their allies. Three engagements took place, in which many died rather than submit and allow our men to plant a colony in their country.

CORTÉS NEEDED LAND and ports on the South Sea, in order to explore that coast of New Spain and certain islands rich in gold, precious stones, pearls, spices, and other desirable and unknown things, and even to bring there the spices of the Moluccas with less trouble and danger. He had already learned something about the South Sea in the time of Moctezuma. The people of Michoacán offered to help him, so he sent four Spaniards there with guides by two different routes, and they traveled as far as Tehuantepec, Zacatula, and other towns, where they took possession of sea and land by planting crosses. They explained their mission to the natives, and asked for gold, pearls, and men to take back and show their captain, whereupon they returned to Mexico. Cortés treated these Indians very kindly, gave them a few things, and sent them back to their king with greetings and messages, with which they departed happily.

The lord of Tehuantepec then sent the Emperor a present of gold, cotton, feathers, and arms, and offered him his person and estate. Not long afterward, he requested Spaniards and horses for an expedition against Tututepec, which was making war on him for submitting to the Christians and showing them the sea. Cortés sent Pedro de Alvarado to him in the year '22 (not '23), with 200 Spanish foot, 40 horse, and two small field pieces. Alvarado marched through Oaxaca, which was now at peace, and in a month arrived at Tututepec, where a few towns offered resistance, but not for long. The lord of the province received him very well and invited him to take up quarters inside Tututepec, which is a large city, in certain houses of his, good, but covered with straw, thinking to burn the Spaniards in them that night. Alvarado, however, either suspecting treachery, or informed of it, refused to stay there, saying it was not good for his horses, but set up his camp below the city, where he detained the lord and a son, who were ransomed for 25,000 castellanos in gold and some pearls, the country being rich in mines and trade. [With the authority of Cortés, he transferred Segura de la Frontera from Tepeaca to Tututepec.] Alvarado returned to Mexico to see Cortés about the new town, but during his absence the settlers quarreled, abandoned the place, and went to Oaxaca. Cortés had

Diego de Ocampo, its alcalde mayor, investigate, and Ocampo condemned one man to death. The case was appealed to Cortés, who commuted the sentence to exile. The lord of Tututepec died about this time, whereupon several towns of the region rebelled. Pedro de Alvarado marched against them and, although he lost several Spaniards and friends, reduced them to their former state. Segura, however, was never reoccupied.

151. War in Colima

As soon as Cortés had access to the coast of the South Sea and had friends there, he sent forty Spanish carpenters and sailors to build two brigantines at Zacatula, to explore the coast and search for the passage to the South Sea which was then believed to exist; also, to build two caravels to explore a route to the islands of spices and pearls, and make a voyage to the Moluccas. He sent to Zacatula the iron fittings, anchors, sails, cordage, and the large store of rigging and gear he had at Vera Cruz, employing [as carriers] a great number of men and women for this long and costly journey. Later he sent Cristóbal de Olid to superintend the construction of the ships, and to explore the coast with them when they were completed.

Olid set out at once from Tzintzuntzan for Zacatula, with more than 100 Spanish foot, 40 horse, and a force of Indians from Michoacán. On his way he learned that the rich towns of Colima had risen, so he marched against them and fought for several days, but was defeated and humiliated, the men of Colima having killed three Spaniards and a large number of his friends. Cortés immediately dispatched Gonzalo de Sandoval there, with 25 horse, 60 foot, and many Indian friends, between warriors and bearers, to avenge this defeat and chastise the people of Impilcingo [Yopelcingo], who had made war on their neighbors for being friendly to the Spaniards. Sandoval marched against Impilcingo and fought many engagements with its people, but was unable to conquer them, the terrain being too rough for the horses. From Impilcingo he went to Zacatula, inspected the ships, picked up more Spaniards, and went on to Colima, 70 leagues away, pacifying several towns along the way. The men of Colima advanced against him at the same place where they had defeated Olid, thinking to defeat him likewise. Both sides fought stubbornly, and ours won, although at the cost of many wounded men and horses, but no deaths except among the Indian friends. (I always mention the horses killed or wounded because of their great importance in these wars, which in most cases were won with their help; also because they were very expensive.)

The men of Impilcingo had been so badly mauled in this battle that they did not stage another, but gave themselves up as vassals of the Emperor, and induced the people of Colimotl, Cihuatlán, and other places to do likewise. [The villa of] Colima was then founded by 25 horse and 120 foot, among whom Cortés distributed its territory. Sandoval and his companions heard that ten suns distant from there was an island of Amazons, a rich land; but these women were never found. In my opinion the error arose from the name of Cihuatlán, which means "place of women."

152. Cristóbal de Tapia

A LITTLE AFTER the capture of Mexico, Cristóbal de Tapia, Veedor of Santo Domingo, set out [for Mexico] with the title of Governor of New Spain. He landed at Vera Cruz and presented his credentials, thinking to have them honored because of his favor with the Bishop of Burgos [Juan de Fonseca], who had sent him; he also counted on the support of the friends of Diego Velázquez [in Mexico]. He was told that his orders would be obeyed, but that, with respect to their fulfillment, the citizens and regidores of the villa [of Vera Cruz], who were then occupied with the rebuilding of Mexico and with other conquests, would do whatever was necessary for the service of the Emperor and King, their lord. Tapia was furious and suspicious at this reply, wrote a letter to Cortés, and soon departed for Mexico.

Cortés wrote Tapia that he was very happy at his coming because of their ancient association and friendship, and that he would send Fray Pedro Melgarejo de Urrea, commissary of the Crusade, to accompany and inform him of the state of the country and the Spaniards, for Melgarejo had been present at siege of Mexico. Cortés gave the friar his instructions and ordered that Tapia was to be well provided for on his journey. In order, however, to keep Tapia out of Mexico, Cortés decided to meet him on the road, abandoning a journey to Pánuco that he had planned. The captains and attorneys of all the villas, however, opposed his going, so he sent his authorization to Gonzalo de Sandoval, Pedro de Alvarado, Diego de Soto, Diego de Valdenebro, and Fray Pedro Melgarejo, all of whom were in Vera Cruz, to negotiate with Tapia, whom they obliged to return with them to Cempoala. There he again presented his papers; but they appealed to the Emperor, saying they did so in the interest of the royal service and for the peace and well being of the conquerors and the country. They even told Tapia that his orders had been dictated by favoritism and were [therefore] null; moreover, that he was incompetent and unworthy of governing such a great country.

When Cristóbal de Tapia saw himself confronted with such opposition and otherwise threatened, he returned whence he had come, very insulted, and possibly bribed. In Santo Domingo the Audiencia and the Governor attempted to remove him from office, on the ground that he had gone to New Spain to stir up a revolt, although he had been forbidden, under heavy penalties, to go.

Juan Bono de Quexo, who had been with Narváez as sailing master, also came [from Spain] with dispatches from the Bishop of Burgos for Cristóbal de Tapia. He brought a hundred letters, all alike, and some in blank, all signed by the same bishop, filled with promises for those who would receive Tapia as Governor and saying that the Emperor had been disserved by Cortés; also a letter for Cortés himself, promising him great favors if he would turn the country over to Tapia, and threatening him if he should refuse.

These pleasant letters stirred up a great row, and if Tapia had not departed there would have been trouble. Some say that Mexico was on the brink of rebellion, as had happened in Toledo [in the war of the comuneros], but Cortés wisely and tactfully put a stop to it. The Indians themselves were thrown into a turmoil, and those of Cuixteco, Coatzacoalcos, Tabasco, and other places rebelled, to their great cost.

BEFORE MOCTEZUMA'S DEATH, and again when Mexico was destroyed, the lord of Pánuco had offered to accept the service of the Emperor and the friendship of the Christians, for which reason (this was at the time of Cristóbal de Tapia's arrival) Cortés planned to found a colony on the [Pánuco] River, which was said to be navigable and to have deposits of gold and silver. He was also moved by a desire to avenge the deaths of Francisco de Garay's men, who had been killed there, and also to forestall Garay himself who, it was rumored, was seeking the government of Pánuco and preparing to settle and conquer the river and coast. Thus it was that Cortés, who had written to Castile much earlier requesting the government of Pánuco for himself, now asked for men to help him against his enemies. At the same time he denied responsibility for the loss of Garay's soldiers and others who had gone to Vera Cruz and met with misfortune. So he took 300 Spanish foot, 150 horse, and 40,000 Mexicans and set out [for Pánuco].

Cortés met the enemy at Ayotchquitlatlán and, since the terrain was smooth and level, where he could make good use of his horse, he quickly won a victory, inflicting heavy losses on his adversaries. Many Mexican [friends] died there, and 50 Spaniards and several horses were wounded. Cortés stayed there four days to take care of his wounded, and during this time many towns of the alliance [of Pánuco] came to offer their submission and to bring gifts. He went to Chila, five leagues from the coast, where Garay had been defeated, and sent messengers to all the people of the river country, begging for peace and permission to preach. But they, trusting in their numbers and the protection of the lagoons, or thinking to kill and eat the men of Cortés as they had done with those of Garay, paid no heed to his appeals, warnings, and [offers of] friendship; rather, they killed several messengers and threatened him who had sent them.

Cortés waited two weeks, hoping to persuade them peacefully, and then attacked. Since, however, he could not harm them by land, they having taken refuge in their lagoons, he adopted a different tactic, gathered up some canoes, and crossed by night (so as not to be detected) to the other side of the river with a hundred foot and forty horse. He was seen at daybreak, when he was assailed by a large number, who fought more furiously than the Spaniards had ever seen Indians fight in the open. They killed two horses and badly wounded ten more, but in spite of all that they were routed and pursued for a league, and a great many of them died.

Our men slept that night in a deserted town, in the temples of which they found the garments and weapons of Garay's men hanging, and their faces, flayed and tanned and still wearing their beards, fastened to the walls, a mournful sight, for some of them could be recognized. It was evident that the men of Pánuco were as fierce and cruel as the Mexicans had said, speaking from experience, for they had often been at war with them. Cortés then marched against a handsome town, where many men were under arms, as if in ambush, to take him within the houses with their bare hands. But they were seen by the cavalry who were scouting on ahead, whereupon they sallied out and fought so stoutly that they killed one horse and wounded twenty others, as well as many Spaniards. They resisted so stubbornly that the encounter lasted a good while. They were repulsed three or four times, and as often reformed in excellent order, wheeling, kneeling on the ground, and shooting their darts, arrows, and stones in complete silence—a very rare thing among the Indians. When they tired they jumped into the river and swam across, a few at a time, which Cortés was pleased to see. They reformed their ranks on the far side and remained there fighting with great spirit until nightfall.

Our men retired to their camp, ate the slain horse, and slept under heavy guard. The following day they scoured the country and came upon four deserted towns, where they discovered many jars of the wine commonly drunk there, carefully stored in cellars. For the benefit of the horses they slept in the maize fields. They continued their march for two more days, but, not encountering any people, returned to their camp at Chila.

None of the people who dwelt along the river came to see the Spaniards, or to attack them. Cortés regretted this on both counts, and, in order to entice them out in one way or another, he sent his horse, foot, and friends across the river to assault a large town on the shore of a lagoon. They made a night attack by land and water, and did a great deal of damage. The Indians were terrified at this and at once began to yield, and within twenty-five days all the people of the region and the river had submitted.

Cortés founded Santiesteban del Puerto near Chila, leaving there one hundred foot and thirty horse, among whom he distributed its provinces. He named alcaldes, regidores, and the other officers of the council, and appointed Pedro de Vallejo his lieutenant. He destroyed Pánuco, Chila, and the other towns for rebellion and the cruelty they had practiced on Garay's men, and then returned to Mexico, which was being rebuilt. The expedition cost him sixty thousand pesos because there were no spoils. Horseshoes sold for a gold peso, or for twice as much in silver.

At that time a ship bringing provisions and supplies to Vera Cruz was sunk, only three Spaniards escaping to a little island, five leagues from land, where they survived for many days by eating the seals that crawled up on the beach to sleep; they also ate a fruit resembling figs.

Tututepec of the North [in the modern state of Hidalgo] rebelled about this time, along with many towns in the province of Pánuco, and their lords burned or destroyed more than twenty towns friendly to the Christians. Cortés marched against them and put down the uprising. Many of our Indian stragglers were killed, and a dozen horses foundered in the mountains, a loss that was severely felt. The lord of Tututepec and his captain-general for that war were captured and hanged, because they had submitted as friends, had already rebelled once and been pardoned, and had repudiated their word and oath. Two hundred of his men were sold at auction as slaves, to compensate for the loss of the horses. With this punishment and the election of a new lord, brother of the deceased, the people submitted quietly.

154. Expedition of Garay to Pánuco

FRANCISCO DE GARAY first went to Pánuco in the year '18, when the people of Chila defeated him, ate the Spaniards they had killed, and even hung their skins in the temples as mementos or votive offerings, as you have just learned. The following year, according to some, he returned with more men and was again expelled from the river. Then, to salvage his reputation and seize the wealth of Pánuco, he sent Juan López de Torralba to Castile with an account of his expenses and the discovery he had made, and Torralba obtained the governorship of Pánuco for him.

With this authority, in the year '23, he fitted out nine ships and three brigantines, and put on board a force of 145 horses and 850 Spaniards, and some islanders from Jamaica, where he had readied his fleet. He armed it with many guns, 200 arquebuses, and 300 crossbows, and, since he was a rich man, he stocked his ships plentifully with meat, bread, and merchandise. He even founded on paper a town that he named Garay, and appointed Alonso de Mendoza and Fernando de Figueroa as alcaldes, and Gonzalo de Ovalle, Diego de Cifuentes, and a certain Villagrán as regidores. He named a constable, a clerk of weights and measures, and an attorney, and provided for the other offices customary in a villa of Castile. He had them and the captains of the army swear that they would not abandon or oppose him. Then he sailed from Jamaica for Puerto Rico, touching at Xagua, a good port in Cuba, where he learned that Cortés had founded a colony in Pánuco and conquered the province, a piece of intelligence that annoyed and frightened him, lest he should suffer the fate of Narváez. Thinking to make an arrangement with Cortés, he wrote to Diego Velázquez and the Licenciado Zuazo about it, and asked Zuazo to go to Mexico and represent him. Zuazo consented gladly, went to Xagua to meet Garay, and each went his way.

Zuazo encountered bad weather and suffered severely before he reached New Spain. Garay also ran into a storm, and it was the Day of St. James [July 25] before he came to the [Pánuco] River. He anchored there with his whole fleet, since he could do nothing else, and sent his kinsman Gonzalo de Ocampo up the river with a brigantine to explore the country, the people, and the towns along its banks. Ocampo ascended the river for fifteen leagues, marked the many tributary streams, and returned after four days, reporting that the country was very poor and uninhabited. He was believed, although he did not know what he was talking about. Then Garay landed four hundred companions and the horses, and ordered Juan de Grijalba to take his ships up the coast, while he marched along the beach in battle order to Pánuco. For three days he struggled through uninhabited country and bad swamps; he crossed the river called the Montalto (because it flows down from high mountains), by swimming and on rafts; he entered a large deserted town well stocked with maize and guava trees; he made the circuit of a great lagoon, and then dispatched messengers (whom he had captured at Chila and who knew Spanish) to a town requesting that he be received in peace. There Garay was lodged and provided with bread, fruit, and fowl, these last being caught in the lagoon. The soldiers were on the point of mutiny because they were not allowed to put the place to the sack. They crossed another river which was at flood, and eight horses were drowned, after which they got themselves entangled in some great lagoons, from which they barely escaped. Indeed, if there had been any warriors about, not a man could have survived. They finally emerged on firm ground, after suffering great hunger and hardships, eaten alive by swams of mosquitoes, bugs, and bats, and reached Pánuco, which they very much desired to do. There, however, they found nothing to eat, because of the wars that Cortés had waged or, as they thought, because their enemies on the far side of the river had carried off the provisions.

For this reason (also because the supply ships had not appeared) the soldiers scattered to look for food and clothing. Garay sent Gonzalo de Ocampo to Santiesteban del Puerto to discover the feeling of Cortés' men. Ocampo returned and reported that it was good and that [Garay] could go there. Garay, however, very improperly approached the Indians and, to win their support, told them he had come to punish the soldiers of Cortés for harming and molesting them. The Spaniards at Santiesteban, knowing the terrain, sallied out secretly and fell upon Garay's cavalry at Nochapalán, a very large town, and there arrested Captain Alvarado and forty men as usurpers of the land and as clothing thieves. Garay was badly hurt and much annoyed by this, and, since he lost [at the same time] four ships, the rest being at anchor in the mouth of the Pánuco, he began to fear the good fortune of Cortés. So he sent word to Pedro de Vallejo, Cortés' lieutenant [at Santiesteban] that he carried the authority and permission of the Emperor to found a colony, and that [Vallejo] should restore his men and horses. Vallejo answered that he would believe it when he saw [Garay's] credentials; but in the meantime he ordered the ships' masters to put into the port, to avoid the fate of the others, for a storm was blowing up, and that, if they should refuse, he would consider them pirates. But [Garay] and they replied that they would do no such thing merely on his word, but would do whatever seemed best to them.

155. Death of the Adelantado Garay

As SOON AS Pedro de Vallejo saw Garay's fleet arrive, he notified Cortés; he also informed him of what had passed between them, so that Cortés might send him in time more men, supplies, and advice about what to do. At this intelligence, Cortés abandoned the expeditions he was preparing for Honduras, Chiapa, and Guatemala, and made ready to leave for Pánuco, although he was suffering from an injured arm. As he was on the point of departure, however, Francisco de las Casas and Rodrigo de Paz arrived in Mexico, bearing letters from the Emperor and decrees appointing [Cortés] to the government of New Spain and all the land he had conquered, particularly Pánuco. For this reason Cortés did not go to Pánuco, but sent his alcalde mayor, Diego de Ocampo, with the new decree, and a large force under Pedro de Alvarado.

Garay and Ocampo argued back and forth: the former said the land was his as a gift of the King; the latter denied it, on the ground that the King had forbidden anyone to intrude, since Cortés had founded a colony there, and that, anyway, such was the custom in the Indies. Garay's men suffered in the meantime, for they coveted the wealth and abundance of their opponents, while they perished at the hands of the Indians and their ships were being riddled by worms and exposed to storms. For this latter reason, or possibly through connivance, Martín de San Juan, of Guipúzcoa, and a certain Castromocho, both of them sailing masters, secretly summoned Pedro de Vallejo and surrendered their ships to him. When he had them in his possession he notified Garay to anchor in the port, according to maritime usage, or sail away. Garay answered him with gunfire. When, however, the notary Vicente López repeated the warning, and Garay saw his other ships entering the port, he sailed in with his flagship. Vallejo put him under arrest, but Ocampo freed him immediately and seized the ships, which meant the disarming and ruin of Garay, who, nevertheless, demanded the restoration of his ships and men, and exhibited his royal decree, by virtue of which he notified them that he purposed to found a colony at Río de las Palmas. At the same time he complained of Gonzalo de Ocampo, who had made an unfavorable report about that site, and the officers of his army and council, who had opposed his planting a colony there on the ground that it would stir up trouble with Cortés, now prosperous and highly regarded.

Diego de Ocampo, Pedro de Vallejo, and Pedro de Alvarado persuaded Garay to write to Cortés and propose an arrangement, or to found his colony at Río de las Palmas, which [they said] was just as good a site as Pánuco, whereupon they would restore his ships and men, and supply him with provisions and arms.

Garay wrote to Cortés, accepting the proposal, and so it was announced by crier that all should embark at once on their ships, on pain of a whipping for the foot soldiers, and loss of arms and horses for all others, and that those who had purchased arms should relinquish them. At this the soldiers began to grumble and object; some of them made off into the country and were killed by the Indians; others went into hiding, by which the army was greatly reduced; still others made the excuse that the ships were rotten and worm-eaten, and said they were not obligated to follow [Garay] farther than Pánuco; nor did they wish to die of hunger, as several of their company had done. Garay begged them not to abandon him, promised them great things, and reminded them of their oath; but they were deaf, and many disappeared between dusk and dawn, fifty in one night. Garay was now desperate. He sent letters to Cortés by Pedro Cano and Juan Ochoa, putting his life, honor, and remedy in Cortés' hands. As soon as he received a reply he set out for Mexico. Cortés ordered that he be well provided for on the journey, and received him well. After exchanging many complaints and excuses, they reached an agreement: that Garay's eldest son should marry Doña Catalina Pizarro, a bastard daughter of Cortés; that Garay should plant a colony at Río de las Palmas; that Cortés should supply and aid him. In this wise they were reconciled and became bosom friends. Both attended matins on Christmas Eve, in the year 1523, and took breakfast together after Mass in great merriment. Shortly afterward Garay fell ill of *dolor de costado* [pneumonia], which he had caught from the cold wind upon leaving the church. He made his will, appointed Cortés his executor, and died two weeks later, some say four days. There was some gossip to the effect that his death was not an accident, for he was lodged with Alonso de Villanueva, but it was false, for he died of *dolor de costado*, as was sworn to by Dr. Ojeda and the Licenciado Pedro López, the physicians who treated him.

So died the Adelantado Francisco de Garay, poor and unhappy, in the house of a stranger and the land of his adversary, when he' might, if he had not been restless, have died rich and happy, in his own house, surrounded by his wife and children.

156 Pacification of Pánuco

WHEN GARAY LEFT for Mexico, Diego de Ocampo ordered, by public crier, the captains and officers of Garay's army to leave Santiesteban, to prevent their disturbing the country and people, for many of them were close friends of Diego Velázquez, men such as Juan de Grijalba, Gonzalo de Figueroa, Alonso de Mendoza, Lorenzo de Ulloa, Juan de Medina, Juan de Avila, Antonio de la Cerda, Taborda, and many others. For this reason, and because they were left without a head (although a son of Garay was among them), the army had no discipline and got out of hand. The men invaded the towns, took whatever clothing and women they could, and, in short, wandered about like vagabonds.

The Indians were enraged by their conduct and plotted to kill them, and within a short time had killed and eaten four hundred Spaniards. In Tamiquil alone they cut the throats of a hundred, an event that so saddened Garay that it hastened his death; but it filled the Indians with such daring that they attacked Santiesteban itself and brought it to verge of destruction. The men, however, were allowed to break into the open, where, after many attacks, they routed the Indians. In Tucetuco one night the Indians burned to death 40 men and 15 horses belonging to Cortés, who, as soon as he had word of it, sent Gonzalo de Sandoval there with four guns, 50 horse, 100 Spanish foot, and two Mexican lords, each of whom commanded 15,000 Indians, men and women. (I mention the women because, whenever Cortés or his captains undertook a campaign, they brought along many women for breadmaking and other services; besides, many Indians refused to go without their wives or mistresses.)

Sandoval made his way to Pánuco by forced marches, had two engagements with the people of the province, defeated them, and entered Santiesteban, where only 22 horses and 100 Spaniards were left, and, if he had been delayed a little longer, he would not have found them alive, so starved and battered were they. Sandoval at once divided his men into three companies, each of which was sent on an expedition to the interior, killing and robbing, and burning everything they encountered. In a short time they had done a great deal of damage, burning many towns and killing an infinite number of people. They captured 60 lords of vassals and 400 rich and noble men, not counting those of lower rank. They were all tried, their confessions taken, and were condemned to be burned alive. After consulting Cortés, Sandoval released the commoners, but burned the 400 captives and the 60 lords. He summoned their sons and heirs to witness their execution and to learn a lesson, and then restored their seigniories in the name of the Emperor, taking their oath that they would remain friends of the Christians and Spaniards—an oath that they honored in the breach, the Indians being by nature frivolous and turbulent. Finally, however, Pánuco was pacified.

157 Misadventures of the Licenciado Zuazo

UPON SAILING from Cape San Antón in Cuba for New Spain, the Licenciado Alonso Zuazo ran into a storm that drove his caravel off its course, and it was wrecked on Las Víboras, where some of the crew were devoured by sharks and sea lions, while the licenciado and several of his companions survived by eating tortoises, which are fishes shaped like shields, each one of which is capable of carrying six men on its shell while swimming. They lay six hundred small eggs in the sand, which had to be eaten raw for lack of fire. Zuazo spent several more days on another sand bar, where he survived by eating birds raw and drinking their blood. He must soon have perished from thirst and the excessive heat; but he made fire with sticks, as the Indians do, which was of much help to him. On still another bar he managed to find water, by immense effort, and burned wood covered with stone [coral?], a novel thing. He constructed a skiff with the timbers of a wrecked caravel, and in it sent Francisco Ballester and Gonzalo Gómez, with an Indian for bailing (these men having vowed perpetual chastity during the storm), to Cortés with word of his misfortune. They touched at Quiahuixtlán, at Vera Cruz, and finally at Medellín, where Diego de Ocampo readied a ship for them and sent them back for Zuazo. When Cortés learned of it he confirmed the orders and said that, if Zuazo should arrive, he was to be well provided for. He sent a servant to Medellín to wait for Zuazo and give him ten thousand castellanos, clothing, and horses for his journey to Mexico. There Zuazo was cordially received by Hernán Cortés and his misfortunes had a happy ending.

158. Pedro de Alvarado Conquers Utlatlán

AFTER THE FALL of Mexico, the people of Guatemala, Utlatlán, Chiapa, Soconusco, and other towns of the south coast had offered their submission, giving and receiving ambassadors and presents; but in their fickleness they did not keep the peace; rather, they made war upon those who did. For this reason, and because he expected to find rich lands and strange people in that direction, Cortés dispatched Pedro de Alvarado against them with 300 Spanish foot armed with arquebuses, one hundred seventy horse, four guns, and several Mexican lords with some warriors and carriers, for the road was long. Alvarado departed from Mexico on the sixth of December, 1523, and marched by way of Tehuantepec to Soconusco, to reduce certain mutinous towns. After admonishing and advising the rebels many times [to yield], he punished them with slavery. He spent many days in combat at Zapotitlán, a large and strong place, where many Spaniards and several horses were wounded, and an infinite number of Indians were killed on both sides. From Zapotitlán he marched to Quetzaltenango in three days: on the first day he crossed two rivers with great difficulty; on the second he mounted a very steep pass five leagues long, in an angle of which he discovered the remains of a woman and a dog that had been sacrificed, which, according to the interpreters and guides, was meant as a challenge. In a canyon he met some four thousand of the enemy, and farther along thirty thousand more, and defeated them all, for they took to their heels at the approach of a horse, an animal that they had never seen before.

They made a stand and fought near some springs, and were again routed. Reforming their ranks on the slope of a mountain, they turned upon the Spaniards with a great yelling, much spirit, and boldness; there were even many among them who would lie in wait for one or two horses, and others who would seize a horse by the tail and wound it. In the end, however, the horse and the arquebuses inflicted such losses upon them that they fled very prettily. Alvarado pursued them for a great distance and killed many as he overtook them. One of the four lords of Utlatlán, captain-general of their army, died. Several Spaniards died also, and many of them and many horses were wounded.

The next day Alvarado entered Quetzaltenango, but found it deserted. He rested there while he scoured the country. On the sixth day a large army advanced in good order from Quetzaltenango to attack the Spaniards. Alvarado met them with ninety horse, two hundred foot, and a fair number of friends. He took up a position on a wide plain, an arquebus shot from his camp—this in case he should need help. Each captain placed his men according to the disposition of the terrain, and the two armies then attacked. Ours prevailed. Our horse pursued the enemy for more than two leagues, while our foot did incredible carnage among them as they were crossing a stream. The lords and captains, and many eminent men assembled on a hilltop to fight, and were there taken and killed.

When the lords of Utlatlán and Quetzaltenango saw the destruction, they summoned their neighbors and friends, and gave hostages to their enemies [in exchange] for aid, so they were able to amass another large force. They sent word to Pedro de Alvarado that they wished to be his friends and renew their obedience to the Emperor, and that he should come to Utlatlán. It was all a stratagem to catch the Spaniards within the walls and burn them that night, for the city was extremely strong, its streets were narrow, its houses built close together, and it had only two entrances, one up a stairway of thirty steps, the other over a causeway, which had been cut in many places to prevent the use of horses. Alvarado believed them and went there, but as soon as he saw the broken causeway and the great strength of the place, and noticed the absence of women, he smelled treachery and left, not so quickly, however, that he escaped injury. Nevertheless, he pretended not to have noticed the trickery, spoke with the lords, and, as the saying goes, *One traitor is worth two scoundrels,* he plied them with soft words and gifts to put them off their guard, and then seized them. But not on this account did the war terminate; rather, it was waged even more bitterly, because the Spaniards were, so to speak, bottled up, and could not go abroad for fodder and wood without a fight, and our Indian friends and even some Spaniards were killed every day.

Our men were unable to scour the country to burn and destroy crops and orchards, because of the many deep ravines by which their camp was surrounded. In this situation, Alvarado, thinking it would speed the conquest, burned the lords he had taken and threatened to burn the city. For this purpose, and to discover the disposition of the Guatemalans, he asked these for help; they sent him four thousand men, and with them and the rest of his forces he pressed the enemy so closely that he drove them out of their own country, whereupon the nobles and commoners of the city came to ask his pardon and to submit, laying the blame for the war upon the lords who had been burned, as, indeed, these had confessed before they died in the fire. Alvarado received [the delegation] and took their oath of fealty. He then released two sons of the dead lords whom he held as prisoners, and restored them to the rank and estate of their fathers. Thus that land was subjugated, and Utlatlán was reoccupied. Many other prisoners were branded and sold as slaves, the fifth part [of the price] being reserved for the King and collected by the treasurer of the expedition, Baltasar de Mendoza.

The country is rich and heavily populated and has many towns and an abundance of foodstuffs. It has mountains of alum, and others that yield a substance resembling oil, as well as such excellent sulphur that our arquebusiers made very good powder out of it, without refinement or admixture of any kind. The war in Utlatlán ended on the first day of April, 1524. During it, horseshoes sold at 150 castellanos the dozen.

159. Conquest of Guatemala

FROM UTLATLÁN Alvarado went to Guatemala, where he was well received and provided for. Seven leagues away, on the shore of a lake [Atitlán], stood a very large city that was at war with Guatemala, Utlatlán, and other towns. Alvarado sent two Guatemalans there to beg them not to injure their neighbors, his friends, and to admonish them to accept peace and friendship [of the Spaniards]. But they, trusting to their strength on the water and their multitude of canoes, killed the messengers fearlessly and without compunction. So Alvarado went there with one hundred fifty Spanish foot, sixty horse, and many Guatemalans; but the enemy would neither receive nor speak to him. With thirty horse he rode as far as he could along the shore of the lake toward a rocky islet, where he descried a squadron of armed men. He attacked them, put them to flight, and pursued them as far as a narrow causeway, which the horses could not pass. His men all dismounted and followed the enemy to the rock. His foot soon arrived, and in a short time he took it and killed many men, while the others sprang into the water and swam to another small islet. Our men sacked the houses and then retired to a plain covered with maize, where they pitched camp and slept that night.

The next day they entered the deserted city [of Atitlán], and were astonished to find it abandoned, for it was a strong place. The reason was the loss of the rocky island, which was its fortress, and the ease with which the Spaniards penetrated wherever they pleased. Alvarado scoured the country and captured several men, three of whom he sent to the lords [of Atitlán] begging them to come in peace, and assuring them they would be well treated; otherwise, he would pursue them and destroy their orchards and fields. They replied that their country had never been subjugated by force of arms up to that time, but that since he had done so with such valor they desired to be his friends. So they came and shook hands with him, and thenceforth they kept the peace as friends of the Spaniards.

Alvarado returned to Guatemala, and three days later [representatives of] all the towns of the lake came and offered him their persons and estates. They said they wished to be at peace with everyone to escape the burden of war and quarrels with their neighbors. At the same time many other peoples of the south coast submitted to Alvarado, to gain his support, for they told him that the province of Ixcuintepec would not allow anyone friendly to the Christians to pass through their territory. Alvarado took his whole army there, slept three nights in the open, and penetrated within the limits of the city. Since, however, no one had any commerce with it, there was no open road to it bigger than a cattle path, and even this was all grown over by the thick jungle. Alvarado approached the town undetected and caught the inhabitants in their houses, because the heavy rains had kept them off the streets. He captured and killed some, for they were caught off their guard and had not been able to assemble or arm themselves. Most of them fled, but the rest fortified themselves in their houses, killed many of our Indians, and wounded a few Spaniards. Alvarado burned the town, warned its lord that he would do the same with its grain fields, and even with the Indians themselves, if they refused to yield, whereupon its lord and all of them came at once and submitted. Alvarado spent a week in these activities, during which all the towns roundabout offered him their friendship and services.

From Ixcuintepec Alvarado marched to Atiquipac, which speaks a different language, and from there to Taxisco and Nancitlán. On this journey many of our Indians were killed while straggling, and a great part of our baggage was captured, with all the fittings and strings for the crossbows—no small loss. To recover it Alvarado sent his brother Jorge in pursuit, with forty horse, but Jorge, regardless of his speed, failed. These men of Nancitlán carried little bells in their hands while fighting.* Alvarado tarried in this town for a week, but was unable to persuade its inhabitants to surrender, so he went on to Pasaco, which he was treacherously invited to enter—this so they might kill him in safety—but on the way there he noticed many arrows stuck in the ground, and at the entrance of the town several men quartering a dog, both of which circumstances are signs of war and enmity. A body of armed men soon sallied forth, and he fought with them until he got them away from the town, and then pursued them and killed many. Thence he went to Mopizalco and Acajutla, on the shore of the South Sea, where he was met by a multitude of warriors who, warned of his approach, had come out to fight, looking very fierce. Alvarado had two hundred fifty Spanish foot and one hundred horse, but, seeing the enemy so strong and well organized, did not dare to close with them. They, on the contrary, attacked him as he passed, even seizing the horses' stirrups and bridles; but the cavalry, soon followed by the rest of the army, turned upon them and left hardly an enemy alive, not only because the enemy fought fiercely and stood their ground, but because their armor was so heavy that when a man fell he could not get up again, so that flight was out of the question. Their armor consisted of a kind of sack made of hard twisted cotton, three fingers thick. The sacks were white or colored, and the Indians made a brave show with them and the plumes they wore on their heads. Their arrows were long and their lances thirty spans in length.

Many Spaniards were wounded that day, and Pedro de Alvarado himself was struck in one leg by an arrow, which left that leg four fingers shorter than the other. Later he encountered a larger and more formidable force, which was armed with very long poisoned lances, but he vanquished and destroyed it also. He then marched to Miahuatlán, and from there to Atecuán, where the people of Cuzcatlán [Salvador] came and offered him their submission—falsely, as it turned out, to put him off his guard. Their plan was to

---

* This nonsensical statement is owing to one of Gómara's rare misreadings of his sources, in this case Alvarado's report to Cortés on the Guatemalan campaign. Alvarado had written: "Y ninguna cosa de lo perdido se pudo cobrar, porque la ropa ya la habían hecho pedazos, y cada uno traía en la guerra su pampanilla de ella." Gómara mistook pampanilla (breechclout) for campanilla (little bell). The sentence should read: "These men of Nancitlán wore breechclouts in battle."

kill the Spaniards, who were so few that the Indians thought it would be easy to capture and sacrifice them. Alvarado learned of their evil purpose and begged them to yield peacefully, but they abandoned their city and remained hostile. In this war they killed eleven horses, which Alvarado had them pay for by selling his prisoners as slaves. He stayed there for twenty days without being able to persuade them to submit, and then returned to Guatemala.

In this campaign Alvarado covered four hundred leagues. He got no spoils to speak of, but he did pacify and reduce many provinces. He suffered greatly from hunger, endured many hardships, and crossed rivers so hot that they could not be waded. Pedro de Alvarado took such a fancy to this land of Guatemala and its people that he decided to stay there and colonize, following in this the instructions of Cortés. So he founded a city and named it Santiago de Guatemala, appointing two alcaldes and four regidores, and filling all the offices necessary for the good government of a town. He built a church of the same name on the site of the present cathedral of Guatemala. He distributed many towns in encomienda to the citizens and conquerors, and sent a report of the whole expedition and his plans to Cortés, who gave him two hundred more Spaniards, confirmed his encomiendas, and backed him in his demand for the government [of Guatemala].

160. War in Chamula

ON THE EIGHTH of December of the year '23, Hernán Cortés sent Diego de Godoy, with thirty horse, one hundred Spanish foot, two guns, and a considerable force of friends to the villa of Espíritu Santo against certain rebellious provinces of that region. He did not give him more men because the region was between Chiapa and Guatemala, where Pedro de Alvarado was campaigning, and [near] Honduras, where Cristóbal de Olid was to lead an expedition.

Diego de Godoy had a prosperous journey and, with the lieutenant [governor] of the new villa, undertook several expeditions and forays. He reached Chamula, a large town, capital of a province, strong and built on a hill that the horses could not climb. It was surrounded by a wall nearly three fathoms high, made of stone and earth, with a center of timbers. Godoy attacked it two days running, with great risk and hardship for his companions, and took it in the end, because the inhabitants, seeing that resistance was useless, packed up their effects and left. At the beginning of the assault they threw over the wall a piece of gold, mocking the Spaniards for their cupidity and madness, and inviting them to come in and get [their gold], for they had a plenty. To disguise their flight they leaned many lances against the wall, to give those on the outside the notion that they were staying; but even so they did not escape without being observed, and our men captured and killed a great many of them, mostly women and children. The spoils were scanty, but a large store of provisions was taken. The principal arms of these Indians were the lance and a round shield made of spun cotton, with which they covered the whole body, and which they could roll up on the march, and unroll for fighting. Chiapa, Huehueistlán, and other cities and provinces were visited and trampled in this expedition of Godoy, but nothing else worthy of note occurred.

161. Cortés Sends Olid to Honduras

BEFORE FRANCISCO DE GARAY'S [last] expedition to Pánuco, Cortés had planned to colonize Hibueras and Honduras,* which were said to be rich in gold and land, although they were distant from Mexico, but he was not able to do so for fear of losing [to Garay] the river and land [of Pánuco] that he had already colonized. But as soon as he was free of that powerful competitor, and had in hand the Emperor's order (signed at Valladolid on the sixth of June of the year '23) to explore both coasts and search for the supposed strait, he set about making preparations. He gave Alonso de Contreras 6,000 gold castellanos with which to purchase horses, arms, and supplies in Cuba, and to recruit men. Then he sent Cristóbal de Olid, in five well-armed ships and a brigantine, with 400 Spanish foot and 30 horse [to Honduras].

Cortés ordered Olid first to go to Havana to pick up the men,

* Hibueras (or Higueras) and Honduras were identical, so far as is known.

horses, and provisions purchased by Contreras, and then to found a colony on the Cape of Hibueras [Honduras], from which he was to send Cortés' cousin, Diego Hurtado de Mendoza, to explore the coast between there and Darién and search for the strait that everyone supposed existed. With further orders of Cortés for his expedition, Cristóbal de Olid departed from Chalchiuhcuecan [Vera Cruz] on January 11 of the year '24, according to some, while Cortés sent two ships to explore the coast between Pánuco and Florida to look for a strait, and two brigantines as well to sail [along the south coast] from Zacatula to Panama for the same purpose. The two brigantines had, however, been burned before the order arrived, so that search was given up.

162. Conquest of Zapotecas

WHEN MEXICO WAS DESTROYED, the two large and warlike provinces of Zapotecas and Mixtecas [Oaxaca] withdrew their obedience to Cortés, and were joined by many others in rebellion against the Spaniards, which resulted in many killings and much harm. Cortés sent Rodrigo de Rangel there, but he, either from lack of horses or water, or because the people were valiant, was unable to subdue them; rather, he lost several Spaniards in the expedition, by reason of which [the natives] became much fiercer than before, and destroyed and sacked many towns subject and friendly to Cortés, which complained bitterly to him and demanded help and the punishment [of their enemies].

Cortés again sent this same Rangel, with one hundred fifty foot (since the terrain does not permit the use of horses), four small guns, and many Tlaxcalans and Mexicans. Rangel set out on the fifth of February of the year '24. He admonished [the Indians] to submit peacefully and, when they refused to listen, waged stern war upon them, killing many and capturing a large number, whom he branded and sold for slaves. He found a great deal of clothing and gold among them, which he brought back to Mexico. In short, they were so thoroughly chastized that they never again rebelled.

Cortés and his captains undertook other expeditions and conquests on their own account, but the ones described were the most important. They subjugated the whole Mexican Empire and many other great kingdoms of New Spain, Guatemala, Pánuco, Jalisco, and Honduras, which are now governments in their own right.

163. Rebuilding of Mexico

CORTÉS PLANNED to rebuild Mexico, not so much because of the majestic situation of the city, as because of its fame and renown; also because he wanted to repair the damage he had done. Thus he strove to make it greater and more populous than it had been. He named alcaldes, regidores, clerks of the market, an attorney, notaries, constables, and the other officers that a city council has need of. He drew up a plan of the city, distributed lots to the conquerors, and reserved sites for churches, squares, arsenals, and other public and community buildings. He ordered that the Spanish quarter should be separate from that of the Indians, and divided the water supply between them.

To reduce the expense of building, he brought in a number of Indians. At first this was difficult, because many lords, kinsmen of Cuauhtémoc, and other prisoners were mutinous; they brought in all their captains in an attempt to kill Cortés and liberate their king. Cortés sought to seize and punish them, but they were lucky enough to get away in time. He appointed Don Carlos Ahuaxpitzatzin lord of Texcoco, with the consent and approval of that city, to replace his deceased brother, Don Fernando, and ordered him to bring the greater part of his vassals to the work [of reconstruction], for they were carpenters, masons, and artisans. He distributed and promised homesites, exemptions, and other privileges to the natives of Mexico and to all who would come and settle there, and he invited many.

He released the *cihuacoatl,* that is, the captain-general, put him in charge of the people and the construction, and gave him command of a district. He gave command of another district to Don Pedro Moctezuma, son of Moctezuma—this to win the good will of the Mexicans. He appointed other gentlemen as lords of the islands and streets of the city, [with the duty of] bringing in people. He divided the place among them, while they distributed building lots and land as they thought best, and began the work of reconstruction with great diligence and enthusiasm. Upon hearing that Mexico–Tenochtitlán was being rebuilt, and that the citizens were to be free, so many people came that there was hardly room for them to stand for a league roundabout. They worked so hard and ate so little that they sickened, the pestilence attacked them, and an infinite number died. The work was heavy, because they had to carry in on their backs, or drag, the stone, earth, lumber, lime, bricks, and all other materials. Nevertheless, their songs and music, their invocations of their city and lord, and their exchanges of pleasantries were something to hear. The shortage of food was caused by the late siege and war, during which they could not plant as they customarily did. Also, their great numbers alone brought famine, pestilence, and death. Still, little by little, they rebuilt Mexico, with 100,000 houses better than the old ones, while the Spaniards erected many good houses after our fashion. Cortés built a magnificent one on the site of Moctezuma's palace, from which he enjoyed a rent of 4,000 ducats and more. In Cortés' residencia, Pánfilo de Narváez charged that Cortés had felled whole forests to build it, and had used 7,000 cedar beams. Here this seems like a great thing, but there, where the forests are of cedar, it is nothing. Indeed, one garden in Texcoco is enclosed by 1,000 cedars. It is worthy of note that a single cedar beam in Cacama's house in Texcoco was 120 feet long and 12 feet thick throughout its length, this after it had been squared.

Several very good sheds were built for the safety of the brigantines, and served equally as fortifications. They were partly on land and partly over the water, with three naves, in which the brigantines are kept today as a memento. The old canals were not restored, but new ones were dug through the dry ground. In this respect Mexico is not what it was. The lake has been subsiding since the year '24, and it sometimes stinks. Otherwise, however, the city is a most healthful place to live in, tempered as it is by the surrounding mountains and sustained by the fertility of the soil; having, moreover, convenient access by water. Thus it is that Mexico is more heavily populated than before. It is, indeed, the greatest city in the world and is the noblest of the Indies, in military strength and orderliness, for it has 2,000 Spanish citizens and a like number of horses in their stables, with rich harness and armor. It has, moreover, a great deal of trade, with officers in charge of silk, cloth, glass, casting, and coining, and a studium* established by Don Antonio de Mendoza. The citizens of Mexico are justly proud of these things, although, to be sure, there is a great difference between the conqueror-citizen and the plain citizen, for, as soon as [the rebuilding of] Mexico had begun, but had not been completed, Cortés, along with the conqueror-citizens, took up his residence in Coyoacán. The fame of Cortés and Mexico's greatness spread abroad, and within a short time there were as many Indians in it as we have said, and so many Spaniards that they were able to conquer 400 leagues of land and more, and all the provinces we have mentioned, while Hernán Cortés governed from Mexico.

---

* Probably the school of Santa Cruz de Tlatelolco for Indian boys.

164. Cortés' Plans for Ennobling New Spain

THE GLORY AND FAME of having conquered New Spain and the other kingdoms, it seemed to Cortés, would not be fulfilled unless he adorned it and made it strong. For this [first] purpose he brought to Mexico Catalina Xuárez (who had remained in Cuba during the wars) and her company, in great pomp. He also induced the citizens of Mexico and those of the other villas he had founded to send for their wives, while he advanced the money to bring maidens, ladies, and Old Christian women* from Spain. At his expense he brought many married men with their daughters, such as the Comendador [of the Order of Santiago] Lionel de Cervantes with his seven, who made rich and honorable marriages.

Cortés sent to the islands of Cuba, Santo Domingo, San Juan de Boriquén [Puerto Rico], and Jamaica for brood stock: cows, sows, sheep, goats, she-asses, and mares, although at that time and even before it had been forbidden to ship horses from the islands—this

---

* Not old women, of course, but those without taint of Moorish or Jewish blood, usually limited to the four grandparents.

to enhance their value, in view of the wealth and need of Cortés. [His purpose was to use these animals] for meat, milk, wool, and hides, and for pack animals, and war and draft horses. He sent to the same islands for sugar cane, mulberry trees for silk, vine cuttings, and other plants, and to Spain for arms, iron, guns, powder, tools, forges for fabricating implements, and for olive pits, seeds, and nuts, which do not yield in the islands.

Cortés cast five [bronze] guns, two of which were culverins, at great expense because of the scarcity and high price of tin. Tin, indeed, was worth its weight in silver, because it was mined at Taxco, twenty-six leagues from Mexico, where it is found in little pieces no larger than coins. On the other hand, while it was being extracted, a vein of iron ore was discovered, much to Cortés' pleasure. With these five guns, and with those he had bought at auction from Juan Ponce de León and Pánfilo de Narváez, he accumulated thirty-five bronze pieces and seventy of cast iron, which he used for the fortification of Mexico. Afterward, more men came out from Spain armed with arquebuses and breastplates.

He also sent exploring parties to all the conquered territory to search for gold, and many abundant mines were discovered which enriched the country, although at the cost of the lives of many Indians who were forcibly brought like slaves to the mines.

He transferred the port and wharf of Vera Cruz to a place two leagues from San Juan de Ulúa, on a lagoon with inlets where boats are sheltered [from the northers]. He relocated Medellín there (where a great jetty is now being constructed to protect the ships), and set up a Board of Trade. He also smoothed the road to Mexico, for the pack animals bearing merchandise.

165. The Bishop of Burgos Is Challenged

JUAN RODRÍGUEZ DE FONSECA, Bishop of Burgos, felt such enmity and hatred for Cortés, and such love and partiality for Diego Velázquez, that he belittled [Cortés'] deeds and services, and concealed them [from the Emperor]. Thus Cortés was defamed, when he deserved greater fame, and neither his father, Martín Cortés, nor Francisco de Montejo, nor his cousin, the Licenciado Francisco Núñez, nor any of his attorneys could get from the bishop any decision or order covering the needs of the conquest of New Spain, or for the satisfaction of the conquerors. The bishop was in sole charge of the affairs of the Indies; the King was occupied in Germany with his duties as Emperor; and [Cortés'] men had no recourse, or even a hope of getting their business attended to. So it was that they determined to challenge [the bishop], however ugly and difficult [a task] it might be. They spoke to Pope Adrian [VI] (who had governed this kingdom before his elevation), and to the Emperor when he returned. The Pope, at the supplication of M. de la Chau, [Chamberlain] of the Emperor's council (who had been sent to Spain to felicitate the Pope upon his election), wished to make a thorough investigation of the matter because of the very high position of the bishop. He already favored Cortés because of [the conqueror's] renown, and, both sides having been heard, he ordered the bishop (who was then at Zaragoza) to cease his activities in the affairs of Cortés, and, as it later appeared, relinquish his charge of the Indies, for the Emperor, guided by the Pope's exposition of the case, issued such an order.

The charge brought and proved [against the bishop] was that he had always hated Cortés, whom he had publicly denounced as a traitor; that he had suppressed Cortés' letters and misrepresented his services to keep the King in ignorance of them; that he had commanded Juan López de Recalde, Auditor of the Board of Trade at Seville, not to allow men, arms, clothing, tools, and other things to be shipped to New Spain; that he had appointed unworthy men, such as Cristóbal de Tapia, to office; that he was a violent partisan of Diego Velázquez (who had married Doña Petronila de Fonseca, the bishop's niece); that he had permitted and approved the false reports against Cortés, fabricated by Andrés de Duero, Manuel de Rojas, and others, and sent in by Diego Velázquez. This last is what hurt and dishonored the bishop most, because it sounded very bad for him to deny the true account and approve the false. Because of this challenge the bishop retired from the court, unhappy and angry, and Diego Velázquez was condemned and removed from his government of Cuba (only he had died meanwhile), and Cortés was enabled, with great honor, to announce himself as Governor of New Spain.

Juan Rodríguez de Fonseca was absolute ruler of Indian affairs for about thirty years. When he began he was Dean of Seville [Cathedral], and when he retired he was Bishop of Burgos, Archbishop of Rosana, and Commissary-General of the Crusade. He might even have been Archbishop of Toledo if he had bestirred himself, for he was an exceedingly wealthy cleric and had served a very long time, and was, moreover, supported by his brother, Antonio de Fonseca [Chief Auditor of the Council of Castile]; but he had become over-confident, so the miter was stolen from him, it is said, by his nephew, Don Alonso de Fonseca, Archbishop of Santiago (the same who had financed the Fuenterrabía affair*), so the two were not on speaking terms thereafter.

---

* Fuenterrabía, a Spanish town near the Bay of Biscay, was taken by the French in 1521 and held until 1524. This is probably the episode that Gómara alludes to. Alonso de Fonseca was made Archbishop of Toledo in 1524.

166. Cortés Is Made Governor

AFTER THE BISHOP OF BURGOS had been challenged, the Emperor appointed a commission to look into the differences and suits between Hernán Cortés and Diego Velázquez. [The commission was composed of] Mercurino Gattinara, the Grand Chancellor, an Italian; M. de la Chau; Dr. de la Roche, a Fleming; Fernando de Vega, Lord of Grajales and Comendador Mayor of Castile; Dr. Lorenzo Galíndez de Caravajal; and the Licenciado Francisco de Vargas, Treasurer-General of Castile. They convened for many days at the house of Alonso de Argüello, where the Grand Chancellor was residing. They heard Martín Cortés, Francisco de Montejo, Francisco Núñez, and the other attorneys of Cortés; and they heard Manuel de Rojas, Andrés de Duero, and the other attorneys of Diego Velázquez. After studying the case, they found in favor of Cortés, guided thereto by law and justice, rather than by admiration of his power, although they did praise his deeds and services, and approve of his fidelity. They quashed the claims of Diego Velázquez to the government of New Spain, but left him free to sue Cortés for debts. I even believe they removed him from the government of Cuba for having dispatched Pánfilo de Narváez [to New Spain] with a fleet. The defense of Cortés, the right and justice of his suit, and his appointment to the government of New Spain—all this is recorded in the history. He was charged with having undertaken his expedition of discovery, trade, and conquest with the money and authority of Diego Velázquez; that he had refused to share the profit [with Velázquez] or render him obedience; that he had blinded Narváez in one eye; that he had refused to receive Cristóbal de Tapia; that he had disobeyed the royal provisions; that he had not paid the royal fifth; and that he had tyrannized over the Spaniards and mistreated the Indians.

Acting on the decision and advice of these gentlemen, the Emperor named Cortés Adelantado, Distributor [of land and encomiendas], and Governor of New Spain and of all the territories he should conquer, while he praised and confirmed him in everything he had done in the service of God and the King. He signed the decree at Valladolid on the twenty-second of October of the year 1522. It was countersigned by Don García de Padilla and notarized by Francisco de los Cobos, Secretary. Cortés was also directed to expel turncoats [converted Moslems and Jews] and lawyers from New Spain: the latter, so as to keep down the number of lawsuits; the former, so as not to spoil the work of conversion. The Emperor also wrote him a letter, thanking him for the hardships he had undergone in the conquest, and for his service to God in casting down idols. To encourage Cortés in further enterprises of the kind, he promised him great favors, and the bishops, secular priests, and friars for the conversion that Cortés had asked for. [He further undertook] to support all the other measures [initiated by Cortés] for the strengthening, cultivation, and ennoblement of the land.

Francisco de las Casas and Rodrigo de Paz set out at once with these welcome dispatches of His Majesty. At Santiago de Baracoa they informed Diego Velázquez, by public crier, of these decisions and orders (this was during the month of May of the year '23), which upset Velázquez so badly that he died of chagrin. He died sad and poor, having once been rich, and after his death his heirs never demanded anything of Cortés.

FOLLOWING THE CUSTOM of the Indies, Cortés always distributed the land among its conquerors, trusting that he would be named Distributor-General of the conquered territory; or pehaps he did so to favor his friends, of whom he had great ones. So as soon as he received the Emperor's order authorizing him to distribute and give New Spain in encomienda to its conquerors and settlers, he made many and large allotments. At the same time he ordered the encomenderos to maintain a priest or friar in every town or provincial capital, and to instruct the Indians of their encomiendas in the Christian doctrine and undertake their conversion, for many had begged to be baptized. He did not give everyone an encomienda, which would have been impossible and excessive; nor were the ones he did give as big as they desired and demanded, for which reason some were humiliated, while others complained. Nothing, indeed, stirs up and irritates the conquerors more than this business of encomiendas, and nothing has brought more hatred and enmity down upon the heads of captains and governors. So true is this that, although [the governorship] is a necessary and honorable post, it is the most troublesome and invidious.

All kings and republics that have subjugated many lands have distributed them among their captains and soldiers, or citizens, founding towns for the conservation and perpetuity of the state, and as rewards for the hardships and services of the men. This has been the rule in Spain ever since it had kings, and was observed by the Catholic Monarchs, Ferdinand and Isabella, and even by the Emperor (until he was advised to stop it), for in a decree signed at Madrid in the year '45 he ordered the encomiendas to be made perpetual, which is a much greater thing [than distributing lands], and he did so with the approval and advice of his Council of the Indies, and with that of many Dominican and Franciscan friars, and other men learned in the law, as many say. Men who go on conquests are put to great expense, for which reason they are given honors and riches, and become noble and famous, for it is a fine thing to be a conquering knight. If I had the space I should here name all the conquerors, but, since that cannot be, let each one do so in his own house.

WHENEVER CORTÉS entered a town he cast down its idols and forbade human sacrifice—this to remove an offense to God and injury to one's neighbors. In the first letters he wrote to the Emperor, after taking Mexico, he begged His Majesty and the Council of the Indies to send bishops, priests, and friars to preach to and convert the Indians. Later he wrote to Fray Francisco de Los Angeles (of the Quiñón family), General of the Franciscan Order, to send him friars for the work of conversion, whom he would pay out of the tithes of that country. [Fray Francisco] sent him twelve friars, under the charge of Fray Martín de Valencia de San Juan, of [the convent of] San Gabriel, a most holy man credited with miracles. Cortés also wrote to Fray García de Loaysa, General of the Dominicans, who sent none until the year '26, when Fray Tomás Ortiz went over with twelve companions. Bishops were slow in going, and there were few secular priests, for which reason, and because he thought it expedient, Cortés begged the Emperor to send many friars to build monasteries, attend to the conversion, and collect tithes; but His Majesty was better advised and refused to request it of the Pope, who would not have consented, nor would it have been to his interest.

Fray Martín de Valencia, the Pope's vicar, arrived in Mexico in the year '24, with twelve companions. Cortés received him with gifts, services, and honor. Whenever he spoke to them it was with cap in hand and one knee on the ground, while he kissed their robes as an example to the Indians who were to be converted; he did so also because he was himself devout and humble. The Indians were amazed to see one whom they worshiped abase himself in this fashion, so they always treated [the friars] with great reverence. He told the Spaniards, especially those who had unconverted Indians in encomienda, to show the friars great honor, which they did by giving abundant alms in expiation of their sins, although he was told by some that he was acting in behalf of those [the friars] who would destroy them once they got established in the kingdom—words which he had occasion to remember thereafter.

As soon as the friars arrived, the work of conversion was actively undertaken. The idols were cast down, and, since there were many

priests and friars in the encomienda towns, as Cortés had commanded, a great harvest of preaching, baptizing, and marrying was
reaped. There was some difficulty in discovering which of the many
wives of the neophytes were to be married at the church door, as is
the custom of our Holy Mother Church, either because they were
unable to decide, or because our people did not understand them.
For this reason, in that same year of '24, Cortés convoked a synod,
the first to be held in the Indies, to consider this and other matters.
Thirty men attended it, of whom six were learned in the law, some
laymen, one of whom was Cortés, five clerics, and nineteen friars.
Fray Martín, as vicar of the Pope, presided. They decided that for
the time being [the Indians] should marry whom they pleased, since
they were unacquainted with our marriage rites.

169. Cortés Sends the Emperor a Silver Cannon

ON THE FIFTEENTH of October of that same year of '24, Cortés
wrote the Emperor, thanking him for the favors and honors accorded
him. [In it] he pleaded for the conquerors, and begged exemptions
and privileges for the villas he had founded, and for Tlaxcala,
Texcoco, and the other towns that had assisted and served him in the
wars. He remitted to the Emperor 70,000 castellanos in gold by the
hand of Diego de Soto, and a silver culverin worth 24,000 gold pesos
—a beautiful piece, more in its appearance than in value. It was
heavy, but was made of silver from Michoacán. It bore in relief the
device of a phoenix, with an inscription to the Emperor, as follows:

> *As this [phoenix] was born without equal,*
> *As I am without equal in your service,*
> *So are you without equal in the world.*

I shall refrain from describing the feather, hair, and cotton articles
that Cortés sent at that time, for the cannon quite outshone them;
nor [shall I mention] the pearls, or the tigers, or the other good
things of that land, unknown here in Spain. But I must add that the

cannon, because of its inscription, brought down upon him the envy and dislike of certain courtiers, although the common people praised him to the skies. I believe that this silver cannon of Cortés was the only one of its kind ever to be cast. He composed the inscription himself, for he was not a bad versifier when he put his mind to it. Many unsuccessfully tried their hand at [a rejoinder]; thus Cristóbal de Tapia, referring perhaps to the 3,000 castellanos spent on the casting alone, wrote:

> *This gun, I here submit,*
> *More folly shows than wit.*

Cortés also sent 25,000 castellanos in gold and 550 marks of silver to Martín Cortés, to cover the cost of his wife's voyage [to Mexico]; and also asked him to ship him arms, artillery, and tools, and to send ships loaded with sails, cordage, anchors, clothing, plants, legumes, and the like, for the improvement of the land he had conquered. The King, however, seized it all, as he seized everything then brought from the Indies.

Even with the money that Cortés sent the Emperor, the royal treasury remained empty and [the Emperor] without a penny, because of the heavy sums he had spent on armies and fleets, as you have read in the history. At this same time there arrived in Mexico many royal servants and officers: Alonso de Estrada, Treasurer, from Ciudad Real; Gonzalo de Salazar, Factor, from Granada; Rodrigo de Albornoz, Contador, from Paradinas; and Peralmíndez Chirinos, Veedor. Since these were the first to be sent to New Spain, and since many conquerors had sought the offices, [the latter] felt themselves wronged and complained of Cortés. So they examined the accounts of Julián de Alderete and the others appointed by the city council [of Mexico] to hold and collect the King's fifth, and his rents and property, and they did not overlook certain sums, amounting to about 60,000 castellanos, which had been given to Cortés; but he proved that he had spent them in the service of the Emperor as well as some 50,000 pesos of his own that he had deposited with them, so the account was liquidated.

Still, the royal officers clung to the notion that Cortés possessed vast treasures, for they had heard in Spain that Juan de Rivera had offered the Emperor in his name some 200,000 ducats; also, there was no lack of whisperers who told them that the Indians brought him in daily gold, silver, cacao [beans], pearls, featherwork, and other valuables; that he had hidden Moctezuma's treasure and stolen that of the Emperor and the other conquerors, using for the purpose Indians who secretly took it out at night by the wicket of his house. So it was that, not taking into account what he had sent to Castile or spent in the wars, they wrote many stories to Spain (especially Rodrigo de Albornoz, who carried instructions in cipher to make secret reports on anything that struck his fancy), accusing Cortés of avarice and tyranny. They believed all this because they did not know him, and were badly informed, and found there many persons who bore him a grudge for not granting them encomiendas, or such as they demanded.

170. Search for a Strait

IN CASTILE it was desired to discover a strait in the Indies through which to sail to the Moluccas, and thus to remove [the cause of] the conflict with Portugal over the Spice Islands. With this in mind, the Emperor ordered Pedrarias de Avila, Cortés, Gil González de Avila, and others to make a search from Veragua to Yucatan, because ever since Christopher Columbus had discovered Tierra Firme a strait was believed to exist, a belief that was strengthened when Vasco Núñez de Balboa discovered the other sea and learned how narrow the land was between Nombre de Dios and Panama.

Thus it happened that all three undertook the search at the same time, although Pedrarias sent Francisco Hernández rather to colonize than look for a strait. This Hernández founded a colony in Nicaragua and got as far as Honduras. Hernán Cortés sent Cristóbal de Olid, as we have already said. Gil González [de Avila] set out with the same object in the year '23, founding San Gil de Buenavista, destroying Francisco Hernández, and beginning the conquest of that country [of Nicaragua].

171. Olid Rebels Against Cortés

FOLLOWING CORTÉS' INSTRUCTIONS, Cristóbal de Olid first sailed to Cuba, and at Havana took on board the horses and provisions that Contreras had purchased at excessive prices. [For example], a fanega of maize sold for two pesos gold; a fanega of beans, four; of garbanzos, nine; an arroba of olive oil, three; of vinegar, four; of tallow candles, nine; of soap, also nine; a quintal of tow, four pesos; of iron, six; a string of garlic, two; a belt, one; an arquebus, 100; a pair of shoes, one; a cowhide, twelve; while a sailing master earned 800 pesos a month. Notwithstanding these high prices, Cortés outfitted this and other fleets, spending on this last one some 30,000 castellanos.

While the ships were being loaded with provisions and wood and water, [Olid] arranged a plot with Diego Velázquez to rise against Cortés. Among the plotters were Juan Ruano, Andrés de Duero, the Bachiller Parada, the Provisor Moreno, and others whose identity was learned after the death of Velázquez and Olid. [Olid] took what Contreras and Velázquez gave him, and made land fifteen leagues beyond Puerto de Caballos [in Honduras], after a stormy and dangerous passage. Since he arrived on the third of May, he named the town he traced out Triunfo de la Cruz. He appointed as alcaldes, regidores, and officers the men Cortés had indicated in Mexico; he took possession and performed the other ceremonies in the names of the Emperor and Cortés, whose authority he bore. He did all this as later became evident, to quiet the kinsmen and servants of Cortés, and to fortify himself and make a reconnaissance of the country. But he soon discovered a hatred for Cortés and his affairs, and threatened to hang anyone who opposed him or grumbled.

By promising offices, bishoprics, and judgeships to many, he was soon without opposition. He abandoned the search for a strait and set about expelling Gil González de Avila from those parts, the latter having, as I have just said, founded the town of San Gil de Buenavista. Olid killed a number of Spaniards in the process, among them his own nephew, Gil de Avila, as well as many others, in order to have that rich country to himself.

When Cortés got word of these activities of Cristóbal de Olid, he forthwith dispatched Francisco de las Casas, in two well-manned vessels, with authority and orders to arrest him. Cristóbal de Olid sighted the ships and guessed their mission, so he filled two caravels with men and fired upon [Las Casas] to prevent his landing. Las Casas hoisted a peace flag, but it was not heeded, so he launched two boatloads of armed men, to fight and make a landing if they could find an entrance, while he manned his guns and managed to sink one of his opponent's caravels, for Olid's malice and suspected rebellion were manifest in his refusal to recognize [Las Casas' signal]. No men were drowned. Las Casas, however, did not dare to make port, but stood at anchor to await Cristóbal de Olid's next move, while [the latter] recalled the men he had sent against Gil González. Meanwhile, a violent storm blew up and wrecked Francisco de las Casas' ships at a place where his men were easily taken without bloodshed. They were kept three days in the water and cold, without food, and more than forty of them died.

Cristóbal de Olid forced [the survivors] to swear on the Bible (as he had done with the men of Gil González) that they would never oppose him and would never again follow Cortés, whereupon he released them all except Francisco de las Casas, whom he took with him to Naco, a fine town [later] destroyed by [Diego de] Albítez and [Andrés de] Cereceda. In this fashion Cristóbal de Olid captured Francisco de las Casas, as he had already captured Gil González de Avila, although some say this was later. However it was, it is certain that he held them both as prisoners at the same time in his own house, and that he was very proud to have such eminent ones, not only on account of their renown and reputation, but because he thought that through them he could reach an accommodation with Cortés and be left in sole possession of the country. Things, however, turned out quite the contrary.

Francisco de las Casas begged him many times, in the presence of all the Spaniards, to release him to make his report to Cortés, since his person and presence there were of no advantage [to Olid]. But Olid always refused, although Las Casas warned him that his life was in jeopardy—a bold and daring thing for a prisoner to say. But Cristóbal de Olid, who fancied himself a valiant man, and who held the others unarmed and surrounded by his servants, ignored the threats, so the two prisoners plotted to kill him. While they were at table dining (others say while they were strolling about the room), they seized two table knives (or desk knives), and Francisco de las Casas seized him by the beard and held him, and they stabbed him many times, saying: "It is time we put an end to this tyrant!" Olid finally escaped and managed to conceal himself among some Indian huts, thinking that, when his men came to eat, they would kill Francisco de las Casas and Gil González de Avila. But these shouted: "Here, you men of Cortés!" and, within a short time they had taken, without much opposition, the arms and persons of all the Spaniards in his company, and captured several of Cristóbal de Olid's henchmen. Olid himself was summoned by crier; his hiding place was discovered; he was seized, tried, and sentenced by the two; and, a few days after his arrest, he was publicly beheaded at Naco. So he lost his life because he despised his opponent and did not take his enemy's advice.

After the death of Cristóbal de Olid, Francisco de las Casas and Gil González de Avila took charge of the men and the country, and no one [of Olid's captains] removed his men. Francisco de las Casas founded the villa of Trujillo on the eighteenth of May of the year '25, and, after arranging many matters of advantage to Cortés, he returned by land to Mexico, taking Gil González de Avila with him.

The Audiencia of Santo Domingo had the Emperor's orders to punish anyone who should become insubordinate and stir up trouble among the Spaniards of Honduras, so they at once sent the Bachiller Pedro Moreno, their prosecutor, with letters and authority; but, by the time he arrived, Cristóbal de Olid was dead and the killers had departed for Mexico, and nothing could be done about it. Anyway, it was said that Moreno was more merchant than judge.

172. Cortés Marches Against Olid

CORTÉS WAS FURIOUS with Cristóbal de Olid for having risen against him and did not fail to say so on all occasions, for Olid had been his friend and owed him his career. Nor did Cortés have much confidence in the diligence of Francisco de las Casas, for Olid had many friends, so he determined to go there himself. He notified his friends, prepared for his departure, and made public his decision. The royal officers begged him to give up the expedition, because [they said] the security of Mexico was more important than that of Honduras, and that his absence might give the Indians an excuse for rebelling and killing the few remaining Spaniards. Indeed, they were convinced that the Indians had this in mind, because the Indians were always going about bemoaning the deaths of their fathers, and the imprisonment and captivity of their lords. [The royal officers] felt that if Mexico should fall, the whole country would be lost; that the Indians feared and respected Cortés more than all the rest together; and that he should leave the punishment of Cristóbal de Olid to time, Francisco de las Casas, and the Emperor. Besides, they told him, the journey was long, difficult, and profitless, and would moreover cause civil strife among the Spaniards.

Cortés answered that if he neglected to punish [Olid] it would encourage other rascals to rise, as he greatly feared, because there were many other captains scattered about in New Spain who would, perhaps, follow Olid's example and become insubordinate; that they would commit excesses in the land and stir up a general rebellion; and that afterward neither he nor anyone could win it back again. The royal officers then made a formal demand of him in the name of the Emperor not to go, and he promised to go no farther than Coatzacoalcos and other rebellious provinces near by. At this they withdrew their request and demand, and he prepared for his departure, but with great prudence, because all the affairs of the country, for good or evil, depended upon him, and this gave him much to think about and to provide for. He arranged the many affairs of the government; he ordered the conversion of the Indians to be pursued with all possible and necessary zeal; he wrote to the councils [of the villas] and the ecomenderos, charging them to cast down all idols; he distributed encomiendas to the royal officers and to many others (this to make everybody happy); he left behind as lieutenant-governors the Treasurer Alonso de Estrada and the Contador Rodrigo de Albornoz, thinking these two would be competent; he put Alonso Zuazo in charge of dispensing justice; and, to keep Gonzalo de Salazar and Peralmíndez Chirinos from feeling hurt, he took them along with him. He appointed Francisco de Solís captain of the artillery and warden of the brigantines, which he had well supplied with arms and ammunition, against possible need.

He decided to take with him the lords and nobles of Mexico and Culhúa, who might disturb the country and rebel during his absence. Among them were King Cuauhtémoc; Coanacoxtzin, former Lord of Texcoco; Tetlepanquetzal, lord of Tacuba; Ocuitzin, lord of Atzcapotzalco; and Xihuacoa, Tlacatlec, and Mexicalcinco, very powerful men who, if left behind, would have been capable of staging a rebellion. All this having been arranged, Cortés departed from Mexico in October of the year 1524, thinking all would be well; but all went badly, except the conversion of the Indians, which was immensely successful and well done, as we shall relate at greater length.

173. Mutiny of Cortés' Lieutenants

NO SOONER had Cortés left the city than Alonso de Estrada and Rodrigo de Albornoz began to bicker and quarrel over questions of precedence and seniority. One day at a council meeting they drew their swords over the appointment of a constable, and little by little they reached the extreme of failing to fulfill their duties. The council sent a report of the matter to Cortés, but, since the letters were delivered to him on the road, he did not take action. Instead, he wrote [to Estrada and Albornoz], reprimanding them for their error and folly, and warning them that if they did not mend their ways and obey [his instructions], he would remove them from office and punish them. They, however, did not even on this account abandon their feud; rather, their rancor and hatred increased, because Estrada, who boasted of royal blood,* despised Albornoz, and Albornoz, who was touchy about his honor, would not be put upon. So their discord grew, and the city [council] warned Cortés to come back quickly to remedy the situation and pacify the citizens, Indians as well as Spaniards, who were getting restive with the quarreling of these two. Cortés, then, so as not to interrupt his expedition, decided to give the Factor Gonzalo de Salazar and the Veedor Peralmíndez Chirinos de Ubeda equal authority with the other two, so that all four of them could govern without offense to any of them. He also issued secret orders for [Salazar and Chirinos], in case they thought it necessary, to take over the government jointly with the Licenciado Zuazo, and suspend

* Estrada was reputed to be the natural son of Ferdinand the Catholic.

from office Alonso de Estrada and Rodrigo de Albornoz, whom they should punish if guilty.

This secret order that Cortés had issued with such good intentions was the source of violent hatred and quarrels among the royal officers, and of a civil war in which many Spaniards died and Mexico reached the very brink of destruction. Armed with their authority and secret instructions, Salazar and Chirinos took leave of Cortés in the villa of Espíritu Santo (although not in Grace),† and returned to Mexico, which they had no intention of governing jointly with the others, but alone; so they initiated an investigation, gathered information, and put [Estrada and Albornoz] under arrest. They sent the Licenciado Zuazo a prisoner, loaded with irons and a chain, to Vera Cruz, there to be put on board a ship and taken to Cuba to make an accounting of a certain residencia [that he had presided over]. Their treatment of Estrada and Albornoz was even worse. Acting as if there were no King, they persecuted everyone who failed to please them. [For example], acting in the belief that Cortés would never return to Mexico, and impelled by their excessive cupidity (although they advertised that they were acting in the Emperor's service), they arrested Rodrigo de Paz, cousin and major-domo of Cortés and chief constable of Mexico, whom they tortured most barbarously to make him divulge the location of the treasure, and whom, when he did not do so, for he knew nothing of it, nor even that it existed, they hanged. Then they took possession of the houses of Cortés, with the artillery, arms, and other things contained therein—an act that shocked the whole city. (For this act they were later condemned to death—although the sentence was not executed—by the oidores and licenciados Juan de Salmerón, Ceynos, Quiroga, and Maldonado, under the presidency of Sebastián Ramírez de Fuenleal, Bishop of Santo Domingo, and by the Council of the Indies. Very much later, while Don Antonio de Mendoza was Viceroy, the same Audiencia of Mexico condemned them to pay for all the artillery and the other things they had removed from the house of Cortés.)

These fine governors became as dissolute as they were absolute. Things being in this state, the people of Oaxaca and Coatlán rebelled and killed 50 Spaniards, and 8,000 or 10,000 Indian slaves who were working in the mines. Peralmíndez advanced against them with 200

† An ecclesiastical pun.

Spanish foot and 100 horse, whereupon the Indians took refuge upon five or six pinnacles, and later upon a very high one, with all their clothing and gold. Chirinos besieged them for forty days because the Indians had a great golden serpent, many shields, necklaces, flyflaps, precious stones, and other rich jewels; but, undetected by him, they escaped one night with their whole treasure.

Gonzalo de Salazar had himself proclaimed, by public crier and drums, Governor and Captain-General of all New Spain. Meanwhile, a letter was sent off to Cortés by the hand of Captain Francisco de Medina; but Medina was cruelly put to death by the Indians of Xicalanco, who thrust many pitch pine splinters into his body and burned him slowly, while they forced him to march around a pit—a ceremony performed by sacrificial victims. They also killed his Spanish companions and his Indian guides and carriers.

Diego de Ordaz was sent out soon afterward to search for Cortés, but turned back when he heard of the death that Medina had suf-fered. Then, to avoid being accused of cowardice, or perhaps thinking that Cortés had also been killed by the Indians, he reported that Cortés was dead, a story that caused a great part of the trouble. His report, coupled with the bad news of the many hardships and perils that Cortés and his company were undergoing, convinced the whole city that Cortés was dead. Many wives mourned their husbands, and certain kinsmen, friends, and servants of Cortés paid him funeral honors. But Juana de Mansilla, the wife of Alonso Valiente, said that Cortés was alive and, word of it coming to the ears of Gonzalo de Salazar, he ordered her whipped through the public and customary‡ streets of Mexico—the senseless act of a tyrant. (When Cortés returned, he restored the woman's name by carrying her behind him on his horse through Mexico and addressing her as "Doña Juana." In certain lines composed later, in imitation of those of the Provincial, it was said that adding a *doña* to her name was as absurd as putting a nose on her arm.)

About this time, six or seven ships touched at Medellín, belonging to certain merchants who, attracted by the stories of the riches of Mexico, had come to sell their wares. Gonzalo de Salazar wanted to use these ships to send certain monies to the Emperor (which were the touchstone of his affair), and write to the Council of the Indies

‡ That is, the streets officially designated for this purpose.

and [Francisco de los] Cobos, to take care of his interests; but he was not without opponents, who said that he could not [lawfully] do so without the approval and letters of the Governor, Hernán Cortés.

Francisco de las Casas, accompanied by Gil González de Avila, arrived, and, since he was a brave and haughty gentleman and a brother-in-law of Cortés, he took a very strong stand against [the royal officers] and even insulted them one day and abused Rodrigo de Albornoz. Then he sent to Medellín to have the anchors and sails removed from the ships, so that [the officers] would have no means of sending false, lying, and mischievous reports, as he termed them, back to Spain. But the Factor Salazar was too clever for him, and arrested both him and Gil González, charging them with the killing of Cristóbal de Olid and with disobedience and disrespect in the business of the ships; also because [Las Casas] was an obstacle in the way of his plans. He sentenced them to death and would have beheaded them, even though they appealed to the Emperor, if it had not been for their good pleaders. Even so, he sent them prisoners to Spain, together with the process and sentence, in a ship belonging to Juan Bono de Quexo, in which he also forwarded some 12,000 castellanos in bars and gold jewels by the hand of Juan de la Peña, his servant. It was his bad luck, however, to have the caravel sunk off the island of Fayal, one of the Azores. The letters and documents were lost, but the men and treasure were saved.

174. The Factor and Veedor Are Arrested

WHILE GONZALO DE SALAZAR was enjoying his triumph in Mexico, and Peralmíndez Chirinos was besieging the rock of Coatlán, as I have related, Martín Dorantes, the page of Cortés, arrived at the city, with many letters and orders of the Governor, appointing Francisco de las Casas and Pedro de Alvarado as [lieutenant] governors, and removing from office and punishing the Factor and Veedor. Dorantes went secretly to the convent of San Francisco and, as soon as he learned from the friars that Francisco de las Casas had been sent a prisoner to Spain, he summoned Rodrigo de Albornoz and Alonso de Estrada and delivered Cortés' letters to them. They read them at once and called together all Cortés' adherents, who forthwith elected Alonso de Estrada Cortés' lieutenant, in the name of the Emperor, because neither Pedro de Alvarado nor Francisco de las Casas, to whom the letters were addressed, was present.

The news that Cortés was alive flew through the city; there was great jubilation and all left their houses to see and talk to Dorantes. The rejoicing caused by these good tidings made Mexico a different place from what it had been. Gonzalo de Salazar, excessively afraid of the fury of the people, appealed to many not to abandon him in his need. He placed guns at the doors of Cortés' house, where he had been living since the execution of Rodrigo de Paz, and fortified himself with some two hundred Spaniards. Alonso de Estrada attacked the house with all his company, and, when the two hundred Spaniards saw the whole city descending upon them, they decided it was better to go over to Cortés, who was alive, than to support the Factor; and to save their lives they began to desert Salazar and let themselves down from the windows and galleries of the house. Among the first to escape was Don Luis de Guzmán, and soon [Salazar] was left with only ten or fifteen men, who must have been his servants. The Factor did not yield on that account; rather, he encouraged those who remained, and prepared to resist. He himself touched off a gun with a burning stick, but it did no harm because his enemies opened ranks to let the ball pass. Then Estrada and his men attacked, entered the house, and seized the Factor in a bedroom, where he had retired. They bound him with a chain and paraded him through the square and streets for all to see, not without vituperation and insult. Then they locked him in a cage under heavy guard, after which Estrada and Albornoz went to that same house [of Cortés].

Estrada was properly against [the Factor], but Albornoz acted deviously. It is said that he spoke to the Factor and promised him that he would be neither for nor against him, but [was only interested] in peace. Upon his return he spoke with Estrada, who was on his way to attack the house, and had [Estrada] give him a horse in exchange for the mule he was riding, and arms for himself and servants, so that he might put on a show of force in case the Factor should win.

Peralmíndez Chirinos, as soon as he learned that Cortés was alive and had revoked his authority as governor, abandoned the war he was engaged in and set out for Mexico at top speed to lend support to his friend Gonzalo de Salazar. Before he arrived, however, he learned that [Salazar] had been arrested and caged, so he went on to Tlaxcala and sought refuge in the convent of San Francisco, thinking to be safe there and escape from the hands of Estrada and the party of Cortés. But as soon as this was discovered in Mexico, he was sent for and put into another cage next his companion, without benefit of sanctuary.

Upon the arrest of these two, the scandal came to an end, and Estrada and Albornoz governed very peacefully in the name of the King and the people; although it happened that certain friends and servants of Gonzalo de Salazar and Peralmíndez got together and plotted to kill Albornoz and Estrada on a designated day, and have the guards free the prisoners. But, since the keys [to the cages] were in the hands of the governors, the plot could not be carried out without making duplicates, besides which it would have been impossible to break open the cages without detection and arrest, for they were constructed of heavy beams. So they let a certain Guzmán, son of a locksmith of Seville and maker of crossbow strings, in on the secret. This Guzmán, who was a good man and a follower of Cortés, informed himself in detail of who and how many the plotters were, in order to denounce them and be believed. He promised them keys, files, and picklocks whenever they wanted them, and begged them to see him every day and tell him what was going on, because [he said] he wanted to be present at the liberation of the captives and prevent their being killed. They foolishly and ingenuously believed him, and often came to his shop. Guzmán informed the governors of the business and named the plotters, and [the governors] at once investigated and found it was all true, so they ordered the arrest of the conspirators and took their confessions, in which the latter admitted they had wanted to free their masters and kill [the governors]. Their leader, a certain Escobar, and several others were hanged; others had their hands cut off; others, their feet; still others were flogged; and many were exiled—in a word, they were all well punished. From that time onward no one disturbed the city, or the government of Alonso de Estrada.

In this fashion, just as I have described it, the civil war between Spaniards in Mexico was brought to an end, Hernán Cortés being absent—a war brought on by the King's officers themselves, who were the most to blame. And never again, during an absence of Cortés, did any soldier of his rebel, nor was there a repetition of such disturbances. It was wonderful that the Indians did not rise at that time, for they had the means to do so, and even the arms. Some of them, to be sure, did show signs of rising; but they were waiting for Cuauhtémoc to send them word that he had killed Cortés, as he attempted to do on the journey, as will be related below.

175. Cortés Sets Out for Honduras

IMMEDIATELY AFTER he had dispatched Gonzalo de Salazar and Peralmíndez from the villa of Espíritu Santo with his authority to assume the goverment of Mexico, Cortés sent word to the lords of Tabasco and Xicalanco that he was there and that he wished to march by a certain route, and he requested them to lend him men who knew the coast and the back country. These lords at once sent him twelve of the most respectable persons of their towns, and sent him merchants also, with the safe-conducts they customarily carry. They, when they thoroughly understood Cortés' plan, painted him a canvas on which they depicted the whole route from Xicalanco to Naco and Nito, where the Spaniards were, and even as far as Nicaragua, which is on the South Sea, and the place where Pedrarias, Governor of Tierra Firme, resided. This [map] was a remarkable thing, because it showed all the rivers and mountains that had to be crossed, and all the large towns and inns where they stopped when they attended the fairs. They told him, however, that they no longer went to the fairs as they had formerly done, because the people had fled to the forests, the wandering Spaniards having burned many towns.

Cortés thanked them for the painting and gave them a few trinkets in payment for it and for the intelligence of [the land] he was in search of; indeed, he was astonished at their knowledge of such distant places. Having secured a guide and an interpreter, he now paraded his troops and found he had one hundred and fifty horse and an equal number of foot, in battle trim, with three thousand Indians, men and women, to serve them. He had a drove of swine, which are very hardy animals for traveling and endurance, and which multiply rapidly. He loaded three caravels with the four pieces of artillery he had brought from Mexico, with beans, [salt] fish, and other provisions; with many arms and munitions, and all the wine, oil, vinegar, and dried beef from Vera Cruz and Medellín. He sent the ships down the coast as far as the River of Tabasco, while he set out by land, thinking to keep close to the sea. Nine leagues beyond the villa of Espíritu Santo he crossed a wide river in canoes and entered Tonalá. A like distance farther on he crossed another river, called the Aquiualco [Ahualulco?], which the horses swam. The next one he came to was so wide that, to keep the horses from drowning, he had to build a wooden bridge, not half a league from the sea, 934 paces [⅖ mile] long, a work which amazed the Indians, while it exhausted them. He reached Copilco, capital of the province, after a march of thirty-five leagues, during which he crossed fifty rivers and swampy lagoons, over which he built an equal number of bridges, for his men could not have passed otherwise. This country is thickly populated, although it is very low and covered with swamps and great lagoons, navigated by many canoes. It is rich is cacao, breadstuffs, fruit, and fish. This route turned out to be very profitable; the people remained friendly to the Spaniards of Espíritu Santo, among whom the land was partitioned.

From Anaxaxuca, the last town of Copilco before Cihuatlán, Cortés traversed many difficult mountain ranges and a very wide river called the Quetzalapan, which flows into the River of Tabasco, now called the Grijalba. He brought supplies from the caravels, utilizing twenty canoes manned by two hundred Tabascans; he also used them to cross the river, in which a Negro drowned and some four arrobas of precious horseshoes were lost. (It was here, I think, that Juan Jaramillo married Marina while drunk. Cortés was criticized for allowing it, because he had children by her.) The Indians fled, and during the twenty days he was there Cortés could find no one to guide him, nor did anyone come except two men and several women, who informed him that their lord and all the rest of the people were hiding in the woods and lagoons, where they could move only by canoe. They were asked if they knew Chilapan, which was marked on the map, and they pointed to a mountain range some ten leagues distant. Cortés, using many timbers thirty and forty feet in length, built a bridge 300 paces long, by means of which he crossed a great swamp, for he could not get out of the town without traversing water. He slept [that night] on high, dry ground, and entered Chilapan the next day. It was a large town in a fine situation, but it had been burned and destroyed. He found there only two men, who guided him to Tamaztepec, otherwise known as Tepetitlán, but to get there he had to cross a river called, like the town, the Chilapan. Another slave was drowned here, and a great deal of baggage was lost. It took him two days to cover six leagues, and the horses were almost always up to their knees in water and mud, and in many places even up to their bellies. The hardships and perils endured by the men were excessive, and three Spaniards were drowned. Tamaztepec was deserted and destroyed.

Nevertheless, our men rested there for six days, finding fruit and green maize in the fields, and grain in the bins—which was a vast relief and refreshment, given the condition of both men and horses. How the pigs managed to get there was a miracle. From Tamaztepec Cortés made it to Ixtapa in two days, through swamps and quagmires, in which the horses sank to their cinches. The people of the town fled at the sight of mounted men; also because the lord of Cihuatlán had told them that the Spaniards killed everyone they caught. They even burned many of their houses and carried off their clothing and women to the far side of the river that flows through the town, many of them drowning in their haste to escape. A few were captured. They said they had acted in this fashion because of the fright that the lord of Cihuatlán had given them.

Cortés then summoned the people he had brought from Cihuatlán, Chilapan, and Tamaztepec, to bear witness to the good treatment they had received at his hands; and, in the presence of the captives, he gave them some trinkets and permission to go home, and, for their protection, letters addressed to any Christians who might pass that way. The people of Ixtapa were greatly pleased and reassured by his action, and summoned their lord, who came with forty men and proclaimed himself a vassal of the Emperor. Moreover, he provided abundantly for our army during the week it spent there. He requested the return of the twenty women who had been captured at the river, and they were at once given him.

While Cortés was there, it happened that a Mexican ate the leg of an Indian of the town who had been hacked to death. As soon as Cortés heard of it, he ordered the Mexican forthwith to be burned in the presence of the lord, to whom, through his interpreter, he explained the reason for it. He even preached the lord a long sermon, to the effect that he had come to those parts on behalf of the best and most powerful Prince on earth, whom the whole world recognized as sovereign, as the lord himself had done; that he had come to punish those wicked men who, like this Mexican, ate human flesh; that [he had come] to teach the law of Christ, which commands us to believe in and worship a single God, not numerous idols; that [he had come] to warn men of the deceit practiced upon them by the devil, whose purpose it was to carry them off to hell, where they would be tormented in terrible and everlasting fire. Cortés likewise explained to the lord the many mysteries of our Holy Catholic Faith and painted for him the joys of paradise, and in this fashion pleased and astonished him.

From this same lord Cortés obtained three canoes which he sent down the river to Tabasco, with three Spaniards, whose instructions were to have the caravels wait at the Bay of Ascensión, and then to send these canoes and others up the estuary to Acalán, with meat and bread from the ships. The lord also gave Cortés three manned canoes, in which Cortés sent several Spaniards up the river to pacify the land and clear the road—no small mark of friendship.

It was at this time that dismal reports were brought to Mexico, to the effect that Cortés would never return, thus giving Gonzalo de Salazar and Peralmíndez the opportunity to disclose their accursed intention.

176. The Priests of Tatahuitlalpan

FROM IXTAPA Cortés went to Tatahuitlalpan, where he found no one at all, except in a very large and well-adorned temple on the far side of the river, some twenty men who must have been priests.

They said they had remained there in order to die with their gods, the gods having told them that the bearded men would kill them— this because Cortés always destroyed the idols and replaced them with crosses. So when they saw the Mexican Indians with ornaments taken from the idols, they said, weeping, that they no longer wished to live. Then Cortés and the two Franciscan friars, speaking through the interpreters, repeated what they had told the lord of Ixtapa, that is, to abandon that mad and wicked belief of theirs. They replied that they wished to die in the law of their fathers and grandfathers. One of the twenty, the principal, pointed out Huatecpan on the map, but said he was not permitted to walk [there] on the ground—a very great piece of foolishness, but one with which they lived contented and carefree.

Shortly after the army left this place, Cortés crossed a swamp half a league wide, and then a deep estuary, over which he had to construct a bridge; and farther on, another swamp a league wide; but, since it was fairly firm underfoot, the horses crossed it with little difficulty, although they did sink to their cinches and, even in the best places, up to their knees. [The Spaniards] were now in such a dense forest that they could see only the sky above them and the ground they trod, the trees being so tall that it was impossible to climb them and survey the country. They wandered about lost in it for two days, when they noticed pasture on the shore of a lagoon where the horses could graze. That night they slept and ate little, and some thought they would die before reaching an inhabited place. Then Cortés brought out a compass and mariner's card that he carried for such occasions, and, remembering the place that had been pointed out to him at Tatahuitlalpan, he took his bearings and decided that if he followed a northeast course they would come out at Huatecpan, or very close to it. So they opened a road by hand in that direction and, as God willed, hit the place squarely, after much hardship. There they refreshed themselves with fruits and other things, and the horses did no less, with green maize and the beautiful grass of the banks.

The town was deserted. Cortés could find no trace of the three canoes and the Spaniards he had sent up the river; but, while walking through the town, he saw a crossbow bolt stuck in the ground, by which he gathered that the men had gone on ahead, unless they had been killed by the natives. Several Spaniards crossed the river in canoes, looking for the people in the orchards and fields, and at last came to a great lagoon, where all the people of the town were in canoes or on the islands. As many as forty of them, laughing happily, approached Cortés and told him they had abandoned the town because of what the lord of Cihuatlán [had said]; that certain bearded men had gone up the river with the men of Ixtapa, who had vouched for the good treatment that the strangers accorded the natives, and that a brother of their lord had gone with them in four canoes filled with armed men, to protect [the strangers] from the people upstream.

Cortés sent for the Spaniards, and they came the next day, in many canoes loaded with honey, maize, cacao, and a little gold, which filled everyone's eyes with joy. People came also from four or five other towns to bring provisions for the Spaniards and to gape at them because of the wonderful things they had heard. As a token of friendship they brought a bit of gold, which all [the Spaniards] wished had been more. Cortés treated them with much courtesy and begged them to be friends of the Christians, which they all promised to be. Then they returned to their homes, burned many of their idols because of the preaching they had listened to, and their lord gave what gold he had.

177. Cortés Builds a Bridge

FROM HUATECPAN Cortés set out for the province of Acalán, taking a trail made by the merchants, who, according to them, were almost the only persons to travel from town to town. He crossed a river by canoe; a horse was drowned and several loads of baggage were lost. He marched three days over some very rough mountains, where the army suffered acutely from fatigue, and then came to an estuary five hundred paces wide, which put our army in the direst straits, for they had no boats and could not touch bottom. Their situation was so bad that they tearfully begged God's mercy, because it seemed impossible to get across except by flying, and to turn back, as most of them wanted to do, was to perish, for the floods caused by the heavy rains had washed out the bridges they had built. In a canoe with two Spanish sailors, Cortés took soundings of the whole bay and estuary, and everywhere they found four fathoms of water. They strung pikes together and sampled the bottom, which was covered with two more fathoms of mud and slime, making the total depth six fathoms, so building a bridge seemed to be out of the question.

Cortés, nevertheless, determined to try it. He asked the Mexican lords to have their Indians fell trees, fashion long beams, and drag them [to the bank] for building a bridge by which to escape. They did so, and the Spaniards, mounted on rafts and their three canoes, sank the beams one by one in the mud. Their exertion and irritation were so great that they cursed the bridge and even their captain, grumbling loudly at the man who, with his great cleverness and knowledge, had got them into a spot from which he could not extricate them. They said the bridge would never be finished, and even if it should be they would themselves be finished; that, therefore, they should retreat before their provisions were exhausted, for in any case they would turn back before reaching Honduras. Cortés had never been more perplexed, but, in order to keep the peace, he did not oppose them, but begged them to allow him five days only, and promised that if he had not built the bridge by the end of that time, he would turn back. They replied that they would wait, even if they had to eat stones. Thereupon Cortés told the Indians to consider the necessity they were all faced with, because they had either to get across or perish. He inspired them to work by telling them that just beyond the estuary was Acalán, a land full of friends, where the ships were waiting with a store of provisions and refreshments. He also promised them great rewards back in Mexico if they built the bridge.

All of them, especially their lords, agreed. They formed themselves into squads: some to gather roots, herbs, and fruits in the forest; others, to fell trees; others, to trim them; others, to drag them; still others, to sink them in the estuary. Cortés was the master architect of the work and put such diligence into it, and they such hard work, that within six days the bridge was completed, and on the seventh the whole army and the horses crossed—a thing that seemed impossible without the help of God. The Spaniards were greatly astonished, and even did their share, for, although they grumble, they work well. The task was performed in common, and the cleverness of the Indians was amazing. As many as a thousand beams were used in it, eight fathoms long and five or six spans thick, and many smaller ones to surface it. For lack of nails, because they had only horseshoe nails and wooden pegs, they lashed it together with vines.

The universal rejoicing at having crossed the estuary in safety was not, however, of long duration, because they immediately came to a frightful morass, though not a wide one, in which the horses, without their saddles, sank to their ears, and the more they struggled the deeper they sank, until there seemed to be no hope of saving them. Bundles of twigs and grass were inserted under their breasts and bellies to bolster them up, but did not suffice. While they were in this state a channel opened and they swam across, but were so exhausted they could not stand. [The Spaniards] thanked Our Lord for His great mercy, for without horses they were lost indeed.

At this juncture four Spaniards who had been sent on ahead returned, with eighty Indians, from the province of Acalán, loaded with fowl, fruit, and bread, and God knows how delighted everyone was, especially when they were told that Apoxpalón, lord of the province, and all the people were waiting for them in peace, and would be happy to receive and lodge them. Certain of these Indians presented Cortés with little gold articles on behalf of their lord, and told him how glad they were at his coming to their country, because for many years they had heard of [the Spaniards] through the merchants of Xicalanco and Tabasco. Cortés thanked them for their good will and gave them some Spanish trinkets for their lord, and sent some Spaniards with them to show them the bridge. They were astonished at its structure, not only because of its size (for nothing like it had ever been seen in those parts), but because they were convinced that nothing was impossible to the Spaniards.

The next day [the army] reached Tizatepec, where the citizens had a great feast spread for the men, and a quantity of grain, grass, and roses for the horses. The army rested there for six days, recuperating from their recent hardships and hunger. A youth of fine appearance and well-attended, who said he was the son of Apoxpalón, waited on Cortés. He brought him many fowl and some gold, and offered his person and his country, on the pretext that his father was dead. Cortés consoled him with kind words, although he suspected the lad was lying, for [the father] had been alive only four days previously and had sent him a present. Nevertheless, he took off a necklace of Flemish beads he was wearing and gave it to the youth, who was greatly pleased with it, while Cortés begged him to stay.

178. Apoxpalón, Lord of Izancanac

FROM TIZATEPEC [the Spaniards] marched to Teutiercas, six leagues, and were well received by its lord and lodged in two temples. There were many beautiful temples, one of which, the largest, was dedicated to the goddess to whom lovely virgins were sacrificed, for, if they were not [virgins], it was said, she became very angry. For this reason girls were selected in childhood and reared in great luxury. Cortés explained to them, as best he could, what was proper for Christians to do, and what the King had commanded, whereupon he cast down the idols, to the grief of the townspeople.

The lord of Teutiercas held long conversations with the Spaniards, having taken a great liking to Cortés, who told him at length what the Spaniards were seeking and the road they were to take. [The lord] told him as a great secret that Apoxpalón was alive and wished to lead him by a roundabout but not bad road and show him his towns and wealth. He ·begged [Cortés] to keep his secret if he wished to see [Apoxpalón] alive in his wealth and state. Cortés thanked him heartily and promised, not only to keep his secret, but to treat him as a friend. Then he summoned the youth I have mentioned and interrogated him. [The youth] could not deny the truth and admitted that his father was alive. He summoned him at [Cortés'] request, and on the second day brought him there.

Apoxpalón excused himself very shamefacedly [for the fabrication], on the ground that he had been afraid of the strange men and animals, until he should learn whether or not they were benevolent and would not destroy his towns. Now, however, that he saw they harmed no one, he begged Cortés to go with him to Izancanac, a populous city where he resided. Cortés departed the next day. He gave Apoxpalón a horse to ride, at which Apoxpalón showed great pleasure, although at first he almost fell off. Cortés and Apoxpalón were given a great reception in the city and were lodged in a house which also held the Spaniards and the horses. The Mexicans were distributed among the other houses. The lord fed them all bountifully the whole time they were there, and gave Cortés some gold and twenty women; also a canoe to take him down the river to the sea, where the caravels were, to see a Spaniard who had recently arrived from Santiesteban de Pánuco with letters, accompanied by four Indians with other letters from the villa of Espíritu Santo and Mexico, written before Gonzalo de Salazar and Peralmíndez had arrived there. Cortés wrote in reply that he was doing well enough, although he had suffered some hardships. He also wrote to the Spaniards in the caravels instructing them what they were to do and where they were to await him.

In the land of Acalán, so they say, the people have the custom of choosing as their lord the most prosperous merchant, which is why Apoxpalón had been chosen, for he enjoyed a large land trade in cotton, cacao, slaves, salt, and gold (although this was not plentiful and was mixed with copper and other things); in colored shells, with which they adorn themselves and their idols; in resin and other incense for the temples; in pitch pine for lighting; in pigments and dyes with which they paint themselves for war and festivals, and stain their bodies as a defense against heat and cold; and in many other articles of merchandise, luxuries or necessities. For this purpose he held fairs in many towns, such as Nito, where he had agents and separate districts for his own vassals and traders.

Apoxpalón proved himself a good friend of the Spaniards, building a bridge for them over a swamp, and giving them canoes in which to cross an estuary. He also supplied them with guides who knew the land. And for all of this he asked in return only a letter from Cortés to any Spaniards who might pass that way, to the effect that he was their friend. Acalán is densely populated and rich; Izancanac is a large city.

179. Death of Cuauhtémoc

CORTÉS HAD BROUGHT along Cuauhtémoc and many other Mexican lords, to keep them from causing an uprising in the city and country; likewise, some three thousand Indians for transport and service. Cuauhtémoc resented being kept under guard and, since he still had the spirit of a king and saw that the Spaniards were far from help, weak from their march, and in an unknown country, he plotted to kill them, especially Cortés, in revenge, and then to return to Mexico, proclaim liberty, and make himself king again. He informed the other lords of his plan and sent word back to the Mexicans [in the city] that they were to kill in a single day all the Spaniards there, who numbered only two hundred and had only fifty horses, and who, moreover, were quarreling among themselves. If he had had the ability to act as he had planned, he might have succeeded, for Cortés had few men with him, and those in Mexico were also few and on bad terms. Their numbers were reduced because some had gone with Alvarado to Guatemala; others, with [Francisco de las] Casas to Honduras; [still others], to the mines of Michoacán. The Indians of Mexico had agreed that when they saw the Spaniards off their guard, and received the second order of Cuauhtémoc, they would make a great noise with drums, fifes, conches, and horns. This, being louder than usual, alarmed the Spaniards, who inquired the reason for it, for they were suspicious of [the Indians], I know not whether from indications or knowledge, and always went about armed, even in the funeral processions they held for Cortés, and kept their horses by them, saddled and bridled.

Mexicalcinco (who afterward took the name of Cristóbal) revealed to Cortés the conspiracy of Cuauhtémoc, and showed him a paper with the glyphs and names of the lords who were plotting his death. Cortés praised Mexicalcinco, promised him great rewards, and arrested ten of the men named in the paper, none of whom was allowed to communicate with the others. He inquired of them how many were implicated in the conspiracy, and told each of them he had already been informed by the others. The case, according to Cortés, was so clear that they could not deny [the conspiracy], and so all confessed that Cuauhtémoc, Coanacoxtzin, and Tetlepanquetzal had originated the plot; that the rest, although they were in favor of it, had not really given their consent, nor had they participated in the talks; that it was not a bad thing or a sin for them to desire their liberty; that it seemed to them that they would never have a better opportunity, or place in which to kill him, since he had few companions and no [Indian] friends with him; and that they were not afraid of the Spaniards in Mexico, who were new to the country, unskilled in the use of arms, and were fighting among themselves (this really worried Cortés); but that, since their gods did not love them, Cortés should kill them.

After this confession, Cortés tried them and forthwith sentenced Cuauhtémoc, Tlacatlec, and Tetlepanquetzal to be hanged, whose execution was a sufficient lesson to the rest, for they all truly expected to be killed and burned, since even kings were not spared. They further thought that the conspiracy had been revealed to Cortés by the compass and mariner's card, not by a man. They firmly believed that their thoughts could not be concealed from it, since it had exposed this affair and indicated the road to Huatecpan. Many of them, therefore, came to Cortés and told him to look in the mirror (which was their name for the compass), where he could see that they wished him well and had no evil intentions. So frightened were they that Cortés and the other Spaniards were convinced they were telling the truth. The execution took place at Izancanac during Lent of the year 1525.

Cuauhtémoc was, as history tells us, a valiant man, and in every adversity proved his royal heart and courage, in favor of peace at the beginning of the war, and in perseverance during the siege; at the time of his arrest, and when he was hanged, or was tortured to reveal the treasure of Moctezuma. (His feet were smeared with oil and exposed many times to the fire; but [his torturers] gained more infamy than gold.) Cortés, indeed, should have preserved his life as a precious jewel, for Cuauhtémoc was the triumph and glory of his victories; but Cortés did not wish to keep him alive in such a troubled land and time. It is true that he thought highly of him and that the Indians held him in the same honor and reverence in which they had held Moctezuma; and I believe it was for this reason that Cortés always had Cuauhtémoc in his company when he rode through the city, or went on foot.

Apoxpalón was terrified at the punishment of such a very great king, and, either from fear or because of what Cortés had told him about his many gods, he burned an infinite number of idols in the presence of the Spaniards, and promised not to worship them from that time onward. He promised, moreover, to be a friend of the Spaniards and a vassal of the King.

180. Canec Burns His Idols

FROM IZANCANAC, the capital of Acalán, our Spaniards marched to Mazatlán. (The town is known by a different name in their language, but I do not know how it should be spelled. Although I have made every effort to learn the names and their proper spelling of the places through which our army passed on its expedition to Honduras, I am not quite satisfied. Let no one be surprised, therefore, if they are not correctly written.) Taught by his past experience, Cortés had provisions packed for a six-day march, although he was to be on the road only three days, or four at the most. He sent four Spaniards on ahead with the two guides Apoxpalón had given him. He crossed the swamp and estuary by the bridge and in the canoes built and supplied by that same lord, and, after a march of five leagues, met the four Spaniards on their way back. They informed him that there was a good road through grassy and cultivated land—a welcome piece of news for those who had struggled with bad ones.

Cortés dispatched fast runners to capture a few of the inhabitants and learn from them how they regarded the coming of the Spaniards. Two men of Acalán were brought back as prisoners, who, to judge by their packs of clothing, were merchants. They said that there was no knowledge of such men [as the Spaniards] in Mazatlán, and that the town was full of people. Cortés released the two guides he had brought from Izancanac and replaced them by the two merchants. That night he slept in the woods, as he had done the night before. The next day the Spanish scouts came upon four men from Mazatlán, lookouts, armed with bows and arrows, who, as soon as they sighted our men, loosed their bows, wounded one of our Indians, and fled to the woods. The Spaniards pursued them, but were able to capture only one, whom they left in the hands of the Indians, and then went on ahead to see whether there were more; but, as soon as the Spaniards had gone, the three who had taken refuge in the woods fell upon our Indians, who were equal in number, and took their prisoner from them. Humiliated by this affront, [our Indians] ran after the others, engaged them again, and wounded one of the men of Mazatlán with a great gash in the arm. Him they seized, and the others fled because the army was approaching. The wounded man said that in his town nothing was known of the bearded men; that [he and his companions] had been posted as lookouts, as is their custom, to prevent their enemies (of whom they had many in that region) from making a surprise attack on the town and its farms; and that the town was not far distant.

Cortés spurred forward to arrive there before nightfall, but was unable to make it, so he slept that night in a hut at the edge of a swamp, without water to drink. At dawn Cortés had branches and underbrush laid across the swamp to make a passage, over which the horses were led without much trouble. Three leagues farther on he came upon a town built on a high rock, well planned for defense; but he encountered no resistance because the inhabitants had fled. [The Spaniards] found a great quantity of turkeys, honey, beans, maize, and other provisions. The town was strong because of its position on the rock; it had only one approach which, however, was level; it was flanked on one side by a lagoon and on the other by a very deep stream that flowed into the lagoon. Its moat was very deep, and it had besides a wooden parapet, breast-high; behind [the parapet] was a wall of boards and beams, two fathoms high, pierced with many loopholes for arrows, and at intervals towers that stood a fathom and a half above the wall, well stocked with stones and arrows. Even the houses were built like forts, their traverses and loopholes commanding the streets. In short, everything was strong and well-planned for the arms of that country, so that, since it had been abandoned in spite of its strength, our men were much pleased, especially because it was a frontier post and had had a garrison of soldiers. Cortés sent one of the men of Acalán to summon the lord and the people.

The governor came [instead], saying that the lord was only a child, and a scared one at that. He invited [Cortés] to go with him to Tiac, six leagues farther on; but, by the time they arrived, the frightened citizens had fled to the woods. Tiac was a large town, but weak, being situated on a plain. It had three districts, each of which had its own wall, while another wall enclosed them all. Cortés was unable to persuade the people to return while the army was inside, although they did give him provisions, some clothing, and a guide, who told him he had seen other bearded men and their stags (which was their name for horses). Now that Cortés had such an excellent guide, he paid off the men of Acalán and gave them leave to return to their own country, with warm greetings for Apoxpalón.

From Tiac Cortés went to Xuncahuitl, where he spent the night. This was also a walled and fortified town, like the others. He found it deserted but well stocked with food. There our army collected provisions for a five-day march through unpeopled country (as the new guide informed them it would be) to Taica. They spent four nights in the mountains, which they crossed by a difficult pass which they named Pass of Alabaster, because all the peaks and stones were of that material. On the fifth day they arrived at a very large lake [Petén], in the middle of which, on an island, was a big town. This, according to the guide, was the capital of the province of Taica, inaccessible except by water. The scouts captured a man of the place in a canoe, which they could not have done but for the help of their dog. He said that in the city nothing was known of such men [as the Spaniards], and that if they wished to see it they should go to certain grain fields on the shore of the lake, where they could take many of the farmers' canoes. With twelve crossbowmen, Cortés set out on foot, guided by the man, but he was caught in a downpour that drenched him to the knees and beyond and was so long delayed that he was unable to approach unseen, so the farmers spied him and took to the water in their canoes. Cortés made camp in the open, fortifying himself as best he could, because the guide told him that the people of the city were very practiced in war and were feared by all their neighbors; but that, if Cortés so wished, he would himself go to the island in his little canoe and speak to the lord of Taica, Canec, whom he knew from other times, and explain to him Cortés' reason for coming. Cortés let him go with the owner of the canoe.

He did not return until midnight. He could not come sooner because it was two leagues from the shore to the island and their paddles were bad. He brought back two persons, evidently men of importance, who said they had come on behalf of Canec, their lord, to visit the captain of the army and discover his intentions. Cortés answered them joyfully and gave them a Spaniard as hostage to induce Canec to come to the camp. They were infinitely pleased to observe the horses, the dress, and the beards of our men. They departed, and the next morning the lord came, with thirty men in six canoes; he also brought the Spaniard, and showed no sign of fear or hostility. Cortés greeted him cordially, and to entertain him and show him how the Christians honored their God, he had a solemn Mass sung and had the acolytes play their pipes. Canec listened attentively to the playing and singing, and closely observed the ceremonies and services at the altar. He seemed to enjoy them thoroughly, and he praised the music highly, something he had never heard. When the divine service was over, the priests and friars approached him very respectfully and, through the interpreters, preached him a sermon. He replied that he would gladly destroy his idols, and would like very much to know how to honor and serve the God they had told him about. He asked them for a Cross to erect in his town, and they said they would give him one (as they did in every place they came to), and would soon send him missionaries to teach him the law of Christ, but could not do so at the moment. After the sermon, Cortés spoke to him briefly of the greatness of the Emperor and urged him to become a vassal, as the people of Mexico–Tenochtitlán had already done. Canec replied that from that time on he would consider himself as such. He also said that, several years before, some Tabascans who were traveling through his country on their way to the fairs had told him that certain strangers like [the Spaniards] had come to their town, that they had fought bravely with them, but had been vanquished in three battles. Cortés then told Canec that he was the captain of the men spoken of by the Tabascans, as Canec could verify by inquiry.

At this the conversation ended and they sat down to eat. Canec had fowl, fish, cakes, honey, fruit, and gold (although little of this), and strings of the colored shells that they prize brought from the canoes. Cortés gave him a shirt, a black velvet cap, and some iron articles such as scissors and knives, and asked him whether he knew anything about certain of his Spaniards who were on the coast not far from there. Canec answered that he had often heard of them, because some of his vassals had passed very near them, and that, if Cortés wished, he would give him a guide to take him there without losing his way, but that the road was very rough and difficult on account of the high mountains, and it would be easier to go by sea.

Cortés thanked him for the intelligence and the guide, but said that the canoes could not carry the horses, baggage, and so many men, for which reason he would have to go by land, and would Canec tell him how to get past the lake? Canec said that Cortés would be free of it three leagues from there; that meanwhile he should come to the city to see his house and watch the burning of his idols. Cortés, over the protests of his companions, did so, taking with him some twenty crossbowmen—a very foolhardy thing to do. He remained in the town until the afternoon, amidst the rejoicing of the citizens. He witnessed the burning of the idols; he took a guide; commended to their care a horse he had left behind, crippled by a stake that had penetrated its foot; and so departed, to sleep in the open, after making the circuit of the lake.

181. Our Men Make an Arduous March

THE DAY AFTER his departure, Cortés advanced over level ground, where our horsemen lanced eighteen deer, so plentiful were they; but two horses were so weak that they died in the chase. Four Indian hunters carrying a dead lion [panther] were captured. Our men were astonished, because they thought it a remarkable thing for four little men to kill a lion with arrows alone. They came to an estuary, wide and deep, within sight of the town toward which they were heading. Having no means of crossing, they waved their capes at the towns-people, who were milling about packing their effects preparatory to taking refuge in the woods. Two men came over in a canoe, bringing about a dozen turkeys, but, disregarding entreaties, refused to land, whereupon a Spaniard put spurs to his horse, dashed into the water, and swam after the Indians, who were so alarmed and frightened that they could not work their paddles. Then two other

Spaniards, good swimmers, joined in the pursuit and captured the canoe. These two Indians led [the Spaniards] around the head of the estuary, a league, and so to the town, where our men arrived exhausted, having marched eight leagues. They found no people there, but did find an abundance of provisions.

The name of the town was Tlecán; that of its lord, Aimohán. The army halted there for four days awaiting the return of the lord and the inhabitants. They did not appear, so [Cortés] collected rations for six days (this, according to the guide, being the time they would be in unhabited country). The army set out and slept six leagues away at a large inn belonging to Aimohán and used by merchants. There our men rested a day, for it was the feast of the Mother of God; they fished in the river, drove a large number of shad into a pocket and caught them all—which, besides being a fine bit of fishing, was very profitable. The next day they covered nine leagues and killed seven deer on the plain. They crossed a difficult pass, two leagues of climbing and descending, where the horses lost their shoes, necessitating a day's delay to get them reshod. The next day's journey brought them to a village called Axuncapuin, belonging to Canec, where they stopped two days. From Axuncapuin they went on to Taxaitetl, another village of Canec's, where they spent the night and found a great deal of fruit and green maize, and men to guide them. After two leagues of smooth going the next day, they began the ascent of an extremely rough range, eight leagues, which took them a week to cross, and seventy-eight horses died from falling off precipices or from foundering, and those that survived were so battered that they did not recover for three months.

During this whole time it rained continuously, day and night, and it was remarkable how the men suffered from thirst in the midst of so much water. A nephew of Cortés broke his leg in three or four places in a fall, and they had a very difficult time bringing him out of the mountains. This was not the end of their troubles, for they were soon confronted with a very big river [the Polochic?], swollen by the rains, and so swift that it filled the Spaniards with dismay, for there were no canoes, and even if there had been they would not have served. To build a bridge was impossible; to turn back, death. Cortés sent several men up the river to see whether it narrowed and could be forded, and they returned very joyful, having found a passage. I cannot describe to you the tears of joy shed by our Spaniards at this piece of good news. They embraced each other, gave many thanks to Our Lord God, who had succored them in their need; they sang the *Te Deum Laudamus* and the Litany, and, since it was Holy Week, they all confessed.

The ford was a slab of level rock, smooth, and as wide as the river, with more than twenty fissures in it through which the water flowed—a thing so extraordinary that it seemed more like a fable, or an enchantment out of *Amadís de Gaula,* but it was most true. Others describe it as a miracle; but it was the work of nature, which opened these channels for the water, or it was the work of the water itself, which in its constant flow cut the rock in that fashion. The men now set to work felling timber, for there were many trees about, and they brought in more than two hundred beams and many withes, which, as I have said elsewhere, were used as ropes. This time no one shirked. They spanned the channels with the beams, tying them together, and so built their bridge, which took them two days to finish. The water rushing through the crevices made so much noise that it deafened the men. The horses and swine swam across below the ford, where the water flowed more calmly because of its depth.

That night they slept at Teucix, one league away, where they found several good houses and green fields, but there was room for only twenty persons and not enough food for all. This was a great disappointment to them because they were starving, not having eaten anything for a week except palm buds, little thin dates, and herbs cooked without salt. The men of Teucix told them that a day's journey up the river there was a large town in the province of Teuicán [Taniha?], which had a quantity of fowl, cacao, maize, and other provisions; but, to get to it, it would be necessary to cross the river, which they did not know how to do, it was so high and furious. Cortés answered that it could be passed, and told them to give him a guide, whom he sent out with thirty Spaniards and a thousand Indians. They made many trips back and forth, and supplied the camp with food, though with great difficulty. While at Teucix, Cortés sent out several Spaniards with a native guide to survey the road to Azuzulín [Acuculín], the lord of which was called Aquiahuilquín. They had proceeded ten leagues when they came upon seven men and a woman in a hut (which must have been an inn), and then returned, reporting that the road, as compared with the last one, was very good.

Among the seven men was one from Acalán, a merchant, who had dwelt a long time in Nito, where the Spaniards were. He said that many bearded men, on foot and horseback, had entered the town a year since and sacked it, mistreating the citizens and merchants, causing the flight of the brother of Aquiahuilquín (who had a storehouse there) and all the other merchants. Many of them had asked Aquiahuilquín's permission to settle and trade in his country, for the fairs had been destroyed and the merchants ruined by the foreigners. This [permission] was what the man from Acalán was now negotiating. Cortés begged the merchant to lead him there, and promised to reward him well, as, in fact, he did. Cortés then released the prisoners on his own responsibility, paid off the other guides, and dismissed them. He sent four of the seven men, with two from Teucix, to beg Aquiahuilquín to remain and speak with Cortés, who would do him no hurt. But by dawn the next day the man from Acalán, along with the other three, had disappeared, and Cortés was left without a guide. But he finally departed and slept that night in a wood five leagues distant. A horse was crippled on this bad stretch of road. The next day the army marched six leagues and crossed two rivers, one of them by canoe, where two mares were drowned. That night found them in a village of perhaps twenty houses, all new, belonging to the merchants of Acalán, who had fled. From it [the Spaniards] proceeded to Azuzulín, which they also found deserted and without provisions, a doubly painful thing for them.

They searched the country for guides, and in eight days picked up only some prostitutes, who were of little use in that respect; on the contrary, they caused trouble, because one of them said she could lead them to a town two day's journeys away, where they would get news of what they were seeking. Several Spaniards went there with her, but found no one, and returned very downcast. Cortés was in despair, for, even with his compass, he could not decide upon his course, so high were the mountains ahead of him, and so devoid of traces of human life.

Then by chance they captured a youth who was crossing the mountains, and he guided them to a village in the province of Tuniha, which was marked on their map. This took two days, after which they were guided for two more by an old man who could not run away, to a town where they captured four men, the rest having fled. These said that Nito and the Spaniards were two suns farther on, and, to convince [the Spaniards] that they were telling the truth, one of them fetched two women, who gave the names of the Spaniards they had served. This was a great consolation to the hearers, in view of their condition, for they had expected to die of hunger in that land of Tuniha, having eaten nothing but palm buds, green or cooked with fresh pork, without salt; and even of this they could not get enough, because it took two men a whole day to fell a palm tree, and only half an hour to eat the shoot or bud at its top. Juan de Avalos, a cousin of Cortés, rolled down a mountain with his horse during the last stage and broke an arm.

182. Nito

AS SOON AS CORTÉS knew how close he was to Nito, he dispatched fifteen Spaniards with one of the four men, to see whether they might not meet some Spaniard or Indian of that town and learn from him whose party he belonged to, and how many men there were in it. The fifteen got as far as a big river [the Motagua?], where they seized a canoe belonging to some Indian merchants. After waiting there for two days, they saw a boat put out, with four Spaniards who were fishing. These they captured without being heard in the town, and learned from them that there were sixty Spanish men and twenty women in it, most of whom were sick; that they [belonged to the party of] Gil González; that their captain was Diego Nieto; that Cristóbal de Olid was dead; and that Francisco de las Casas and Gil González, who had killed him, were on their way back to Mexico by way of the territory and government of Pedro de Alvarado. God knows how pleased Cortés was with these tidings! He notified Diego Nieto of his presence and his desire to see him; he told Nieto to have some canoes at hand for crossing the river, and at once set out. It took him three days to get there, and five more to transport his army over the river, because there were only one skiff and one or two canoes.

Cortés' arrival was a great consolation for everyone: for those who accompanied him, because they were at the end of their strength; for those who stayed behind, because they were sick and had nothing to eat. He had to provide for all these men, so he sent off [parties] in all directions, but the only things they brought back were broken heads. He sent them out again, and again they found nothing, save only an important merchant and four slaves, whom they captured in their canoes. Thus it was that with so many mouths to feed and so little food for them, the men were perishing of hunger; and truly they would have perished if it had not been for the few pigs that had survived, and for the herbs and roots gathered by the Mexicans. But it was the will of God (who forgets no one) that a ship should put in at that time, bringing 30 Spaniards (without counting the sailors), 13 horses, 75 pigs, 12 casks of salt pork, and many loads of maize. All gave heartfelt thanks to Jesus Christ and at once fell to and filled their bellies.

Cortés purchased the ship and all the provisions (but not the horses, which were kept by their owners). Then he reconditioned a virtually worthless ship belonging to the Spaniards [of Nito], and with the timbers of several other wrecks he put together a brigantine, so that he soon had the means to navigate when he should choose to do so. The diligence and alertness of Cortés in all his affairs was amazing.

After his arrival, the men of Nito reconnoitered the country, which they had not dared or been able to do before, and, wandering from one place to another, discovered a trail leading to Lequela over some very rugged mountains. Lequela was a large town, well provided with food, but, since it was 18 leagues away by a very bad road, it was impossible to obtain supplies from it.

Noting the miserable and unsuccessful attempts at colonizing, Cortés readied his three vessels for a voyage to the Bay of San Andrés. He sent Gonzalo de Sandoval with almost all his men and horses, except two, to Naco, 20 leagues, to placate the Spaniards there, who were still disturbed by the recent troubles. He did not wish to sail without more supplies, in case the voyage should be prolonged. He took forty Spaniards and fifty Indians, and embarked with them in the brigantine, two skiffs, and four canoes. He set off down the river and sailed into a gulf or estuary some twelve leagues in circumference, but with no towns whatever on its shores, which were very swampy. From it he sailed into another gulf, perhaps thirty leagues in extent—a remarkable thing, since it was surrounded by very high mountains. Landing with thirty Spaniards and an equal number of Indians, he made his way to a town, where he found neither people nor bread. So he went back to his vessels with the maize and chili he had been able to collect. He sailed across the gulf, encountered a storm, and lost one canoe and one Indian drowned.

The next day Cortés ran into a small estuary, where he left his canoes and the brigantine under a Spanish guard, while he and the rest went inland. After half a league he came to a deserted and ruined village (a condition that many of them were in because of the proximity of the Spaniards). The next day he advanced five leagues through the woods, on all fours most of the time, coming out in some cleared land, where he took three women and a man in a hut, evidently owners of the clearing. The man led him to another, where he captured two more women. Then he came to a village of some forty miserable huts, though new, where he found some fowl running loose, quail and pheasants in coops, and some dried maize; but of salt, which was what they were mostly seeking, there was none; nor were there any men either. At that moment, two citizens, not expecting to find such guests in their houses, appeared and were captured. They guided Cortés over a worse road than the previous one, overgrown and closed, where within seven leagues he had to cross forty-five rivers, not counting the many creeks. All of them flowed into the gulf. At sunset our men were startled by a great noise. Marina inquired [of the Indians] what it was about, and they replied that it was festivals and dances. Cortés did not dare enter the town, but remained awake and under heavy guard, sleep being out of the question on account of the mosquitoes, the pounding of the rain, and the thunder and lightning of the night. At dawn he entered the town and caught the citizens asleep, and, if it had not been for a Spaniard who, either frightened or startled at seeing so many armed men gathered in a house, began to shout "Santiago! Santiago!", this would have been a pretty raid, perhaps without bloodshed. As it was, some fifteen men and twenty women were captured, and as many more were killed, among them the lord. They were lying under a roof without walls, where they had assembled to dance, as at a council house.

No maize was found here either, so two days after their arrival, [the Spaniards] set out for a larger town which, according to the prisoners, was well-stocked with all manner of provisions. They marched eight leagues, captured a few woodcutters and eight hunters; they waded a river breast-deep which was so swift that many would have been in danger of drowning if they had not joined hands. They slept in the open, but [were awakened by a loud alarm], at which they rushed into the square, while the citizens fled. In the morning they searched the houses and found a great deal of raw cotton, mantles, and other clothing, and a quantity of dry maize and salt—this last being the principal object of their search, for they had had none for many days. They also found a store of cacao, chili, fruit, and other provisions, such as turkeys, many pheasants, quail, and dogs, in coops. If the boats had been at hand, they could have been well-loaded, and even the ships; but, since these were twenty leagues away and the men were very tired, hardly anything could be taken.

This town had temples like those of Mexico, though its language was very different. A river runs by it that flows into the gulf, so Cortés sent two Spaniards, with one of the eight Indians as guide, to fetch the brigantine and boats up that same river and have them loaded with provisions. Meanwhile, he put together four large rafts, each of which could carry fifty loads of grain and ten men. The two Spaniards returned, having left the boats far downstream because of the swift current. The rafts were loaded; Cortés went with them, while he sent his men down by land. [The rafts] encountered some dangerous going before reaching the brigantine, and were shouted and shot at from the banks; but, although Cortés and many others were wounded, none died. Of those who went by land, one Spaniard died almost instantly from the effect of a certain herb he had eaten. They had with them an Indian from the coast of the South Sea, who said that Nito was no more than sixty leagues from his country—a welcome piece of news.

The shore [of the gulf] was lined from one end to the other with cacao trees and many orchards, and with many beautiful gardens and estates. In short, it was one of the best places of those parts. The rafts traveled twenty leagues in a day and a night, and Cortés not only procured the maize and provisions I have mentioned, but got even more from the towns [along the way], and with them stocked his ships fairly well. It took him thirty-five days to get back to Nito.

183. Naco

IMMEDIATELY upon his return, Cortés embarked with all the Spaniards, his own men as well as those of Gil González, for the Bay of San Andrés, where the men he had sent to Naco were awaiting him. There he remained for twenty days, and, because it was a good port and there were indications of gold in the vicinity, established a colony of fifty Spaniards, including twenty horse, and named it Natividad de Nuestra Señora. He appointed a council and built a church, which he gave in charge to a priest and furnished with all the appointments for celebrating Mass. Leaving behind several small guns, he set sail for the Port of Honduras and Trujillo, sending there by land (since there was a good road, although several rivers had to be crossed) twenty horse and ten crossbowmen. The voyage took nine days because of contrary winds, but he finally arrived and was carried bodily from his skiff by the Spaniards already there, who plunged happily into the water. He at once went to church to give thanks to God for having brought him to the place where he so desired to be. They gave him a complete account of everything that had happened to Gil González de Avila, Francisco Hernández, Cristóbal de Olid, Francisco de las Casas, and the Bachiller [Pedro] Moreno, as I have already related. They begged his forgiveness for having followed Cristóbal de Olid, alleging they had no alternative, and asked him to help them, for they were ruined. He did pardon them, restored offices to their first holders, appointed others, and began to erect houses. Two days after his arrival, he sent one of the Spaniards, who understood the language, and two Mexicans to two towns seven leagues distant called Chapaxina and Papaica, provincial capitals, to inform them that Captain Cortés had arrived from Mexico–Tenochtitlán.

The townspeople listened attentively to the message, and sent several men back with the Spaniards to learn in detail whether it was true. Cortés received them warmly and gave them trinkets, addressing them through Marina, and begging them to bring their lords to see him (a thing he greatly desired, since he could not go there himself, for fear of their running away). The messengers were very glad to talk with Marina, because their language and that of the Mexicans are not very different, except in pronunciation. They promised Cortés they would do what they could, and departed. Five days later, two noble personages appeared, bringing fowl, fruit, maize, and other provisions, which they told the captain to accept on behalf of their lords, and to tell them what he wanted of them and what he was seeking in their country; also, that the lords had not come to see him because they were afraid they would be carried off to the ships, as had happened to others a short while before. (As was learned later, these were [the ships of] the Bachiller Moreno and Juan Ruano.)

Cortés answered that he was not there to harm them; on the contrary, that he had come to promote the well-being of the lords and their people, if they would listen to him and believe, for his purpose was to punish the slavers and rescue the citizens; that the lords, therefore, should appear before him without fear, and they would learn that he was there to secure their persons and estates, and to save their souls. So saying, he dismissed them, but begged them to send him workers to make a clearing in the woods. Many men soon appeared from more than fifteen independent towns, bringing provisions, to work wherever he should direct.

At this time Cortés dispatched four ships: the three that he had brought with him and the small caravel we have mentioned. In one he sent invalids back to New Spain, with letters to the councils of Mexico and all the other towns, giving them an account of his expedition and informing them that, in the interest of the Emperor's service, he had to stay where he was for a few days. He strongly urged them to conduct their governments for the peace of all. He ordered his cousin Juan de Avalos, captain of the ship, to stop at Cozumel and pick up the sixteen men who had been abandoned there by a certain Valenzuela when he sacked Triunfo de Cruz, which had been founded by Cristóbal de Olid. The ship picked up the Spaniards at Cozumel, but was wrecked on Cape San Antón in Cuba. Juan de Avalos, two Franciscan friars, and more than thirty other men were drowned. Of those who escaped and made their way inland, eating roots, only fifteen survived and reached Guaniguanico. Eighty men, without counting a few Indians, died on this voyage.

Cortés sent the brigantine to Española, with letter for the oidores [of the Audiencia], announcing his arrival [at the Bay of San Andrés] and informing them of the Olid affair. He begged them to order the Bachiller Moreno to release the Indians of Papaica and Chapaxina he had carried off as slaves. The [other two vessels] he sent to Jamaica and Trinidad in Cuba for meat and clothing and bread. They also had a bad voyage, but were not wrecked.

184. Dissensions in Mexico

THE OIDORES of Santo Domingo, in view of the repeated rumors that Cortés was dead, sent to make inquiries, utilizing for the purpose a merchant ship that had come from New Spain with a cargo of thirty-two horses, a great deal of harness, and many other things to sell. [The master of] the ship, when he learned from the men of the brigantine at Trinidad that Cortés was alive, changed his destination from Medellín to Trujillo, thinking to sell his merchandise there at better prices.

By this same ship the Licenciado Zuazo wrote to Cortés how badly things were going in Mexico; that there were factions and feuds between the Spaniards and the royal officers Cortés had left there as his lieutenants; that Gonzalo de Salazar and Peralmíndez had proclaimed themselves governors and had circulated the story that Cortés was dead. They had arrested the Treasurer Alonso de Estrada and the Contador Rodrigo de Albornoz, had hanged Rodrigo de Paz, and appointed new alcaldes and alguaciles; that they had sent [Zuazo] himself a prisoner to Cuba to stand a residencia for the time he had served there as judge; and that the Indians were on the verge of rebellion. In short, he told Cortés everything that had happened in the city. Cortés read the letters and almost burst with rage and grief. "Put a scoundrel in power," he said, "and you will soon know what he is. I deserved this because I honored strangers and not the men who had risked their lives for me!"

He retired to his chamber to think, and even to mourn over the sad business. He could not decide whether it would be best to go to Mexico himself, or to send someone else, to prevent the ruin of that fine country. For three days he held processions and had masses of the Holy Ghost said, and begged guidance for the better service of God. In the end he set aside everything else in order to go to Mexico and remedy this great evil, for he was very angry with those who had caused it. He left his cousin Hernando de Saavedra in charge at Trujillo, with fifty Spanish foot and thirty-five horse. He sent word to Gonzalo de Sandoval to leave Naco and take his company to Mexico over the road that Francisco de las Casas had taken, that is, by the coast of the South Sea and Guatemala, an established route, level and safe. Cortés himself embarked for Medellín in the same ship that had brought him the bad news.

While the ship, however, was riding on only one anchor, ready to sail, the weather turned unfavorable, so Cortés went ashore to put down an uprising among the inhabitants of a certain town, which he did by punishing the rebels. Two days later he rejoined the ship, which set sail with a fair wind; but not two leagues from port the main yard broke, and he had to put back. After three days spent in fitting a new yard, the ship sailed again, and with a fine wind made fifty leagues in two nights and a day, but then a norther blew up, so strong and contrary that it broke the foremast off at the cap, and the ship had to put back again to the same port, which it made with great difficulty and danger.

Cortés again had masses said and processions held, but it occurred to him that, since he had started so many times in fair weather and as many times had returned to port, God did not want him to leave that country and go to Mexico. So he decided to remain and to send his servant Martín Dorantes in his stead in that same vessel, which was bound for Pánuco, giving him written instructions (to be delivered to whomever it seemed best) for Francisco de las Casas to take over the government of Mexico. He also revoked all the powers he had issued up to that time. He sent with Dorantes several gentlemen and other persons from Mexico to establish the fact that he was not dead, as had been published. This Martín Dorantes, as I have mentioned in another place, after many hazards, did get to Mexico at the time Francisco de las Casas was on his way as a prisoner to Spain; but the arrival of Dorantes convinced those of the city that Cortés was alive.

185. War in Papaica

AFTER THE SHIP had been dispatched, Cortés ordered Hernando de Saavedra, with thirty foot and thirty horse, to make a reconnaissance in the back country. Saavedra set out and marched thirty-five leagues through a fine valley, well-provided with good pasturage and many houses stocked with every kind of provisions. He met no opposition and persuaded many towns to accept the friendship of the Christians. Some twenty lords presented themselves to Cortés, offering to be his friends, and every day they brought provisions to Trujillo, both as gifts and for trading. The lords of Papaica and Chapaxina were still in rebellion, although they did send representatives of their towns. Cortés admonished them repeatedly to submit peacefully, assuring them that their persons and goods would be respected, but they refused to heed him. By a clever stratagem Cortés seized three lords of Chapaxina and put them in irons, giving them a certain time in which to repeople their towns, in default of which they would be severely punished. So they ordered all the people and goods to be brought back, and he thereupon released them. Their names were Chicueilt, Potlo, and Mendereto.

But neither the people of Papaica nor their lords would obey his summons, so one night he sent out a company of Spanish foot and horse, with many Indians, and they fell upon Pizacura, one of the lords of the city, and captured him. He, when asked why he had been wicked and disobedient, said that he would have submitted, save that Mazatl had more influence in the community and would not consent to peace or friendship with the Christians; but that, if Cortés would release him, he would spy upon Mazatl and have him seized and hanged; and that, if he would do so at once, the country would be pacified and repeopled. It did not, however, turn out in this fashion, although Pizacura was released and Mazatl captured. Mazatl was told what Pizacura had said, and was ordered to bring his vassals in from the mountains within a certain time and repeople Papaica. Since Mazatl could not be got rid of, he was brought to Trujillo, tried, sentenced to death, and executed. This act filled the other lords and towns with great fear, and they at once came out of the woods and returned to their houses, with their children, wives, and goods; that is, all except [the town of] Papaica, which tried to fortify itself after the release of Pizacura. He was also accused of opposing the peace, and the townspeople were accused of refusing to return to their city; so, after they had been warned to yield peaceably and threatened with punishment if they did not, war was declared upon them. In the city some hundred persons were captured and enslaved. Pizacura was taken, and, although he had been condemned to death, he was not executed, but kept a prisoner, in company with two other young lords and a youth. This youth was apparently the rightful lord, instead of Mazatl or Pizacura, who, abusing their position as his guardians, had usurped his power.

About this time some twenty Spaniards of the parties of Gonzalo de Sandoval and Francisco Hernández came to Trujillo from Naco. They reported that a certain captain, with forty companions, had come to Naco, claiming to represent Francisco Hernández, the lieutenant of Pedrarias, and that he was coming to the port or Bay of San Andrés and the villa of Natividad de Nuestra Señora in search of the Bachiller Moreno. Moreno had written to Hernández to hold the men, land, and government of Natividad in the name of the Audiencia of Santo Domingo, not in that of Pedrarias. This had caused trouble among the Spaniards, who thought that Hernández was rebelling against Governor Pedrarias—which could well have been true, because it was very common in the Indies for lieutenants to strike out on their own. Cortés wrote to Hernández to hold his encomienda of land and people in the name of Pedrarias and the King, and sent him four mule loads of horseshoes and mining tools— and this was one of the reasons for which Pedrarias later beheaded Francisco Hernández.

When these men had gone, certain Indians came from the province of Huitclato, which is 65 leagues from Trujillo, complaining to Cortés that Spaniards were taking their women, goods, and workmen, and committing many other outrages, and begged him to help them, since he had helped everyone else in such troubles. Cortés, who had already been informed of this, dispatched a constable and two of the Indians to Gabriel de Rojas, the captain of Francisco Hernández, with written orders for him to leave the land of Huiclato in peace, and to set free the men he had taken. This Rojas, either because Hernán Cortés was near by, or because he was summoned by Francisco Hernández, returned at once whence he had come, for, it appeared, Francisco Hernández was in a predicament because of the mutiny of captains Sosa and Andrés Garabito. These had risen against him because he had tried to free himself from Pedrarias. Cortés, therefore, in view of these dissensions and disturbances among the Spaniards, and because he had in mind the wealth of the province of Nicaragua, which was close at hand, took a notion to go there, and began to prepare himself and clear the road over a very rough range of mountains.

186 Cortés Returns to New Spain

WHILE CORTÉS was thus engaged, his cousin Fray Diego Altamirano, a man of importance and honor, came to bring him back to Mexico, to put out the fire that was raging among the Spaniards. He urged Cortés, therefore, to leave at once. He told him of the death of Rodrigo de Paz, the arrest of Francisco de las Casas, the whipping of Juana de Mansilla, the plundering of his house, the evil doings of the Factor Salazar, the departure of Juan de la Peña with money for the King and letters for Cobos; in short, he informed Cortés of everything that had taken place. Among other things, Salazar had himself addressed as "Lordship," sat on a dais under a canopy, and had salutes fired in his honor, which up to that time he had not done. His excuse was that, while he was not addressed as "Governor," but treated as a plain citizen, many held him in little respect.

Cortés was extremely upset by these very true tidings, but found some comfort in the conversation of Fray Diego, who loved him and was wise and courageous besides. He called back the many Indian workmen he had gathered to clear the road to Nicaragua, and sent them with several Spaniards to open the road to Guatemala, thinking to go back to Mexico by the same route Francisco de las Casas had taken. He sent messengers to all the cities along the way to inform them of his plans and to beg them to store up food for him and to keep the roads open. They were all very pleased that Malinche (as they called him) was to pass through their lands, because they held him in the highest respect for having taken Mexico–Tenochtitlán. So they cleared the roads as far as the valley of Ulancho and the mountains of Chindón, which are very rugged; and all the caciques were ready with provisions to feast and entertain him in their towns.

Fray Diego Altamirano, however, importuned him to give up that long journey, and Cortés himself was still shaky from the one he had made from the villa of Espíritu Santo to Trujillo, where he now was, so he decided to go to New Spain by sea. He at once set about supplying two ships, and providing the new towns of Trujillo and Natividad with necessities. Meanwhile, several Indians arrived from Huitila and other islands, called the Guanajos (which are between Puerto de Caballos and Puerto de Honduras, rather far off the coast), to thank Cortés for the favor he had done them, and to ask him to give them a Spaniard for each island, with whom, they said, they would be safe. But, not having any Spaniards to spare, and not wishing to delay his departure, he gave each a letter for their protection, and charged Hernando de Saavedra, whom he was leaving in charge at Trujillo, to send them help as soon as he had finished the war in Papaica. Their reason was that a ship had been fitted out in Cuba and Jamaica to capture these islanders for work in the mines, sugar cane, and fields, and to serve as shepherds. Cortés, learning of this, sent a caravel with many men (in case force should be necessary), to beg the captain of the ship, a certain Rodrigo de Merlo, not to seize these poor wretches and, if he had already done so, to release them. Rodrigo de Merlo, in view of promises that Cortés made him, went to Trujillo to live, and the Indians were restored to their islands.

Getting back to Cortés, I say that when his ships were ready, he embarked in them with twenty Spanish foot and twenty horse, many Mexicans, and Pizacura, with the other lords of the vicinity, to show them how obedient Mexico was to the Spaniards, so that when they returned they would do the same. But Pizacura died before they returned.

Cortés sailed from the port of Trujillo on the twenty-fifth of April, 1526. The wind was favorable until he rounded the point of Yucatan and passed the Alacranes, when he ran into a heavy wind and hove to in order not to be driven back; but the wind grew stronger every hour, as it usually does, so much so that it threatened to destroy the ships. Thus he was forced to sail to Havana, where he remained ten days, amusing himself with his old acquaintances, and inspecting his ships, which were in need of attention.

There he learned, from some vessels that had just arrived from Spain, that Mexico had been at peace since the arrest of the Factor Salazar and Peralmíndez, which gave him no little comfort. He set sail from Havana and, with a favorable wind, arrived a week later at Chalchiuhcuecan. He was unable to enter the port, either because of a change in the weather or because of a strong offshore wind, so he anchored two leagues out and came ashore in the ship's boats. He walked to Medellín, five leagues, and went to the church to give thanks to God for having brought him safely back to New Spain. The people of the villa, who were still asleep, soon learned of his arrival and, with great haste and pleasure, arose to meet him, for they could not believe it, and many did not recognize him, so sick was he of a fever and battered by the sea. In truth, he was exhausted and had suffered much in body and spirit. He had traveled at hazard some five hundred leagues, while it is only four hundred leagues from Trujillo to Mexico by way of Guatemala and Tehuantepec, which is the most direct and frequented route. During many months he had eaten only herbs cooked without salt and drunk bad water, of which many Spaniards and even Indians had died, among them Coanacoxtzin. (It may be that not many will enjoy reading the account of this journey of Cortés, because it contains no novelties that delight, but rather hardships that frighten.)

187. Mexico Rejoices

As soon as Cortés reached Medellín, he dispatched messengers to every town, principally to Mexico, announcing his arrival, and in all of them there was great rejoicing at the news. The Indians of the north coast and vicinity at once came to him loaded with turkeys, fruits, and cacao for him to eat, and brought him plumes, mantles, and silver and gold, while they offered their help in case he should wish to kill those who had vexed him. He thanked them for their presents and love, but told them he was not going to kill anyone, because the Emperor would see that justice was done. He remained in Medellín eleven or twelve days, and was two weeks in reaching Mexico. He was welcomed at Cempoala, and wherever he passed, even though most of the country was uninhabited, he found an abundance of food and drink. Indians came to greet him from eighty leagues away, bringing presents, offering their services, and even making complaints. They showed the greatest joy at his return; they swept the road and scattered flowers before him, so beloved was he; many bewailed the hardships they had suffered during his absence; and some, like those of Oaxaca, begged vengeance.

Rodrigo de Albornoz, who was in Texcoco, advanced a day's journey, accompanied by many Spaniards, to meet him, and in Texcoco he was most joyously received. His entrance into Mexico was the occasion for the greatest outburst of jubilation that you can imagine. All the Spaniards, with Alonso de Estrada [at their head], sallied forth in military array, while the Indians flocked to see him as if he had been Moctezuma himself. They filled the streets to overflowing; they showed their joy by dancing, by the beating of drums and the blowing of conches, trumpets, and many fifes; and all that day and night they surged through the streets making bonfires and illuminations. Cortés was greatly moved to see the happiness of the Indians, the triumph they offered him, and the peace and quiet of the city. He went straightway to the convent of San Francisco, there to rest and give thanks to God, who had brought him through so many hardships and perils to this repose and security.

188. Residencia of Cortés

AT THAT TIME Cortés was the most famous man of our nation. Nevertheless, many defamed him, especially Pánfilo de Narváez, who was then at court bringing charges against him. The members of the Council of the Indies, since they had had no word from Cortés for a long time, suspected, and even believed, that all the evil stories told of him were true. Thus it was that they appointed Admiral Don Diego Columbus Governor of Mexico, with the stipulation that he should take or send a thousand men at his own expense to Mexico to arrest Cortés. (Don Diego was then engaged in a suit with the King, claiming the right to that government and many others.) At the same time they appointed Nuño de Guzmán Governor of Pánuco, and the Portuguese Simón de Alcazaba Governor of Honduras. They were greatly helped in this by Juan de Ribera, secretary and attorney of Cortés, who had quarreled with Martín Cortés over the 4,000 ducats he had brought him but refused to deliver; so he went around spreading a thousand wicked stories about his employer which were widely credited. Ribera, however, while busying himself in these matters died one night from the effect of some Cadahalso bacon he had eaten.

The acts of the Council could not be kept so secret, nor could the newly appointed officers keep so silent, that the matter was not noised about the court (which was being held in Toledo), and many who thought highly of Cortés took it very badly. The Comendador Pedro de Piña spoke to the Licenciado Núñez, and Fray Pedro Melgarejo (who was also lodged in the house of Gonzalo Hurtado) revealed it to the Trinitarians. So the acts were appealed, and a stay of a few days was requested, pending news from Mexico. Don Alvaro de Zúñiga, Duke of Béjar, strongly supported the party of Cortés, to whom he had betrothed his niece, Doña Juana de Zúñiga. He put up security for him, guaranteed his fidelity, and placated the Emperor. At this juncture, Diego de Soto arrived at Seville, with sixty thousand castellanos and the silver cannon, which, because of its novelty and value, became the talk of Spain and even other realms. This treasure, to tell the truth, was what saved the government of Mexico for Cortés. Upon its receipt, the Council decided to send a judge to take the residencia of Cortés, and for it sought a man of learning and position to carry out the order and impose respect, because soldiers are bold. While still in Toledo, the Council heard of the standing of the Licenciado Luis Ponce de León, lieutenant and kinsman of Don Martín de Córdoba, Count of Alcaudete and corregidor of that city. Ponce de León, though young, had a good reputation, so they sent him to New Spain with sufficient powers and backing.

To avoid making mistakes and to get everything done as well as possible, he took with him the Bachiller Marcos de Aguilar, who had resided for several years in the island of Santo Domingo, acting as alcalde mayor for Admiral Don Diego Columbus. The Licenciado Luis Ponce de León set forth at once and, thanks to favorable weather, reached Vera Cruz only a little after Cortés had left Medellín. Simón de Cuenca, Lieutenant Governor of that villa, immediately informed Cortés that some investigators and judges had come to take his residencia, and his letters were carried by relay so quickly that they reached Mexico in two days' time. Cortés was at the convent of San Francisco confessing and receiving Holy Communion when the letters arrived. He had already appointed new alcaldes, and had arrested Gonzalo de Ocampo, with other bandits and supporters of the Factor, and was engaged in making a secret investigation of their actions. Two or three days later, on the Day of St. John [June 24], during a bullfight, another messenger arrived at Mexico, with letters from the Licenciado Luis Ponce, and one from the Emperor, informing Cortés of the purpose of Luis Ponce's visit. Cortés at once wrote to Luis Ponce, inquiring what road he was taking, the one through populated country or the other.

The Licenciado did not reply. He wished to spend a few days at Vera Cruz, for he was greatly fatigued from the sea voyage, which was his first. Meanwhile, however, he heard a rumor, to the effect that in his absence Cortés intended to execute the Factor Salazar, Peralmíndez, and the other prisoners, and that Cortés would not receive him; rather, that Cortés would arrest him on the way (which was Cortés' alleged reason for inquiring about his route). So Ponce posted off with some of the gentlemen and friars of his company and, to avoid being molested and insulted, took the longer route through the towns. Such is the power of gossip! He rode so quickly that he reached Ixtapalapa in five days, which prevented Cortés' servants, who had gone out to meet him on both routes, from arranging a proper reception for him, and from providing food and lodging.

At Ixtapalapa Ponce was received with a great banquet and festivities. After the banquet, the Licenciado and almost all those of his company vomited up everything they had eaten, and then were attacked by diarrhea. They thought they had been poisoned, a story repeated by Fray Tomás Ortiz, who affirmed that the poison had been administered in curds, and that the Licenciado had offered him a dish of them. Andrés de Tapia, who was officiating as host, said to him: "There will be more for Your Reverence." To which the friar replied: "Not that or anything else!" This is the malicious story alluded to in the verses of the Provincial, which I have already mentioned,* and which was brought up in the residencia. But it was false, as I shall explain below. The Comendador Proaña, who was in Ponce's company as alguacil mayor, ate everything that the Licenciado ate, including the same dish of cheese or curds, and did not vomit or suffer any ill effects. In my opinion, the men were hot, tired, and hungry; they ate too much and drank very cold water, which upset their stomachs and brought on the diarrhea and vomiting. The Licenciado was offered a rich present from Cortés, but refused to accept it.

Accompanied by Pedro de Alvarado, Gonzalo de Sandoval, Alonso de Estrada, Rodrigo de Albornoz, and the whole of the city council and gentry of Mexico, Cortés sallied forth to receive him, and led him by the hand straight to the convent of San Francisco, where they heard [early] Mass, for Ponce had arrived in the morning. Cortés asked Ponce to show his orders, but was told he could see them the next day, so Cortés took him to his house and put him up very comfortably. The following day the city council and all the citizenry gathered in the cathedral, where Luis Ponce officially presented his orders, and relieved the alcaldes and alguaciles of their staves of justice. Then he gave them all back again, and said quite politely: "I shall retain for myself the staff of the Lord Governor."

Cortés and all members of the city council kissed the letters of the Emperor and placed them upon their heads, and said they would comply with whatever was contained therein, as the command of their King and Lord. Their act was duly registered. The residencia of Cortés was announced by the public crier, and all who had grievances against him were invited to present them. Then you should have seen the bustling and the trafficking, as each and all looked after their own interests, some fearful, some hopeful, and others sowing discord!

---

* See above, chap. 173. The verses have not been preserved.

THE LICENCIADO attended Mass one day at the convent of San Francisco, and returned to his lodgings suffering from a high fever, occasioned by the *modorra*.* He took to his bed and was unconscious for several days, his fever and drowsiness increasing the while. He died on the seventh day, after receiving the sacraments. In his testament he named the Bachiller Marcos de Aguilar his successor. Cortés mourned him as a father and had him buried in the convent of San Francisco, with much pomp, lamentation, and many candles.

Cortés enemies spread the rumor that the Licenciado had died of poison; but the Licenciado Pero López and Dr. [Cristóbal] de Ojeda, who attended him, treated him for *modorra,* and swore that it was the cause of his death. They even testified that in the afternoon before he died he had the drums rolled for the dying, and that during the ceremony he kept time with his feet, as was witnessed by many. Then he lost the power of speech and died that night before dawn. Few have died dancing as this lawyer did!

Of the hundred persons who had embarked with the Licenciado Ponce de León, most died at sea, or on the road within a few days of landing; of the Dominican friars, two. It was believed that a pestilence struck down and killed the others. Many nobles and gentlemen were in his company, such as Proaño, an officer of the King (whom I have already mentioned), and Captain Salazar de la Pedrada, who had been appointed military governor of Mexico. Fray Tomás Ortiz, who was [later] at Bocas del Dragón [Venezuela] for seven years,† accompanied him as Provincial of the Dominican friars. For a religious, Ortiz was scandalously loose-mouthed. He it was who started two very wicked stories: In one he affirmed that Cortés had poisoned the Licenciado Ponce; in the other he said that Luis Ponce carried ex-

* *Modorra,* in modern usage, is a disease that attacks sheep. The victim falls to the ground and cannot be aroused. There are numerous allusions to *modorra* in early Spanish medical history, but it .is defined too vaguely for identification. An epidemic of *modorra* killed 700 men (out of 1,500) at Darién in 1514, according to Pascual de Andagoya (Mario Góngora, *Los Grupos de Conquistadores en Tierra Firme: 1509-1530* [Santiago, Chile, 1962], p. 18). See also H. Harold Scott, *A History of Tropical Medicine,* 2 vols. (Baltimore, 1939). Vol. 1, pp. 129 and 288.

† Tomás Ortiz was made Bishop of Santa Marta, Venezuela, in 1529, and died there in 1531.

press orders of the Emperor to behead Cortés as soon as he had relieved him of his staff of justice. Indeed, before Ortiz got to Mexico, he sent word of [this order] to Cortés by the hand of Juan Xuárez, Francisco de Orduña, and Alonso Valiente. After arriving, he repeated the story in the convent of San Francisco, in the presence of Fray Martín de Valencia, Fray Toribio [de Benavente], and other religious. By this action the friar expected thanks on the one hand, and rewards, on the other. But Ponce died, and Cortés gave Ortiz nothing.

190. Cortés Is Exiled from Mexico

AFTER THE DEATH of Luis Ponce de León, the Bachiller Marcos de Aguilar began to govern and to proceed with the residencia of Cortés. Some rejoiced thereat; others not: the former wishing to destroy Cortés, the latter to save him. These said that the powers of Aguilar were illegal and hence that all his acts would be void, for Luis Ponce did not have the right to transfer his authority. For this reason the city council of Mexico, and the attorneys of the other villas who were present, appealed from the government of Aguilar and protested it. Moreover, they made a formal demand on Cortés in the presence of a notary, to take over the government and the administration of justice until His Majesty should otherwise provide. He, however, trusting to his unblemished record of service and loyalty to the Emperor, refused to do so. On the contrary, he defended and supported Marcos de Aguilar in the office and urged him to proceed with the residencia. But the Bachiller Aguilar, although he did dispense justice, was extremely reluctant to perform his duties as governor. The council, since it could do nothing further, appointed as his assistant Gonzalo de Sandoval, the close friend of Cortés, to look after the latter's interests; but Sandoval, with the approval of Cortés, also refused to serve.

Marcos de Aguilar governed with great difficulty and trouble. I know not whether it was because of his infirmities, the perversity of others, or because he was swamped in the deep sea of administration. He got very thin, fell ill of a fever, and, since he had long suffered from syphilis, he died two months or so after Luis Ponce de León.

(A son of his, who had been ill from the voyage, died two months earlier.) Aguilar named as his successor and Justicia Mayor, the Treasurer Alonso de Estrada, for Albornoz had returned to Spain and the other two royal officers were in jail. The city council and almost everybody else disapproved of the substitution, which seemed to them a piece of favoritism, so they appointed Gonzalo de Sandoval Estrada's assistant and put Cortés in charge of Indian affairs and war. These negotiations lasted several months.

The Emperor, with the advice of his Council of the Indies and Rodrigo de Albornoz (who had left Mexico after the death of Luis Ponce and while Marcos de Aguilar was ill), ordered that the government should be provisionally exercised by whoever the Bachiller Aguilar had named. Thus it happened that Alonso de Estrada governed by himself. He did not observe toward Cortés the respect due his person for having won the city and conquered so many lands, nor did he show any gratitude to Cortés for having made him governor earlier. Indeed, he thought that by virtue of being a regidor of Mexico and Royal Treasurer, and holding that office [of governor] (although it was only a borrowed one), he was Cortés' equal, and that he could precede and command him, and legally administer justice. Thus it happened that he treated Cortés with great discourtesy, and addressed him in terms that would have been improper in either of them. All this caused a good deal of friction between them, and they got so angry with each other that the matter threatened to become worse than before. Alonso de Estrada, recognizing that in a quarrel with Cortés he would be the loser, courted the favor of Gonzalo de Salazar and Peralmíndez by giving them hope of their release, which was an improper thing for a good judge to do and an insult to the person of the Catholic King, which was so much revered.

Now it happened that several retainers of Cortés stabbed a captain during a quarrel. One of them was arrested, and that very day Estrada had the man's right hand cut off and sent him to jail into the bargain —this to show his scorn of Cortés. He also exiled Cortés to prevent him from releasing the prisoner—such a scandalous act that Mexico was on the point of bloodshed that day, and even of ruin. Cortés, however, met the situation by leaving the city to begin his exile. If he had had the spirit of a tyrant, as he was accused of having, what better opportunity could he have had than the one now presented to him, when almost all the Spaniards, and all the Indians, would have taken up arms in his favor and defense? This was not the only occasion, for there were many others when he could have raised the country in rebellion. But he refused to do so and, I believe, never harbored such a thought, as his actions prove. He could, to be sure, safely boast of his loyalty to the King when, if he had been disloyal, he would have been punished. Even so, his many and powerful rivals, who enjoyed favor at court and in the Council [of the Indies], as I have said elsewhere, accused him always of disloyalty and applied even uglier terms to him, such as tyrant and traitor. They expected to be credited, for many Spaniards in the Indies gave daily evidence of their lack of respect for the King. Cortés, however, always fell back upon two old sayings: *Let the King be my fighting cock,* and *Thou shalt give thy life for thy loyalty and thy King.*

The very day that Cortés' man had had his hand cut off, Fray Julián Garcés, a Dominican, arrived at Texcoco. He had been named Bishop of Tlaxcala, the diocese of which was called Carolense, in honor of our Lord and King. Learning of the fire that was raging among the Spaniards, he embarked in a canoe with his companion, Fray Diego de Loaysa, and arrived in Mexico four hours later. All the priests and friars of the city, bearing crosses, came out to welcome him, for he was the first bishop of the country. He at once intervened between Cortés and Estrada, and with his wisdom and authority induced them to be friends, with which the factions ceased.

A little later orders were received from the Emperor to release the Factor Salazar and the Veedor Peralmíndez, and to restore them to their offices. Cortés was no little pained by this, because he would have liked to receive some compensation for the death of his cousin, Rodrigo de Paz, and the restitution of the property that had been removed from his house. He had failed to heed the proverb: *He who favors his enemy dies at his hands,* and *A dead dog never bites.* For he could have beheaded them before the arrival of the Licenciado Luis Ponce de León, as several had advised him to do while he had the power. His reasons for not doing so were various: He wished to avoid talk; he did not wish to act as judge in his own cause; he was a man of courage; and their guilt in having unjustly put Rodrigo de Paz to death was manifest. So he was confident that any judge or governor would execute them for the civil strife they had stirred up and for the outrages they had committed. A further reason for his sparing them was that, as the saying goes, *The magistrate was their father-in-law,* for they were henchmen of Secretary Cobos, whom Cortés did not wish to offend, lest he suffer in other and more important matters.

191. Expedition to the Spice Islands

IN A LETTER dated at Granada, June 20, 1526, the Emperor ordered Cortés to send the fleet he had at Zacatula in search of the ship *Trinidad** and Frey García de Loaysa, Commander of the Order of St. John, who had gone to the Moluccas; also to search for [Sebastian] Cabot, and to explore a route from New Spain to the Spice Islands by way of the South Sea, as Cortés had promised to do. Cortés had written that he would either go himself or send a fleet of such strength that it could hold its own against any princely power in the islands, even the King of Portugal; that he would occupy them, not only to trade for spices and other merchandise, but to hold them for himself, and erect fortresses and Christian towns, which would subjugate the islands and all the lands lying within the royal domain, as delimited by the Line of Demarcation, such as Gilolo, Borneo, the two Javas, Sumatra, Malacca, and the whole coast of China—all this with the stipulation that the Emperor would grant Cortés certain rights and privileges.

This proposal having been made, and approved by the Emperor, Cortés, who at the moment had no war on his hands or anything else to do, decided to fulfill his promise by sending three ships to the Moluccas, or to make the voyage himself. Meanwhile, during the illness of Marcos de Aguilar, a certain Hortunio de Alango, of Portugalete, had landed at Zihuatanejo [on the south coast], in a patache belonging to Loaysa's fleet, driven there perhaps by contrary winds,

---

* The *Trinidad* was one of Magellan's fleet. Her crew had been abandonded in the Moluccas and imprisoned by the Portuguese. Frey Juan García Jofre de Loaysa (not to be confused with his kinsman, Cardinal García de Loaysa, General of the Dominican Order, confessor of Charles V, and President of the Council of the Indies), was sent by Charles V, in 1525, to rescue them. Loaysa failed and died at sea, but among his crew was the Basque Andrés de Urdaneta, who, forty years later, was to discover the Eastward Passage across the Pacific, from Manila to Acapulco.

or because he did not know of the route to Tidore. So Cortés launched his three vessels, in the flagship of which, called the *Florida,* he put fifty Spaniards; in the second, called the *Santiago,* he put forty-five, under Captain Luis de Cárdenas, of Córdoba; and in a brigantine, under Captain Pedro de Fuentes, of Jerez de la Frontera, he put fifteen. He armed them with 30 guns, stocked them with an abundance of provisions (necessary for such a long and unknown voyage), and many articles for trading. He appointed as captain of the fleet his kinsman Alvaro de Saavedra Cerón, who set sail from Zihuatanejo on all Souls' Day of the year 1527, or the day before. According to the pilot's log, he sailed two thousand leagues, although by the direct route it is not more than fifteen hundred. With only his flagship, the others having been scattered by the winds, Cerón reached a large group of islands, which he named Los Reyes, after the day [January 6] of his arrival. They are some eleven degrees, more or less, this side [north] of the Equator.

The inhabitants are large of body, long-faced, dark, and heavily bearded. They wear their hair long; they use canes for spears; they make very fine mats of palm fiber which from a distance look like gold; they cover their private parts with breechclouts of the same, but otherwise go naked; they go about in large canoes.

From the islands of Los Reyes, Cerón sailed to Mindanao and the Bisayas, which lie at eight degrees [north]. They are rich in gold, pigs, chickens, and rice. The women are beautiful, the men white. All wear their hair long. They are armed with iron cutlasses, cannon, long arrows, and blowguns, with which they shoot poisoned darts. They wear cotton armor, and breastplates made of fish scales. They are warlike. They conclude peace by drinking the blood of their new friends, and they even sacrifice men to their god Anito. Their kings wear crowns on their heads, as ours do. The name of their reigning sovereign was Catonao. He it was who killed Don Jorge Manrique, Don Jorge's brother Don Diego, and others.

A Portuguese, one Sebastián del Puerto (married at Coruña), who had been with Loaysa, took refuge in Alvaro de Saavedra's ship. He had served as translator, and said that his master had brought him to Cebú, where he learned that eight or more Spaniards of Magellan's crew had been taken to China and sold as slaves. In short, he gave an account of the whole voyage. Saavedra ransomed two other Spaniards, of Loaysa's party, on an island called Candia, for seventy gold castellanos. Here he made peace with its lords, with whom he drank blood drawn from their arms, as is the custom there, as it is among the Scythians. He passed Terrenate, where the Portuguese have a fortress, and reached Gilolo, where he encountered Fernando de la Torre, of Burgos, captain over a hundred and twenty Spaniards of Loaysa's party, and commandant of a castle. There Alvaro de Saavedra repaired his ship, took on supplies and every kind of necessary gear, and twenty hundredweight of cloves of the Emperor's share, which Fernando de la Torre gave him.

He set sail June 3, 1528, and wandered about aimlessly for a good while. He touched at the Ladrón Islands, and at others where some of the people were black and kinky-haired; others, white, bearded, and tattooed on the arms—all this within such a short distance that it was quite astonishing. He was forced back to Tidore, where he remained for many days. He sailed for New Spain on May 8, 1529, but died at sea on October 19 of that same year. Owing to his death, the shortage of hands, and unfavorable winds, the ship put back to Tidore, with only eighteen of the fifty men who had embarked at Zihuatanejo. By this time Fernando de la Torre had lost his castle [to the Portuguese], so the eighteen made their way to Malacca, only to be seized there by [the Portuguese] Don Jorge de Castro, who kept them in prison for two years, during which time ten of them died. Such is the treatment that the Portuguese mete out to the Castilians! So only eight were left, and this was the end of the expedition that Cortés sent to the Spice Islands.

192. Cortés Returns to Spain

NOW THAT ALONSO DE ESTRADA, obeying the Emperor's orders, was governing in the place of Marcos de Aguilar, it seemed to Cortés, in view of His Majesty's action, that the only way for him to recover his office was to go in person to negotiate it—a painful decision for him to take, because he still considered himself blameless, and he fumed at the many adversaries he had in Spain, the evil tongues, and his lack of favor, for in his absence he counted for nothing. So he made up his mind to go to Castile to dispatch his many affairs, which were important to himself, the Emperor, and New Spain. I shall speak of a few of them. One was to find a wife, for he had children and was getting old; another was to appear before the King in person and give him a full account of the vast territory and the many peoples he had conquered and partly converted, and inform him by word of mouth of the quarreling and dissension among the Spaniards in Mexico, for he suspected that the King had not heard the truth; another was to demand of him rewards commensurate with his merits and services, and a title that would set him above the others. He had, moreover, a number of profitable suggestions for the good government of New Spain which he had thought out and written, and which he wished to present to the King.

While he was considering these things, he received a letter from Fray García de Loaysa, the Emperor's confessor and President of [the Council of] the Indies, who later became cardinal, in which Loaysa urged and advised him to come to Spain, to see him and become acquainted with His Majesty, promising Cortés his friendship and influence. Upon receipt of this letter, Cortés hastened his departure, abandoning his project of establishing a colony on the Río de las Palmas, which is beyond Pánuco, although he had already planned the expedition and dispatched in advance some two hundred Spanish [foot] and sixty horse to the land of the Chichimecas, along with a number of Mexicans. If that land proved to be good (as he had been informed), and rich in silver mines, he meant to plant a colony there. Otherwise, if the Spaniards were not received in peace, he intended to make war upon them and enslave them, for they were barbarous people.

He wrote to Vera Cruz to have two good ships readied for him, and sent there for the purpose one Pero Ruiz de Esquivel, an hidalgo of Seville, who, however, did not arrive. A month later his body was discovered buried on a small island in the lagoon, with one hand exposed and gnawed by dogs and birds. He was clad in doublet and hose. He had a single knife wound on his forehead. The Negro who escorted him never appeared; nor did two bars of gold, or the boat; nor was it ever learned who had killed him, or why.

Cortés made an inventory of his personal goods, which were valued at 200,000 gold pesos; he left behind as manager and major-domo of his estate, his kinsman the Licenciado Juan Altamirano, Diego de Ocampo, and a certain Santa Cruz. He fitted out the two ships quite completely and offered free passage and fare to all who wished to go with him. He put on board 1,500 marks of silver and 20,000 pesos in fine gold, as well as 10,000 pesos in base gold and many very rich jewels. He took with him Gonzalo de Sandoval, Andrés de Tapia, and some of the noblest and most renowned of the conquistadores; also, a son of Moctezuma and a son of Maxixca, this latter now baptized as Don Lorenzo, and many gentlemen and lords of Mexico, Tlaxcala, and other cities; eight tumblers, several very white Indian men and women, and dwarfs and monsters. In short, he traveled as a great lord. Besides the above, he brought along as exhibits: tigers, albatrosses, an *ayotochtli* [armadillo], an animal called a *tlacuachi* [opossum], which carries its young in a pouch while running and the tail of which, according to the Indian women, is of great help in childbirth. For gifts he carried a large quantity of feather and hair mantles, fans, shields, plumes, stone mirrors, and the like. He arrived in Spain toward the end of the year 1528, while the court was sitting at Toledo. The whole kingdom was agog with his fame and the news of his coming, and everyone wanted to see him.

193. The Emperor Rewards Cortés

THE EMPEROR received Cortés very cordially and, to show him greater honor, even went to visit him at his lodgings, Cortés being ill and despaired of by the doctors. Cortés submitted to His Majesty his thoughts [on the government of New Spain] and gave him the notes he had written. He even accompanied the Emperor as far as Zaragoza, while the Emperor was on his way to embark for Italy and his coronation.* The Emperor, in recognition of his services and the worth of his person, made him Marqués del Valle de Oaxaca, as Cortés had requested, on July 6, 1528 [1529], Captain General of New Spain and the provinces of the South Sea coast, Discoverer and Founder of

---

* Charles V was crowned Emperor of the Holy Roman Empire, at Bologna on February 24, 1530, by Pope Clement VII, who placed upon his head successively the golden crown of the Romans and the iron crown of Lombardy.

that same coast and its islands, with the right of retaining the twelfth part of what he should conquer, in perpetuity for himself and his descendants. The Emperor offered him the habit of Santiago, but Cortés would not accept it without a commandery. Cortés further requested [and was granted]: Cuernavaca, Oaxaca, Tehuantepec, Coyoacán, Matalcingo, Tacubaya, Toluca, Oaxtepec, Utlatepec(?), Etla, Jalapa [del Marqués, Oaxaca], Teuquilayacoyán(?), Calimaya, Yautepec, Tepoztlán, Cuilapan, Yecapixtla, Cuetlaxca(?), Tuxtla [San Andrés, Vera Cruz], Tepeaca, Atloxtán(?), and Ixcalpan [La Rinconada, Vera Cruz], with all their villages, territories, citizens, civil and criminal jurisdiction, *pechos* [taxes paid by by commoners], tributes, and rights.† These are all large towns, and their lands are extensive. The Emperor also granted Cortés other favors and privileges, but those I have named were the greatest and best.

194. Marriage of Cortés

DOÑA CATALINA XUÁREZ had died without issue. When the news of her death reached Castile, many undertook to find a wife for Cortés, who was now famous and very rich. Don Alvaro de Zúñiga was particularly diligent in this, and succeeded in arranging a match between Cortés and his niece, Doña Juana de Zúñiga, daughter of Don Carlos Arellano, Count of Aguilar, using for the purpose a power-of-attorney [that Cortés had sent to his father] Martín Cortés. Doña Juana was a beautiful woman, and Count Alonso [Carlos?] and his brother were valorous men, high in the favor of the Emperor. So Cortés considered himself to be well-betrothed and well-connected, because these men were the cream of the ancient nobility.

Cortés had brought with him, among the gems he had got from the

---

† Gómara's list (like that of the grant) is corrupt and incomplete. In 1532, the second Audiencia of Mexico restored to the Crown some sixteen towns and 29,619 tributaries. In 1569, even so, the income of the Marquesado, including tributes in cash and kind, was about 86,000 pesos a year, paid by 60,903 tributaries and *pecheros*, which means that in 1529, when the grant was made, the total number was at least four times as great (against the 23,000 allowed in the grant), which gives an original population of perhaps a million. The area of the reduced Marquesado (after 1532) was about 25,000 square miles. (See Simpson, *The Encomienda in New* Spain, 1950 edition. pp. 164-167.)

Indians, five exceedingly fine emeralds, thought to be worth 100,000 ducats. One was carved in the form of a rose; another, like a horn; a third, like a fish, with golden eyes, a marvellous piece of Indian workmanship; a fourth, like a little bell, set in gold, with a rich pearl for a clapper, and engraved with the words "Blessed be he who made thee!"; the last was a tiny cup on a gold base, with four little chains by which to hang it caught in a long pearl button; it had a gold spout and was engraved *Inter natos mulierum non surrexit major.* For this single piece, which was the best of them, certain Genoese at La Rábida offered him forty thousand ducats, thinking to sell it to the sultan of Turkey. But Cortés would not part with the emeralds for any price, although he lost them later in Algiers, when he went there with the Emperor, as we related in the history of the naval wars of our time. He had been told that the Empress wished to see these gems, and that she would ask him for them and would have the Emperor buy them from him. For this reason he sent them to his betrothed wife, along with many other things, before arriving at court, and was thus able to excuse himself when asked about them. He presented the gems to his betrothed, and they were the best that ever a woman had in Spain. He married Doña Juana and took her, along with his title of Marqués, back to Mexico with him.

195. The Emperor Establishes the Audiencia

WHILE PÁNFILO DE NARVÁEZ was in Spain negotiating the conquest of Río de las Palmas and Florida, where he died [1527], he did nothing at court but bring complaints against Cortés, and even presented the Emperor with a memorial of many chapters, in one of which he swore that Cortés had as many bars of gold and silver as there were iron ingots in Biscay, and he offered to prove it. The charge was not true, but it left a suspicion. He demanded the punishment of Cortés for blinding him in one eye, and for poisoning the Licenciado Luis Ponce de León and Francisco de Garay. As a result of his numerous petitions, it was proposed to send to Mexico Don

Pedro de la Cueva, a stern and severe man, majordomo to the King (and, later, general in the artillery and Comendador of Alcántara), for the purpose of beheading Cortés in case the charge was proved. Meanwhile, however, Cortés' letters, dated at Mexico September 3, 1526, arrived, together with the testimony of Dr. Ojeda and the Licenciado Pedro López, who had attended Luis Ponce, so the matter was dropped. When Cortés arrived in Castile, he and Don Pedro de la Cueva had a hearty laugh over the business, and Cortés remarked: *"Long journeys, long lies!"*

The Emperor and his Council of the Indies now set up a chancellery [Audiencia] for Mexico, to which all the people of New Spain might repair for the adjustment of their suits and affairs. And so, to put an end to the dissensions and punish the offenders, to take the residencia of Cortés (of whose services and guilt he wished to satisfy himself), and to investigate the royal officials and the treasury, the Emperor ordered Nuño de Guzmán, Governor of Pánuco, to serve as President, and four licenciados as oidores. Nuño de Guzmán went to Mexico early in 1529 and at once entered upon his duties, in the company of the Licenciados Juan Ortiz de Matienzo and Diego Delgadillo, the other two having died meanwhile. He began a terrible residencia and persecution of Cortés and, since the latter was absent, thrust his lance into him up to the hilt. The Audiencia held a public auction of Cortés' goods, which they sold at ridiculous prices. They had the town crier read a summons for him; they proscribed him, and, if he had been present, his life would have been in danger, although, on the other hand, *Chin to chin, honor is respected.* It is a common thing for judges to talk fiercely against the absent.

But these judges, it seems to me, would have harassed Cortés in any case, because they abused his friends to such an extent that the latter did not dare walk through the streets. For example, they arrested Pedro de Alvarado, who had recently arrived from Spain, for having spoken [there] in defense of Cortés, and they accused him of being responsible for the rebellion of Mexico in the time of Narváez. [Nuño de Guzmán] also arrested Alonso de Estrada and many others, insulting them openly. Within a short time, indeed, the Emperor had received more complaints of him than of all other past [officials], so he removed him from office in the year '30. Nuño de Guzmán gave proof of his prejudice and hatred, not only in Mexico, but even at court, for in many towns of Castile the Licenciado Francisco Núñez [a kinsman?] persecuted men from Mexico in the same fashion. Later, the oidores and President who succeeded Nuño de Guzmán and the Licenciados Matienzo and Delgadillo denounced them for their hatred and prejudice against Cortés, and condemned them to compensate him for his goods they had sacrificed.

When Nuño de Guzmán learned that he was to be removed from the presidency, he became uneasy and organized an expedition against the Teuchichimecas and to explore Culiacán which, some say, is where the Mexicans came from. He assembled five hundred Spaniards, most of them mounted. Some were prisoners and others joined against their will, while those who went freely, as well as those who had come with him [from Pánuco], were new to the country. In Michoacán he seized King Cazonci, the friend of Cortés, servant of the Spaniards and vassal of the Emperor, even though he was at peace. He took from him, it is said, ten thousand marks of silver and a large quantity of gold, which done, he burned Cazonci and many other gentlemen and nobles of that kingdom at the stake, to keep them from complaining, for *A dead dog does not bite.* Taking six thousand Indians as bearers and servants for his army, he carried the war into Jalisco and conquered it, naming it New Galicia, as I have related elsewhere. Nuño de Guzmán remained in Jalisco until the Viceroy, Don Antonio de Mendoza, and the Audiencia had him arrested and sent back to Spain [1537], to make an accounting of his actions, and he was never allowed to return. If Nuño de Guzmán had been as good a governor as he was a warrior, he would have had the best place in the Indies; but he behaved badly both to Indians and Spaniards.

In that same year of 1530, in which Nuño de Guzmán left Mexico, Sebastián Ramírez de Fuenleal went there as President,* to inspect and reform the Audiencia, the city, and the country. He was a native of Villaescusa and had been bishop and President in the island of Santo Domingo. For oidores he was given the Licenciados Juan de Salmerón, of Madrid; Vasco de Quiroga, of Madrigal; Francisco Ceynos, of Zamora; and Alonso Maldonado, of Salamanca. These

---

* Gómara's chronology is confused. Nuño de Guzmán left Mexico for the conquest of New Galicia on December 22, 1529. The oidores of the second Audiencia did not arrive in Mexico until December 23, 1530; President Fuenleal, a year later.

ruled the land in justice. They founded the city of Los Angeles [Puebla], called by the Indians Cuetlaxcoapan, or "Snake-in-the-water," otherwise, Huicilapan, or "Bird-in-the-water"—this because of two springs there, one of bad water, one of good. It is twenty leagues from Mexico, on the road to Vera Cruz.

The bishop [rather, the oidores] began to free the Indians, because of which many Spanish settlers abandoned the country and went to seek their fortunes in Jalisco, Honduras, Guatemala, and other parts where there were wars and expeditions.

196. Cortés Returns to Mexico

MEANWHILE, Cortés arrived at Vera Cruz [July 15, 1530]. As soon as word of his arrival got around, and that he was coming as Marqués and was bringing his wife, a multitude of Indians and almost all the Spaniards in Mexico took this as an excuse for going to meet him. In a few days he was joined by more than a thousand Spaniards, who complained that they had nothing to eat, for the Licenciados Matienzo and Delgadillo had ruined them and him too, and they begged Cortés' permission to kill them and the rest [of his enemies]. But Cortés, knowing what an ugly affair this would be, reprimanded them severely. On the other hand, he gave them hope of relief from their want, in the expeditions he was planning to make, and, to keep them from open mutiny or a sack, he entertained them with feasting.

The President and oidores [rather, the two oidores] ordered all the Spaniards to return at once to Mexico, and each citizen to his own town, on pain of death—this to separate them from Cortés, whom the Audiencia was on the point of arresting and sending back to Spain as a disturber of the peace. In view of the speed with which the lawyers were moving, he had himself proclaimed by public crier in Vera Cruz as Captain-General of New Spain, and had his orders read, which twisted the noses of the oidores in Mexico. Thereupon he set out straight for Mexico with a large company of Spaniards and Indians, and an abundance of horses.

When he reached Texcoco, the Audiencia ordered him, on pain of confiscation of his property and the pleasure of the King, not to enter

Mexico. With the prudence befitting the service of the Emperor and the good of the country that he had won with such hardships, he obeyed and complied. In Texcoco he was surrounded by people, and his court was as large as that of Mexico, or larger. He wrote to the President and oidores [oidores alone, as above] to bear in mind his good intentions and not to give the Indians a pretext for rising; they could rest easy about the Spaniards.

The Indians, seeing how things stood, killed all the Spaniards they could catch off their guard, and within a few days had killed more than two hundred, in the towns and on the roads, as they had con-spired to do. Several of them, however, divulged the plot to the bishop [Zumárraga]. He was alarmed and sought the advice of the oidores and the rest of the citizens of the capital, who, recognizing that there was no better remedy or surer defense than the person, renown, valor, and authority of Cortés, summoned him to Mexico. He at once went there at the head of a large body of troops, and truly he looked like a Captain-General. Everyone poured out to greet him, for he was accompanied by the Marquesa, and the day was one of great rejoicing. The Audiencia consulted him about the evil situation, and Cortés took the offensive, arrested many Indians, burned several, had others torn by dogs, and punished so many that in a short time he had pacified the country and secured the roads—a deed worthy of a Roman reward.*

197. Cortés Explores the South Sea Coast

AFTER CORTÉS HAD RESTED a while, the President and oidores ordered him to send a fleet to explore, [the coast of] the South Sea, as his instructions specified, and as he had agreed in his capitulation with the Emperor, executed in Madrid on October 29, of the year '29, and signed by the Empress Doña Isabel [with the proviso] that in case of his refusal, His Majesty would make a contract with someone else. The purpose of the Audiencia was as much to get Cortés out of

---

* Gómara's chronology is again faulty. The Indian uprising occurred in 1531, after the new Audiencia had taken over. In its suppression Vasco Porcallo, one of Cortés' lieutenants, took and branded two thousand Indians, mostly women and children, who were at once released by the Audiencia.

Mexico as to have fulfill his agreement with the Emperor. They well knew that he always had many carpenters and vessels at his shipyards, but they wanted him to go there in person. Cortés replied that he would do so, and he speeded the construction of two ships he was building at Acapulco.

Meanwhile, an epidemic of measles (called by the Indians *zahuatl-tepiton*, "little leprosy") broke out, and many Indians died of it. It was a result of the smallpox brought in by the Negro of Pánfilo de Narváez; it was also a new disease, never seen before in that land.

When the ships were finished, Cortés manned them with adequate crews, armed them with guns, and stocked them with provisions, arms, and merchandise. He appointed as their commander his cousin Diego Hurtado de Mendoza. One of the ships was named the *San Miguel*, the other the *San Marcos*. He appointed Juan de Mazuela treasurer; Alonso de Molina, veedor; Miguel Marroquino, military commander; Juan Ortiz de Cabex, chief constable; Melchor Fernández, pilot. Diego Hurtado sailed from the port of Acapulco on Corpus Christi Day [June 30] of the year 1532. He followed the coast westward, according to plan, and reached the port of Jalisco [Matanchel], where he intended to take on water—not that he was in need of it, but to fill his empty jars. Nuño de Guzmán, the Governor, sent men to prevent his entering, either because Hurtado belonged to the party of Cortés or because Nuño would allow no one to enter his jurisdiction without permission. Diego Hurtado left without the water and sailed a good two hundred leagues farther, following the coast as well as he could. A number of his men having mutinied, he put them on board one of his ships and sent them to New Spain, so that he might pusue his way in safety and without worry. He continued his voyage in the other ship, but accomplished nothing of note that I know of. He was not heard of for a long time.

The mutineers ran into contrary winds on their way back, and their water gave out, so they were forced to anchor in a bay called Banderas, where the natives were up in arms because of the ill treatment they had suffered at the hands of Nuño de Guzmán's men. Our men landed there and were attacked by the Indians when they tried to get water, but the Indians outnumbered them and killed all the men from the ship, save only two who escaped.

As soon as Cortés heard what had happened, he went to Tehuantepec (one of his villas, a hundred and twenty leagues from Mexico) and there fitted out and equipped two vessels that the shipwrights had just completed. He named as captain of one of them Diego Becerra, of Mérida, and as pilot Fortún Jiménez, a Basque. Of the second he named Hernando de Grijalba [captain], and a Portuguese, [Martín de] Acosta, pilot. I believe they set sail a year and a half after Diego Hurtado [actually, on October 30, 1533]. Their aims were three: to avenge the murdered men, to seek out and rescue the survivors, and to learn the secrets and extent of that coast.

The two vessels were separated on the first night out and never sighted each other again. Fortún Jiménez, who had quite likely quarreled with Diego Becerra, conspired with a number of Basques (sailors as well as landsmen), killed him, and badly wounded several others. Jiménez then sailed to Motín, where he put ashore the wounded men and two Franciscan friars. Taking on water, he sailed to the Bay of Santa Cruz [La Paz, Lower California], where he landed, only to be killed by the Indians, along with twenty other Spaniards. Two sailors in the ship's boat brought the news to Chiametla. They also told Nuño de Guzmán that they had found good evidence of pearls [at La Paz], so he went back there to salvage the ship—which done, he put a crew on her and sent her off to look for pearls.

Hernando de Grijalba [in the second ship] sailed three hundred leagues to the northwest without sighting land, for which reason he stood out to sea in the hope of finding islands. He did come upon one, which he named Santo Tomás [Socorro], after the day on which he discovered it. According to his account, it was uninhabited and waterless on the side by which he approached. It lies at 20° [N. Lat.]; it has beautiful woods and a cool climate, many doves, partridges, falcons, and other birds.

Such was the fate of the four ships that Cortés sent on voyages of exploration.

198. Misadventures of Cortés on the South Coast

WHILE THESE EVENTS were transpiring, Cortés constructed three more very good vessels at Tehuantepec, because he always kept many men there building ships in order to fulfill his agreement with the Emperor; also, because he thought he might discover rich lands and islands with them. As soon as he received word [of the fate of his ship], he filed charges against Nuño de Guzmán with the President and oidores, and begged them in justice to have his ship restored to him. They did issue a decree and followed it with a letter [to Guzmán], all to do no purpose. Then Cortés, who was irritated at Nuño de Guzmán because of the residencia Guzmán had presided over and the goods he had confiscated, dispatched three ships to Chiametla, named the *Santa Agueda,* the *San Lázaro,* and the *Santo Tomás,* while he set out overland from Mexico with a large company. When he arrived at Chiametla, he found his ship* destroyed and stripped of everything, which, with the hull, had cost him altogether 15,000 ducats. His three vessels arrived, and he embarked in them with all the men and horses they could carry; the rest he left [at Chiametla] under the command of Andrés de Tapia, for he had brought some 300 Spanish troops, 37 women, and 130 horses.

He sailed to the place where Fortún Jiménez had been killed [La Paz] and landed there on New Year's Day of 1536. In honor of the day he named the high cape there, Sierras de San Felipe, and an island that lay three leagues offshore, Santiago. Three days later he entered a very fine port, large and protected from all winds, which he named the Bay of Santa Cruz. It was there that Fortún Jiménez and the twenty Spaniards had been killed. As soon as he landed he sent for Andrés de Tapia, who embarked and sailed before the wind as far as two rivers, now known as the San Pedro and the San Pablo. All three ships were blown off their course immediately. The smallest sailed to [the Bay of] Santa Cruz; the second, to the Guayabal River; and the one called the *San Lázaro* was wrecked, or rather, ran aground, near Jalisco, and its crew returned to Mexico. Cortés waited three days for his ships, and, when they failed to appear, began to suffer from want of the provisions they carried; for in that country [of La Paz] the people do not cultivate maize, but live on fruits and herbs, game and fish. It is said that the Indians there fish from rafts made of five logs lashed together, like a hand, using arrows and pointed sticks. In the circumstances Cortés decided to take his one

* This was the murdered Becerra's ship, the *Concepción.*

ship and go in search of the others and, if he failed to find them, at least to bring back provisions.

So he embarked with some seventy men, many of them smiths and carpenters, and brought along a forge and materials for making a brigantine if it should be necessary. He crossed the sea [Gulf of California], which resembles the Adriatic, and coasted for fifty leagues, and one morning found himself so badly involved among reefs and shoals that he could find neither entrance nor exit. While he was taking soundings in search of a passage, he approached the shore and sighted a vessel anchored in a bay. He tried to get to it, but could not find a channel, for the sea was breaking over the shoals in every direction. The men in the other ship† also sighted his and, suspecting whose it was, sent over a boat with their pilot, Antón Cordero. Cordero came alongside, greeted Cortés, and came on board to guide him. He said there was depth enough through the breakers, where his ship had passed; but he hardly spoken when he ran the ship aground two leagues from shore, where it stuck, dead and broken.

Then you should have seen the bravest in tears, and heard how they cursed the pilot Cordero! Commending their souls to God, they stripped, thinking to escape by swimming, or on planks. They were on the point of doing so when two seas washed the ship into the channel the pilot had spoken of, although the ship was holed; but, by pumping and bailing, they got it to the anchored vessel. Then they disembarked and unloaded everything, and, with the capstans of both ships, they pulled her out. They set up their forge and made charcoal. Working at night by the light of torches and candles, for there was a great deal of wax at hand, they soon had her repaired. At San Miguel [Culiacán], seventeen leagues from the Guayabal, which flows into the Culiacán, Cortés purchased a quantity of provisions and grain. Each calf cost him thirty castellanos of fine gold; each pig, ten; each sheep and each fanega of maize, four. He set sail again, but the *San Lázaro* struck her sternpost on a shoal and fouled her rudder; so again they had to make charcoal and repair her.

Cortés sailed [for the Bay of Santa Cruz] in the larger ship, leaving Hernando de Grijalba in command of the other, which was not ready. Two days later, in fine weather, the lashings of the mizzen yard parted (the sail being furled), and the yard fell and killed the

---

† This was one of Andres de Tapia's ships, which had been scattered by the winds.

pilot Antón Cordero, who was sleeping at the foot of the mast. Cortés himself then had to act as pilot, for there was no one else competent to do so. He steered for the island of Santiago, already mentioned, but a heavy northwester blew up and prevented his entering the bay, so he followed the coast to the southeast, hugging the shore and taking soundings. He dropped anchor and landed on a sandbank to look for water. Not finding any, he dug wells in the sand and filled eight pipes. Meanwhile, the northwester stopped, and he sailed with favorable winds to the Island of Pearls (so named by Fortún Jiménez), which lies close to that of Santiago. The wind died, but soon freshened again, so he made it to the port of Santa Cruz, not without risk, for the channel is narrow and the water shallow.

The men he had left there were emaciated from hunger, and more than five of them had died, for they were so weak that they could not gather shellfish or catch fish, which is what they had lived upon. They ate without salt the plants used in the making of glass.‡ and wild fruits, although not so many as they needed. Cortés fed them very sparingly, lest they should sicken, for their stomachs were weak; but in their hunger they ate too much and many more died.

Hernando de Grijalba was so delayed (Antonio de Mendoza having arrived meanwhile in Mexico as Viceroy, as Cortés had been informed at San Miguel), that Cortés decided to leave Francisco de Ulloa in command at Santa Cruz and go on to Tehuantepec, thinking to send ships and men to Ulloa, to explore the coast and look for Hernando de Grijalba.

At this juncture one of Cortés' caravels arrived from New Spain in search of him, and he was told that it would be followed by two large ships bringing many men, arms, guns, and provisions. He waited for two days and, when they did not appear, set out with his single vessel and encountered them at anchor off the coast of Jalisco. He brought them into that same port [of Matanchel], where he found Hernando de Grijalba's ship aground on a sandbar, her stores rotted. He had her cleaned and washed. The men who were engaged in it and unloaded the meat, had their faces and eyes so swollen from the

---

‡ *Hierba de que hacen vidrio*. Professor Carl Sauer suggests that this could have been the *huaje*, a species of acacia, which is common in the La Paz area. The green pods of the *huaje* are still sold in the markets of Oaxaca. A further guess is that the dry wood of the *huaje* was used by the smiths for stoking their forge, since it would make a very hot fire. It seems doubtful that they would have taken the time to burn charcoal in their emergency.

stench and effluvium that they could not see. Cortés raised the ship, got her into deep water, and discovered that she was sound and had no leaks whatever. He had yards and masts cut, for there were good trees near by, and put her in running order. Then he set sail with all four ships for Santiago de Buena Esperanza, in Colima, where he was joined by his other two ships. These had been sent in search of him, for he had been away so long that the Marquesa was badly worried. So, with all six ships he sailed to Acapulco, in the land of New Spain.

Many tales are told of this voyage of Cortés, which to some seems like a miracle; to others, a dream; but I have told nothing but the truth and what is credible. While Cortés was at Acapulco, about to depart for Mexico, a messenger arrived from Don Antonio de Mendoza, advising him of Mendoza's arrival as Viceroy of those lands, and bringing him a copy of a letter from Francisco Pizarro, written to Pedro de Alvarado, Adelantado and Governor of Guatemala (as Pizarro had written to other governors), informing him that he was besieged in Ciudad de los Reyes [Lima], with a large number of men, and was in such straits that he could escape only by sea, that he was being attacked daily, and that if he was not relieved he would be lost.

Cortés then abandoned his search for Francisco de Ulloa and sent two ships, loaded with provisions and arms, silk garments for the person of Pizarro, two chairs of state, a robe of marten fur, velvet cushions, trappings for horses, and some household ornaments that Cortés had brought along for use on his expedition but no longer had much need of, now that he was back in his own country. Hernando de Grijalba departed [for Peru] and arrived in good time. He sent one of the ships back to Acapulco, while Cortés gathered sixty men in Cuernavaca and eleven pieces of artillery, seventeen horses, sixty coats of mail, many crossbows and arquebuses, tools, and other things, which he sent to Peru, but was never repaid, because Francisco Pizarro was killed not long afterward. Pizarro did send, however, many rich gifts to the Marquesa, but Grijalba made off with them.

199. The Sea of Cortés, Also Called the Red

IN THE MONTH OF MAY of that same year of 1539, Cortés dispatched three more ships, well-armed and supplied, under Francisco de Ulloa (who meanwhile had returned with all the others), with orders to follow the coast of Culiacán, which trends toward the north. These ships were named the *Santa Agueda,* the *Trinidad,* and the *Santo Tomás.* They sailed from Acapulco; they touched at Santiago de Buena Esperanza to take on supplies; from the Guayabal they crossed over to California to search for a ship, and recrossed the Sea of Cortés (which others call the Red). They followed the coast [northward] more than two-hundred leagues to the bay at the end [of the Gulf of California], which they named the Ancón de San Andrés, after the saint's day of their arrival. Francisco de Ulloa took possession of the land for the King of Castile, in the name of Hernán Cortés.

This bay lies at 32° N. Lat., or a little higher, the sea there is vermilion in color; the tides rise and fall regularly. Along the coast are many little volcanoes; the hills are barren; it is a poor country. Ulloa found specimens of sheep, I mean bighorns, for they have very heavy twisted horns. There are many whales in this sea. The natives fish with hooks made of the thorns of trees and the bones of tortoises; these are large and plentiful. The men go about naked and shorn, like the Otomí of New Spain, and wear on their breasts polished shells resembling nacre. They utilize the stomachs of seals for water vessels, although they also have pots of good clay.

From the Ancón de San Andrés, following the opposite [west] coast, Ulloa reached California, rounded the cape [San Lucas], and sailed north to the parallel of San Andrés, at a point he named Cape Disappointment [Punta Baja], where he turned back to New Spain because of contrary winds and shortage of provisions. This voyage took him a whole year, and he brought back no word of a good new land. *The game was not worth the candle.*

In the belief that there were some very large and rich islands between New Spain and the Spice Islands, Cortés had thought he might discover a second New Spain on that coast and sea, but in spite of all the ships he had fitted out, and even commanded in person, he accomplished nothing but what I have said. According to the account he rendered, he spent some two hundred thousand ducats on these voyages of exploration, for he sent out more ships and men than he had anticipated. This was the reason, as we shall explain later, for his return to Spain, his falling out with the Viceroy, Don Antonio de Mendoza, and his suit with the King over [the number of] his vassals. But no one ever spent so much and so zealously in such enterprises.

[Chapters 200 to 248, inclusive, have been omitted. See Introduction.]

249. New Spain Compared with Peru

THE SILVER AND GOLD taken by Cortés and his companions in the conquest of New Spain was very little in comparison with what was later extracted from the mines. All, or very nearly all, was brought to Spain. Although the mines [of New Spain] have not been so rich, or the remittances so heavy, as those of Peru, yet they have been continuous and great, and for twice as long a period. Even allowing for the years of the civil wars, when nothing was shipped, the amount is still three times as large, although this cannot be confirmed except by the Board of Trade at Seville. It is, however, the opinion of many. Leaving out of the reckoning the gold and silver, a great deal of sugar and cochineal has been brought over (two very rich articles), and the feathers and cotton, as well as many other things, are of some value. Few ships sail there which do not bring back cargoes. This cannot be said of Peru, which is still lacking in such profitable trade. So New Spain has been as great a source of wealth for Castile as Peru has been, although Peru has the reputation. It is true that not so many men have come back rich from Mexico as from Peru, but on the other hand not so many have died.

In the conversion and conservation of the natives, New Spain has a great advantage over Peru, and is more settled and full of people. The same holds true for cattle-raising and farming. Indeed, New Spain ships horses, sugar, meat, and twenty other things to Peru. It may happen that Peru will become peopled, and as enriched with our things as New Spain has been, for it is a good land where it has sufficient rain. Irrigation is general.

I have made this statement because of the rivalry between the two sets of conquerors.

250. The Viceroys of Mexico

THE GREATNESS of New Spain, the majesty of its capital, and the quality of the conquerors demanded a person of high place and valor to head its government. Thus it was that the Emperor appointed as Viceroy Don Antonio de Mendoza, brother of the Marqués de Mondéjar [Don Luis Hurtado de Mendoza, Captain-General of Granada and, later, President of the Council of the Indies]. Sebastián Ramírez [de Fuenleal] returned to Spain; he had governed well, and was soon made President of the Audiencia of Valladolid and Bishop of Cuenca. Don Antonio de Mendoza was appointed, I believe, in the year '34.* He brought with him many master craftsmen to ennoble his province, especially Mexico. He also introduced type and a printing press, glass (unknown to the Indians), and dies for coining money. He expanded silk culture and ordered all the silk to be brought to Mexico for manufacture. As a result there are [in Mexico] many looms, and in [New Spain] an infinite number of mulberry trees, although the Indians harvest little silk and do it badly, on the pretext that it is too laborious—this because they are lazy and enjoy too much liberty and freedom [to move around].

Mendoza convoked the bishops, secular priests, friars, and other men of law, to discuss matters pertaining to the Church and the indoctrination of the Indians. They ordered that the Indians were no longer to be taught Latin, which they learned readily, or even Spanish, which they speak unwillingly. They take well to music, especially the flute, but their voices are bad for singing in tune. They might have become priests, but are not allowed to. Don Antonio

---

* Mendoza was appointed Viceroy on April 17, 1535. Bishop Sebastián Ramírez de Fuenleal was named President of the Audiencia of Mexico on April 11, 1530, but did not take office until September, 1531. He served until Mendoza's arrival, returning to Spain early in 1536.

founded several towns, after the fashion of Roman colonies, in honor of the Emperor, engraving the Emperor's name and the year in marble. He began the construction of a mole for the port of Medellín, an expensive but necessary operation. He reduced the Chichimecas [Otomí] to civilized life and granted them self-government, which they had not exercised before, nor, I believe, did they desire or need it. He spent a great sum on the [Coronado] expedition to Cíbola, as we have already related, without any return whatever, except to make an enemy of Cortés. He had a great stretch of the south coast of Jalisco explored, and dispatched an expedition to the Spice Islands, in which he lost his ships. He conducted himself very prudently at the time of the promulgation of the New Laws of the Indies [1544], when Peru revolted because of the many impoverished and dissatisfied men there who chose rebellion and war.

The Emperor sent him [1551] to Peru with the same office of Viceroy, the Licenciado [Pedro de la] Gasca having returned to Spain.† Mendoza governed well, although the citizens of New Spain made some complaints of him to the Emperor. Mendoza would have preferred to remain in Mexico, with which he was now familiar; nor did he wish to leave the Indians, with whom he got on very well. (They had cured him of the gout by means of baths and herbs.) Nor did he wish to give up his estates, cattle, and other interests. Nor did he wish to know new men and face new conditions, for he was aware that the [Spanish] Peruvians are rough men. In the end, however, he was obliged to go, making the journey overland from Mexico to Panama, more than five hundred leagues, in the year 1551. In that same year Don Luis de Velasco, former Inspector General of the Army and a gentleman of much experience in government, came to Mexico as Viceroy.

This Viceroyalty is a very important post, in honor, authority, and profit.

---

† La Gasca had been sent to Peru to suppress the revolt of the encomenderos under Gonzalo Pizarro. His success was spectacular, and the city of Cuzco voted him the title of "Father, Restorer, and Pacifier."

CORTÉS AND Don Antonio de Mendoza quarreled bitterly over the expedition to Cíbola, each claiming it as his own by the Emperor's order: Don Antonio as Viceroy, Cortés as Captain-General. They exchanged such words that they were never reconciled, although they had been close friends. As a result they wrote a thousand complaints of each other, which damaged and diminished them both.

Cortés had a suit over the number of his vassals with the Licenciado [Juan de] Villalobos, Fiscal of the [Council of the] Indies, who had challenged his privileges, so the Viceroy began to count his vassals—an evil thing, even by the Emperor's order—which forced Cortés to return to Spain in the year '40. He took with him his heir, Don Martín, who was about eight years old, and Don Luis, and placed them in the service of Prince Philip [later Philip II]. Cortés returned rich and well-attended, although less so than the first time. He became a close friend of Cardinal Loaysa and the Licenciado Cobos, Fiscal [of the Emperor's Council], but this did him no good with the Emperor, who had departed for Flanders, by way of France, to settle the Ghent business.*

In the year '41 the Emperor attacked Algiers with a great fleet and a force of cavalry. Cortés, with his sons Don Martín and Don Luis, and with a great many servants and horse, accompanied him to the war. The fleet was destroyed by a storm, Cortés being in the galley *Esperanza,* of Don Enrique Enríquez. For fear of losing his money and jewels in the wreck, he tied in a handkerchief the five precious emeralds, which, as I have said, were worth one hundred thousand ducats; but, either through his carelessness, or because he could not avoid it, they were lost in the heavy mud, where many men were also lost. So the war turned out to be more costly for him than for anyone save His Majesty, although Andrea Doria lost eleven galleys. Cortés was much grieved at the loss of his jewels, but he was even more grieved when he was not invited to participate in the council

---

* Ghent revolted in 1539, in protest against the imperial exactions. Charles suppressed the uprising the following year with terrible ferocity: twenty-six of its leading citizens were executed, many more were exiled, and a heavy fine was levied on the city, which was reduced to a mere dependency of the Empire. Incidentally, Charles V was born in Ghent.

of war, to which others, of less age and experience, were summoned. This caused some grumbling in the army. The council of war decided to raise the siege and withdraw, to the great disappointment of many, and I, who was present, was astonished.

Cortés then offered to take Algiers with the Spanish, German, and Italian troops, if the Emperor would consent. The soldiers were delighted and praised him highly; but the sailors and others did not heed him. The Emperor, I think, did not hear of the offer, and so retreated.

For many years thereafter Cortés followed the court, vexed by the suit over vassals and privileges, and even by the residencia taken by Nuño de Guzmán and the Licenciados Matienzo and Delgadillo, which was reviewed in the Council of the Indies. The suit was never decided, which was a great consolation for him. He went to Seville intending to return to New Spain and die in Mexico. There he met his daughter, Doña María Cortés, whom he had promised in marriage to Don Alvar Pérez Osorio, son and heir of the Marqués de Astorga, Don Perálvarez Osorio, endowing her with one hundred thousand ducats and her wardrobe. But, through the fault of Don Alvar and his father, the marriage was not consummated.

Cortés fell ill of diarrhea and indigestion, which lasted a long while. His condition worsened, and he died at Castilleja de la Cuesta on December 2, 1547, at the age of 63. His body was interred with those of the dukes of Medina Sidonia.

Cortés had three daughters and a son by Doña Juana de Zúñiga. He named his son Don Martín. Don Martín inherited the estate and married Doña Ana de Arellano, his cousin, daughter of the Count of Aguilar, Don Pedro Ramírez de Arellano, in fulfillment of the agreement Cortés had made. The daughters were Doña María Cortés, Doña Catalina, and Doña Juana, the youngest, who was bethrothed to Don Felipe de Arellano, with a dowry of seventy thousand ducats, according to an agreement made with Don Felipe. Cortés left another son, Don Martín, whom he had by an Indian woman [Doña Marina], and Don Luis Cortés, by a Spanish woman, and three daughters, each by a different mother, all Indians.

Cortés founded a hospital in Mexico [the Hospital de Jesús], where in his will he directed that his bones be sent, as a charge on the entail. He ordered a school built there, and a nunnery at Coyoacán.

He endowed each of these foundations with four thousand ducats a year (the rent of his houses in Mexico), and two thousand more toward the support of the pupils.†

252. Portrait of Cortés

HERNÁN CORTÉS was of a good stature, broad-shouldered and deep-chested; his color, pale; his beard, fair; his hair, long. He was very strong, courageous, and skillful at arms. As a youth he was mischievous; as a man, serene; so he was always a leader in war as well as in peace. He was once elected alcalde of Santiago de Baracoa [Cuba], which is the highest honor a city can bestow upon a citizen. There he earned the reputation that he later made good. He was much given to consorting with women, and always gave himself to them. The same was true with his gaming, and he played at dice marvelously well and merrily. He loved eating, but was temperate in drink, although he did not stint himself. When necessity demanded, he could suffer hunger, as he proved on the Honduras expedition, and on the sea that he named for himself. He was a very stubborn man, as a result of which he had more lawsuits than was proper to his station. He spent liberally on war, women, friends, and fancies, although in other things he was close, which got him the name of new-rich. In his dress he was elegant rather than sumptuous, and was extremely neat. He took delight in a large household and family, in silver service and dignity. He bore himself nobly, with such gravity and prudence that he never gave offence or seemed unapproachable. It is said of him that as a boy he was told that he would conquer many lands and become a very great lord. He was jealous in his own house, but free in his neighbors'—the mark of a

---

† Gómara inserts at the end of this chapter some funeral verses ascribed to Cortés' son, now a lad of fifteen:

Don Martín Cortés a la Sepultura de su Padre.
Padre, cuya suerte impropriamente
aqueste bajo mundo poseía;
valor que nuestra edad enriquecía,
descansa agora en paz eternamente.

"Father, whose fortune an ungrateful world undeserving shared, whose valor enriched our age, rest now in eternal peace."

libertine. He was devout and given to praying; he knew many prayers and psalms by heart. He was a great giver of alms and, when he was dying, he strongly urged his son to emulate him. He ordinarily gave a thousand ducats a year to charity, and sometimes lent money for alms, saying that with the interest he would expiate his sins. Over his doors and on his coat of arms he caused to be inscribed: *Judicium Domini apprehendit eos, et fortitudo ejus corroboravit bracchium meum.* (The judgment of the Lord overtook them; His might strengthened my arm.)

Such, just as you have heard, was Cortés, Conqueror of New Spain. Since I began the *Conquest of Mexico* with his birth, I shall end it with his death.

Glossary

ADELANTADO. Provincial governor; a Crown appointment of considerable power and prestige. Pedro de Alvarado was made Adelantado of Guatemala.

ALCALDE. Mayor of a town; there were usually two of them.

ALCALDE MAYOR. Governor of a province (alcaldía mayor); a Crown appointment. Cf. Corregidor.

ALGUACIL. A constable; alguacil mayor, chief constable.

ARROBA. Twenty-five pounds.

AUDIENCIA. The highest tribunal of New Spain; also referred to as a chancellery (cancillería). It was composed of a President and four oidores, or associate judges. In the absence of the Viceroy, the Audiencia assumed executive functions, the President being the *de facto* Viceroy, as in the case of Nuño de Guzmán (1529).

BACHILLER. Lowest of the academic degrees, comparable to our A. B. Like those of Licenciado and Doctor, it was heavily swathed in dignity and privileges, notably the right to be heard in an ecclesiastical court for most charges.

BRIGANTINE. A small, partially decked pinnace, propelled by oars and sails. The brigantines of Cortés had a small gun mounted forward and carried a crew of twenty-three.

CABILDO. Town council; also known as regimiento.

CAPTAIN-GENERAL. Military commandant, as opposed to civil governor and Justicia Mayor. Cortés was elected to all three offices by the cabildo of Vera Cruz in 1519.

CARGA. Load carried by an Indian bearer (*tameme*); two arrobas or fifty pounds.

CASTELLANO. The peso de oro, peso de oro fino, or peso de minas, valued at 450 maravedís. *See* Peso.

COMENDADOR. The commander of a military order, such as those of Santiago and Calatrava.

COMUNERO. The revolt of the free cities of Castile (comunidades) against Charles V in 1520-1522 gave rise to the use of "comunero" as a synonym for rebel or troublemaker.

CONTADOR. Accountant; one of the four treasury officials assigned to New Spain to look after the Crown's fiscal interests. The other three were the Veedor (inspector), Factor (business agent), and Tesorero (treasurer).

CORREGIDOR. Governor of a city or province (corregimiento). The corregidor was a royal official with functions not easily distinguished from those of an alcalde mayor.

CULHÚA. The "Mexican Empire," or Triple Alliance of Texcoco, Tacuba, and Mexico-Tenochtitlán. Gómara uses "Mexican" and "Culhúan" indiscriminately, although "Mexican" should be restricted to the inhabitants of Mexico–Tenochtitlán.

FACTOR. *See* Contador.

FANEGA. Dry measure of a hundredweight, about 1.6 bushels.

HIDALGO. A noble.

JUSTICIA MAYOR. Chief magistrate. *See* Captain-General.

LEGUA. A league. The standard Spanish league was 1/25 of a degree of latitude measured on the earth's surface—at least in theory—which comes to about 2.6 miles, but in practice it tended to vary with the difficulty of the terrain. Ordinarily, a day's journey on horseback (*jornada*) was reckoned as seven leagues.

LICENCIADO. Licenciate, the second of the academic degrees. *See* Bachiller.

MEXICO. As used in the text, Mexico is always the City of Mexico. The country itself, until Independence, was known as New Spain.

NAO. A fully decked vessel, larger than the caravel. Columbus's flagship, the *Santa María,* was a small nao of about one hundred tons.

OIDOR. Associate justice of the Audiencia.

PESO. Spanish coinage of the time is too complicated to be gone into here. The common unit of value was the maravedí, 450 of which made up the castellano, or peso de oro, which in turn was divided into eight tomines or reales. The ducat (ducado) was worth eleven tomines. The silver peso of 278 maravedís did not become standard until much later. Gómara apparently uses the silver peso as the equivalent of half a castellano.

REGIDOR. Alderman. The Spanish town council (regimiento or cabildo) had a varying number of regidores, depending upon the importance of the place. Some were elected annually (on January 1), while others were appointed regidores perpetuos by the Crown as a reward for distinguished services. Bernal Díaz del Castillo was a regidor perpetuo of Guatemala.

RESIDENCIA. A trial to which royal officers were subjected, either at the expiration of their terms or, as in the case of Cortés, at the King's pleasure.

TAMEME (Aztec *tlameme*). A bearer. Owing to the absence of pack animals the *tamemes* were an important part of Aztec economy.

TIBURÓN. The great shark of the West Indies and the Pacific coast of North America, much feared for its ferocity.

VEEDOR. Inspector. *See* Contador.

VILLA. A municipal corporation, one step below the city (ciudad) in importance. Most of the Spanish towns of New Spain were organized as villas and enjoyed the considerable privileges of their Castilian prototypes. Their prestige and authority, though not precisely defined, were nevertheless great and were recognized, even by the Crown, as a kind of birthright. Cortés made use of the Villa Rica de la Vera Cruz to legitimize, more or less, his illegal invasion of New Spain.

VISITADOR. The royal visitor was an ancient institution going back to the time of Charlemagne. By it the Crown kept an eye on its servants. Of all the royal officers, the visitor was the most dreaded, for he represented the King's person and was sometimes vested with the awful authority to execute justice by his own hand. That Cortés was able to flummox Cristóbal de Tapia, the first royal visitor sent to New Spain (1521), is a monument to his genius for intrigue and to his effrontery.

Bibliography

BANCROFT, HUBERT HOWE, *History of Central America* (San Francisco, 1882-1887), 3 vols.

———, *History of Mexico* (San Francisco, 1883-1888), 6 vols.

BENAVENTE, TORIBIO DE (MOTOLINÍA), *History of the Indians of New Spain,* trans. F. H. Steck (Washington, D. C.: Academy of American Franciscan History, 1951).

———, *Memoriales,* ed. Luis García Pimentel (Mexico, 1903).

CHAMBERLAIN, Robert S., *The Conquest and Colonization of Honduras* (Washington, D. C.: Carnegie Institution, 1953).

———, *The Conquest and Colonization of Yucatan* (Washington, D. C.: Carnegie Institution, 1948).

CHAVERO, ALFREDO, ED., *El Lienzo de Tlaxcala.* In *Antigüedades Mexicanas* (Mexico, 1892).

CORTÉS, HERNÁN, *The Letters of Cortés,* trans. Francis A. McNutt (New York and London, 1908), 2 vols.

———, abridgement of same, ed. J. Bayard Morris (New York: Robert M. McBride, 1929).

DEL RÍO, ANGEL, *Historia de la Literatura Española* (New York: Dryden Press, 1948), 2 vols.

DÍAZ DEL CASTILLO, BERNAL, *True History of the Conquest of Mexico,* trans. A. P. Maudslay (London: Hakluyt Society, 1908-1916), 5 vols. Numerous abridged versions, particularly that edited by Irving A. Leonard (New York: Farrar, Strauss, 1956).

GIBSON, CHARLES, *Tlaxcala in the Sixteenth Century* (New Haven: Yale University Press, 1952).

IGLESIA, RAMÓN, *Cronistas e Historiadores de la Conquista de Mexico: El Ciclo de Hernán Cortés* (Mexico: El Colegio de México, 1942).

————, *El Hombre Colón y otros Ensayos* (Mexico: El Colegio de México, 1944).

LAS CASAS, BARTOLOMÉ DE, *Historia de las Indias,* ed. Agustín Millares Carlo, 3 vols. (Mexico: Fondo de Cultura Económica, 1951).

LÓPEZ DE GÓMARA, FRANCISCO, *Annals of the Emperor Charles V,* trans. Roger Bigelow Merriman (London: Oxford University Press, 1912).

————, *Chrónica de los Muy Nombrados Omiche y Haradín Barbarrojas* (Madrid, 1853).

————, *Historia de las Guerras Navales.* MS, but the materials, according to H. R. Wagner (q. v., below), are included in the *Chrónica* just mentioned, and in the *Annals of the Emperor Charles V.*

————, *La Istoria de las Indias y Conquista de México,* ed. H. Barcia. In *Biblioteca de Autores Españoles,* Vol. 22 (Madrid, 1877).

————, *Historia de la Conquista de México,* ed. Joaquín Ramírez Cabañas, 2 vols. (Mexico: Editorial Pedro Robredo, 1943).

————, *The Pleasant Historie of the Conquest of Weast India,* etc., trans. Thomas Nicholas (London, 1578). This is a truncated version of the second part of Gómara's *Istoria de las Indias.*

————, *De Rebus Gestis Ferdinandi Cortesii,* trans. Joaquín García Icazbalceta. In *Colección de Documentos para la Historia de México* (Mexico, 1858-1866), 2 vols. Vol. 1, pp. 309-356. Gómara's authorship is established by Ramón Iglesia in his *Cronistas e Historiadores* (q. v., above). Iglesia also reprints Icazbalceta's translation.

MORISON, SAMUEL ELIOT, *Admiral of the Ocean Sea: A Life of Christopher Columbus* (Boston: Little, Brown, 1942), 2 vols.

Morley, Sylvanus G., *The Ancient Maya* (Stanford, Calif.: Stanford University Press, 1946).

OROZCO Y BERRA, MANUEL, *Apuntes para la Historia de la Geografía en México* (Mexico, 1881).

————, *Historia de la Dominación Española en México* (Mexico: José Porrúa e Hijos, 1938), 4 vols.

PRESCOTT, WILLIAM HICKLING, *History of the Conquest of Mexico* (New York, 1843), 3 vols. Numerous reprints.

SAUER, CARL O., *Colima of New Spain in the Sixteenth Century, Ibero-Americana: 29* (Berkeley and Los Angeles: University of California Press, 1948).

SIMPSON, LESLEY BYRD, *The Encomienda in New Spain,* 2d ed. (Berkeley and Los Angeles: University of California Press, 1950).

————, *Many Mexicos,* 3d ed. (Berkeley and Los Angeles: University of California Press, 1957).

SPINDEN, HERBERT J., *Ancient Civilizations of Mexico and Central America* (New York: American Museum of Natural History, 1917).

THOMPSON, J. ERIC, *Mexico Before Cortez* (New York: Charles Scribner's Sons, 1933).

VAILLANT, GEORGE, *The Aztecs of Mexico* (New York: Doubleday, Doran, 1941).

VALDÉS, JUAN DE, *Dialogo de la Lengua,* ed. José Montesinos (Madrid: Clásicos Castellanos, 1928).

WAGNER, HENRY RAUP, "Francisco López de Gómara and His Works." In *Proceedings of the American Antiquarian Society,* October, 1948 (Worcester, Mass.: American Antiquarian Society, 1949).

———, *The Rise of Fernando Cortés* (Berkeley, Calif.: Cortés Society, 1944).

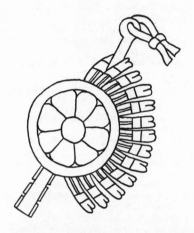

Index

NOTE.—I have limited the references to the more significant persons and places. I have omitted all references to Hernán Cortés, whose name appears on virtually every page. Where feasible, I have added identifying labels in parentheses after the main entries. Place names are identified by the modern Mexican state in which they occur, or by country if non-Mexican.

420